EGYPT IN LATE ANTIQUITY

ROGER S. BAGNALL

Egypt in Late Antiquity

PRINCETON UNIVERSITY PRESS

Copyright © 1993 by Princeton University Press
Published by Princeton University Press,
41 William Street, Princeton, New Jersey 08540
In the United Kingdom: Princeton University Press,
Chichester, West Sussex

Library of Congress Cataloging-in-Publication Data

Bagnall, Roger S., 1947-
Egypt in late antiquity / Roger S. Bagnall
p.   cm.
Includes bibliographical references and index.
ISBN 0-691-06986-7
1. Egypt—Civilization—332 B.C.-638 A.D.   I. Title.
DT93.B33 1993
932'.022—dc20   92-40332

Publication of this book has been aided by the
Stanwood Cockey Lodge Fund of Columbia University.

This book has been composed in Palatino, using Nota Bene 4,
on a Hewlett-Packard LaserJet 4M.
The publisher would like to acknowledge Roger S. Bagnall
for providing the camera-ready copy from which
this book was printed.

Printed in the United States of America

1 3 5 7 9 10 8 6 4 2

Contents

List of Illustrations

Plates

(following page 180)

Map

Preface

The reader should be told immediately of two chosen limitations of this work—the definition of its title, in fact. The first is of time: My "late antiquity" begins with the emergence of Egypt from the difficulties of the third century and ends in the middle of the fifth century, after which the term "Byzantine" is arguably more appropriate (though traditionally used in the study of Roman Egypt for everything after 284 or sometimes 312). The second is of place: Alexandria figures here only as seen from the countryside, the *chora* of Egypt. It is the cities, villages, and fringes of that countryside that form the subject of the book. These choices are not the result of any lack of interest on my part in either post-Chalcedonian Egypt or in that great metropolis on the sea. Rather, the confines reflect a conviction that the world described in this book forms a unity of its own worth attention. "Late antique" or "late Roman" are in any event historically more defensible terms than "Byzantine" for the period treated here, and the middle of the fifth century is a significant boundary from more than one point of view.[1] Equally, these choices owe something to a conviction that not to place such limits would take the book beyond my competence, swell it to unpublishable length, and make its gestation time still more prolonged than it has been already.[2]

The roots of this book lie in an act of generosity by Naphtali Lewis. When I came to Columbia in 1974, he turned over to me his transcriptions of the fourth-century Karanis papyri in the Columbia collection, copies he had made more than three decades earlier but for the most part never published. At the time, I knew absolutely nothing of the papyri or history of this period, but I have not been able to escape its fascination in almost two decades since then.

Many other acts of generosity have contributed to the writing of the book itself. The National Endowment for the Humanities made possible the first stages of direct work, the creation of a database on fourth century documents, with a fellowship for independent study

---

[1]See A. Giardina, "Egitto bizantino o tardo antico? Problemi della terminologia e della periodizzazione," *Egitto e storia antica* (Bologna 1989) 89-103. For the middle of the fifth century as something of a watershed in contract types, cf. A. Jördens, *P.Heid.* V, pp. 371-75. I have, however, cited sixth-century material when it has seemed particularly illuminating.

[2]Christopher Haas's forthcoming *Late Roman Alexandria* will offer a separate treatment of that subject.

and research in 1984-85. A fellowship from the John Simon Guggenheim Memorial Foundation in 1990-91 allowed the completion of the first draft of the book. To Columbia University I owe, apart from normal sustenance, sabbatical leaves during those years and generous continuing research support from the office of the vice president for Arts and Sciences. During the second of these leaves, my colleague Paul Anderer gave me real freedom to pursue this work by serving in my place as dean of the Graduate School of Arts and Sciences. His superb leadership and the forbearance of my staff gave me the ability to concentrate on scholarly rather than administrative pursuits. I am also grateful for the constant help of numerous members of the staff of the Columbia University Libraries.

Various parts of this book have begun and developed as lectures and papers over the past decade, at the University of Florence, Bar Ilan University, Hebrew University, Brooklyn Museum, University of Toronto, York University, University of Strasbourg, University of Warsaw, and Bryn Mawr College. For the invitations that provoked their writing and revision I am indebted to Manfredo Manfredi, Ranon Katzoff, Baruch Halpern and Deborah Hobson, Richard Fazzini and Robert Bianchi, Timothy Barnes, Anna Swiderek, Jean Gascou, and Richard Hamilton; and I am equally grateful to the audiences on all these occasions for many helpful comments.

The complete draft of this book was read—again, with that generosity that makes work in papyrology a joy—by a number of friends, whose comments on matters great and small greatly assisted the work of revision: Alan Bowman, Willy Clarysse, Georgina Fantoni, Ann Hanson, Deborah Hobson, James Keenan, Naphtali Lewis, Leslie MacCoull, Dominic Rathbone, Jane Rowlandson, Dorothy J. Thompson, and Klaas Worp. It has also benefited from a reading by my parents and from a checking of references by my research assistant, Denise Gilpin. I am grateful to all who gave permission to reproduce illustrations and who supplied photographs. They are acknowledged in the list of illustrations (p. viii), but I thank particularly Robin Meador-Woodruff of the Kelsey Museum for intelligent, cheerful, and patient help beyond the call of duty.

                                                    Roger S. Bagnall
                                                    February 1993

A Note on References and Abbreviations

Modern works cited more than once (and some cited only once) are included in the Bibliography and indicated by author's name and date of publication; those cited only once are given in full. Abbreviations for journals and standard works may be found in *L'année philologique* and the *American Journal of Archaeology*; deviations should be transparent. Papyri and related works are cited according to J. F. Oates et al., *Checklist of Editions of Greek and Latin Papyri, Ostraca and Tablets*, 4th ed. (*BASP* Suppl. 7, 1992). Provenance and date are provided where they seem useful. Papyrus references are to volume (roman numerals) and papyrus (arabic numerals), except where references to page numbers are specifically so indicated. Critical work on papyri published up to about 1986, as recorded in the various volumes of the *Berichtigungsliste der Griechischen Papyrusurkunden aus Ägypten*, is indicated simply with the letters *BL*; the precise references can be found for each papyrus in W. Clarysse et al., *Konkordanz und Supplement zu Berichtigungsliste Band I-VII* (Leuven 1989) for the material in volumes 1-7, and in *BL* 8 for subsequent work. Critical work since 1986 is cited in full.

For conventions used in this book for the indication of dates, see Appendix 1. For abbreviations used for units of money and measures, see Appendix 2.

Besides these I have used the following abbreviations:

ApPatr = *Apophthegmata Patrum*; the numbering is cited from B. Ward, trans., *The Sayings of the Desert Fathers*, 2d ed. (London and Oxford 1981)

CSBE = R. S. Bagnall and K. A. Worp, *The Chronological Systems of Byzantine Egypt* (Stud.Amst. 8, Zutphen 1978)

CTh = *Codex Theodosianus*: ed. T. Mommsen, *Theodosiani libri XVI cum constitutionibus Sirmondianis* (Berlin 1905)

EpAm = *Epistula Ammonis*, ed. James E. Goehring, *The Letter of Ammon and Pachomian Monasticism* (Patristische Texte und Studien 27, Berlin 1986)

HL = Palladius, *Historia Lausiaca*, ed. G. J. M. Bartelink, *La storia Lausiaca*, tr. M. Barchiesi (n.p. 1974)

HM = *Historia Monachorum in Aegypto. Édition critique du texte grec et traduction annotée*, by A.-J. Festugière (Subsidia Hagiographica 53, Brussels 1971)

MonEpiphanius = The Metropolitan Museum of Art Egyptian Expedition. *The Monastery of Epiphanius at Thebes* II: *Coptic Ostraca and Papyri*, ed. W. E. Crum (New York 1926)

Naldini = M. Naldini, *Il Cristianesimo in Egitto. Lettere private nei papiri dei secoli II-IV* (Florence 1968)

NewDocs = *New Documents Illustrating Early Christianity*, ed. G. Horsley, 1 (1981)-5 (1989)

Porter-Moss = B. Porter and R. L. B. Moss, *Topographical Bibliography of Ancient Egyptian Hieroglyphical Texts, Reliefs, and Paintings* (Oxford 1927-)

RFBE = R. S. Bagnall and K. A. Worp, *Regnal Formulas in Byzantine Egypt* (*BASP* Suppl. 2, Missoula 1979)

VAnt = *Vita Antonii*, cited from *La vie primitive de S. Antoine conservée en syriaque* II, *Discussion et traduction*, ed. R. Draguet (Corpus Scriptorum Christianorum Orientalium 418, Scriptores Syri 184, Louvain 1980)

EGYPT IN LATE ANTIQUITY

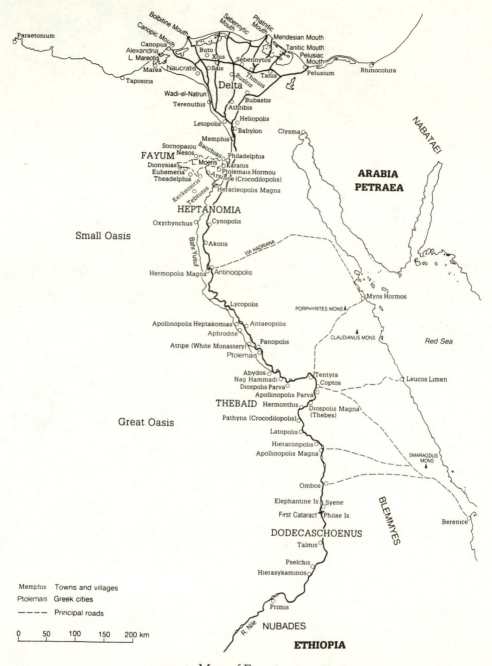

Paraetonium

Bolbitine Mouth
Sebennytic Mouth
Phatnitic Mouth
Canopic Mouth
Mendesian Mouth
Canopus
Tanitic Mouth
Alexandria
Buto
Pelusiac Mouth
L. Mareotis
Xois
Sebennytos
Marea
Naucratis
Sais
Thmuis
Tanis
Pelusium
Rhinocolura
Taposiris
Busiris
Delta

Wadi-el-Natrun
Bubastis
Terenuthis
Athribis
Letopolis
Heliopolis
Memphis
Babylon
Clysma
Socnopaiou
Nesos
Bacchias
Philadelphia
FAYUM
Dionysias
L. Moeris
Karanis
Euhemeria
Ptolemais Hormou
Theadelphia
Arsinoe (Crocodilopolis)
Kerkeosiris
Tebtunis
Heracleopolis Magna

HEPTANOMIA

NABATAEI

ARABIA
PETRAEA

Small Oasis
Oxyrhynchus
Cynopolis

Akoris
VIA HADRIANA

Bahr Yusuf
Hermopolis Magna
Antinoopolis

Myos Hormos

Lycopolis
PORPHYRITES MONS

Apollinopolis Heptakomias
Antaeopolis
Aphrodite
CLAUDIANUS MONS
Red Sea
Atripe (White Monastery)
Panopolis
Ptolemais

Abydos
Nag Hammadi
Tentyra
Leucos Limen
Diospolis Parva
Coptos
Apollinopolis Parva
THEBAID
Hermonthis
Diospolis Magna
Pathyris (Crocodilopolis)
(Thebes)

Great Oasis
Latopolis
Hieraconpolis
Apollinopolis Magna
SMARAGDUS
MONS

Ombos

Elephantine Is.
Syene
BLEMMYES
First Cataract
Philae Is.
Berenice
DODECASCHOENUS
Talmis

Pselchis
Hierasykaminos

Memphis   Towns and villages
Ptolemais Greek cities
– – –   Principal roads

0   50   100   150   200 km

Primis

R. Nile   NUBADES

ETHIOPIA

Map of Egypt
(from A. K. Bowman, *Egypt after the Pharaohs*, Fig. 1)

Introduction

Egypt in the era of Greek and Roman dominance offers the ancient Mediterranean historian opportunities unmatched in any other part of that world as a result of the tens of thousands of papyri and ostraka found there during the past century and a half. These opportunities have, however, only occasionally been taken in a manner that contributes significantly to the broader historical picture of the world around Egypt.[1] This book seeks to assess the society, economy, and culture of Egypt in the fourth century of our era in the context of the later Roman Empire.

This century has always been the center of much interest among both Roman historians and students of early Christianity. It was the time of a widespread revival in the empire after the tribulations of the middle of the third century, and it was the period in which the practice of Christianity was first officially recognized by the emperor and subsequently became in effect the established religion of the empire. But the fourth century's press has been mixed, at best. Tagged conventionally as the transition from the principate to the more absolutist monarchy of the later empire, the era has been seen as decisive for the transformation of a free peasantry, groaning under rapidly increasing taxation, into one tied to both the land and the patronage of great magnates. It has been thought to be a time of unparalleled corruption in government and the military, both of which have been deemed to be growing rapidly. Declining cities have been regarded as graveyards for social mobility. The fourth century from such points of view was a time of decline, a major way-station in the decline and fall of the Roman Empire.

To readers familiar with the scholarship of the last quarter-century, such characterizations may sound quaint. Late antiquity generally has received much better notices in recent years, and the fourth century in particular has been justly recognized as a time of great vitality and interest. The title of the series of books edited by Peter Brown for the University of California Press, The Transformation of the Classical Heritage, is a representative witness to the change in thinking. This more positive approach is, however, by no means

---

[1] A range of assessments can be found in *Egitto e storia antica dall'ellenismo all'età araba: bilancio di un confronto*, ed. L. Criscuolo and G. Geraci (Bologna 1989). The best survey is A. K. Bowman, *Egypt after the Pharaohs* (London 1986; paperback ed. with addenda 1989). Two exemplary recent studies using archival evidence are D. J. Thompson, *Memphis under the Ptolemies* (Princeton 1988) and Rathbone 1991.

universal, and it certainly has some limits. It has, for one thing, tended
to focus—like most writing of ancient history—on that apex of the
political, social, and economic pyramid represented in and responsible
for the literary sources. This is true even with the much-broadened
range of literature studied in recent years.

Fourth-century Egypt, then, has the obvious attraction of offering
a society documented by thousands of nonliterary sources and
capable of being investigated at social and economic levels well below
those available for scrutiny elsewhere. Even if, as we shall see, there
are still serious limits to our evidence and its ability to illuminate the
lower reaches of this hierarchical society, Egypt provides a unique
opportunity to look with some depth at a particular time and place in
late antiquity. Egypt was, moreover, a mature provincial society in a
Greek-occupied land under Roman rule. What it has to tell us should
thus have a considerable bearing for much of the Greek East. The
limits of this book would be greatly surpassed by any general attempt
to demonstrate the significant applicability of its findings for other
parts of the late Roman world, and for the most part the drawing of
such conclusions is therefore left to the reader. Obviously much differed from place to place; much that was Egyptian was peculiarly so.
But much also enters the realm of the basic questions about Roman
provincial society in this period.

These questions include the relationship of the cities to their surrounding rural districts and villages; the extent of continuity and
change in the basic realities of life, such as diet; the ways in which
power was organized and used; the character of the urban economy
and the extent to which the city is to be seen as a "consumer" or
"service" center; the structures of landholding and the management of
agricultural enterprises; the interactions of the international languages
and cultures (Greek and Latin) with indigenous ones; and the paths
by which the ancient world moved from being predominantly pagan
to mostly (but far from entirely) Christian. For all these subjects the
papyri, complemented by other evidence, have much to tell us when
properly interrogated. But there are limits, which should be faced
squarely.

Sources: The Limits of Abundance

The literature of ancient history is rich in laments over the poverty of
its source material. Papyrologists, blessed with a wealth of documentation beyond the lot of ordinary ancient historians, take refuge in

complaining about the limits of the papyri as evidence. It is not my purpose here to add to that dismal chorus. True, there are subjects on which we are scarcely informed, aspects of human life that are but dimly illuminated by the papyri. These are obvious from the pages that follow. So too should be the hazardous and approximate character of the attempts at quantification throughout this book.

But the reader deserves a word of caution about a more insidious characteristic of the evidence. Almost all of it comes from the viewpoint of the propertied classes of the cities of Egypt, the metropoleis of the nomes. Most documents cited in this book come from Oxyrhynchos or Hermopolis, fewer from Antinoopolis, Panopolis, or Arsinoe, and very few indeed from other cities. These reflect the preoccupations of those who were literate in Greek or could pay scribes who were: transactions petty and large in money or commodities, leases, loans, deliveries, payments; legal complaints and records; the voluminous documentation of tax collection on behalf of the imperial authorities and the management of the finances and services of the towns; private letters.

A papyrological voice may be heard objecting that this description ignores the archives of Arsinoite villages, principally Karanis and Theadelphia. That is only partly true. These archives are rich in documents emanating from the same apparatus and processes at work in the cities: the villages sent their taxes to the cities, urban residents lent money or grain to villagers at high interest, and villagers tried to move the machinery of the cities to do something on their behalf. In other words, village archives are largely the result of demands and relationships originating from the cities. How much would be left of the archive of Aurelius Isidoros if his liturgical work, tax payments, leases, and loans were removed?

If the Greek papyri of late antiquity are largely the voice of the urban population and those struggling to cope with the requirements the city dwellers placed on them, whether on their own behalf or that of the imperial government, one may be tempted to look to the Coptic texts for the voice of the others. Those hopes too are destined to be disappointed, for the documents of daily life do not become common in Coptic until much later, long after Chalcedon. As we shall see, Coptic in the fourth century is still largely the instrument of one milieu, the Christian monasteries. To that limited extent, we see from another point of view. But it must not be forgotten that this too is not the viewpoint of the poor. The creators of Coptic were bilingually literate men, not products of the peasantry. If they were poor as monks (and many were not), it was the deliberate, voluntary poverty of choice. And the monasteries are no more the voice of the villages than the cities are.

Archaeology is almost impartially poverty-stricken for all settings, as if to mock the riches of the written record.[2] No city of Hellenistic or Roman Egypt has been excavated for more than a small fraction of its area; only where a papyrus gives us a tour, in Hermopolis, do we even know the bare outline of a town.[3] Of villages, not one has been fully excavated.[4] Some of those that lacked modern habitation on top, like Karanis, were partly ruined by sebbakh-diggers; others were damaged by papyrus-hunters.[5] Probably the large majority of those still extant a century ago were destroyed in the first two decades of the twentieth century.[6] Other villages and towns alike offer tempting mounds covered with modern habitation. Even the apparently most promising, however, have never been properly excavated. Tehneh (Tenis-Akoris, an ancient nome capital become a large village of the Hermopolite) was barely scratched by excavators. When it failed to yield substantial numbers of papyri, it was abandoned.[7] The history of archaeology in Egypt is all too much a matter of digging for papyri, excavating cemeteries, or clearing temples. It would ill become a papyrologist to complain about the excavation of papyri, but papyri as the object of excavation have led to little of archaeological worth.[8] Grenfell and Hunt found many papyri in the rubbish heaps of Oxyrhynchos, but the 1908 plan of the town printed in *Oxyrhynchus Papyri* L (p.vii), contains hardly any information about its layout or character. And one major problem not of human making deserves mention: the Nile has—in some regions at least—continued to move its course over the past two millennia, in general toward the east; as a result, many villages must have been

---

[2]See R. S. Bagnall, "Archaeology and Papyrology," *Journal of Roman Archaeology* 1 (1988) 197-202.

[3]See below, p. 45, for description and bibliography.

[4]Cf. Butzer 1976, 71: "Quite apart from selective destruction of sites by the Nile, practically none of the occupied town mounds of the Nile Valley have been investigated and only a minority of abandoned *koms* has ever been visited."

[5]Nowicka 1969, 10-13, describes both the poor record of excavation and also the dismal fate of even those villages that have been partly excavated with archaeological investigation in mind.

[6]See the despairing remarks of F. W. Kelsey in *Cd'E* 3 (1927-28) 78-79 about the more than 99 percent reduction of the mounds of Arsinoe between 1914 and 1920.

[7]See Lesquier 1911. The renewal of excavations there by the Japanese since 1981 gives hope that this site may yet experience a better fate.

[8]Lest anyone think that papyrus-hunting as the purpose and method of an excavation is a matter of the dim past, Bresciani describes the excavations at Medinet Madi (1966-1969) as "principalmente ed esplicitamente papirologico": Bresciani 1968, 25.

forced to move, and the ancient sites must have been wiped out, their debris now scattered and buried in the Delta or the Mediterranean under tons of silt.[9] In general, villages in the "black" land have probably survived in disproportionately small numbers.[10]

Still, survey work could even now have value. For example, it would be good to know how similar the metropoleis of the nomes were in size. Were only a few substantial Roman cities, and many just small towns of an Egyptian character? Or was there a relatively uniform spread of Graeco-Roman urbanism? How was the countryside organized? Were there many small villages, or fewer large ones? At what distances from one another?

More excavations, carried out not for a few trenches but for a considerable extent, might make it possible to see how much craft production was centralized in the towns or carried on in the villages; might give a better sense of how much the fourth-century church developed a physical presence in the towns and in the villages as compared to the monastic establishments on the edge of the desert; might help provide a better basis for that thorny problem, the dating of Coptic art; might show more clearly the relationship between the organization of space and the cultural forces at work; might clarify the relative expenditure of local resources on public and private construction.[11]

The third major source of information for the period is perhaps the most problematic yet. The literature of the Egyptian church, written originally in Greek or Coptic but preserved in some cases in Latin, Syriac, or Arabic, is voluminous. Much is still unpublished, poorly edited, or untranslated. Only a small part of it has anything to offer for social history. As a scholar far more learned than I in such matters put it, "Despite very vast and attentive reading, I have not been able to draw much from hagiographic literature. To be sure, I cite it rather often, I draw from it information which, in almost every case, has never been put to use by historians of the church; but if I compare the

[9]Butzer 1976, 36: "The economic base for east-bank towns along this sector has changed dramatically and the actual settlement sites corresponding to many cemeteries now preserved on the eastern desert edge must have been destroyed by the river."

[10]Cf. Smith 1972, 705, who points out that most excavated sites are in the desert, not on the alluvial plain, even though most of the population lived on the alluvium. A further distorting factor: desert edge settlements were mostly laid out from scratch and were thus not necessarily typical. In sites on alluvium, most excavation has been of large complexes built of stone, which survives better.

[11]Renewed excavations at Tebtunis also give hope of a more comprehensive view of one village: Cl. Gallazzi, "Fouilles anciennes et nouvelles sur le site de Tebtynis," *BIFAO* 89 (1989) 179-91.

mass of texts which I have read with the number of passages that I
have been able to make use of, the poverty of these texts from the
point of view of my research leaps to the eyes."[12]

For the most part, I have drawn on this literature at second hand,
benefiting from the work of specialists, although I have read a number
of the earlier and more rewarding texts, which are valuable mainly
when tossing out bits of circumstantial detail not particularly germane
to the theme of the work.[13] These texts pose, however, special problems when dealing with matters central to their purposes, such as the
role of the monastic establishments in church life or the relationship
between Christianity and paganism. For such subjects they need a
most critical scrutiny of the writers' aims, and that they have rarely
received. Even scholars of the first rank, perhaps in reaction against
earlier blanket skepticism, have often taken the preaching of the
famous monk Shenoute (to give but one example) at something close
to face value. Here, if ever, a "hermeneutics of suspicion" will be warranted. That approach has informed chapter 8 particularly.[14]

Methods of Understanding

It is not uncommon to be admonished that "the historian of antiquity,
no less than the one of more contemporary societies, must place his or
her theoretical framework first."[15] Such basic notions as informed this
work from an early stage concerned the nature of the ancient sources
and what questions could reasonably be asked of them. These matters
are treated in general terms in the previous section and, as they affect
individual questions, in the various chapters. For the rest, any broader
framework emerged to view only piecemeal along the way, with
flashes of what seemed, at the moment, like insight. To say this is not
to endorse a view of the whole business as "inductive" and emerging
from itself; rather, it has been an iterative process, with study of the
evidence and intuition of hypotheses feeding on one another.[16]

[12]Wipszycka 1972, 22 (my translation). Cf. her similar remarks on the canonical
collections (ibid., 19).

[13]Even these, however, may be fabricated. For an example, see the brilliant note
of E. Wipszycka, "Saint Antoine et les carrières d'Alexandrie," *Études et Travaux* 15
(1991) 460-63.

[14]Cf. F. Thelamon, *Païens et chrétiens au IVe siècle* (Paris 1981) 279: "Comme cha-
que fois que nous abordons le paganisme à travers les textes d'auteurs chrétiens, il
est indispensable de ne jamais utiliser un document sans tenir compte du contexte et
du dessein de l'auteur." (She is writing about Rufinus' account of conflict in fourth-
century Alexandria.)

[15]Shaw 1983, 135.

[16]A lucid description of this process from a scientist's point of view can be
found in Peter Medawar, *Pluto's Republic* (Oxford 1982), especially "Induction and

It may be useful to say something in a broader context about the nature and limits of the evidence, as they appear in retrospect, and how the evidence may legitimately be used. Some, or even all, of these observations may seem obvious, but their persistent disregard by some scholars justifies a bit of table-pounding. The most elementary is that the documents must be analyzed by time and place to have any meaning. Village and city, Upper and Lower Egypt acquire their distinctiveness only by this procedure. Any hope of distinguishing change in a land so marked by continuities (cf. below, p. 13) rests on chronological stratification. It is largely this that gives value and life to the virtually endless task of detailed, seemingly antiquarian, critical study of the individual documents.

Time and place are not the only important axes. The social and economic matrix of individuals and transactions is equally critical and perhaps still more often overlooked. It is curious that a profession so addicted to complaining about students' blind trust in anything printed is itself so prone to take at face value anything written, provided that its author has been dead for a very long time. The seeming authenticity of documents has tended to give them a particular credibility sometimes denied to literary works, the authors of which may be suspected of tendentiousness. This credence, justified perhaps in cases like tax receipts, is unduly extended to petitions and similar texts, which tend to be the basis of vast generalizations about the state of things. That is natural enough because petitions themselves often generalize, thus saving the modern scholar the trouble of independent analysis. But even apart from the rhetorical and literary elements in such texts,[17] it must be remembered that they always represent the self-interest of the petitioner and thus are inherently suspect. It is clear, moreover, that these users of the system of justice come predominantly from the upper levels of society, both urban and village (below, p. 168). Their claims must be scrutinized for the assumptions of status and wealth. The rich are no more likely to have looked at matters disinterestedly in antiquity than today.

A different temptation comes from the abundance of the documents,[18] which may lead the inquirer to conclude that there is ade-

---

Intuition in Scientific Thought," 73-114.

[17]Cf. Arkady B. Kovelman, "From Logos to Myth," *BASP* 28 (1991) 135-52.

[18]The data base for this book included more than 3,500 documents, omitting some uninformative texts (principally ostraka). Abundance is of course relative; a tabulation only of dated papyri from the second century that had been published as of thirty years ago (Duncan-Jones 1990, 68-71) shows an average per year triple that of this entire data base for the period 275-450.

quate evidence for many, if not all, subjects. Any such hopes are dashed again and again throughout this study; a thousand points of light do not of themselves add up to illumination. For one question only a particular place is documented, for another a brief period. Other matters—above all subjective, conceptual, and personal—simply are not documented at all. For still others, the only evidence comes from hagiographic and monastic literature and must be heavily filtered. In the face of this paradox—much information but limited understanding—it is natural to look to comparative study for insight.[19]

Just what late antique Egypt is to be compared with, however (other than the rest of the later Roman world), is anything but obvious. Classical historians have tended to favor anthropology as a source for models and frameworks. Anthropologists have, historically, displayed a systematic bias in favor of studying societies sheltered from the "outside world," groups detached from larger entities and unaffected by cosmopolitan culture. Their preference for small-scale and relatively egalitarian communities (or at least what were perceived to be such) is also noteworthy.[20] Egypt in the fourth century, however, was none of these things. Although such anthropological studies can offer interesting suggestions of both questions and patterns, neither can they be pressed very far, nor in many cases can hypotheses be tested. Given a complex and developed society, integrated into a Mediterranean empire and culture, then, the comparative study of "primitive" societies is not likely to be a consistently enlightening method.

More may be gained from consideration of similar but better-documented historical societies, mainly from the medieval and early modern periods. The reader finds some such comparisons sprinkled here and there in the various chapters. No great weight should be placed on these flavorings. More such study would no doubt be interesting and valuable, but the route by which it could really illuminate an account of fourth-century Egypt would be indirect. An example or two may thus suggest questions or help to confirm an indistinctly visible pattern, but any real light must come from a wider casting of the net coupled with more profound study of the structural interconnections of institutions and practices in the societies in question. That, however, is a different inquiry. The focus here, rather, is on dis-

[19]Cf. the exhortations of Deborah Hobson, "Towards a Broader Context for the Study of Greco-Roman Egypt," *EMC* 32, n.s. 7 (1988) 353-63.

[20]Cf. Bagnall 1989a for some problems posed for a particular question by these characteristics.

tinguishing what was distinctive about the fourth century from the flowing continuum of Roman and Byzantine Egypt—what place it occupies in the formation of the synthesis visible in the Christian Egypt of the sixth century.[21]

The abundance of documents offers another peril besides that of failure to see the gaps or inadequate attempts to fill them, a danger that goes to the heart of the difficulty of using papyri to write history. This is the distinction of signal from noise, of pattern from events, of theme from complex and confusing setting. In much of ancient history, this difficulty is insignificant: there are few truly primary sources, and secondary works—ancient historians—are the main basis of study. With their synthetic accounts, they leave the modern student signal and theme, but they usually still lack much of the data on which they were based and often offer little means of forming any independent interpretation. With the papyri, the situation is reversed. It is much as described by one student of the birds of tropical rain forests: "Phenomena . . . don't jump out at you. They're buried in the intricacies of what's going on, and the overwhelming mass of detail makes any generalizations hard to detect."[22] Only patchily can the historian of Egypt imitate the scientist in providing a quantitative description of patterns, and still more rarely is it possible to give a hypothesis any true test against newly acquired or inspected data, although new evidence occasionally arrives like a thief in the night to correct and refute.

As the comparison to nature is meant to suggest, the problem involves more than managing evidence. Natural and social processes alike are made up of countless individual events; these are not neatly arranged in obvious and rigid ranks where each event leads tidily to the next and the whole presents a clear and linear appearance, but are apparently random, individually determined, and often in conflict. Order in nature and to some extent in society may be discovered and mathematically expressed as tendencies and distributions. The papyri, like all historical documentation, present an imperfect (and certainly not a random) sample of the events of the time from which they come; they thus differ fundamentally from narrative secondary sources.[23] These bits of evidence thus partake of another basic characteristic of

[21]See the sensitive evocation in MacCoull 1988, 147-59, of this distinctive "way of being human."

[22]Jared Diamond, "Bach, God, and the Jungle," *Natural History* (December 1990) 22-27 at 26, with an evocative parallel to the patterns of Bach's organ music.

[23]The obvious and often-remarked truth that the historian's choice of questions to be asked and way of asking them are both subjective and creative represents another kind of selection.

the underlying events, that many are bloody and violent, and others are failures of different sorts. Modern scholars, with genteel sensibilities, tend to regard the casualties of social and economic struggle as signs of societal failure. That attitude is unjustified. To some degree such casualties are universal, but beyond that they may as well be a product of economic and social freedom; individual actors regularly use their freedom to push the limits and create pressures, with inevitable losses for some, even for many.[24] The analytic character of the documents thus places heavy demands on the interpreter in seeking to understand which social or economic casualties are noise, no more significant for broad historical questions than an individual human killed by a lion is for the lines of evolution, and which are the signal.

This is all the more important in that modern interpretation of late antiquity has tended to see a diminution of social and economic freedom. Paradoxically, however, that perception—always a negative judgment—has been fed in part by a revulsion from some phenomena of the documents; that judgment stems in turn from an intolerance for the casualties inherent in a free society—by, that is, a preference for a visible tidiness that could result only from an authoritarian ordering of the economic and social scene. Late antique Egypt certainly could not be described as a politically liberal society, but there is no justification for characterizing it as economically and socially fixed and unfree.[25] It thus offends antimarket liberal authoritarianism comprehensively, but it has a fair claim to be typical of much of the Roman world in these respects. Like almost all ancient, medieval, and early modern societies, in fact, Egypt in late antiquity was a traditional, hierarchical society and should be judged within the context of such societies.

[24]This is hardly an original observation. For an interesting discussion of the intellectual debt of Darwinian theory to Adam Smith's economic analysis, see Stephen Jay Gould, "Darwin and Paley Meet the Invisible Hand," *Natural History* (November 1990) 8-16. Gould remarks (16), "I call Darwin's system more relentless than Adam Smith's because human beings, as moral agents, cannot bear the hecatomb of such a system applied without restraint to our own affairs. We therefore never let laissez faire operate without some constraint, some safety net for losers. But nature is not a moral agent, and nature has endless time."

[25]From at least the fourth century B.C. on, the economies of the ancient world were, despite modern interpreters, predominantly free of state control. For fourth-century B.C. Athens, cf. Cohen 1992. Even Ptolemaic Egypt, that one-time model of a statist economy, has come apart under critical scrutiny; see particularly the subtle analysis of Jean Bingen, "Le Papyrus Revenue Laws—Tradition grecque et Adaptation hellénistique," *Rheinisch-Westfälische Akademie der Wissenschaften, Vorträge* G231 (Opladen 1978).

Nor are the absence of complete security and the presence of a high level of risk necessarily inimical to a vital society. It is hardly surprising that it was an Israeli scholar who pointed out "the general truth, insufficiently realized in modern western countries, that advanced and orderly societies may survive and even thrive while yet suffering from various endemic forms of insecurity."[26]

Continuity and Change, Particular and General

It is a truism of literature about Egypt that many facets of life have been little altered by the passage of twenty or forty centuries. Indeed, the continuity of both material and human existence has forcibly struck every traveler to Mediterranean lands. To attempt to describe the society and economy of a region in a particular period, then, leaves a writer open to obvious risks. A balanced account of life will be dominated by things that would have been as true for an earlier or later period as they were for this; but a description of what is peculiar to a period must see things through a distorted lens. This historian's dilemma is not that only of ancient Mediterranean history, of course. Every writer must find a means of balancing the claims of the elements of human existence shared with the people of the past and those of the uniqueness of each time and people. But for late antiquity, the abundance of papyri from the first three centuries of Roman rule makes a balancing act more difficult than for almost any other period. To write about the time from Diocletian to the Council of Chalcedon (451) is, time and again, to face a stark choice: Either leave out of account the far more plentiful evidence for most subjects in the papyri of the era from Augustus to Aurelian, or find the late antique evidence buried in the greater mass of earlier documentation. For some novelties—the rise of Christianity, for example—the problem is trivial. For many more areas, ranging from the physical character of the cities to the nature of the village agricultural economy, it is acute. There is no satisfactory way out. For the most part, I have chosen to concentrate on the documents from late antiquity, even at the risk of providing a less full context than might emerge from a fully synoptic view. I am conscious that I cannot have succeeded at all points in balancing continuity and change.

Something of the same balancing act is involved in trying to give a general picture of Egyptian society without neglecting the details. Despite many technical monographs, a considerable volume of articles, and many commentaries to published papyri, the field is still far

[26]Isaac 1990, 98.

from the point where a responsible historian can describe his perspective as "that of the parachutist, not the truffle hunter."[27] In some
areas, it is possible to rely on excellent recent work, while in others
almost all remains to be done. I have tried to control the assertions of
others from the original sources, but where subjects remained essentially untreated I have cited the documents more fully and tried to
indicate some problems of detail raised by them. The results are
unlikely to be fully satisfactory to any class of reader, but they may at
least have the merit of making it clearer where further work is needed.

Organizing the Subject

Choices have had to be made in presenting the results of this study.
The most fundamental is between places and topics as a basic organizational framework, but there is as well a constant tension between
description and argument in setting out in general terms a subject in
which so much is still the stuff of controversy. The results are com-
promises. The most descriptive chapter is the first, in which the
general background of life in Egypt is presented—geography, climate,
food, clothing, transportation, and other elements of material existence. These form the greatest constants in the historical picture, but
even there some striking changes may be observed over the centuries
of Greek and Roman rule, and some of these are clear for the first time
in the period covered by this book.

Chapters 2 and 3 describe the two key physical settings for Egyptian society in late antiquity, cities and villages. These chapters contain
much that might well have been presented elsewhere by topic. This
organizational choice reflects my conviction that the differences and
relationship of the city and the village are absolutely crucial to
understanding how Egypt from the third century on came increasingly to resemble other parts of the eastern Mediterranean world and
differ from more ancient Egypt. The tones of description and continuity in these sections, then, to some extent mask an undercurrent of
argument about change that finds its completion in what follows.

The remaining chapters are essentially topical. Although chapter 4
deals explicitly with some particular relationships between cities and
villages, that relationship is in general critical to each of the following
chapters, which are more overtly argumentative than chapters 1, 2
and 3. Only the foundations laid earlier make possible this superstruc-
ture.

[27]Cannadine 1990, 7.

CHAPTER 1

The Environment

The Nile, Valley and Delta: Geology, Ecology

Egypt captured the imagination of ancient visitors and readers just as it has of modern. It is a land predominantly of desert, dry land with little vegetation, which occupies more than 96 percent of the area of modern Egypt. Except along the Mediterranean shore, where the climate resembles that of the rest of the lands around that sea, Egypt has virtually no regular rainfall to moisten the soil; nor, apart from a number of oases, does the desert offer water for human consumption. The climate is mostly mild in winter, rarely colder than freezing, but its summer daytime highs in Upper Egypt, coupled with windstorms carrying sand,[1] elevate the thermometer to 100° F (38° C) daily for months on end: "like the furnace of Babylon," says Palladius.[2] Only the low humidity prevents the heat from paralyzing activity altogether.

Moving through this desert from south to north (to the bewilderment of the ancients) flows the Nile River, fed by rains far to the south of Egypt. Although the eastern and western deserts, with their oases, their Red Sea ports, their nomads, and their trade routes, enter the picture from time to time (especially pp. 145-47 below), this is predominantly an account of life in the Nile Valley. That valley divides conveniently into two parts, the Delta that begins just north of modern Cairo and the ribbonlike valley to the south. There was a certain balance between Lower Egypt and Upper Egypt,[3] for each was anciently divided into approximately twenty nomes, or districts; the exact number varied from period to period.[4] The quirks of preservation of papyrus described in the Introduction have destroyed this balance in historical perspective, for almost no evidence survives from the Delta towns and villages. Here and there it is possible to compensate for this loss, but admittedly we do not even know if our pic-

---

[1]Cf. the painting of the approach of the *khamsin*, by David Roberts in his *Egypt*, vol. 3 (1849) pl. 26, and the descriptions in *Flaubert in Egypt* 103.

[2]*HL* 22.12.

[3]Lower and Upper refer to the direction of movement of the Nile, not to our north-oriented maps.

[4]See Appendix 3. As we shall see, the Delta was in fact larger and came to have more nomes.

ture of ancient Egypt would differ greatly if the evidence were more evenly distributed. To a large degree, then, this is not the story of the entire Nile Valley, but merely of the long ribbon of the upper part of that valley, from Aswan to Memphis: less than one percent of the area shown by modern maps as constituting "Egypt."

That valley is a narrow (from 1 to 20 km wide) river plain, which until the construction of dams at the First Cataract at Aswan was seasonally inundated.[5] What the ancients could perceive locally at ground level we can now appreciate globally from satellite photography: a thin dark band (what the Egyptians called "the black land") through an immense expanse of barren terrain. The Nile's floodwaters reached their peak in the south by the middle of August, in the north a month or six weeks later. When the water topped the banks, it spilled out into flood basins. In a good year, all but the low levees above the alluvial flats, on which settlements were concentrated, would be covered with water for six to eight weeks. Evaporation is vigorous in the dry, hot climate of the Nile Valley, and when it had done its work the nutrient-rich silt of the river flood would be left behind for the planting of the new crops. In its most primitive, undeveloped state, perhaps two-thirds of the valley surface was cultivable without human intervention through irrigation or drainage. Productivity could be improved by maintaining dikes in appropriate places, using canals to see that water went where it was supposed to and stayed there as long as possible, and restricting settlement to levees or land on the desert fringe.

Nature was not uniformly benevolent. The quantity of the Nile flood varied from year to year, sometimes too much and, more threateningly, sometimes too little. A poor flood would leave some basins empty, while reaching others but not giving them sufficient moisture for long enough. It is not surprising, therefore, that the Nile was not only worshiped as a divinity but also monitored like a patient in intensive care.[6] The high-water mark was carefully recorded at various points,[7] and at crucial moments measurements might be taken from day to day.[8] More broadly, because all life depended on the Nile's water, the papyri document a constant concern for all aspects of managing that water.

[5]The account that follows is based principally on Butzer 1976.

[6]See generally Bonneau 1964.

[7]For example, inscriptions at Akoris (Hermopolite): *I.Akoris* 29-39 (284-295 or somewhat later); 41 (4c); 40 (379-383, see K. A. Worp, *ZPE* 78 [1989] 137). Those of the tetrarchic period refer to the Nile as divine, while the fragmentary later texts do not.

[8]*P.Aberd.* 18 = *SB* XIV 11474 (Arsinoite?, 292). See generally D. Bonneau, *Le fisc et le Nil* (Paris 1971).

The central task was maintaining dikes and channels. Their function was not so much to irrigate land, in a modern sense, as to manage
the floodwaters. The system was local; no nome was particularly
dependent on any other for its water supply, and no high-level
management was required. That does not mean that it could not be
directed and exhorted from on high: circulars of the *strategos* and
dioiketes to the *dekaprotoi* concerning work on the dikes and cleaning of
the canals emphasize giving the dikes a proper depth and breadth,
filling up holes so that the flood will be contained, and cleaning the
canals up to the markers so that the flow of water will reach the fields
for irrigation.[9] A hierarchy of officials at the nome and village level
coordinated the efforts of corvée labor in the months before the flood,
directed mostly to cleaning debris and vegetation out of the channels
and piling up this and other material on the dikes to raise and streng-
then them.[10] The apportionment of this labor was based on landholdings.[11] True canal irrigation was not brought into use in Egypt until
the nineteenth century, with the one exception of the Fayum basin
(the ancient Arsinoite Nome), which is at some distance from the river
and not reached directly by its flood.[12] There the supply was limited
and the canal system long, complex, and vulnerable. It is not an accident of preservation that virtually all evidence for disputes over water
supply and rights comes from the Fayum, along with much of the
evidence for canal work.[13]

The development of more sophisticated means of artificial irrigation is a product of Hellenistic and Roman Egypt. It became possible
to water some land not reached by the flood in a given year, as well as
land on the large dikes, by water-lifting equipment. The more primi-

[9]Cf. *P.Oxy.* XII 1409 (*BL*) (278), and W. L. Westermann, *Aegyptus* 6 (1925) 121-29.
For the reporting back to the top that ensued, cf. *SB* XIV 11647 (prov.unkn., 280/1), a
letter of the *strategos* of the Memphite to his superior, forwarding a survey of dike
and canal works carried out by a public surveyor. See generally on this subject Butzer 1976, 20.

[10]The documentation is abundant; cf. Bonneau 1964. A good example of the
planning efforts is *SB* XIV 12108 (Oxyrhynchos, 3/4c), in which responsibility for a
canal of 250+ schoinia (seven miles) is divided among fourteen villages in two toparchies. See the commentary by H. C. Youtie in *ZPE* 24 [1977] 133-37 = *Scr.Post.* I 395-
99, particularly on the relationship of the Tomis river (Bahr Youssef canal) to Nile.

[11]A sample receipt is *P.Col.* VII 168 (Karanis, 373).

[12]Butzer 1976, 47. He points out that the gentle gradient of the Nile makes its
valley mostly unsuitable for radial canalization.

[13]Some examples from the abundant material: *P.Wisc.* I 32 (*BL*) (Philadelphia,
305); *P.Col.* VII 174 (Karanis, ?342); *P.Sakaon* 32, 33, 35, 42, 45 (all Theadelphia). See
particularly *P.Haun.* III 58 (Karanis, 439), a declaration concerning water rights, with
the detailed commentary by Bonneau 1979.

tive of these devices, the *shaduf*, was within the reach of many
farmers,[14] but the *saqiya*, the waterwheel generally called *mechane* in
the Greek papyri,[15] was a major capital investment. Such wheels,
driven by animal power, appear increasingly commonly in papyri of
the fourth century and later.[16] One such machine could irrigate a substantial amount of land, and its spread no doubt increased cultivable
land area considerably.[17]

At the other end of the spectrum of wetness were lands usually
covered partly or wholly by water and cultivable only some of the
time. Such was the land by the edge of Lake Moeris in the Fayum;
such also were marshland[18] and a variety of spaces occupied by water
in time of flood (and perhaps much of the rest of the time, too) but dry
in some seasons or years.[19] There was also a need to store water for
human consumption; although those who lived by the Nile could perhaps count on its water throughout the year, others could not. Hence
the frequent mention of cisterns, a ubiquitous feature of life from
Alexandria to rural villages.[20]

Just as the Nile dominates the habitable landscape, so it organizes
space. Along the ribbon of the valley, towns and villages were spread
in a pattern controlled by the longitudinal character of the land.[21]
Movement was almost entirely by river except for local travel (see p.
34). The average distance from one nome capital to the next was

[14]For an illustration, see Butzer 1976, 43.

[15]Picture in Butzer 1976, 45.

[16]Oleson 1984 includes an exhaustive catalogue of the textual and archaeological information, with illustrations. Terminology is often problematic: cf. esp. Oleson
126-40. All types of water-lifting wheels become dramatically more common in the
documentation after the middle of the third century of our era.

[17]*P.Mich.* XI 611 (*BL*) (Plelo, Oxy., 412) is the lease of a *mechane* and 30.75
arouras of land with it. *P.Mil.* II 64 (*BL*) (Oxyrhynchos, 441) is an example of an
increasingly common document type, requests and acknowledgements for parts for
wheels.

[18]Cf. *P.Charite* 8 (Hermopolis, 348), a receipt for rent on seven arouras of land in
the marsh near a canal.

[19]See *SB* XIV 11853 (prov. unkn., 3/4c), a private letter mentioning the need for
careful instructions to workers on the *koilas*, a watercourse dry during part of the
year. For the *koilas*, cf. *BJRL* 61 (1979) 308. In *CPR* V 8 (*BL*) (Hermopolite, 320) there is
a lease of a canal in an embankment, by the sluice; the bed will presumably be dry
during cultivation.

[20]See, e.g., *P.Oxy.* XLVIII 3409 (360-375?), where a vault of a *lakkos* has collapsed. In *P.IFAO* II 12 (*BL*) (Oxyrhynchite, 5c), the landlord is informed that the
lakkos at a farmstead has been measured, including the vault, at 113 *naubia* (about
278 m^3).

[21]Butzer 1976, 101, suggests that density of settlement was largely a function of
the ratio of Nile frontage to total land: the deeper the floodplain, the lower the
density.

around 40 km, with only a few trips more than 60 km.[22] This is a distance readily traversed in a day by river, and many towns were within a half day's travel of the next town. The total trip from Aswan to Memphis might take two weeks or a bit more, the reverse journey upriver an additional week, but by ancient standards that was reasonable. And, because transport was almost all by water, it was not unduly expensive.

At a more local level, travel was mostly by land. But the distance from riverbank to the border of the cultivated land with the desert was hardly anywhere more than a few hours' walk. And travel to a neighboring village was no great task. The Hermopolite Nome, one of the largest, had about a hundred villages in the fourth century;[23] the average area attached to a village must have been therefore a bit more than 1,000 ha, with the average distance to the next village perhaps about 4 km. Even allowing for some detouring to follow the dikes, and accounting also for a normal level of heat-induced lethargy, that is little more than an hour's trip. Villages were, of course, not all of average size. To judge from tax assessments, the largest might well have had fifteen times the land of the smallest. Visiting the nome metropolis from a village might be only a matter of an hour's walk or as much as a trip from one metropolis to the next. In most cases, trips longer than a few hours would be more efficiently carried out by going to the next river port and taking a boat to the metropolis.

A glance at the map (p. 2) might lead one to suppose that conditions were radically different in the Delta. Here, after all, there is a solid expanse of irrigated land, gradually broadening to almost 200 km at its widest point. The corridorlike character of the upper valley, it might seem, gives way here to something more like broad plains. But it was not so. The land was dissected by the major branches of the Nile and secondary watercourses. Like the upper valley, it was marked by natural dikes and alluvial flats, with lower floods and levees than further south.[24] There were more perennial or seasonal swamps than in Upper Egypt. The Delta's overall size in antiquity was not greatly different from now, although the sandy fringe on the sea was settled only in Hellenistic times, and it had a recently reclaimed swampy hinterland behind it. Only the northernmost part of the Delta was uninhabitable. It is difficult to be sure how much of the Delta's total area was usable for agriculture, but in late antiquity it may have amounted to twice the arable land of the upper valley.

[22]See App. 3 for distances.
[23]*P.Col.* IX 247 records seventy villages in ten *pagi*, an area equal to about two-thirds of the nome.
[24]See Butzer 1976, 22-27, for the Delta.

Travel in this expanse seems not to have differed much from that upriver. Movement laterally across the country was rendered difficult by the north-south orientation of the river delta, as invaders of Egypt like Perdiccas and Antigonos the One-Eyed found to their dismay. Individual nomes were pockets between branches, linked with others best by river—often meaning travel back up the Nile and down another branch—but probably internally organized by roads on dikes. The average size of nomes was evidently somewhat larger than those of Upper Egypt; but by the time of the high Roman Empire a process of subdivision, advancing perhaps with the reclamation of land, had turned the traditional twenty nomes of Lower Egypt into something more like thirty-five. If usable land in the Delta amounted to about 15,000 km^2 (compared to somewhat over 8,000 in the upper valley), the average nome would in fact have been only slightly larger than those in the south.[25] As the center of gravity in the country shifted to the north,[26] the Delta's political, economic, and religious importance grew, camouflaged though it is by the defective surviving documentation.

Seasons and Calendar

Although Egypt has climatic seasons, with varying temperature and to some extent rainfall, seasons do not claim the dominant role that they play in temperate zones. Rather, they are a secondary theme in a composition built on the regime of the Nile, itself in turn a creation of the seasons of precipitation in the regions of its sources in Ethiopia and Uganda. The rhythm of the Nile provided the Egyptians' own conception of the seasons of the year, which they divided into three seasons of four months each: inundation, germination (winter), and harvest. This year was thought of as beginning with the swelling of the Nile around the time of the rising of Sirius on or around July 19, but because the Egyptian year counted 365 days and lacked a means for taking account of the extra quarter day of the astronomical year, the year slipped a month every 120 years or so.[27] When Augustus stabilized the year by adding leap years, the beginning of the civil year already fell somewhat more than a month later than the start of

[25]The total Delta area was something like 23,000 km.^{2} Supposing that 15,000 of these were usable, and that thirty-five nomes divided the area, the average nome had about 430 km^2 in area, compared with about 370 for the valley (8,100 divided by 22).

[26]Butzer 1976, 95, thinks that the Delta had overtaken the upper valley by the Ptolemaic period.

[27]See Gardiner 1957, 203-206, for a basic discussion.

the Nile's rise. Inundation, then, corresponded approximately to the Egyptian months Mesore to Hathyr, or late July to late November; winter to the period from Choiak to Phamenoth, or late November to late March; and harvest to Pharmouthi through Epeiph, or late March to late July. In reality, of course, the Nile's rise was later in the downriver areas to the north than at the first cataract in the south, so that the real activities associated with the seasons varied from place to place by a few weeks, and some tasks could be deliberately scheduled by choosing earlier or later planting dates.[28]

The Nile's behavior affected principally the broad fields reached by the floodwaters. The counterpoint was provided by the crops grown on elevated ground, which matured according to the climatic season and not the river's rise and fall. These were the crops of tree and vine, fruits, nuts, olives, and grapes. They occupied far less land than field crops like wheat and barley, but their value was high and, mercifully, their demands for attention came mainly at times of the year when the grain fields gave the farmer leisure. The intertwined calendar, however, had that characteristic known to farmers of every time and place, relentlessness. "The season requires," one writer says;[29] "the time of the gathering of the crops calls," says another.[30] A letter terms the time a *kairos*, the decisive moment that must be seized now.[31]

During the inundation, much of the country was under water. In August, September, and much of October, no work in the fields was possible. Precisely these months, however, were the time for harvesting orchard crops,[32] and Hathyr 1 (28 October) was the start of the new year for the cycle of work on vineyards, as owners and workers turned their attention from the harvest to preparing the vines for winter.[33] Those whose lives centered around fields of wheat could catch up on other work; some served as water-guards, making sure that the life-giving water was not inadvertently or maliciously diverted from the fields where it was supposed to stand.[34] One

---

[28]See Rathbone 1991, 212-64, esp. summary calendar on 260-63, for the Appianus estate's handling of such matters.

[29]*P.Fay* 135 (Euhemeria, 4c).

[30]*P.Cair.Preis.* 4 = *CPR* XVIIA 9a-b (Hermopolis, 320).

[31]Naldini 57 = *P.Lips.* 111 (4c).

[32]The vintage apparently followed close on the harvest, as one would expect; deliveries are normally due in August, see the table in *CPR* XIV, pp. 31-32. Cf. *P.Oxy.* VI 940 (*BL*) (5c), indicating variability in the date of the vintage.

[33]Cf. *P.Oxy.* XIV 1631 (*BL*; *Sel.Pap.* I 18) (21 December 280, a work contract drawn up almost two months after the start of the period that it covers).

[34]*P.Cair.Preis.* 15 (cf. *ZPE* 45 [1982] 221) (Hermopolis, 362?), a surety document for a man to serve as guard until the end of the watching of the waters and their release. The date is 20 August, near the height of the flood.

important activity of this period was making contracts. While the water stood in the fields, owners and tenants drew up leases of land, laborers entered into work contracts, and owners of animals made agreements for their short-term lease by farmers who needed them for plowing.[35] As the waters receded in October and the land dried out,[36] plowing and sowing could begin, tasks that continued in the early part of the next season.

Winter began with the completion of the sowing in November. Fields planted with fodder crops (often in rotation with wheat or barley) would start yielding green fodder by January,[37] while maintenance work like hoeing, trenching, thinning, and watering went on in the vineyards and orchards. The grainfields too needed attention as the season progressed, but such work generated little paper and is thus poorly documented.

The harvest came on with April and continued into May.[38] It was certainly the most intensive period of work during the entire year. Priority of attention no doubt went to wheat and other time-sensitive crops; flax, which came ripe in early April, was more tolerant and could be put off.[39] By Pauni, crops were being threshed, and rents and taxes paid.[40] The administration introduced around 330 a system whereby the grain paid in taxes was delivered by taxpayers directly to collectors in the harbors rather than, as before, to village granaries; the receipts for such payments are heavily concentrated in the period from May to August.[41] But threshing floor space was no doubt limited, and the authorities wanted it supervised. Threshing would therefore continue throughout the summer and even into the period of inundation.[42] At the same time, most of the year's work on

[35]For example, *P.Michael.* 22 (*BL*) (Tebtunis, 291), a lease of three cows for plowing dated 29 September. The relatively early date may be owing to the fact that the Fayum was not directly flooded like the valley.

[36]For a graphic representation of the flood at Aswan, see Bonneau 1964, 22, Graph VI.

[37]Cf. *P.Michael.* 22 (above, n. 35), where part of the rent for the oxen used in plowing is to be paid in green fodder in Tybi (January).

[38]It was in Pharmouthi (27 March-25 April) that the "call" of the crops quoted above (n. 30) was heard.

[39]See *CPR* XIV 5 introd.

[40]In *P.Oxy.* X 1255 (13 June 292) the komarchs of Ision Panga declare under oath to the *strategos* that they will, on his orders, "keep in safety the crops at the threshing-floors in our lands until the *dekaprotoi* have received payment in full of the public taxes."

[41]See *P.Col.* VII, p. 99, for a graph.

[42]*P.Cair.Isid.* 66 (Karanis, 299) shows Isidoros with grain still on the public threshing floor (where it was maliciously burned) on 20 August.

maintaining dikes and canals would be carried out during the harvest months, particularly the period from Pauni to Mesore, just in advance of the arrival of the Nile waters, for the proper use of which a properly cared-for system of earthworks would be critical.[43] As the waters of the river rose, the agricultural year properly speaking came to its close, while the arboricultural and viticultural year moved to its climax, the harvest of grapes and other fruit.

Food and Clothing: Necessities and Luxuries

The papyri offer a rich diet of foodstuffs, but one would be ill-advised to swallow the menu whole. The documentation is, perhaps even more than usually, biased. The major source of mentions of food crops is the enormous body of receipts, accounts, reports, and correspondence connected with the collection of taxes; next comes the documentation of private transactions in the production cycle, leases and receipts above all. The main taxable crops dominate the texts, and no doubt they dominated the diet as well, although not to the same degree; much of the grain, especially of the grain mentioned in the papyri, was exported. The other main source of information is letters and accounts concerning the consumption of the richest stratum of the population. Their tastes, however, and their means, need not be typical of the rest of the people. The eating of ordinary folk is little recorded.

Pride of place goes to the cereal grains, above all wheat. Its growing, taxation, and transportation, its role as a medium of exchange and wealth, are the themes of discussion in several chapters.[44] For the moment, however, wheat as food commands attention.[45] One *prytanis*

[43]The table in Sijpesteijn 1964, 20, shows that "work was carried out all the year round," but of his seventy-four datable work receipts only eighteen belong to the period from Thoth to Phamenoth, forty-one to the Pauni-Mesore period. It must, moreover, be remembered that the lack of direct flooding in the Fayum (the source of all these documents) allowed somewhat more flexibility than in the valley proper.

[44]For wheat production in general, see J. K. Evans, "Wheat Production and its Social Consequences in the Roman World," *CQ* n.s. 31 (1981) 428-42. See Battaglia 1989, 39-51, for terminology.

[45]Just what kind of wheat has been much argued. Jasny 1944 concluded that "the greatly predominant naked wheat of classical antiquity" was *triticum durum*, hard wheat, despite the fact that it is not ideally suited to breadmaking. He thinks that the modern *triticum vulgare* was not known in classical times. A major support of this view is the discovery at Karanis (Boak 1933, 87) of grains identified as *durum*, comprising fifteen of seventeen samples found on that site. That led one student of Islamic agriculture (Watson 1983, 20) to suggest that *t. durum* was "spreading in the centuries just before the rise of Islam," but because that notion is based on Watson's view that *durum* was otherwise unknown in the Mediterranean world before Islam, it seems weakly grounded. The view that the standard wheat of Ptolemaic and

of Oxyrhynchos wrote to the prefect of Egypt, in terms that sound like a commonplace, that the key element in the feeding of the city was the bread supply.[46] As such, it could not be left to chance; the government ensured that the major cities and the military had bakeries supplied with wheat and workers, some of the latter serving a required tour of duty.[47] The most prized bread, sometimes specified, was *katharos*, "clean" or white bread.[48] It appears, however, mainly in the accounts of well-off households and in the context of festive occasions, suggesting (as one might expect) that ordinary bread was less refined. Indeed, it might be made from wheat of the previous year's crop.[49]

Wheat of high quality, from which this bread was made, had not always so dominated Egyptian cereal cultivation. Herodotos claims that the cereal *olyra* was the chief source of bread in Egypt in his time, and while that claim may be exaggerated, an underlying reality is indicated by the numerous references to *olyra* in Ptolemaic papyri. Its identity has been controversial,[50] but it seems certain to have been emmer, another early form of wheat (*T. dicoccum*, Greek *pistikion*).[51] *Olyra*, however, declined in importance in the later Hellenistic period[52] and *pistikion* is mentioned in our period only in a few texts

------

Roman Egypt was *durum* is generally accepted, cf. D. J. Thompson, *CAH*, 2d ed., VII.1, 369, and in Crawford 1979, 140. See also the complex account of Sallares 1991, 313-61, with an evolutionary approach to the grains in question.

[46]*P.Oxy.* X 1252 verso (*BL*) (288-295).

[47]Some documents concerning public bakeries (some if not all surely for military purposes): *P.Sakaon* 23 (for Memphis, 324); *P.Sakaon* 25 (for Alexandria, 327); *P.Oxy.* XLIII 3124 (for Ptolemais, *ca* 322?); *P.Oxy.* VIII 1115 (*BL*) (for Panopolis, 284).

[48]For the terminology of bread types, see Battaglia 1989, 73-99 (81-82 for *katharos*). A white bread bakery owned by a church: *P.Alex.* 32 (*BL*) (5c).

[49]See *P.Oxy.* VII 1071 (5c).

[50]Rathbone 1983 argued for oats and Cadell 1970, 71-75, for sorghum; see Sallares 1991, 495-96 n. 227 for a sufficient refutation.

[51]See Schnebel 1925, 98-99, on *olyra*; he remarks (98) that emmer is also attested in Pharaonic Egypt. Sallares 1991, 368-72, argues that Egyptian emmer survived as a major crop so long because it had evolved into a variety superior to that in use in Greece, with high yield and easy threshing.

[52]See Crawford 1979, 140: "within one hundred and fifty years the switch to *Triticum durum* was almost total. The only cause for surprise is the silence of the sources. The change is well-documented, but no comment on it has survived anywhere in the papyri or the agricultural writers." Sallares 1991, 370-71, supposes that evolution of naked wheats to be more competitive with Egyptian emmer led to the switch, but this view does not take sufficient account of the swiftness of the change or of the other transformations of Egyptian agriculture produced by the need to cater to the tastes of Greek settlers.

from Karanis; one of these specifies that it is delivered for breadmaking.[53]

The other prevalent grain was barley, amply documented in the papyri and found in the Karanis excavations.[54] It is difficult to tell what quantities were produced compared to wheat, but they were substantial; a fair guess might be that barley amounted to one-fifth of the crop.[55] Barley was usually valued at about half what wheat was;[56] it thus represents probably not much more than one-tenth of the total value of grain crops. Its use is not clear. Some was certainly used for breadmaking;[57] some was used for horse or mule feed.[58] It seems likely also that some was used for beermaking, but there is no direct evidence from this period, and, in fact, there is little evidence of beer itself in the papyri from the period after Diocletian. On the whole, it seems likely that barley bread (always a much inferior food to wheat bread) was eaten relatively little, and that by the poor.[59]

Bread, however, was only part of the diet, even for the poor. As in the modern Middle East, various legumes played a significant role. At Oxyrhynchos, the *kemiopolai* (apparently "seed-vegetable sellers") handled several members of the *leguminosa* family. Lentils (*Lens culinaris*, Greek *phakos*) occur commonly in the papyri and were found at Karanis.[60] Various lentil products also occur more rarely: lentil meal, lentil skins, and a mixture of wheat and lentils.[61] Lentils

[53]See *P.Cair.Isid.* 11, introd. (p. 107) for references, all of which come from the archive of Isidoros. The amounts in this account are not large, less than 100 artabas in all, part hulled, part not. For the delivery of emmer for breadmaking, see *P.Cair.Isid.* 40 (*BL*) (prob. 307).

[54]*Hordeum vulgare*: Boak 1933, 87.

[55]Schnebel 1925, 97, stresses the wide variability of the allocation of land to wheat and barley in the evidence known to him, and subsequent publications have not altered this. Karanis in 309 produced 3,715 art. in barley taxes to 4,527 art. of wheat, but it is impossible to say if this ratio reflects the whole crop (cf. the tables in Bagnall 1985a, 293). The wealthy household documented in *P.Lips.* 97 (338) had starting balances of 1,841 art. of wheat, 581 of barley, which thus represents a bit less than one-quarter of the grain.

[56]Cf. Bagnall 1985b, 7, and *P.Oxy.* LIV 3773.

[57]*P.NYU* 5.62-68 (cf. *P.Col.* VII, p. 81) (Karanis, 340-341).

[58]*P.Cair.Isid.* 57 (*BL*) (315), receipts for 80 art. of barley delivered (as a paid requisition) to ships for transport to Alexandria for Hephaistion, called a horse-rearer. In *P.Cair.Isid.* 58, he is called the leader of the Blues in Alexandria. For mule feed, see *SB* VI 9542 (288).

[59]*P.Abinn.* 5 (*BL*), however, suggests giving some barley to workers as a harvest bonus. On traditional Egyptian beer manufacture, from barley dough, see B. J. Kemp, *Ancient Egypt* (London 1989) 120-28.

[60]Boak 1933, 88. See generally Schnebel 1925, 191-93. The quantity of lentils in *P.Lips.* 97 is rather small, 72+ artabas.

[61]Meal: *P.Lond.* VI 1918 (*ca* 330-340); skins: *P.Rain.Cent.* 83 (Hermopolis, 311); mix: *P.Oxy.* XLVIII 3406 (2nd half of 4c).

generally cost somewhere between one-half and three-quarters the price of wheat, or roughly in the same range as barley.[62] Beans (*Phaseolus*, Greek *phaselos*) were available in much the same price range as lentils, and like them are mentioned fairly frequently.[63] Chick-peas (*Cicer arietinum*, Greek *erebinthos*) turn up less frequently but were sold by the same merchants and at much the same price.[64] Flat beans, or vetch (*Vicia faba*, Greek *orobos*), also occur occasionally.[65] There is also evidence for the use of fenugreek (*Trigonella faenum Graecum*, "Greek hay"; in Greek, *têlis*), a leguminous plant the seeds of which can be made into meal and used in baking, as can be seen from one papyrus in which the writer orders that 50 artabas out of a supply of 100 be given to a baker for his use.[66] Lupines (*Lupinus*, which variety is unknown; Greek *thermos*), the seeds of which can be cooked and eaten, are found also in a few documents.[67] Last in this category must be mentioned a kind of flat bean not precisely identified with a modern equivalent but perhaps of the *Vicia* family, called *arakos* by the ancients.[68] Its price was usually close to that of barley, and it appears in the documents in some quantity.[69]

If none of these leguminous crops individually is of the importance of a major cereal, it must be recognized that together they were

[62]Cf. *P.Oxy*. LIV 3773.

[63]See Schnebel 1925, 193-94, to whose references more can now be added. Cf. *P.Oxy*. LIV 3737. In *P.Lips*. 97, the estate has a balance of only 12.75 art. of beans. *P.Cair.Isid*. 21 and 87-91 are particularly interesting for the trade in *phaselos*.

[64]*P.Oxy*. LIV 3737; the reading is not certain. Chick-peas show up along with white lentils in *SB* XVI 12576 (Oxyrhynchos, 308). See generally Schnebel 1925, 189-90. They could be used for meal, cf. *ApPatr* Theodore 7.

[65]*P.Oxy*. LIV 3737, where they command two-thirds the price of chick-peas or beans, and 3745, where vetch has its own guild of retailers. The estate in *P.Lips*. 97 had just over 3 art. of vetch on hand. See generally Schnebel 1925, 190-91.

[66]*P.Oxy*. XII 1572 (*BL*) (299). See generally Schnebel 1925, 195-97, who remarks that it was used in Egypt in his time, mixed with other grains, for a poor sort of bread. The estate in *P.Lips*. 97 had 10+ art. on hand. In *P.Oxy*. LIV 3737, the price is half that of beans or chick-peas. Crawford 1979, 142, notes that it can also be used to make broth.

[67]*P.Lips*. 97 shows over 82 art. on hand, more than most of the minor crops. Boak 1933, 88, reports lupine seeds at Karanis. Several other papyri attest small amounts. See Schnebel 1925, 194-95.

[68]For a detailed discussion of the problem of identification, see Schnebel 1925, 185-89. It could, while still green in the fields, be eaten as fodder by animals: *CPR* XVIIA 16 (321). Crawford 1971, 113, seems to suggest that this was its only use in Ptolemaic Kerkeosiris, but that was at any rate not true in the fourth century, and cf. *Pap.Lugd.Bat*. XIX, p.11.

[69]More than 743 art. in *P.Lips*. 97, behind only wheat and vegetables of the crops. In *P.Oxy*. VII 1056 (360), 40 art. of *arakos* are exchanged for 500 lbs. of meat. For leases of land to be planted in *arakos*, cf. *BGU* III 938 (cf. *RFBE* 43) and *P.Cair.Preis*. 38.

vital to the diet. In one major estate account these six crops together amount to half the volume of wheat.[70] Most legumes offer somewhat more protein than an equivalent volume of wheat, but they supply fewer calories and carbohydrates. Combining bread made of wheat with a legume in a meal improves the variety as well as nutritional value of the incomplete vegetable proteins in both foods. It is impossible to assess the quantity of complete animal protein at the disposal of the average eater, but given the difficulty of preserving meat and dairy foods in the absence of any refrigeration, it is probable that combining cereals and legumes was an important factor in the quality of the Egyptian diet.

That the legumes are only modestly documented, of course, owes much to the fact that they were a medium of neither taxation, like wheat and barley, nor commercial farming, like wine.[71] The same is still more true for other types of vegetables; moreover, like beans these are mostly susceptible of being grown in small quantities in private gardens, unlike the major field crops. It is thus perhaps not surprising that in several thousand papyri from the late third to mid-fifth centuries there are few mentions of cucumbers, cabbage, garlic, mustard greens, anise, artichoke, and cumin,[72] one possible mention of an onion patch,[73] and no other specific vegetable species. What does appear is *lachanon*, in classical Greek a general word for vegetables or garden greens or herbs.[74] It poses a substantial difficulty, not merely in its apparent lack of specificity, but also in its sale by the artaba, sometimes in very substantial quantities.[75] These quantities, in at least one case to be disbursed over a period of months, must be of a com-

---

[70]*P.Lips.* 97.

[71]See Rathbone 1991, 381, on the absence of many fruits and vegetables from estate accounts because they were produced only for local consumption.

[72]Cucumbers: *P.Oxy.* XLVIII 3426 (cf. Bagnall 1985b, 43-44, 62) (*ca* 360-375); cabbage: *P.Oxy.* XIV 1656 (*BL*) (4/5c; perhaps 370s?); garlic: *SB* XII 10938 (early 4c) (cf. Schnebel 1925, 207-10. For a full discussion of garlic growing in Hellenistic and Roman Egypt, see D. J. Crawford, *Cd'E* 48 [1973] 350-63; most of the evidence, however, is Ptolemaic); mustard greens: *P.Lips.* 97 (338); *P.Lond.* II 453 (p. 319) (*BL*) (4c), in this case mustard clover (cf. Schnebel 1925, 205); anise: *SB* XIV 12173 (Arsinoe, 4c) (cf. Schnebel 1925, 206); artichoke: *P.Mich.* XIV 680 (3/4c); cumin: *P.Köln* V 239 (4c); *SB* XVI 12246 (4c); *P.Oxy.* LIV 3765 (*ca* 327); *SB* V 7667 (cf. *BASP* 18 [1981] 49-50) (Oxyrhynchos, 320). Cf. Schnebel 1925, 205-206.

[73]*P.Bon.* 46 reed. in *GRBS* 25 (1984) 83 (?early 5c, perhaps Upper Egypt).

[74]See briefly Schnebel 1925, 210. For usage in monastic texts, see R. Draguet, *Le Muséon* 48 (1945) 60-64.

[75]In *P.Lips.* 97, the estate has more than 875 art. on hand. In *P.Cair.Isid.* 21 (*BL*) (*ca* 314-315 or later), Isidoros collects 29 art. of beans and 7 of *lachanon*. In *P.Mich.* XI 611 (*BL*) (Oxyrhynchos, 412), two arouras are to be planted in *lachanon* at a rent of 6.5 art. per aroura.

modity that can be kept in dried form, a point reinforced by the common juncture of beans and *lachanon*, and by one papyrus in which an official orders the heads of the pertinent guild to furnish someone with a month's rations of *lachanon*.[76] Such an order makes no sense if fresh lettuce, cabbage,[77] or some other perishable item is to be delivered. The existence of a seed denominated by the same word (*lachanon* seed), from which oil is derived, also suggests that in this period the term had some more specific reference, perhaps to the seed rather than to the plant, than in classical Greek literature: perhaps it was a variety of lettuce cultivated for its seeds.[78]

Sources of animal protein are not much easier to assess. Milk is mentioned only in connection with milk-cake, and its perishability kept it from being a commercial product, but families may have consumed it from their own sheep and goats.[79] Cheese, on the other hand, is well attested, sometimes acquired in large quantities.[80] Quality could become an issue, whether because of poor preservation or inherent nature,[81] but in general cheese seems to have been widely available. Barnyard fowl apparently were commonly kept, but it is difficult to say just what kind of eggs are intended when they are mentioned. Poulterers sold both chickens and eggs, sometimes on a substantial scale, but specialized eggsellers are also attested.[82]

Meat again poses problems of keeping. Beef is rarely attested,[83] veal rather more and occasionally in large quantities, even if perhaps for military purposes.[84] The extensive raising of sheep and goats, though primarily for wool, no doubt provided a supply of meat as

[76]*P.Oxy.* VIII 1139 (4c).

[77]So the word is rendered by Karpozelos 1984, 26, in a 13th century Byzantine letter.

[78]Lucas and Harris 1962, 332-33, note the modern use of lettuce-seed oil in Egypt, citing Keimer 1924, 1-6, esp. 4-5, where he says that lettuce is grown in Upper Egypt as a field crop for the seeds, which are pressed for oil. Cf. also Rathbone 1991, 216.

[79]*P.Oxy.* X 1297 (*BL*) (4c). Butter is found: *P.Ryl.* IV 713 (early 4c).

[80]Two hundred cheeses in *P.Ant.* II 92 (4/5c); two jars of cheeses in *P.Oxy.* XIV 1776 (4c late).

[81]Cf. *P.Haun.* II 19 (a 4/5c letter): "The monks say, 'If the cheeses are like that, he shall bring us no more, for they are not yet fit for keeping.'"

[82]*P.Oxy.* XLII 3055 and 3056 are two orders from 285 for delivery of eggs. In *P.Oxy.* I 83 (= *W.Chr.* 430) (327), a public eggseller swears that he will sell only in the public market and not secretly or in his own house. See also the third-century poulterer's archive at *SB* X 10270.

[83]*SB* XIV 12156 (= *PSI* VII 797 verso) (Oxyrhynchos?, end of 3c?).

[84]See *BGU* I 34 (*BL* and cf. *P.Charite* 36, introd.); *P.Stras.* VIII 736 (4c); *P.Oxy.* LIV 3765 (*ca* 327, a price declaration); *P.Mert.* II 86 (*BL*) (296, a receipt for payment of 3500 dr. for 600 lbs. of veal); *SB* VI 9563 (west Delta, end of 4c).

well (cf. below, p. 143). The standard meat of Egypt, however, was pork, of which substantial amounts were consumed by the army. Because army rations often had to be shipped considerable distances and were no doubt stored for extended periods, this pork was sometimes pickled,[85] and perhaps most was salted.[86] Sausages are occasionally mentioned.[87] The bulk of our evidence for meat is in fact from its collection for military rations;[88] the excavations at Karanis did, however, find numerous pig bones along with a small amount of cattle and other animals,[89] and there are many references to pork in civilian contexts.[90] It remains difficult to assess the contribution of meat to the ordinary person's diet, and as generally in the ancient world it was probably mainly a festive food.[91]

In a country dominated by a river, and with cities named after sacred fishes, it is not surprising that fish and fishermen are fairly well documented. It is, of course, much easier to consume a fish than a pig at one meal, but even so, salting no doubt played an important role in storing fish, just as it has in more recent times.[92] The salty fish sauce called *garum* is also well attested, with white and black varieties mentioned, as well as a wine-garum.[93] There was, in fact, a guild of *garum*-sellers at Oxyrhynchos, which duly filed a declaration of the price of their sauce.[94]

One other food group contributed greatly to the caloric level and palatability of the diet, the oils. The third century B.C. Revenue Laws papyrus, where the rules for the oil monopoly under Ptolemy II are set forth, gives the impression of an Egypt heavily planted in sesame, croton, castor, safflower (*knekos*), linseed, and colocynth (pumpkin or

[85]*P.Mil.* II 70; *SB* XVI 12663; *PSI* IX 1073 all mention *oinokreon*, meat pickled in wine. See R. S. Bagnall, *BASP* 27 (1990) 91-92.

[86]Cf. the more than 900 art. of salt on hand in *P.Lips.* 97. For a salt business, see *P.Ryl.* IV 692, 693, 695, and 696 (late 3c).

[87]*P.Lond.* III 1259 (p. 239) (*BL, BASP* 20 [1983] 11-12) (Hermopolite, *ca* 330).

[88]The quality of these was sometimes problematic; cf. *P.Cair.Isid.* 44 (305/6).

[89]Boak 1933, 88-92.

[90]Often called *delphax* or its diminutive, *delphakion*, properly meaning suckling pig; cf., e.g., *BGU* III 949.

[91]Cf. *P.Mert.* I 40 (?Arsinoite, 4/5c).

[92]The numerous texts mentioning fish mostly do not indicate whether the fish is fresh or salted, but salting is mentioned specifically in *P.Oxy.* X 1299 (*BL;* = Naldini 76) (4c). See also the pickled mullet in *P.Coll.Youtie* II 84 (4c) and *P.Oxy.* XXXIV 2728 (*BL*) (3/4c). For salted, pickled and smoked fish in Byzantine letters, cf. Karpozelos 1984, 24-25.

[93]*P.Herm.* 23 mentions white and black garum; *SB* XVI 12246 lists wine garum. Cf. *Kleine Pauly* 2.700-701: black garum was the best.

[94]*P.Oxy.* LIV 3749 (319), priced by the sextarius.

gourd).[95] Of these, sesame and croton were clearly dominant. It is therefore baffling to find only one reference to sesame in our entire period, and that in a list of items for sacrifice from the late third century.[96] Sesame in fact is represented by only a handful of references from the Roman period generally. Safflower, entirely missing from the late third and fourth centuries, is extremely rare from the Roman period except, curiously enough, for a common lease clause allowing the lessee to plant anything except safflower.[97] Croton occurs once, about two and a half artabas in the great agricultural account from 338.[98] Aside from a couple of first-century references, croton is again rare in Roman papyri.[99] Colocynth oil, never common, is absent from the Roman record, though pumpkins themselves turn up occasionally.

Against this record of "disappearing" crops must be set the oils actually found in the papyri of the late Roman period. First, the oil of choice, called "good oil," was olive oil.[100] It does not appear frequently.[101] What the oilworkers mostly sell, according to their price declarations, is oil made from "vegetable seed," *lachanon*-seed.[102] The difficulty of identifying *lachanon* has already been described. Because the different seed crops prevalent in the Ptolemaic period, but rare in Roman times, had greatly varying values,[103] it is hardly likely that the term refers to the group indiscriminately. It has been suggested above (p. 28) that a variety of lettuce productive of seed is more likely. At all events, "oil" without further modifiers appears to refer to this vegetable oil. At the bottom of the scale is the malodorous radish oil,[104] referred to very commonly in the papyri of this period. It is sold

[95]On the various oils, see Schnebel 1925, 197-203; D. B. Sandy, *The Production and Use of Vegetable Oils in Ptolemaic Egypt* (BASP Suppl. 6, Atlanta 1989).

[96]*P.Oxy.* XXXVI 2797.

[97]Apparently because it was a pest to more valuable crops. Some examples: *BGU* XI 2124, XV 2484; *P.Mert.* III 107. There is one account (*SB* XVI 12565) mentioning a significant amount (164.5 art.) of safflower, but it strikes the reader by its rarity.

[98]*P.Lips.* 97.

[99]Note *O.Bodl.* 1086, 1171 (both 1c), 2053, *P.Stras.* IV 267 (both 2c).

[100]For example, *P.Abinn.* 72; *P.Bad.* IV 54 (*BL*); *P.Oxy.* XIV 1753 (40 sextarii per solidus). For the important role of olive oil elsewhere in the empire, see D. J. Mattingly, "Oil for Export?" *JRA* 1 (1988) 33-56.

[101]There are, however, numerous mentions of olives themselves—black, pickled, sweet—preserved and eaten in considerable quantities.

[102]*P.Oxy.* LIV 3760 (*ca* 326). The declaration covers the price of *lachanospermon*, the raw material, as seems to be the case elsewhere in these declarations.

[103]*P.Rev.*, col. 39, gives the prices.

[104]See Lucas and Harris 1962, 335, who describe it as having a disagreeable smell. In *ApPatr* Benjamin 3, its use is a sign of great asceticism.

on one occasion for a third cheaper than olive oil,[105] and the market price in the fifth century was approximately in line with this.[106]

The oils together certainly played at least as important a role in the diet as in the documentation. As in modern eastern Mediterranean cooking, oil does much to make the various legumes palatable in addition to moistening bread and acting as a medium for cooking meat. High in caloric value by weight and bearing valuable unsaturated fats, these vegetable oils helped keep the bulk of cereals and legumes required in the diet within reasonable bounds.

Egypt produced many fruits and nuts. The Karanis excavations found date, fig, hazelnut, filbert, lotus, peach, pine, pistachio, and quince.[107] These were hardly all equally common. The best attested (and ubiquitous today) is the date-palm tree and its fruit, both mentioned in numerous texts and sometimes in considerable quantity. Figs, usually dried, were less common,[108] and of the other fruits found at Karanis only the peach is attested in any papyrus of our period.[109] Nuts generally are sometimes mentioned,[110] and general fruit merchants are also known.[111] Grapes not used for winemaking were sometimes eaten fresh or dried.[112] Apricots and apples were known.[113] Evaluating the contribution of fruit to the diet is difficult without some sense of the quantity eaten; at least it provided some sweetness and vitamins, and dates, the commonest fruit, are rich in iron and niacin among other nutrients.

The major concentrated sweetener, of course, was honey, frequently mentioned; it was a key ingredient in the various kinds of cakes often referred to in letters.[114] The poor, however, probably

[105]*P.Mich.* XI 613 (Herakleopolis, 415), in which a staff officer of the provincial governor receives 150 solidi from two Alexandrian councillors for purchasing 9,000 sextarii of radish oil to be shipped to Alexandria. The solidus thus buys 60 sextarii.

[106]*P.Oxy.* LI 3628-3633, with considerable variation.

[107]Boak 1933, 88.

[108]*P.Oxy.* XX 2273 (*BL*) (late 3c); *P.Wash.Univ.* 52 (4c).

[109]*P.Mich.* XIV 680 (3/4c). An unpublished papyrus of the third century in the Columbia collection mentions pears.

[110]*P.Cair.Isid.* 132 (3c) is a rare example.

[111]Cf. the fruit buyer in *P.Lond.* III 974 (p.115) = *W.Chr.* 429 (Hermopolis, 306), who undertakes on oath to supply the seasonal fruits for his city. A fruitseller in *P.Oxy.* VIII 1133 (*BL*) (396) pays off his debt for a crop bought in advance from an orchard-owner.

[112]*P.Lond.* VI 1918 (*ca* 330-340), apparently fresh; VI 1920, dried.

[113]*P.Mich.* XIV 680 (3/4c).

[114]See the comprehensive treatment by Chouliara-Raïos 1989; add *P.Oxy.* LVI 3860 (late 4c) and 3862 (probably later than the editor's date of 4/5c). For pastries and special breads, see Battaglia 1989, 103-27.

found sweetness more commonly in dates.[115] Cooks could add interest to food otherwise with a wide variety of spices, obtained for the most part by trade from the East but some perhaps domestically produced. Pepper, balsam, cassia, cinnamon, and many other aromatic substances were available. Most of these were undoubtedly expensive luxuries for the rich; it is hard to say how widely they were available to ordinary people to help introduce some variety into a relatively monotonous diet.

It is a curious fact that after centuries of abundant attestation in the papyri, the traditional drink of the Egyptian masses, beer, almost disappears from the documentation in the fourth century.[116] It might be thought that this silence is in part another reflection of the massive shift in the surviving evidence away from the villages and their concerns to the nome metropoleis and theirs, from the lives of peasants to those of middle and upper-class Greek or Hellenized landowners. For what appears, above all, is wine.[117] Expensive wine, ordinary wine, cheap wine, bad wine,[118] and wine vinegar all play a part. People produce wine, buy and sell it, ship it; in wealthy households, it is a major medium of payment for goods and services.[119] Price declarations at Oxyrhynchos record the cost of local wine and vinegar of various types.[120] Clearly wine was widely available and commonly consumed in the middle and upper classes; whether the same was true for the peasant population is more difficult to tell, but the absolute lack of documentation of beer (in Coptic as well), and the widespread assumption in the papyri and in Christian literature that wine was a basic stuff of life, point to the virtual disappearance of beer from the Egyptian diet, a long-term incident of culinary Hellenization comparable to the swifter conquest of durum wheat.[121]

"We go slowly and don't get overtired, living sensibly and clad in flannel from head to foot, even though the temperature indoors is sometimes thirty degrees [C.]." So Gustave Flaubert described his

---

[115]H. Cuvigny, *Cd'E* 65 (1990) 181, who points out that honey was a luxury item.

[116]The only item of any substance is *P.Oxy.* XII 1513, and that concerns supply to the army.

[117]Schnebel 1925, 239-92, gives a general account of wine production. See in particular Rathbone 1991 for commercial wine production on a large estate.

[118]See *P.Iand.* VI 99 (3c): "We tasted the wine of Nikolais on the 28th and found it bitter. Of the jars in the house, most contain vinegar."

[119]E.g., *BGU* I 34 (*BL* and *P.Charite* 36, introd.).

[120]E.g., *P.Oxy.* LIV 3765.

[121]Not to drink wine is a sign of unusual asceticism among monks: cf. *ApPatr* Poemen 19 and Peter Pionites 1.

dress at the start of his Egyptian trip in November 1849.[122] Modern
travelers to Egypt tend to dress as lightly as possible in the heat, that
is, except in winter. They are often, however, struck with the fact that
many Egyptians wear far more extensive and heavier clothing than
foreigners. It is difficult to say from the papyri just what ordinary
dress consisted of in late antiquity, but it is at least clear that the
dominant fabric was wool, with linen an expensive and elegant choice
for dressier garments.[123]

Clothes served more purposes in antiquity than simply covering
the body or even adorning it. Modern consumers think of clothing
primarily as an expense, an outlay for consumption. Good quality
fabrics, however, whether as clothes or as hangings and draperies,
served in antiquity also as a form of storing wealth, of keeping money
in reserve.[124] In that regard they were like items made of precious
metals.

A considerable variety of garments occurs in the texts, largely in
the correspondence of well-off people and in lists of their possessions.[125] There is no ready means of determining for each how much it
was used; for some garments, in fact, it is difficult to determine what it
was. Among the better-known types of clothing were the *chiton*, or
tunic; the *himation*, a woman's dress; the *maphortion* and *faciale*, or
head-cloths; various sorts of cloaks;[126] the *paenula*, or mantle; shoes,
sandals, and slippers;[127] and some more modern-sounding clothes,
shirts and pants, the latter a very unclassical innovation.[128]

---

[122]*Flaubert in Egypt*, 29-30.

[123]Cotton is only rarely attested; cf. H. C. Youtie, *AJP* 65 (1944) 249-58 =
Script.Post. II (Bonn 1982) 665-74.

[124]Because few prices are preserved and the garments they refer to vary widely,
it is difficult to form any detailed sense of the cost of clothing; but in general it seems
to have been expensive. Cf. Karpozelos 1984, 29, for a similar view based on
Byzantine letters six centuries later. Most of the prices in the papyri are in fact payments for military uniforms supplied to the state (see Bagnall 1985b, 69, and *P.Col.*
IX 247, commentary), and these do not in general reflect more than a fraction of the
true cost. In 302, when the true value and the reimbursement had not yet diverged
so much, military garments cost the equivalent of 3 to 4 art. of wheat, or 1.5 to 2
months' average pay.

[125]An example of the proverbial laundry-list in the papyri is *P.Gen.* I 80 (*BL*)
(mid 4c).

[126]Among them the *delmatikon*, *sticharion*, *pallium*, and *chlamys*, along with some
less common types.

[127]Shoes: *P.Gen.* I 80 (*BL*) (mid 4c); *P.Oxy.* X 1288 (*ca* 324-330? *BL*); sandals,
P.Ant. II 92 (4/5c); slippers, *PSI* III 206 (end of 3c, two pairs of women's slippers);
P.Oxy. XXXI 2599 (3/4c, three pairs for the baths).

[128]Breeches: *P.Oxy.* X 1341 (4c); *P.Gen.* I 80 (*BL*) (mid 4c); shirts, also in *P.Gen.* I
80.

The existence of a textile and clothing industry of considerable proportions, ranging from individual craftsmen to larger establishments, is well documented in the papyri. But the letters show also a lively private commerce in the materials of making clothing, from tow and raw wool to finished cloth to dyestuffs. Certainly much clothing was made in the home.[129] It is, however, anything but clear how to assess the relative roles of homemade and commercial clothing in supplying the ordinary needs of the population. Nor is it evident just how easy it was to come by a garment of a particular type at any given time.

Most cleaning of clothes was no doubt done in the home, whether by the women or, in wealthier households, by slaves. But professional cleaners' establishments existed, probably used mainly by the relatively prosperous for more important garments. They were no more immune to destroying clothes than modern cleaners.[130]

Transportation

The dominance of Egypt by the Nile is as marked in transportation as in other respects. From any given point in the country, only the most local of destinations was reachable by land more directly, quickly, or conveniently than by water. Even within a nome, some travel was most efficiently carried out by the river, and all long-distance movement was certainly by boat. This basic situation, reflected in the documents, is strongly reinforced by a second consideration. What Egypt produced was above all grain, a bulky commodity; this grain was in large part destined for export, a policy going back to Ptolemaic need of silver and carried on by emperors needing to feed urban populaces in Rome and later Constantinople. The grain not exported from Egypt remained in Alexandria to feed the large population there, including its garrison. And the government's elaborate system for controlling the transportation and storage of grain ensured the creation of enormous amounts of paperwork.[131] Many papyri are therefore con-

[129]A few examples: *P.Giss.Univ.* III 32 (3/4c, *himatia*); *P.Lond.* VI 1920 (*ca* 330-340, *lebiton*); *P.Meyer* 23 (*BL*) (4/5c, *maphortion*); *SB* XIV 11881 (4c, a pitiful plea for some tow that the recipient can turn into linen and sell to support the orphaned children of her brother); *P.Oxy.* XXXI 2599 (3/4c, face cloth).

[130]Cf. *Pap.Lugd.Bat.* XIII 18 (= Naldini 81; *BL*) (*ca* 312-318), in which a man asks for a new mantle because his has perished at the cleaners. See also *P.Herm.* 12 (4c), where the writer expresses his hope that a garment has been well cleaned by some anticipated "Cretan" earth.

[131]See *P.Wash.Univ.* II 82 (367) introduction, for the paperwork such a transaction would generate.

cerned with river transportation of wheat, barley, chaff, and other goods collected by the government.

The information provided by these texts is highly concentrated on a few points, some of which do not concern transportation itself.[132] About boats we learn the names of types and of some individual boats; the carrying capacities of the boats;[133] and the identity and residence of many of their owners and captains. About the boat types, it is often difficult to be exact. One of the commonest was the *polykopon*, "multioared," with a recorded capacity of 505 to 1,010 artabas (about 15 to 30 metric tons);[134] also common is the *hellenikon*, "Greek" vessel, with a somewhat wider range (350 to 2,000 artabas, or 10.5 to 60 tons).[135] Other specific types include the *zeugmatikon*, perhaps a catamaran,[136] the *lousorion*, a small light galley,[137] *platypegion*, a barge,[138] and other more obscure types.[139] Most boats, however, are not typologically described, being simply boats. Their capacities as cited range from 70 to 5,200 art. (2 tons to about 160 tons),[140] and evidence from earlier periods does not much enlarge that range.[141] Few of these, if any, were capable of sea voyages. The ancients considered boats under 70 to 80 tons unsuitable for sea travel; that would amount to about 2,500 art. burden, a figure exceeded by few boats mentioned in the papyri.[142]

[132]On shipping, see Merzagora 1929, part 1 of an intended longer work which never appeared; this installment covers the types of ships, the cargos they carried, the parts of ships, and insignia.

[133]See Appendix 2 for the weight of wheat.

[134]See Casson 1971, 334; E. Wipszycka in *Cd'E* 35 (1960) 219-20; for examples of capacity, *P.Oxy.* I 86 = *W.Chr.* 46 (338); *P.Oxy.* XXIV 2415 (late 3c).

[135]E.g., *P.Cair.Goodsp.* 14 (*BL*) (343); *P.Oxy.* XXII 2347 (*BL*) (362); *P.Oxy.* X 1260 (*BL*) (286). Cf. Casson 1971, 340.

[136]Casson 1971, 334. The editor of *P.Oxy.* XXIV 2415 suggested a towed vessel; capacity here is 505 art., about 15 tons.

[137]Casson 1971, 333, 340. In *P.Oxy.* VII 1048 capacities of 823 and 2,465 are attested (about 25 and 75 tons), the second being just triple the size of the first; these may have been standard sizes, as perhaps with the *polykopon* in its 505/1,010 modules.

[138]Casson 1971, 334.

[139]The *phikopedalos*, of 900 art. (27 tons) burden in *SB* XIV 11548 (Hermopolis, 343); the *skaphoproron*, perhaps a lighter, 600 art. (18 tons) in *P.Oxy.* XLII 3031 (ca 302); 500 art. (15 tons) in *SB* XVI 12340 (Hermopolis, 312); and the *kontarion*, perhaps a poled vessel; see Casson 1971, 334, 336, 340-41.

[140]The 70-art. boat (the only one under 200 art. attested in this period) occurs in *P.Oxy.* XVII 2136 (291). The 5,200 art. vessel appears in *CPR* XVIIA 7 (Hermopolis, 317); cf. line 2, note.

[141]See Merzagora 1929, 135-36; one 10,000 art. *kerkouros* from Ptolemaic times is attested.

[142]Cf. Casson 1971, 171-72.

Even river boats of such modest size represented a substantial capital investment. The only direct evidence from this period for the value of a boat is a fifty-year lease, virtually a sale, dated 291, of the smallest boat attested, a seventy-artaba boat, for 3.5 talents.[143] That is not an enormous sum,[144] but it is significant. A *hellenikon* of 400 art. burden was lease-purchased in 212 in the same manner for 1 T. 2,000 dr., a sum representing between sixteen and twenty-seven years' wages for various occupations, and perhaps six years' wages even for a well-paid legionary.[145] Put another way, the boat cost approximately the same amount that the wheat to fill it would have. That seems about in line with the cost for the smaller boat in 291, as well.[146] Nor was maintenance negligible; one might have to rent a mast[147] or make repairs.[148] Though the evidence is limited, shipbuilding was certainly a substantial activity.[149]

If the cost of entry into the ranks of boat-owners was minimally the equivalent of several years' income, only the wealthiest can be expected to turn up in the list. Some boats, to be sure, were owned by the government; they are called "treasury" or "public" boats. But those designations are less common in the documents than the names of private owners. Often enough these are no more than names. But a simple list of the titles attached to those who are identified is revealing: a *vir clarissimus*, a *vir spectabilis*, *speculatores*, a *comes*, an *a commentariis ducis*, *princeps*, a former *logistes*, city councillors, a bishop who owns four boats, a bishop's son, the church of Alexandria, and a priest.[150] The owners, in short, are the municipal aristocracy, high-

---

[143]*P.Oxy.* XVII 2136.

[144]Price information for this period is not extensive; but cf. the 16.5 tal. (five times as much) paid in 289 for one top-quality camel: *BGU* I 13 (cf. *BL* 2.2.14, = *M.Chr.* 265)—admittedly a very high price, because one camel sold in 302, after significant rises in prices, for 9 tal. (*P.Grenf.* II 74).

[145]*P.Lond.* III 1164h (p. 163). Compare wage levels in *BGU* II 362, two to three years later, analyzed by Johnson 1936, 309.

[146]The 500-artaba *hellenikon phikopedalon* sold in 581 (*P.Monac.* 4/5 verso) commanded only 19.67 solidi, which would normally purchase about 200 artabas of wheat, thus a considerably lower (though hardly low) price.

[147]*P.Corn.* 45 (Oxyrhynchos, 299).

[148]*P.Oxy.* XIV 1752 (378), wine paid to sawyers for renewal of a boat; *P.Oxy.* XLVIII 3427 (2nd half 4c), payment for boat repair.

[149]See P. van Minnen and K. A. Worp, *ZPE* 78 (1989) 141-42.

[150]Respectively: *P.Oxy.* VII 1048; *P.Oxy.* XLIX 3481; *P.Oxy.* XLII 3079; *SB* XIV 11551 (on the staff of the governor of the Thebaid); *P.Col.* VII 160 and 161; *P.Harr.* I 94; *P.Col.* VII 160 and 161; *P.Oxy.* XLVIII 3395; *P.Harr.* I 94; *P.Oxy.* I 87 = *W.Chr.* 446 (BL); *P.Oxy.* VII 1048; *P.Col.* VII 160 and 161; *P.Harr.* I 94 (priest, bishop's son); *W.Chr.* 434 (Hermopolis, 390: church of Alexandria). Another bishop appears in *P.Oxy.* XXXIV 2729 (cf. n. 156 below). Monasteries also owned boats; cf. Chitty 1966, 37; Gascou 1976a, 184.

ranking imperial officials, and the upper clergy,[151] the major holders
of all forms of wealth and power in this society.[152] They were distributed all over Egypt; in just one account of boats we find a remarkable range of home ports: the Kynopolite, Hypselite, Lykopolite,
Upper Kynopolite, Oxyrhynchite, Metelite, Prosopite, Herakleopolite,
Apollonopolite, Arsinoite, Phthenote, Lower Diospolite, Elearchia,
Hermopolite, and Nilopolite.[153] There are no figures available for the
total number of such boats, but if the average boat carried 1,500 art.,
made six round trips per year, and the total to be carried was
8,000,000 art., about nine hundred boats would have been required.

This was not the only Nile traffic. The government also operated
an official post, the *velox cursus*, via cutters manned by sailors and
rowers provided by the municipal governments.[154] And there was
abundant shipping in private hands for commercial purposes. Much
of the evidence concerns boats, mostly small craft, owned by *geouchoi*,
large landowners, and used for transporting goods between parts of
scattered holdings and from country estates to the city.[155] A bishop is
again named as a boat-owner,[156] and monasteries and churches also
own boats.[157] Those who did not own boats sometimes chartered them
for particular occasions.[158] There were also opportunities to ship
goods and to travel on third-party boats traveling up and down the

[151]Hollerich 1982 discusses the various forms of church and clergy involvement
in the "grain trade" (as he inaccurately calls it), concluding (205-6) that the origin of
such ownership was satisfaction of liturgical obligations and not investment. But his
belief that river shipping was a compulsory service rests on a misreading of Johnson
and West 1949, 157-58. The liturgy mentioned there is of providing sailors for the
public boats used for transportation of high officials, a very different matter. See
Sirks 1991, 193-95, for the distinction between river and sea transportation of tax
grain.

[152]For similar investment in shipping in the Ptolemaic period, cf. D. J. Thompson, "Nile Grain Transport under the Ptolemies," in *Trade in the Ancient Economy*, ed.
P. Garnsey et al. (Berkeley 1983) 64-75, esp. 66-68.

[153]*P.Oxy.* XXIV 2415 (late 3c).

[154]Among documents concerning this service: *P.Oxy.* XXXIII 2675; *P.Oxy.* LI
3623; *P.Oxy.* VI 900 (= *W.Chr.* 437); *PSI* X 1108; *P.Grenf.* II 80-82 (*BL*) (Hermopolis,
402-403).

[155]*P.Oxy.* IX 1223 (= *Sel.Pap.* I 164) (*ca* 360-375, *BL*); *P.Oxy.* XLVIII 3406 (2nd half
4c); *PSI* VIII 948 (*BL*) (Arsinoite, 345/6).

[156]*P.Oxy.* XXXIV 2729 (*BL*; Bagnall 1985b, 17, 45-46; J.-M. Carrié, *Aegyptus* 64
[1984] 203-27) (*ca* 352-359). Klaas Worp points out that the bishop named here,
Theodoros, is attested in Athanasius' *Festal Epistle* for 347.

[157]*P.Ross.Georg.* III 6 (*BL*) (Oxyrhynchos?, 4c), mentioning two sailors of the
church. In *SB* VIII 9683 (prov.unkn., end of 4c), a monk complains about a soldier's
removal of "the anchor of our brothers," perhaps a reference to a part from a boat
owned by a monastic establishment. The Pachomian establishments certainly owned
boats.

[158]*P.Flor.* III 305 (Hermopolite, 4c); *SB* XII 11155 (4c).

Nile,[159] but it was not always easy to find such boats when they were wanted, and there are several references either to travelers' difficulties in finding a boat to take them where they wanted to go at a particular time or to their concerns with security or breakage on board.[160] Adverse winds[161] or the state of the Nile's flood[162] also made water travel more difficult for individuals, even on canals. Nor should it be forgotten that crossing the Nile always involved a ferry.[163]

The nearest land equivalent of the boat was the wagon. It involved a capital investment in construction and required animals to haul it. Although not terribly fast, the wagon had a capacity well in excess of that of any animal. There are few references to wagons in the papyri of the fourth century, and all occur in the context of the estate management operations of large landowners.[164] To obtain maximum capacity, wagons needed to be drawn by oxen, and these too were expensive, owned principally for plowing and rented out to others for that purpose once the owner's plowing was accomplished.[165] The scarcity of wagons may be explained, apart from their expense, by the dominance of water transport for the movement of bulky items and by the character of the Egyptian countryside, extensively chopped up by canals and dikes.[166]

Land transportation, of both goods and people, was primarily the province of the donkey. The cost of a donkey varied considerably in real terms,[167] ranging in rough terms perhaps from about the equivalent of five to ten months' average income. It was still a capital investment of some substance, but obviously at an order of magnitude

[159]Some examples: *P.Stras.* VI 558 (*ca* 300); *P.Oxy.* XIV 1749 (4c); *P.Lips.* 102 (?Hermopolite, end of 4c) (an expense record for a trip to Alexandria, stay there, and trip back).

[160]*P.Oxy.* XLVI 3314 (4c); *P.Amh.* II 144 (5c); in *P.Mich.* III 214 (Koptos, 297), a husband urges a wife not to wear her gold ornaments on the boat. Breakage of a jar on board: *PSI* VII 829 = Naldini 71 (4c).

[161]*P.Oxy.* XIV 1682 (Naldini 52) (4c); a calm is mentioned in *P.Oxy.* IX 1223 = *Sel.Pap.* I 164 (*ca* 360-375, BL).

[162]Cf. *VAnt* 0 (p. 3.29): "Because the time was limited in which boats travel from Egypt to the Thebaid and from there to here, and the carrier of the letter was in a hurry . . ." For canal travel, see *P.Oxy.* LVI 3860 (late 4c).

[163]Cf., e.g., *ApPatr* Ammonas 6.

[164]*CPR* VI 31 (?before 300/1); *SB* XVI 12947 (early 4c); *P.Stras.* VIII 735 (4c). All are apparently Hermopolite, perhaps just an accident of the evidence. There are wagon drivers employed by the great house of *P.Lips.* 97, also.

[165]Cf. *P.Gen.* I 76 (BL) (3c). See also *P.Oxy.* XXXVIII 2849 (296) and *P.Oxy.* XLVIII 3407 (2nd half of 4c), in which oxen are needed for the heavy work of moving stone.

[166]For a general assessment see Bagnall 1985c.

[167]See Bagnall 1985b, 67-68, for prices.

lower than even the very smallest of boats. There is evidence for a professionalization of the business of buying and selling these animals.[168] Correspondingly, the donkey's capacity was far lower, usually rated at three artabas, or about seventy-five kg.[169] The cost of feed for a mule, which is larger than the donkey, if it could not graze, is set by one document at one (four-choinix) measure of barley per day, or one-tenth of an artaba.[170] Because the value of barley was about half that of wheat, a donkey, eating less and making one round trip per day would consume less than 1.5 percent of the value of a one-way load of wheat.

Considerable evidence for donkeys involves just such transportation of wheat from villages to the city or to river ports, when it is likely that there would have been no return load. The distance coverable on such a trip would rarely need to be more than twenty km, or a forty km round-trip, which seems perfectly manageable. Journeys might, of course, be much shorter; one text shows teams making five round-trips per day.[171] The cost of transport by donkey, naturally, would include also that of the donkeys' drivers; one driver for every three donkeys may have been a common ratio.[172] Donkey drivers were a professional group, although individual farmers certainly owned and used donkeys themselves.

The camel occupied a more specialized niche in the scheme of things.[173] It was the foremost means of long-distance desert transportation, over routes where food and water were not abundant and the animal's endurance and high load capacity were important.[174] Camels were also useful to wealthy landowners, who had greater needs for local transportation than most farmers and sometimes found a mix of camels and donkeys useful in providing flexibility.[175]

[168]See *P.Genova* II App. 1 (319) and *P.Genova* I 21 (cf. *P.Genova* II App. 2) (320); cf. Wagner 1987, 327-28, for a somewhat different restoration of the 319 text, and 319-20, for comment.

[169]See W. Habermann, *MBAH* 9 (1990) 50-94, on the variability of such figures. With panniers it might be 20 percent higher.

[170]*SB* VI 9542 (288), assuming that the figure of three metra for three mules means one each and not three each.

[171]*P.Harr.* I 93 (*BL*) (?Oxyrhynchos, 294).

[172]See for example *O.Oslo* 26 (Fayum, 4/5c), a list of donkeys and drivers totaling (omitting one aberrant case who has six donkeys) thirty-four donkeys and eleven drivers.

[173]See generally Bagnall 1985c.

[174]Among texts connected with transport outside the valley: *P.Sakaon* 22; *PSI* IX 1037; *P.Grenf.* II 74 (*BL*); *P.Abinn.* 9; these concern quarrying operations, the military, and the oases.

[175]See *BGU* I 34 (*BL*); *CPR* VIII 50 (transport from a village to the city); perhaps *P.Oxy.* XVI 1953 (baggage). Three camel drivers are employed by the great house of *P.Lips.* 97. Official use of mixed camels and donkeys is also attested, for example in

Still more specialized in use was the mule, which is mentioned only rarely in a military connection.[176] Horses appear in connection with visits of high officials,[177] with criminal raids where speed was important,[178] and the military.[179] Only a few horse sales are preserved.[180]

By the standards of most of the Roman world, Egypt was an easy country in which to travel and transport goods, principally because of the river system and the shallowness of the inhabited land on either side of the river. Even so, there are signs that people found travel a wearying and dangerous business, to be avoided if possible. One letter says, "we must be very grateful to him because he undertook the trouble of the journey to you although we paid the expenses."[181] Another, summing up feelings deeper than the difficulty of travel, remarks that "it is better for you to be in your homes, whatever they may be, than abroad."[182]

Material Culture: Work and Consumption

Food, clothing, transportation, and shelter (see pp. 49-50 and 112) are the most basic of needs, and most of the Egyptian population enjoyed rather basic forms of them: bread, beans, vegetables, oil, some fish, meat, cheese, and fruit; tunics, cloaks, and sandals; their own feet, perhaps a donkey; a mud-brick house sheltering people and animals together. Set against this is the range of possibilities open to the rich, in more varied food, drink, and clothing; boats, camels, and wagons; larger, better made, and better furnished houses. Some sense of what was available comes in the large vocabulary for these *realia*, much of which is rare and incompletely understood.

That same richness of vocabulary meets the reader of the papyri in other areas of material culture, too. It is, however, deceptive, not just because many things referred to were available to a tiny portion of society, but because on examination they reduce to a few categories

---

P.Oxy. XXXVIII 2859 (301).

[176]*P.Oxy.* XIX 2228 (283 or 285?) deals with the compulsory supply of mules for purchase by the government at a price under discussion. The clear implication is that mules could be found for purchase in the nome. The context of *SB* VI 9542 (288), on feeding mules, is unclear.

[177]*SB* XIV 11593 (*BL*) (Hermopolite, *ca* 340).

[178]*P.Gron.Amst.* 1 (Oxyrhynchos, 455).

[179]Seemingly the context of *P.Amst.* I 82 (prob. *ca* 337-348).

[180]A list is given in Bagnall 1985b, 68.

[181]*P.Wisc.* II 74.

[182]*P.Fay.* 136.

and a simple structure in which raw materials or minimally processed goods predominate and the means by which the necessities of life were produced take pride of place.[183]

Before turning to these specific areas of material culture, however, something must be said about that key underpinning of much of the activity, energy. It will already be obvious that much energy was provided, as in most premodern societies, by human and animal muscles; the contribution of gravity (the Nile's flow downriver) and the winds (sailing on the river) were also not trivial.[184] But there were many activities for which energy from the combustion of fuel was required: cooking, operating baths, metallurgy, baking bricks, tiles, and pottery, glass manufacture, and making plaster. What did the residents of Roman Egypt burn? Modern scholars have, observing the scarcity of trees in early modern Egypt, the paucity of references to wood as fuel in the papyri, and the occasional indication that individual trees were highly valued, tended to assume that ancient Egypt also had little available wood. It is highly likely, however, that Egypt imported wood in considerable quantities, for both construction and combustion, particularly from southern Asia Minor; it certainly did so in later periods of prosperity with shipping technology comparable to that in antiquity.[185] Some was no doubt used in the form of charcoal, and it may have been imported in that form. Chaff from threshing cereal grains was certainly used to heat water in baths and perhaps also for making gypsum plaster.[186] It is also likely that animal dung and garbage were burned, as was the case in Ottoman Aleppo.[187] But fuel for high-temperature combustion must have been comparatively expensive, one of the few ways in which Egypt was a relatively poor country.

First, then, comes the production of food. The land had to be plowed before sowing: hence plows and their parts.[188] For some fields, orchards, and vineyards, irrigation equipment was needed.[189] When

[183]The most useful collection of material on ancient Egyptian material culture is Lucas and Harris 1962, cited below more specifically for some major industries. Reil 1913, though very much antiquated, is still useful for the related crafts.

[184]The scholarly literature is remarkably bare of comment on energy and fuel. Braudel 1981, 334-72, gives a useful survey for early modern Europe, but the resources there differed in several ways from those in Egypt.

[185]Cf. Braudel 1989, 366; L. Robert, *BCH* 108 (1984) 519-20.

[186]Braudel 1989, 366, notes the use of sugarcane stalks in later periods.

[187]Marcus 1989, 262-63.

[188]*P.Amh.* II 143 (4c), in which the courier of the letter is said to be bringing two old plowshares to be made into one new one; *P.Cair.Isid.* 137 (Karanis); *P.Stras.* VI 576 (cf. Index, p. 108) (*ca* 300 ed.; perhaps rather *ca* 325-330 based on price levels), with iron and wooden plows.

[189]See Oleson 1984 for a detailed account.

the wheat and barley had been harvested, they had to be threshed, winnowed, and sifted; the appropriate tools are mentioned.[190] In the orchards and vineyards, pruning and thinning were necessary, with their instruments.[191] The grains, beans, fruit, and wine had to be stored, whether in baskets,[192] sacks,[193] or jars,[194] which might be lined with pitch.[195] To turn grain into flour or seeds into oil, mills were needed, whether simple home devices or self-standing commercial enterprises with more elaborate equipment.[196] The shepherd in the field, watching over the sheep, needed his crook.[197]

Building materials and tools are another important area.[198] Raw materials had to be found and prepared: stone was quarried,[199] bricks made,[200] wooden beams and panels prepared from cut trees,[201] glass made,[202] nails[203] and other metal parts fabricated,[204] and dry lime for mortar prepared.[205] The builders also needed the essential tools, including ropes and baskets.[206]

[190]*P.Lond.* V 1657 (4/5c); *P.Oxy.* X 1290 (5c); *P.Mich.* XIV 680 (3/4c).

[191]*P.Mich.* XV 721 (3/4c); *SB* VIII 9834b.

[192]*P.Mich.* XIV 680 (3/4c); *PSI* VIII 959 (*ca* 385); *P.Vind.Worp* 24 (3/4c); *SB* VIII 9746 = Naldini 36 (4c); *SB* XIV 12080 (4c); *SB* XIV 12140 (3/4c). Baskets, of course, had many possible uses beyond holding food, and the purpose is not always clear.

[193]*P.Abinn.* 68 (hair for sacks); *P.Col.* VII 188 (320, haircloth sacks); *P.Ryl.* IV 606 (late 3c, haircloth and tow sacks); *SB* VIII 9746 = Naldini 36 (4c, haircloth and wool).

[194]Sometimes in large quantities, like the 1,000+ double jars in *P.Lond.* V 1656 (?Arsinoite, 4c). On pottery making, see generally Reil 1913, 37-46; Lucas and Harris 1962, 367-85.

[195]*P.Oxy.* XII 1497 (*ca* 279, pitch and jars); *P.Oxy.* XIV 1753 (390); *P.Oxy.* XIV 1754 (4/5c); *P.Oxy.* LIV 3766 (329). See *CPR* XIV 2.16n. for discussion.

[196]*P.Cair.Isid.* 64 (*ca* 298); *P.Mert.* I 39 (4/5 c); *P.Mich.* XII 627 (Arsinoe, 298); *P.Oxy.* LI 3639 (412).

[197]*P.Wisc.* II 62 (3/4c).

[198]See generally Reil 1913, 25-37, 47-50, 59-93; Lucas and Harris 1962, 48-79.

[199]Stone was expensive because it had to be brought a distance from quarries in the desert; cf. *SB* VI 9230 (Syene?, late 3c); *P.Sakaon* 24 and 25 (325, 327).

[200]*SPP* XX 230 (4c); *SPP* VIII 1023 (4-5c); *PSI* VIII 959 (*ca* 385); *PSI* VI 712 (*BL*) (Oxyrynchos, 295); *P.Haun.* III 63 (4/5c); *P.Ant.* I 46 (? *ca* 337-348, *BL*); *CPR* VIII 22 (Hermopolis, 314).

[201]*CPR* VII 37 (Hermopolis, 4c); *P.Mert.* I 39 (4/5c); *P.Wisc.* II 62 (3/4c); *SB* XIV 11591 (*BL*) (Hermopolis, *ca* 325-330); *SPP* XX 230 (4c).

[202]*P.Oxy.* LIV 3742 (317); *P.Coll.Youtie* II 81 = *P.Oxy.* XLV 3265 (326).

[203]*P.Oxy.* XIV 1658 (4c); *P.Oxy.* XXXVIII 2877 (late 3c); *P.Oxy.* XLIX 3511 (full publ. in *ZPE* 30 [1978] 200-204) (1st half 4c); *SPP* XX 230 (4c).

[204]*P.Flor.* III 384 (*BL*; cf. *GRBS* 25 [1984] 84) (Hermopolis, 5c, fittings of a bathhouse); *SB* VI 9230 (Syene?, late 3c, bronzesmiths working on construction). A bellows is mentioned in *P.Mich.* XIV 680 (3/4c).

[205]*BGU* XIII 2361 (Arsinoite, 4c, distinguishing burnt and unburnt); *P.Cair.Isid.* 59 (*BL*) (Karanis, 318, receipt for unslaked lime); *P.Cair.Isid.* 60 (319); *P.Princ.Roll* 126 (in *Archiv* 30 [1984] 53-82).

[206]*BGU* XIII 2361 (Arsinoite, 4c, poles, staves, shovels); *BGU* XIII 2361 (Arsinoite, 4c, plaited reeds); *P.Harr.* I 97 (4c); *P.Herm.* 36 (4c, palm fiber ropes); *CPR*

And clothing.[207] Most references to the making of clothes are requests for or annoucements of the sending of the raw materials, tow for linen and wool.[208] But the other necessary items are also found, the warp, the woof thread,[209] and particularly dyestuffs.[210] Even in the cities, the generally expensive dyes were probably not always easy to find. Footwear and some clothing required hides.[211]

The dividing line between production and consumption is not easy to draw. But if the home preparation and serving of food can be put on the consumption side, it was no doubt the single most important area for consumer goods. Accounts and letters frequently mention all manner of containers and utensils for storage, cooking, serving, and eating: kettles, frying pans and saucepans, plates and saucers, pots and tureens, casseroles, saltcellars, and so on.[212] Baskets made of reeds were ubiquitous.

Other home furnishings also play a large role. Mostly these seem to have been various creations in fabric: rugs, mattresses, pillows and cushions, bedding, and coverings. Wooden or metal furniture was scarce: a few tables are mentioned,[213] wooden bedsteads,[214] lamp-stands and lamps,[215] and various chests and boxes.[216] A few items of decoration were found in any household, but probably only the wealthy had paintings and sculpture.[217] Generally, homes of the period would seem underfurnished to modern western taste, with most items stacked in a corner much of the time when not in use; the

---

VIII 22 (Hermopolis, 314).

[207]See generally Reil 1913, 93-122; Lucas and Harris 1962, 128-54.

[208]Of numerous examples, note Naldini 93, a fifth-century Christian letter in which a querulous mother, among other requests, wants six pounds of black wool to make herself a veil.

[209]Both found in *P.Lund* IV 14 = *SB* VI 9350 (cf. *BL* 5.65) (Arsinoite); thread also in *P.Oxy.* VIII 1142 (both late 3c). A bobbin in *SB* XIV 12140.

[210]*SB* XVI 12628 (Oxyrhynchos, *ca* 329-331); *SB* I 2251 (Oxyrhynchos, 4c); *P.Stras.* VIII 735 (Hermopolis, 4c); *PSI XVII Congr.* 18 (Oxyrhynchos ?, 4c); *P.Oxy.* LIV 3765 (*ca* 327).

[211]*P.Abinn.* 81 (*ca* 345); *P.Oxy.* LIV 3765 (*ca* 327, oxhide, goatskin, sheepskin).

[212]*P.Cair.Isid.* 137; *P.Oxy.* I 109 (*BL*); *P.Oxy.* XIV 1658; *P.Cair.Isid.* 137; *P.Princ.* II 95; *P.Alex.* 31; *P.Oxy.* XIV 1657; *BGU* XIII 2360; *P.Oxy.* XIV 1657; *P.Alex.* 31; *P.Cair.Isid.* 137; *P.Oxy.* X 1349; *P.Oxy.* XIV 1658; *P.IFAO* II 12b; *BGU* XIII 2360.

[213]*P.Col.* VII 188 (320, bronze); *P.Oxy.* XIV 1645 (308, wooden?).

[214]*P.Oxy.* XIV 1645 (308); perhaps also *P.Oxy.* VIII 1142 (late 3c).

[215]*P.Lond.* V 1657 (4/5c); *P.Oxy.* XIV 1645 (308); *P.Princ.* II 95 (4c ed., perhaps actually 5c); *P.Oxy.* LVI 3860 (late 4c).

[216]*P.Bon.* 38 (3/4c); *P.Ant.* II 93 = Naldini 80 (4c).

[217]*P.IFAO* II 12b (Oxyrhynchos, 5c); *SPP* XX 230 (4c, whether public or private is unclear), both sculpture; *PSI* VII 784 (*Sel.Pap.* I 178) (362), painting.

limited floor area of most people's houses made this practice very natural.

Apart from military equipment, which was needed by only a small part of the population, it remains only to note the presence of writing supplies: papyrus, tablets, pen, and ink. These are mentioned only occasionally, but there may have been no ordinary need for these implements to document themselves.[218]

The final expenditure of the Egyptian life was for funerary expenses. The fourth-century documents are much less informative than those of earlier centuries about such matters, but the materials for mummification and burial appear at times, particularly natron.[219]

[218]*P.Abinn.* 21 (*BL*): "Since I could not at the moment find a clean sheet of papyrus, I have written on this." *P.Harr.* I 97 (4c); *P.Oxy.* VI 895 (*W.Chr.* 47) (305); *P.Oxy.* VIII 1142 (late 3c); *P.Oxy.* X 1297 (*BL*) (4c, both papyrus and wooden tablet mentioned); *P.Oxy.* XVII 2156 (*BL*; Naldini 89) (4/5c, parchment); *SB* XII 11077 (4/5c); *SB* XIV 11593 (*BL*) (Hermopolis, *ca* 340); *PSI* IV 286 (*BL*) (Oxyrhynchos, 3/4c); *PSI* VIII 959 (*ca* 385); *P.Fouad* 71 (*BL*) (5c, after 430; large, rectangular 10-leaf notebook of tablets, Antiochene ink and quill set); *P.Lond.* V 1657 (4/5c, perhaps an inkpot); *SB* XIV 11857-11858 (4/5c, book illumination or external decoration: *Byzantion* 44 [1974] 362-66).

[219]*CPR* X 52 (4/5c, perhaps 370s); *P.Abinn.* 9; *P.Mich.* XIV 680 (3/4c); *P.Wash. Univ.* 52 (4c). See on mummification generally Lucas and Harris 1962, 270-326. For the occupations concerned with funerary practices, see Derda 1991.

CHAPTER 2

The Cities

The Built Environment

A visitor to late third-century Egypt who traveled as far upriver as Hermopolis would disembark at its harbor on the Nile, travel west a few kilometers, and arrive in the city through the Gate of the Sun. The street leading west inside it would offer him a familiar scene, common to hundreds of Roman cities throughout the empire. Colonnades lined this Antinoe Street, leading a pedestrian through a tetrastylon (four monumental pillars marking an intersection), past an exedra and temples of Hadrian and Antinoos, to the central marketplace; then past two nymphaea and temples of Aphrodite and of Fortune (Tyche), through a great tetrastylon where the avenue leading to the great temple of Thoth crossed Antinoe Street, through a third tetrastylon (of Athena), and so to the Gate of the Moon.[1] The careful articulation of space with tetrastyla, the shade-giving colonnades, the way-stations like the exedra and nymphaea (perhaps adorned with fountains), the defined end-points, all would mark Hermopolis for the visitor as a typical Greek city of the Roman Empire—a smaller version of the type represented equally by a metropolis like Ephesos or Antioch.[2] (See Plate 2 for one reconstructed view.) Adjoining, naturally, he would find a gymnasium and baths, those essentials of civilized life, and other civic buildings.[3] As a provincial seat of government, Hermopolis also had offices for imperial officials[4] and storehouses for the products of the land delivered to the government as taxes or requisitions.[5]

---

[1]The main evidence is textual, particularly a building account on a Vienna papyrus, for which see Schmitz 1934. On the archaeological remains, see Roeder 1959, Spencer 1984, and Bailey 1991 (the latter two with up-to-date plans and extensive bibliographies of excavations). A north gate, with public road, appears in CPR XVIIA 18 (321).

[2]For this "armature" of a city of the Roman Empire, see MacDonald 1986. For Egyptian cities, see Bowman 1992.

[3]For bibliography on Roman baths, see J. DeLaine, "Recent Research on Roman Baths," JRA 1 (1988) 11-32; on fuels, see Meyer 1990. The boiler room of the baths of the gymnasium is mentioned in SPP XX 230 (2nd half 4c). There might be multiple gymnasia; there were two at Nikiou in the Delta, see SB I 411 (3/4c). See also P.Oxy. LVI 3856.

[4]A robbery in these offices is mentioned in P.Lips. 34 (ca 375).

[5]Cf. the chaff storehouse of Hermopolis in P.Lips. 84 (late 3c).

Hermopolis was not unique in its self-presentation.[6] Antinoopolis, a consciously Hellenic foundation of Hadrian, only a few kilometers from Hermopolis on the other bank of the Nile, could still be seen as a Roman city when the Napoleonic expedition visited it, with a long street running north-south from the gate to the theater, several transverse streets, and a hippodrome outside the walls.[7] Here too a tetrastylon helped define civic space.[8] At Oxyrhynchos, excavations offer no help, directed as they were entirely at finding papyri. But those papyri inform us unsystematically of Roman buildings: the baths, perpetually in need of work, for example,[9] and the gymnasium. In 283, two brothers who worked joining wooden beams in a colonnade billed the city for their labor in the construction of a street running from the gate at the entrance of the gymnasium toward the south as far as Hierakion Street.[10] The streets running from the several city gates were articulated, as elsewhere, with tetrastyla.[11] For public spectacles, there was the theater.[12] At least some cities had army camps, whether inside or outside the urban core.[13] And for troublemakers, the cities had prisons.[14]

[6]See Lukaszewicz 1986 for a detailed discussion of public buildings and their construction in the cities of Roman Egypt.

[7]Donadoni et al. 1974, Tav. 1, reproduce the plan from *Descr.* in their report on recent excavations.

[8]J. Johnson, *JEA* 1 (1914) 168.

[9]For the baths of Oxyrhynchos, see J. Krüger, *Tyche* 4 (1989) 109-18. *P.Laur.* IV 155 (prob. 282/3) shows the bronzesmiths at work repairing them; in 316, work on the warm baths was still (or again) in progress: *P.Oxy.* I 53. *P.Oxy.* VI 896, Col. I is a report dated to the same year from a painter who had been asked to inspect the warm baths of Hadrian now under repair, to see what needed painting. He informs the logistes that two cold water conductors, a vapor bath, the entrances and exits of the entire colonnade, four passages around the vapor bath in the outer colonnade, and other areas all demand his attention. Ten years later, work was still in progress: *P.Oxy.* XLV 3265 = *P.Coll.Youtie* II 81 (326) is an estimate by the glassworkers for work on the warm baths. The city had more than one bathing establishment, naturally; in *P.Oxy.* VI 892 (338) a city councillor is appointed to be in charge of timber for the baths and north gate currently under construction.

[10]*P.Oxy.* I 55 (= *WChr.* 196). Cf. the gymnasium's guards in *P.Oxy.* I 43 verso iv.8 (early 4c?).

[11]*P.Oxy.* I 43 verso iv.12 (early 4c?), tetrastylon of Thoeris.

[12]*P.Oxy.* I 43 verso iii.6 (early 4c?).

[13]Oxyrhynchos had two quarters named after camps. For Thebes (Diospolis Magna), see Golvin et al. 1986. At Hermopolis, the name *Phrourion* (Fort) for the old temple enclosure speaks clearly enough. An army camp in or near Panopolis is mentioned in *P.Panop.* 8 (338). Perhaps it was, like the *palation*, in the old Triphieion across the river (Borkowski 1990, 29).

[14]*P.Oxy.* XLV 3249 (326); see the valuable commentary.

Hermopolis, Antinoopolis, Oxyrhynchos, no doubt Arsinoe.[15] Little imitators of big cities, sharers in the architectural self-definition of Hellenism under the empire. How far were they typical of the four dozen or so nome capitals of tetrarchic Egypt that called themselves cities, *poleis*?[16] All certainly had the political and social institutions required—the council, the honorable but expensive public offices, the gymnasium. All must have had an agora, a marketplace.[17] An inscription from Athribis, in the Delta, records the erection of a four-fronted arch in 373/4 by a city official.[18] That was another standard Roman architectural form, marking passage from one part of the way to another.[19] (See Plate 1 for an example.) For the rest, neither papyri nor excavations inform us. Probably the elite of every town sought to give it the spatial image of a great city; but their means must have varied considerably and with them the success of this posturing.

Appearances were costly. The councillor appointed to superintend work on the gymnasium porticoes at Hermopolis in 266-67 was allotted 15.5 talents in public funds, or the equivalent of the year's pay for about sixty-five skilled workers.[20] The building account of 263, from which most of the description above of Hermopolis comes, shows a total of more than 65 talents spent on the works along Antinoe Street. These texts record the cost of repairs and improvements to existing buildings and streets. A contemporary equivalent to the 80 talents recorded in these two cases might be put conservatively at $7,000,000 (reckoning $20,000 a year as an average wage), a considerable sum for a city of this size; and this is a partial record of what was spent only for improvements. Hermopolis was not built in a day, any more than any other Roman city; the creation of the basic framework of streets and public buildings in a city might take more than a century. Some of the funds involved probably came from large contributions of the very wealthy, others from rents on the city's land and buildings, but the combination in the case of Hermopolis or any

[15]*P.Turner* 37 (270) mentions the gymnasium quarter and a colonnaded street; but we are poorly informed about the physical realities of this city.

[16]Of these, only Antinoopolis had been a *polis* in the second century, along with the older Greek cities (Naukratis, Alexandria, Ptolemais).

[17]That of the Upper Kynopolite Nome, for example, turns up in documents from elsewhere as a place to buy donkeys: *P.Berl.Leihg.* I 21, *P.Corn.* 13, *P.Oxy.* XIV 1708 (all in 309-311). *P.Herm.* 24 (4/5c) seems to mention a "greatest marketplace" in Hermopolis, and no doubt multiple markets were normal.

[18]*OGIS* II 722 (*SB* X 10697). On Athribis' urban development in the Roman period see L. Dabrowski, *ASAE* 57 (1962) 19-31.

[19]Cf. MacDonald 1986, 87-92.

[20]M. Drew-Bear forth. and earlier Schmitz 1934.

other Egyptian city is obscure.[21]

A different reality greeted the visitor who left the main streets and Roman public buildings. The private houses and shops, with their mix of uses along narrow, twisting streets, had little in common with the public face of the city, though they must have been similar to such quarters of Middle Eastern cities of other periods.[22] No city of Roman Egypt has been excavated extensively enough to allow us to see it whole, but a coherent picture emerges from fragments of evidence. The nome capitals of pharaonic times had been most visibly the centers of cult for the chief god of the nome, and the temple complexes built for these gods, be they of New Kingdom date or as late as Ptolemaic, were imposing structures. In many cases they dominated the whole city. The temple of Hathor at Tentyra (Dendera), for example, is some 110 x 260 m; the pylon of the temple of Horos at Apollonopolis Magna rises 36 m.[23] The temple of Thoeris at Oxyrhynchos, now gone, was described by Grenfell and Hunt as being close in size to that of Dendera.[24] Egyptian architecture was nothing if not massive. These temples, moreover, were surrounded by precincts, walled and filled with smaller temples, other cult buildings, and priests' houses. The precinct of Thoth at Hermopolis amounted to about 26 hectares, the grand sanctuary of Amun at Karnak to about 38 hectares, the enclosed area at Dendera only 8 hectares.

The Egyptian temples were not only large; they were also uncompromisingly Egyptian in style, even those finished by the Romans. A Greek living in a nome metropolis was reminded daily by these temples that the gods of the place were Egyptian, not Greek, even if they were referred to by Greek names—Hermes, Apollo, Aphrodite, and the like—in some cases. Antinoe Street in Hermopolis ran parallel to and just outside the south enclosure wall of Thoth's precinct. The city constructed colonnades, with no buildings behind them, along this wall.[25] The pedestrian was thus spared the intrusion of Egyptian sacred space on his visual perception of Roman public space, but he cannot have forgotten what lay behind that mask of columns.[26]

[21]See Duncan-Jones 1985 (also in Duncan-Jones 1990, 174-84) for an analysis of the sources of the funds for public building in Roman cities, and cf. Drew-Bear forth. On the construction activity of late Roman cities, see A. Lewin, *Studi sulla città imperiale romana nell'orientale tardoantico* (Bibl. d'Athenaeum 17, Como 1991).

[22]See, for example, the description of Ottoman Aleppo in Marcus 1989, 276-84.

[23]See the 1932 aerial photograph reproduced in Baines and Málek, *Atlas* 76.

[24]*EEF Arch.Rep.* 1896-97, 6.

[25]See Drew-Bear forth.

[26]On the physical reflection of organizational change from Ptolemaic to Roman see Bowman 1992.

The matrix of daily life, however, was the dense mass of private buildings.[27] The ready availability, at no cost, of earth for brickmaking, coupled with Egypt's perennial shortage of timber and the expense of bringing stone from quarries at some distance from the Nile, led to a style of housebuilding different from most other lands where Greeks dwelt in numbers. Houses were constructed of sundried bricks, with timber used sometimes for framing and often for roof beams, stone only for foundations and decorative facing. "Houses are constantly being added to, amalgamated, partly demolished, partly reconstructed, divided and partitioned, according to family considerations and pressing domestic and financial needs."[28] Greek and Demotic papyri tell the same story as archaeology. It is cheaper to rebuild and alter than to repair in such an environment. The rooms of today become the cellars of the next generation, topped by new rooms, as the urban mound rises ever higher. Houses built in this way collapsed often enough; sometimes they damaged neighboring properties in the process.[29]

Houses varied in size and quality. An extensive survey of houses in part of Panopolis identifies eight houses as one-storied, suggesting that the rest had two stories above ground.[30] Excavations at Edfu revealed a relatively poor section of town, with few large streets and houses without courtyards.[31] Papyri describe the whole or parts of many houses, particularly at Oxyrhynchos and Hermopolis. One inheritance division[32] partitions a two-story house, which is described in some detail, share by share. There is a basement with four vaulted rooms, a ground floor with one main living room, a pigsty, and a gatehouse; over the gatehouse (but considered first floor) are a living

[27]For houses of Ptolemaic and Roman Egypt, see Husson 1983 and Nowicka 1969.

[28]Smith 1972, 707.

[29]For example, see *P.Cair.Goodsp.* 13 (Hermopolis, 341), sale of a "vacant" lot with a collapsed house on it; *P.Rain.Cent.* 84 (Arsinoe, 315), a complaint about the dangerous condition of a house across the public street from the house of the petitioners; *PSI* V 456 (*BL*; Oxyrhynchos, 276-282), a report on the inspection of a bronzeworker's house complained of by a wealthier neighbor (a prominent athlete); *P.Mil.* II 41 (5c, prov. unknown), a report of the inspection of a small house, revealing that it had become old, threatened to fall down and in part has, and had to be razed to the foundations; *P.Oxy.* I 52 (*BL*), the report of public doctors after examining a girl injured in the fall of a house. On the other hand, in the almost 700 lines, with perhaps half that many identifiable properties, of *P.Berl.Bork.* (*ca* 315-330), only sixteen Panopolitan houses were classified as "in ruin," about 5 percent.

[30]*P.Berl.Bork.* p.21. The same pattern is found at eighteenth-century Aleppo, cf. Marcus 1989, 339.

[31]Described in *Tell Edfou* 1937, 1938, 1939; cf. 1937, 22 for the lack of courtyards.

[32]*P.Lond.* III 978 (p.233) (*BL*; Hermopolis, 331).

room and two small bedrooms, plus a storage room. On the second floor are two large rooms. The house is divided among four siblings, one man and three women, at least two of the latter married. The shares are dispersed over the house to provide each with adequate space; all the women share the use of the pigsty. If one assumes normal family sizes, probably twenty people lived in this house of moderate size.

Virtually every house mentioned in a document had a courtyard and a well, along with storage space for animal feed. Hermopolis and Oxyrhynchos were full of animals: cattle, pigs, donkeys, camels,[33] no doubt goats and the ubiquitous pigeons as well. Quite apart from the disposition of human wastes,[34] then, it is small wonder that leases routinely specify that the house is to be turned back to the lessor free of dung at the end of the term, or that "a vacant dung-covered lot" turns up in the Panopolite register of houses.[35] The inhabitants of Egyptian cities kept the sounds and smells of the country with them, except perhaps for the smell of vegetation. Though some pharaonic towns certainly contained plots of land for growing crops, the more crowded quarters of their Roman descendants did not. Even urban trees were rare enough that the government made a great fuss about protecting the few that existed.[36] The town was, however, immediately surrounded by cropland, close enough that an urban dweller could work such plots and bring their produce into the city for processing; such was the case of oilmakers at Panopolis who leased olive orchards around the city.[37] The overall result was an environment even less healthy than the villages, with (like many other premodern cities) a lower life expectancy than the countryside.[38]

There were other sounds and smells as well. The ground floor front rooms of houses were often workshops or stores. Whole rows of shops might be found on major streets or squares,[39] but large numbers

[33]P.Oxy. X 1280 (BL), perhaps of the last quarter of the 4c, is a partnership agreement for use of a camel shed.

[34]Cf. H. Maehler, BiOr 44 (1987) 688: Mentions of latrines in houses are rare, and a pot in the cellar may have been the common solution.

[35]P.Berl.Bork. i.3, xi.12; cf. ix.31 (a collapsed house partly covered with dung).

[36]For example, P.Oxy. XLI 2969 (323) is one of a series of oaths to protect a neighborhood persea tree, sworn by a bronzeworker, a linen dealer, and a church reader.

[37]See P.Panop. 1-10 for their documents, ranging from 298 to 341. These properties are described as located in a zone called "around the metropolis," evidently not included in the division of the nome into pagi. Its size we do not know.

[38]See Bagnall and Frier, forthcoming; Sallares 1991, 88.

[39]For an example, see the sixth-century shops excavated at Marea: el-Fakharani 1983, 178-80. P.Turner 37 (Arsinoe, 270) is an offer to lease a building with three workshops (ergasteria) on the main street (plateia) and a couple of side rooms, for a

were scattered through the residential quarters where the artisans or shopkeepers lived. These quarters were relatively small clusters of a few streets each, mostly named after local landmarks (especially sanctuaries), ethnic groups, and craft specialties.[40] Registers of payment of taxes on occupations from late third-century Arsinoe show that these trades were no longer concentrated in quarters.[41] Seven fullers lived in seven different neighborhoods, three condiment sellers in three districts, four tinsmiths in four, nine bakers in eight (only two in a quarter called "Bakers'"), five brewers in five, three butchers in three, four myrrh-sellers in four, twelve dyers in eleven quarters. Grains might be brought for milling in the city,[42] or radish-seed for oil production.[43] The range of trades found in the cities is treated below (p. 78), but some sense of how interspersed they were can be found in a papyrus of the late third century, which records the properties found on three sides of a city block.[44] Eighteen properties are enumerated, including those of a *capsarius* (a man who checked clothing at the baths), two fishermen, a builder, an embroiderer, a dyer, a vegetable-seller (no longer resident), a linen weaver, a carpenter, and a baker. Now the *capsarius* and fishermen are not likely to have plied their trades at home, but the rest may well have. A similar hodgepodge of occupations is found in the Panopolite house-register. Nor need establishments house forever the same business; one bakery was turned into a stable.[45] And modest private baths, run for profit, were sprinkled through this mixture,[46] along with the smaller temples.[47]

This basic texture seems to be an inheritance from the character of the living quarters of Egyptian towns of earlier millennia. The nome capitals of the past had been dominated by the enormous temple precincts built on regular, divinely ordained geometric patterns, while

fairly high rent.

[40]Probably very similar to those in Aleppo, where a 365-hectare site was divided into no fewer than eighty-two quarters in the mid-eighteenth century, named after just the same categories (Marcus 1989, 285-89, 317). Arsinoe had at least thirty-six *amphoda* (S. Daris, *Aegyptus* 61 [1981] 143-54).

[41]*BGU* IV 1087 (*BL*; *BGU* XIII 2280b) and *BGU* I 9 (in the same or identical hand though not the same roll). The recto of I 9 contains documents dated 247-248; the register is from *ca* 276.

[42]*P.Laur.* IV 164 (Oxyrhynchos, 4/5c); *P.Wash.Univ.* I 19 (Oxyrhynchos, 287), a receipt for a year's rent on a leased mill.

[43]*P.Oxy.* LI 3639 (412; the lessor of the mill is a *vir clarissimus*).

[44]*P.Oxy.* XLVI 3300 (the document on the other side dates to 271/2).

[45]*P.Vind.Sijp.* 20 (*BL*; 4c).

[46]*P.Flor.* III 384 (5c?, Hermopolis).

[47]Nine of them among several hundred dwellings in the Panopolite census (*P.Berl.Bork.*, pp. 24-26).

the people lived in areas of dense construction and constant rebuilding, with a mixture of houses, stores and workshops, and irregular
streets.[48] In the same way, residential streets of Panopolis had blind
alleys and private entrance lanes sprinkled along the way.[49]

Even along such streets, nothing in these towns was at any great
distance from anything else. The remains of Herakleopolis covered
144 hectares, Hermopolis perhaps 120 hectares, with maximum length
of the city about 1.6 km and width of 1.2 km. Oxyrhynchos was about
2 km by 0.8 km, with an area perhaps a little greater than 100 hectares.
Aphroditopolis (Atfih) was longer but narrower, overall rather smaller; Hibis (in the Oasis) was around the same size. A recent survey of
Naukratis estimated it at 32 hectares, but that does not include areas
excavated earlier and now destroyed. Thmouis (metropolis of the
Mendesian Nome in the Delta) amounted to about 90 hectares, Tanis
some 177 hectares. Athribis covered about 190 hectares. Arsinoe may
have been larger; Kelsey estimated that in 1914 the mounds on the site
covered about 236 hectares, of which almost all was ruined by 1920.[50]
That is the largest of the lot, far larger than most of those known. Most
cities were little larger than a square kilometer; even a not terribly
energetic walker could cover the distance from any part of town to the
central square in no more than thirty minutes (allowing for conges-
tion).

The small areas given, however, may overstate the matter. Considerable areas of most cities were unoccupied in some periods. Apart
from particular lots where no house stood, where dung and rubbish
accumulated, large garbage heaps existed within cities, and new ones
were opened from time to time. Grenfell and Hunt noted that trash
dumps of different periods were sprinkled over the site of Oxyrhynchos.[51] The entire residential quarter excavated at Apollonopolis
Magna by the Franco-Polish expedition in the 1930s was unoccupied
from the late second century to the late sixth.[52] Herakleopolis was a

[48]Cf. Kemp 1972 for an attempt to describe the character of Egyptian towns,
with full awareness of how limited the evidence is.

[49]P.Berl.Bork. pp. 14-16.

[50]Herakleopolis: see Naville 1894.   Hermopolis: a rough calculation from
Roeder 1959, Taff. 88 and 90. Oxyrhynchos: a rough calculation from the imprecise
information in EEF Arch.Rep. 1896-97, 2. Aphroditopolis: EEF Arch.Rep. 1910-11, 6: 3
km x 0.5 km approximately. Hibis: Wagner 1987, 157 n.3. Naukratis: Coulson and
Leonard 1981, 1. Thmouis: Holz et al. 1980, pl. 17; my estimate. Tanis: Yoyotte 1988,
153. Athribis: P. Vernus, Athribis (Cairo 1978) xvi. Arsinoe: Cd'E 3 (1927) 78-79.

[51]These can be seen on the plan in P.Oxy. L, p.vii. See EEF Arch.Rep. 1896-97 for
a description of the site.

[52]See Tell Edfou 1937, 98; Tell Edfou 1939, 110.

mass of rubbish heaps of different periods.[53] The characteristic profile of Egyptian city sites, in fact, before their twentieth-century destruction, was an undulating sea of ancient garbage heaps.

With all this, a papyrus indicates that the West City quarter of Hermopolis had more than 2,300 houses, the East City more than 1,900. A modest estimate for East and West Fort quarters would give the entire city perhaps 7,000 houses.[54] Village houses (see chapter 3) may have held an average of eleven people; numbers in cities were (like the houses) doubtless on average smaller.[55] Some houses were at any time empty, of course.[56] A guess at Hermopolis' population might reasonably fall between 25,000 and 50,000, probably nearer the upper than lower figure.[57] That was probably larger than average, but if the typical metropolis was 80 hectares in area (much lower than the 130 hectare average of those known) and averaged 200 persons per hectare (also a fairly low figure), then it would have had 16,000 inhabitants.[58]

Even apart from the migration of garbage dumps, the physical appearance of the cities did not remain static through late antiquity. The building and refurbishing of the characteristic public structures of the Roman city continued throughout. In 458, five ironsmiths of Oxyrhynchos issued a receipt for two gold solidi given them for nails and other materials for "the future (God willing) public bath."[59] More strikingly, a new type of building came to occupy a central place, spatially and socially: the church. The list of Oxyrhynchite watchmen mentions northern and southern churches; these would occupy a more confident niche as the earliest such buildings listed in a surviving public record if the document were dated, but it is on the reverse of an account dated to 295 and thus might have been written anywhere from a few years to a century later.[60] A church occurs also

[53]Petrie 1905, 26.

[54]Roeder 1959, 107 (estimates by Schmitz). The papyrus is *SPP* V 101. If half of Hermopolis' 120 ha was occupied by houses (the rest being streets, public buildings or vacant), that would mean about 115 houses per ha, or 87 m^2 per house plot.

[55]The average at Aleppo in the eighteenth century is estimated at about nine persons per house, or seven per household: Marcus 1989, 340-41.

[56]Only three, or less than one percent, in the Panopolite register: *P.Berl.Bork.* p. 21.

[57]See Rathbone 1990 for discussion of population estimates.

[58]Aleppo (a larger city at 365 hectares but of similar housing density) is estimated to have had about 200 persons per hectare at its nineteenth-century bottom, more like 350 per hectare at its eighteenth-century peak; cf. Marcus 1989, 338-39.

[59]*P.Oxy.* XXXIV 2718.

[60]*P.Oxy.* I 43 verso i.10, iii.19 (*BL*; = *W.Chr.* 474). U. von Wilamowitz-Moellendorff, reviewing *P.Oxy.* I, in *GGA* 160 (1898) 676, argued that *ekklesia* in this

in the Panopolite register, dated probably to about 315-330.[61]
Archaeology has uncovered the remains of several churches in these
cities, but their dates are even vaguer.[62] It should not astonish that a
city of perhaps 25,000 persons should require eight or a dozen churches. And it may be that the resources they demanded for building
and upkeep came in part from what in the third century was devoted
to the public face of a Roman city. But to a large extent the end of
government and elite support for pagan temples must have made
funds available for the new churches.

The pace at which the old temples were abandoned as places of
cult is treated in chapter 8. The pagan gods began their institutional
retreat at least by the middle of the third century; some fronts collapsed much earlier than others. Some temple precincts had already
been partially overrun by residential construction and trash in prior
centuries.[63] Untended stone temples were wonderful quarries for new
construction; fortunately for the modern visitor, some were instead
converted into churches, others into army camps. Their eclipse by the
churches was perhaps the single most striking physical change in the
cities during the century and a half between Constantine and Chalcedon.

Political Community

The physical city, with its Roman structure and facade overlaid on a
complex amalgam of Greek and Egyptian elements, mirrors a political

---

text could not mean "church" because of the supposed Diocletianic date; he
preferred to suppose it was a place for the popular assembly of Oxyrhynchos to
gather. Such an assembly is unknown in this period, however; and in fact the word
is never used elsewhere to mean a place for such an assembly. Preisigke, *WB* III 256,
interprets it as "church." The date, moreover, may (as noted) be later.

[61]*P.Berl.Bork.* iii.27. Houses of six deacons are listed as well.

[62]The large church at Hermopolis once thought to be the agora was vaguely
dated to the 4th-5th century (Roeder 1959, Taf. 93c); A.H.S. Megaw, in Wace et al.
1959, 74-78, argues for a date *ca* 410-440, largely on the basis of the basilica's place in
the history of the architectural style of Egyptian churches. The chronological indications in Bailey 1991, 46-53, are no better founded. Donadoni et al. 1974, 65, date a
church at Antinoopolis to the last quarter of the fifth century on the basis of a single
coin. Naville 1894 mentions the ruins of several churches at Herakleopolis, and
sculptures presumably from them are discussed (32-34 plus excellent plates), with
nary a hint of a date.

[63]Spencer, Bailey, Burnett 1983 indicate that parts of the area around the temple
of Thoth at Hermopolis had for centuries been used for other purposes. Indeed, the
name *phrourion*, "fort," for the enclosure shows that it had been used for military
purposes at least as early as the beginning of Roman rule (*P.Lond.* III 1168 [p.135],
A.D. 18 attests the term). On residential construction inside precincts, perhaps
originating in priests' houses, see *O.Elkab*, p.16.

community.[64] Offices and institutions, of course, can be invented or abolished faster and more cheaply than can buildings or avenues. Although far more documents of these institutions survive than remnants of the physical structures, their evolution is not for this reason necessarily any clearer. The rapid change in the political form of Egyptian towns, moreover, which began under Diocletian and continued for more than a century, transformed institutions that were themselves not always of much antiquity.

Little is securely known about the metropoleis of the nomes as the Romans found them. They must have seemed bizarre places to the conquerors, most notable for their Egyptian temples and service population, but at least in some possessing a Hellenic stratum devoted to the preservation of the ancestral culture, especially the training of young men in the athletic and martial arts taught by the gymnasium. They can hardly have been recognizable as Greek cities, of the sort the Romans knew in Greece, Asia Minor, and other parts of the East. But, as everywhere in the empire, the usefulness of the upper class for helping administer the country was not difficult to see, and the Romans allowed the elite group who claimed Greek descent and whose life was centered on the gymnasium a certain measure of self-importance through standard Greek magistracies, like the gymnasiarch, the *prytanis*, the *exegetes*, the *kosmetes*, and the *archiereus*, or chief priest.[65]

Not until the beginning of the third century, however, did the Romans take the next step: allowing the creation of city councils, an institution familiar throughout the rest of the Greek world.[66] The well-off landed class, now quite developed, was turned into the basis for a full-fledged city government, although popular assemblies, now on the wane in the Greek world generally, appear never to have been created. Septimius Severus' act of *ca* 201 was not exactly a disinterested benevolence to the Greeks of Egypt, for it made far easier what the Romans had been trying to do for the past century, namely to make the local property-owning class responsible for the orderly and complete collection of the taxes owed to the central government. These third-century councils were in fact an adaptation of traditional Greek councils to the objectives of Roman municipal senates.

[64]On this relationship, see generally Bowman 1992.

[65]The classic description is P. Jouguet, *La vie municipale dans l'Égypte romaine* (BEFAR 104, Paris 1911); cf. A. Bowman and D. Rathbone, *JRS* 82 (1992) 107-27.

[66]Fundamental for what follows is Bowman 1971; see also Drew-Bear 1984 and Bowman 1992, who emphasizes the pre-Severan development necessary for this step. Before Severus only Antinoopolis, Naukratis, and Ptolemais had councils.

Being a *bouleutes*, a councillor, thus had its disadvantages. The wealthy landowners, however, like their counterparts elsewhere, were generally willing to put up with some burdens to gain status, prestige, and a stage for their ambitions, and they paid a substantial entrance fee to do so.[67] Once in, they were part of a small group (probably nowhere more than 100) and served for life.[68] The same competitive foci visible in Greek Asia Minor flourished in Egypt, particularly civic games.[69] Since classical times, the wealthiest elements of Greek cities had, though with constant complaints, managed to live with a system that gave them prominence, prestige, and an arena for competition, in return for accepting financial and managerial burdens: not an ideal life, but clearly better in their eyes than a level of taxation that would allow efficient, anonymous public services, for which they would receive no credit. Just this kind of pattern now becomes standard for Egypt.[70] Modern scholars have tended to take the councillors' endless struggle to enjoy the benefits of the system, without accepting more of its burdens than absolutely necessary, too much at the self-serving evaluation its ancient protagonists put on it. There were indeed serious hazards for the participants, but their whining should not fool the observer into thinking that the rewards were not commensurate with the risks.[71]

It is, however, true that the new council-based system had barely time to get established in Egypt before the difficulties of the third century struck with force, to the point even that with all Egypt's agricultural wealth it was not easy to provide for the food supply of the cities, let alone the uninterrupted functioning of luxuries like the gymnasium. An air of crisis pervades many Hermopolite documents pertinent to the *boule* in the 260s and 270s, and the Oxyrhynchite evidence shows that Hermopolis was not an anomaly.[72] Despite some recovery, it is not surprising that by the reign of Diocletian, a structure

[67]Drew-Bear 1984, 321: a 10,000-drachma fee at Oxyrhynchos in 233.

[68]Bowman 1971, 22-25.

[69]See Drew-Bear 1984, 332, on the role of local pride.

[70]It may be true, as Bowman 1971, 121, says, that the *boulai* of Egypt were little like those in Hellenistic Greece, but they have much in common with the trends of the Roman period in places like Asia Minor.

[71]One of them was an opportunity to try to shunt tax and service burdens onto someone else; cf. the implicit coziness of arrangements in *P.Oxy.* LV 3814 (3/4c). See the sound observations of H. Brandt, *ZPE* 68 (1987) 87-97, on the potential profitability of liturgies. MacMullen 1988, 44-46, seems to swallow the complaints whole, though he recognizes that they were less true in the East than in the West.

[72]Drew-Bear 1984 provides a good summary; cf. especially 316. Bowman 1992 comments on the cities' ability to continue construction and competition through the third century.

that had never enjoyed "normal" times in which to take root seemed ripe for change.

When the Diocletianic changes began, the system offered precisely that combination of Greek, Egyptian, and Roman mentioned earlier. The Greek element was the council, magistrates, and gymnasial class, all well-known throughout the Greek world. They are seen in the form peculiar to the Roman period and can hardly be confused with the institutions of (say) fourth-century B.C. Athens; but they are not the less Greek for that. Intertwined with that was a nome-based administrative structure ultimately going back to pharaonic antecedents, but transformed by the Ptolemies and the Romans. At its head was the *strategos*, an administrative officer drawn from outside the nome and centrally appointed, whose role goes back in many essentials to the later third century B.C. Under him was a detailed structure anchored to the toparchies (administrative districts) and villages of the nome, with a variety of local officials, some salaried and some impressed. The overall Roman administrative armature, described in the next section, included the regional *epistrategoi* and several high officials in Alexandria, headed by the prefect.

The nature of the documentation is such that the role of the *bouleutai* in taxation appears to overwhelm all else. That role indeed offered the greatest dangers[73] and some of the greatest potential rewards to the councillors, and it was the source of most of their dealings with the imperial government (see below, pp. 157-60). Failure to collect and deliver all the taxes due could lead to trial,[74] fines, and even confiscation of one's property by the treasury.[75] A councillor desperate to avoid such fates might invade his wife's dowry.[76] But the council had other responsibilities as well, many of them exercised on a daily basis through specific magistrates.[77] One paper-intensive function was keeping records of the population and of individual

[73]Even physical: *CPR* XVIIA 23 (Hermopolis, 322) shows two overseers of ship-building badly beaten by villagers.

[74]E.g., *P.Oxy.* XII 1417 (4c early), a trial of eutheniarchs.

[75]Such things are mentioned on several occasions. An eloquent testimony is *SB* XIV 11717 = *BASP* 15 (1978) 115-23, in which the lawyer says, "because fate changes everybody's position it happened to him too to become propertyless, because an abominable fate fell upon his father and the most sacred treasury impounded his paternal goods." (This is evidently not the family of Adelphios and his son Asklepiades, see *CPR* XVIIA, p. 66.)

[76]Cf. *PSI* VIII 944 (364/366?).

[77]It is a peculiar, and probably telling, irony that the overwhelming majority of the attestations of all these offices come from private documents, in which they are part of the pompous self-description of former magistrates, rather than from official documents that might tell something of the actual duties of the offices, some of which are in fact poorly known.

status—who was a member of what tribe, who enjoyed a lower-tax category,[78] who was a member of the gymnasium class.[79] The ultimate responsibility here seems to have been that of the *exegetes*, but with a considerable group of responsible officials at the tribe or neighborhood level.[80] The *exegetes*, however, also appears at times with specific responsibility for the city baths.[81]

A cluster of offices surrounds the center of Hellenic culture in the cities, the gymnasium (discussed below). The highest was the gymnasiarch, whose most visible duty was actually providing the oil supply for anointing the ephebes and others. The *kosmetes* was charged with the good order and instruction of the ephebes, and his appearances in documentation of the late third and fourth centuries give little more specificity.[82] The *agonothetes* held primary responsibility for the management of the athletic and musical contests of the city. Civic cults came under the supervision of the chief priest, the *archiereus*.

Another function of civic government was the security of food supplies. Part of this need was discharged by the *agoranomos*, in charge of the orderly and honest operation of public markets;[83] another aspect was in the charge of the *eutheniarches*, who was responsible for seeing that the city had overall an adequate food supply: a difficult office in hard times, an unnecessary one in good.

The council which designated and to which reported all of these officials included many who had held these posts in the past and no doubt had firm opinions about how they were to be discharged. It is thus hardly surprising that the surviving minutes of meetings of this body are lively and even a bit rowdy; a presiding officer (the *prytanis* or *proedros*) might well sit quietly while the members criticized an action of his, until he finally retracted it without comment at the end.[84] But the *prytanis* was all the same a powerful man, calling meetings of

[78]On the city poll-tax, cf. most recently *P.Oxy.* LV 3789 (320), intro.

[79]The records office also had to respond to inquiries from high officials; cf. *P.Oxy.* XLVI 3301 (300), in reply to a request of the prefect.

[80]See Mertens 1958 for a general description of the entire structure by which the population was managed.

[81]*P.Oxy.* VI 891 (*BL*) (294); cf. *P.Oxy.* XXXI 2569 intro.

[82]*P.Oxy.* XLVI 3297 (294) and *P.Ant.* I 31 (347), both notices to a *kosmetes* that his term of office approaches. The latter instructs the recipient "to take thought for the good order (*eukosmia*) of the city as far as possible." The former refers to a festival taking place during the two-week period of responsibility.

[83]Despite the surviving documentation for this office, which shows the *agoranomos* "primarily fulfilling notarial functions rather than the supervision of the market," M. G. Raschke, *BASP* 13 (1976) 17-29 at 20 (with bibliography in n.9).

[84]*P.Oxy.* XVII 2110 (370) is a notable example.

the council, controlling its agenda, introducing business, acting as its executive on a daily basis, and representing it to the outside powers.[85] It is hardly surprising that the term of office was only a year,[86] even if the other councillors might well prefer to avoid taking on the job.[87] There was also a treasurer in charge of the funds of the city council.[88] The range of subjects the council dealt with can be seen from the reports of proceedings; one such mentions the appointment of someone to invite the *epistrategos* to a festival, an advance from bouleutic funds, exhortation of a nominee to become *agonothetes* and another to be gymnasiarch, petitions about appointments, the election of a *kosmetes*, and an approaching imperial visit; it is not surprising that a petition of some priests is postponed till the next meeting.[89] Public works were another area in which the councils had some autonomy and where civic pride spurred them on.[90]

Major changes in the magistracies and council began in the reign of Diocletian. They have generally been seen as signs of the decline of the councils and the bureaucratization of late antique Egypt, but the transformation is more complex than that. The first signs may be the traditional magistracies, which start disappearing.[91] The two traditional market-related magistracies, the *agoranomos* and the *eutheniarches*, though revived under Diocletian, soon disappear, neither attested after about 307.[92] The *archiereus* is not securely attested in the papyri after 309, although two undated references may be as late as 350 and a law of 386 (*CTh* 12.1.112) mentions the position at the provincial level.[93] The *exegetes* is attested only until 330.[94] The gymnasium-related posts drop from the documents one by one, the

[85]Bowman 1971, 53-68, gives a detailed analysis. See also N. Lewis, *BASP* 28 (1991) 164-66.

[86]Holding it was a matter of pride and public display. Cf. *P.Oxy.* XLIV 3202 (3/4c): "The *prytanis* invites you to his crowning tomorrow, Tybi 9th, 8th hour."

[87]Cf. *P.Oxy.* XII 1414 (*BL*) (270-275), in which a *prytanis* complains about his health; the members of the council respond by exhorting him to continue working for them in a manner worthy of his past performance.

[88]See Bowman 1971, 41-42.

[89]*P.Oxy.* XII 1416 (*BL*) (298).

[90]See Bowman 1971, 87.

[91]For what follows, cf. Lenz 1992.

[92]The last evidence for the *eutheniarches* is *P.Oxy.* XII 1417, late third or early 4th century but without absolute date. The role of the *strategos* suggests the very beginning of the fourth century at the latest. Cf. Bowman 1974, 47; N. Lewis, *BASP* 7 (1970) 113-14.

[93]*P.Amh.* II 82 is undated. Former *archiereis* appear in *P.Col.* VII 138 (307/8) and *SB* XVI 12289 (309); undated appearances in *P.Berl.Bork.* (?*ca* 315-330, cf. *BASP* 16 [1979] 164-65) and *P.Panop.* 14 (?*ca* 325-350, id.) are probably somewhat later.

[94]Fittingly enough, the last instance is a petition by someone seeking to escape nomination to the office: *P.Oxy.* XLVII 3350.

agonothetes already in the third century, the *kosmetes* after 347, but the gymnasiarch not until 415.[95] The ephebate itself is not mentioned after 323.[96] The mentions of councillors, *bouleutai*, in general decline sharply after the fourth century.

A dual transformation explains much of this change. The city itself was changing. Pagan cults, already enfeebled in the third century, lost their remaining official protection under Constantine and rapidly found themselves supplanted by Christianity in the public realm. The growing prominence of bishops and other Christian professionals thus represents (among other things) the replacement of the *archiereus*. The ephebate-based gymnasium culture certainly lost ground during the fourth century to other sorts of education and entertainment (cf. below, pp. 104-5), and the disappearance of some offices connected with the gymnasium is thus hardly surprising, although remarkably little is known in detail about the matter.

The second transformation was administrative: the multistage reorganization of city administration in the early fourth century. The most important element of this change was the introduction of the *curator civitatis*, called *logistes* in the Greek documents. This official served as the chief executive of the city and nome government and though chosen from the ranks of the local curial (council) class, was answerable to the central government. Areas that earlier fell under one or another of the other magistrates of the city were now his responsibility. Markets and food supply are the most obvious examples, as the numerous declarations of prices addressed to him manifest.[97] As long as the lower magistrates survived, they reported to the *logistes*.

These changes, however, are not the whole story. A third element is simply a change in the available documentation. The history of city government in Egypt is strikingly tributary to just a few sources. In the third century, the extensive mass of Oxyrhynchite texts is supplemented by the more sharply focused, but extremely valuable, Hermopolite archives of the council.[98] For the fourth century, there is little of direct relevance from any source except Oxyrhynchos, and when the Oxyrhynchite material dwindles, around 370, it is no longer

[95]For the gymnasiarch, see the former gymnasiarch in *P.Rainer Cent.* 90 (Herakleopolis, 414 or 415). A gymnasium wheat-measure (so edd.) also appears in *O.Douch* 38, perhaps of the same period.

[96]*P.Oxy.* I 42.

[97]The extensive documentation, commentary, and bibliography in *P.Oxy.* LIV on this office have greatly improved knowledge of it.

[98]To be reedited by Marie Drew-Bear.

possible to speak with confidence and in a continuous way of the development of institutions.[99]

All the same, a new cadre of officials working with the *logistes* can be defined in the middle third of the fourth century, giving as a group a very different cast to matters and showing that with all its flaws the documentation does allow a coherent picture. The old *strategos*, now transformed into the *exactor* (first attested in 309[100]), has become, instead of an important personage from out of town, a local resident; to him is delegated much of the *logistes*' responsibility for tax collection. Security is in the hands of the *riparius*, and justice is the main province of the *defensor civitatis*, usually called *syndikos* or *ekdikos* in Greek.[101] The latter two, also members of the local curial class, remained in the council after their terms of office. The council itself can be seen in lively existence as late as 370, and it is likely enough that only the lack of evidence masks its continued activity thereafter, even to the seventh century.[102] It may be true, however, that emphasis shifts away from the council *per se* to the class of *curiales*, those with the requisite standing and wealth, even if they are not actually members of the council for some reason.[103]

Within that curial class develops also an inner circle, the group described as the *propoliteuomenoi*, probably rendering the Latin *principales*.[104] Exactly who made up this group is nowhere defined; one is tempted to say that anyone who had to ask was not a member. But this is probably just a failure of the documentation, because it appears to be a formal status.

Outside the city proper there remained the countryside. It was administered after 307/8 by a new system reporting to the *logistes*. The

[99]Hermopolis does provide useful information for the service of *curiales* in offices like that of *praepositus pagi*; and see now P. van Minnen and K. A. Worp, *ZPE* 78 (1989) 139-42, publishing the first proceedings of a council from elsewhere (Hermopolis) than Oxyrhynchos.

[100]See Thomas 1985. A list of *exactores* is given by P.J. Sijpesteijn, *ZPE* 90 (1992) 247-50. He argues (246-47) that the offices were not identical but coexisted for decades, even if often held by the same person.

[101]See below, p. 165, on this office.

[102]See Geremek 1990 for a detailed argument for the continued vitality of the city councils into the sixth century or later. She cites also Rémondon's late thinking in the same direction.

[103]This is the argument of Geremek 1981, who cites evidence to show that *politeuomenos* is not the equivalent of *bouleutes* but a broader term for *curialis*. She does not, however, take account of *P.Amh.* II 82 (*BL*; Lewis, *Cd'E* 29 [1954] 288-91), where a man says that he has never been *politeuomenos* (*oude politeusamenos pote*). He does not mean that he has never held any office, for he is a former high priest. Perhaps this is a non-technical usage. See also *P.Oxy.* LI 3627.1n. on the early attestations of the term.

[104]So Bowman 1971, accepted by Geremek 1981, 234.

old toparchies were divided and probably reconfigured to yield a number of pagi (as many as fifteen in the Hermopolite, later increased to seventeen).[105] Each was governed by a *praepositus*, a member of the curial class of the city who was responsible for not only supervising the tax collection system but also appointing village officials and, indeed, almost anything else.[106] It is in large part this structure, directly under the control of the chief official of the city, which has led to descriptions of the administrative changes of the era as the "municipalization" of the nome. But the nomes did not disappear, and in reality the major change was the replacement of the *strategos* as the chief officer of the nome with the *logistes*, an outsider with an insider more directly linked to the council.[107] These views, in fact, are not in any real contradiction. The rural administration was indeed more closely tied to the cities and their ruling class than it had been before; that ruling class was in turn tied more closely to the imperial government, with more of its power in the hands of a few men (though serving for limited terms) than had been the case before.[108] The combination of growing power but diminished autonomy which the city elites experienced is hardly an unusual phenomenon.[109]

Imperial Government

That imperial government was, except in a few cities serving as seats of governors of regions of Egypt (see below), more absent than present. Its presence lay largely in military units stationed in particular localities (see pp. 174-75). The close binding of the civic governing structures to the empire made it possible to avoid a distributed, permanent professional civil service in individual cities.[110]

[105]*P.Col.* IX 247, commentary.   For the Oxyrhynchite pagi, see P. Pruneti, *Aegyptus* 69 (1989) 113-18.

[106]One of the best known is Aur. Asklepiades, *praepositus* of the 15th pagus of the Hermopolite in 339-341. Cf. *CPR* XVIIA for his papers.

[107]Bowman 1974, 46, rejects the general view of municipalization, on the grounds that the fourth-century documents do not show any greater responsibility for administration of the countryside than before (though he does not seem to consider the *riparii* and their responsibility for security). Cf. also Bowman 1971, 125, where he sees the increased control in the hands of the *logistes* as a sign of the power not of the council but of the imperial government.

[108]A further concentration seems to occur later, with the *logistes* also holding the position of *proedros*, the equivalent of the earlier *prytanis*, or president of the council. Cf. Geremek 1990, and add *ZPE* 71 [1988] 123-26, all concerning the sixth century.

[109]See Cannadine 1990, 166, for similar developments with local government in late 19th- and early 20th-century Britain.

[110]Bowman 1971, 127, argues that this policy of amateurism was a failure, in the sense that it combined ineffectiveness and oppression.

The range of matters in the hands of the *logistes*, in particular, made him almost a full local representative for higher authority: local ser vices, markets, guilds, post, transport, taxes, municipal expenses, public works, gymnastic games, cults, justice, medicine.[111] The imperial government, from a provincial point of view, consisted fundamentally in provincial governorships and their attached offices. This is perhaps why a statement like "the later Roman empire was before all things a bureaucratic state,"[112] though true in its own way for the imperial centers, is far from the mark in describing provincial life. The limited concept of the state and its duties in all premodern societies meant a limited range of state employees.[113]

Except for a brief period, Egypt always had a governor with over-all responsibility for the land, but the sheer volume of business, especially justice, to be dealt with in a country of several millions was too great for one office to handle. Roman Egypt had thus had four *epistrategoi* in charge of regions: the Thebaid, the "Heptanomia" (the northern part of the Nile Valley, or Middle Egypt), and the East and the West Delta.[114]

The fourth century saw a series of experiments in the organization of the country.[115] Diocletian introduced a bipartite division (Egypt and the Thebaid) which lasted until about 314, at which point "Egypt" was divided into two parts: Herculia included the East Delta and the old Heptanomia; Iovia included the Central and West Delta with Alexandria. In 322 Herculia was in turn split, with the old Heptanomia becoming a province called Mercuriana, thus in effect re-creating the old *epistrategiai*. That, however, lasted only until Constantine's victory over Licinius and acquisition of Egypt in 324, when the pre-314 situation was reestablished. In 357 the wheel revolved again, and a tripartite structure resembling the 314-322 arrangement came back, with the province of Augustamnica including the East Delta and Heptanomia, Aegyptus the Central and West Delta, and the Thebaid its normal area (as far north as Hermopolis and

[111]Lallemand 1964, 107-12; cf. above. The most recent lists of *logistai* are *P.Oxy.* LIV, pp. 222-29 (for Oxyrhynchos, 303-346) and *Pap.Flor.* XIX 518-20 (for everything else).

[112]Jones 1964, 563.

[113]The Roman state was, however, considerably more ambitious than the Ottoman; cf. Marcus 1989, 76.

[114]See Thomas 1982 on the *epistrategos*, and Thomas 1984 for the transition from that office to the fourth century.

[115]For what follows, see Lallemand 1964, 41-77; Thomas 1984; *P.Oxy.* LI 3619 intro., LIV 3756 intro. A list of known governors appears in Lallemand 1964, 237-57, with a supplement in P.J. Sijpesteijn-K.A. Worp, *Tyche* 1 (1986) 192-94.

Antinoopolis). From 381 on there was once again a four-part structure, with the Heptanomia split off to form the province of Arcadia, thus once again essentially restoring a third-century structure, all once again under a prefect of Egypt, now called the Augustal Prefect.[116] The governor of one of these parts bore the title of *praeses*.

The competences of the governors are not easily determined. Justice and taxation, not surprisingly, dominate the documentary record. Local officials were the natural court of first resort for most people in most instances, but failure to obtain what one wanted locally often led to petitions to the prefect or *praeses*. All but a few petitions, however, normally resulted in the governor's remanding them to a lower official for further investigation and (usually) disposition. To pursue matters further at a high level, then, one would probably need to travel to the governor's seat and perhaps hire a lawyer.[117] Governors were busy men, and getting their attention took time and persistence. Lawyers and stays away from home were expensive, and only the urban elite could afford such direct access,[118] but anyone could petition in writing.[119]

It was not the travel expenses but the possible consequences that made another type of appearance before the prefect or *praeses* unwelcome. Local officials, especially those responsible for the taxes, might be sent or escorted to the governor's seat if an inquiry was necessary. It could be a long trip; an Oxyrhynchite foreman of eirenarchs was ordered to be sent, along with his brother, to Pelusium, some 400 km away at the northeast corner of the Nile Delta, where the *praeses* of Augustamnica had his headquarters.[120] But the experience was probably not much more welcome when the travel was shorter. The governor of the Thebaid in 372 sent out a circular order for all former *kephalaiotai* from a period of four years preceding the one just past to be sent to his office in Hermopolis. Two members of his staff were dispatched to the various cities in the province (Hypselis, Apollonopolis Mikra, Panopolis, and Ptolemais are documented, but no

[116]The exact authority of the prefect in the various provinces through the various shifts between 298 and 381 is not always easy to determine, but the structure from 381 on clearly reverses the Diocletianic decision to divide power in Egypt and weaken the prefect, cf. Lallemand 1964, 6.

[117]*P.Oxy.* XXII 2343 (*BL*) (*ca* 288).

[118]In *P.Oxy.* XXII 2343, the petitioner is an eirenarch fighting nomination as *dekaprotos*.

[119]The komarchs of an Oxyrhynchite village petition the prefect in *P.Oxy.* XII 1469 (298), complaining about an assistant of the *strategos*. One rather imagines, however, that the prefect simply referred the matter back to the *strategos* for investigation.

[120]*P.Oxy.* L 3576 (341).

doubt others were included) to convey these orders to the local magistrates, who had in turn to see to it that the men in question were sent up.[121] Probably the outcome was benign for most of those summoned, but the summons would not have occurred if some members of the group were not in for serious trouble when the accounts were settled.

Traveling officials from the governor's staff are encountered frequently. Feeding them was an expense for their hosts.[122] Where the nature of their business is clear, it is usually like the summons just described, the transmission of orders to the local authorities and their replies back to the governor.[123] But the *officiales* themselves became directly involved as well, for example in taking sureties for the appearance before the governor of those requested.[124] They were also responsible for gathering up tax funds[125] and for transfers of imperial funds from one place to another, a financially hazardous job. One petition to the emperors tells of the woes of Flavius Isidoros, the best-known specimen of *officialis*,[126] who was detailed by the *praeses* of the Thebaid to transfer 238 solidi (a little over three pounds of gold) to a member of the imperial *comitatus*. About three-quarters of the sum was, he claims, stolen; but he was ultimately held partially responsible and virtually bankrupted (so he says) by having to repay 72 solidi of it.[127] All the same, he eventually wound up in retirement as a landowner.[128]

That Isidoros *could* repay such a sum, with whatever hardship, is in itself instructive. The professional staff of the provincial governors were well compensated, in fees and gifts if not in salary,[129] and they often managed to accumulate a substantial amount of property. The Hermopolite land register shows five such officials (or former offi-

---

[121]*Archiv* 32 (1986) 33-39 (Apollonopolis Mikra, 372), with further references and discussion.

[122]E.g., *P.Ryl.* IV 627.115,129 (*ca* 322-323).

[123]*M.Chr.* 77-78 (Great Oasis, 376-378), two letters of a *politeuomenos* about sureties for persons due to appear for a hearing in the matter of claims against an estate.

[124]*P.Lips.* 46-56 are examples (*BL*).

[125]Cf., e.g., *P.Ant.* I 33 (see *P.Herm.Landl.* p. 19 n. 6 for the date: *post* 350), where eight different *officiales* are booked as receiving payments in solidi for various taxes.

[126]Involved in the episodes just mentioned.

[127]*P.Lips.* 34 (*BL*; Wilcken, *Archiv* 3, 566; 4, 188) (Hermopolis, *ca* 375). *W.Chr.* 187 (*P.Lips.* 61) concerns payment of part of this.

[128]Cf. Jones 1964, 596.

[129]Cf. ibid., 594: "The scale of pay in provincial offices seems to have been miserable." By this, however, he means something like four solidi a year, which most Egyptians would have considered quite decent. On "gifts" and fees to officials, cf. MacMullen 1988, 122-70.

cials) resident in one quarter of Hermopolis, two with small holdings but three with substantial ones (62, 66, and 210 arouras). In Antinoopolis, however, between 15 and 31 of the 205 persons listed belong to this group, and all but a handful of these officials have estates sufficient to support them.[130] This much larger representation (15.1 percent of possible officials at Antinoopolis vs. 2.0 percent at Hermopolis) confirms that Antinoopolis was in fact the capital of the Thebaid in the middle of the fourth century.[131] Because the landholdings of other Antinoites seem (to judge from the land registers) not to have been sufficient to support a civic elite, the presence of the office of the *praeses* was probably important. But it was presumably Hermopolis that was typical.

Only in such a place would one feel the full force of central late Roman bureaucracy. The governor's staff was divided into judicial, financial, and clerical entities, along with flunkies like messengers and ushers.[132] A fairly elaborate scheme of official titles sets out this structure, although its actual workings are poorly known.[133] The generic *officiales*, who are often met traveling like Flavius Isidoros, were presumably at the bottom of the ladder.[134] The officials were theoretically of military rank, and many titles come from the army.[135] Their total numbers are unknown, but evidence from imperial laws pertinent to other provinces indicates that the round number 100 was a typical strength.[136] If so, Egypt had at most 400 professional bureaucrats on the governors' payroll at any given time, or one per 10,000 population. Double it (generously) to allow for other high officials, and one gets to one per 5,000. The ratio in modern New York City, for city employees alone, is about one per 30.[137]

---

[130]*P.Herm.Landl.*; figures are taken from F. The uncertainty about the number derives from the fact that some offices could be either military or civil, the terminology being shared. Most of these are probably civil officials. Of thirty-one total cases, only four have fewer than twelve arouras in the Hermopolite *pagi* included in the register (all but that nearest Hermopolis itself). Of the five cases in Hermopolis, two have small holdings. See Bagnall 1992a for an analysis of the figures.

[131]As suggested by Lallemand 1964, 45-47, on the basis of literary sources.

[132]See Jones 1964, 565-66, for the typical composition of such offices.

[133]For the late fifth century, see the evidence of *CPR* XIV 39 and Fantoni's valuable commentary.

[134]One in *CPR* IX 40 describes himself as "subscribing slowly," i.e., barely able to sign his name.

[135]It is thus not always easy to distinguish, outside official business, a civil from a military official.

[136]Jones 1964, 594. The figure includes the clerks, messengers and so on.

[137]MacMullen 1988, 80, views officials as numerous, partly on the basis of a careless analysis of the Hermopolite registers. See Hopkins 1991, 139, for a better characterization.

There were, in fact, some other high officials, mainly of a financial character, at the provincial level. Unlike the civil administration, the financial saw Egypt whole at all times, a point that suggests the division of the civil administration was for the sake of efficiency, not for protection of the emperor against governors' uprisings.[138] The exact development of these offices is poorly known,[139] but the most prominent, the *katholikos*, was an imperial procurator with wide responsibilities. The office was created in 286, one of Diocletian's earliest acts, and displaced the *dioiketes*.[140] Even when Egypt was divided into multiple provinces the *katholikos* retained authority, in his area of competence, over the whole land. Procurators in charge of imperial property are less well known, but they had similar standing.[141] The official in charge of the food supply of Alexandria also had authority in his sphere in the countryside.[142] All these had *officiales* who traveled the nomes on their masters' business.[143] There were also subordinates of the *dux*, the military commander of the province (see chapter 4).

One other salient feature of the imperial administration was the postal system (as it is generally called), a combination of river boats and land stations with horse relays referred to as the *cursus velox* in Latin. Imperial civil and military officials used this system for official communications and travel throughout the country. Supporting it was a burden for the cities, which were responsible for providing the staff and the animals. These services were theoretically liturgies, but personal services, at least, were generally supplied by the city's hiring someone either with public funds or with funds supplied by a wealthy liturgist.[144]

---

[138]Lallemand 1964, 42, accepted at least partially the notion that defusing prefectorial power was a goal; but that was accomplished by separating civil and military command. For a prosopography of financial officials, see R. Delmaire, *CRIPEL* 10 (1988) 113-38.

[139]See Lallemand 1964, 78-95, with the conclusion that the evolution is poorly documented. The documentation has improved in the intervening years, but not greatly, and the gap between knowledge of governors and that of financial officials has only widened.

[140]D. Hagedorn, "Zum Amt des Dioiketes im römischen Aegypten," *YCS* 28 (1985) 167-210, esp. 187 n. 58 and 197.

[141]In *P.Oxy.* XLVIII 3416 (4c) the *katholikos* and *magister* are coupled. Lallemand 1964, 88, for the *magister rei privatae*.

[142]See *P.Turner* 45 (374), a letter of the *praefectus annonae Alexandriae* to the *exactor* of the Oxyrhynchite, acknowledging receipt of a shipment. Cf. Sirks 1991, 15 n. 28.

[143]An *officialis* of the *magister rei privatae* in *P.Laur.* III 94 (4c) is an example.

[144]See *P.Heid.* V, pp. 185-221, with detailed commentary.

The Seat of Wealth

The governing stratum of the cities of Egypt was a landowning aristocracy, a thin layer of those urban residents who had extensive estates in the countryside. They are part of a phenomenon known throughout the Roman Empire, which found its most extreme expression in the concentrated wealth of the Roman Senate. To say this, however, is by no means to describe the situation adequately. The urban landowning class was not an undifferentiated entity.[145]

Its lowest reaches consisted of city residents with small holdings, those unlikely to be supported by the income from their land. In the Hermopolite list of the middle of the fourth century, they amount to about 53 percent of all urban landholders. With holdings of 10 arouras (about 2.75 ha) or less (many only an aroura or a fraction), they must have depended on other sources of income for most of their support. For them, land held in the countryside was a form of investment of capital that gave them a cushion but not a competence.[146] In the Antinoopolite register, these smallholders amount to 40 percent of the total. Because only about 8.5 percent of the land is registered to women, it is unlikely that aggregating husbands' and wives' holdings would alter the distribution very much. Some of those with small holdings were in the military or civil service of the empire;[147] others probably had occupations. Because the lists mostly record people by name and patronymic, rather than by occupation, with only the occasional occupation given, it is difficult to be more precise about the means of support of this group with small landholdings, of whom only about 12 percent have nonofficial occupations listed.[148]

[145]What follows is largely based on Bagnall 1992b, where detailed numerical analysis and bibliography may be found.

[146]It is true that the absence of holdings from the 7th pagus, nearest the city, may somewhat distort this picture. Some of these people may in fact have had significantly larger holdings when this pagus is counted. There is no reason, however, to think that the *distribution* would change significantly; there were probably many small holders in the 7th pagus who had no holdings at all outside it. Moreover, for an urban resident dependent on rents, eleven arouras is probably not enough to yield a living, given that net after-tax rents seem to average no better than two artabas per aroura in this period.

[147]Lewuillon-Blume 1985 offers an analysis of titles and professions in the registers, but on this point it is vitiated by her amalgamation of civil service functions and *archai*; the latter are offices held by landowners without profession, not a salaried profession in themselves, whereas the imperial civil service functions were salaried.

[148]Of the lowest 100, 11 do; of the next 100, 13. Lewuillon-Blume 1985, 141, thinks that rigid rules applied to the indication of occupational status in these lists; but if this were true, it would be difficult to find any hypothesis for the livelihood of the small landowners without supposing an inverted distribution in the 7th pagus, with the rich holding little and the small folk dominant; cf. previous note.

A broad middle group was better able to live off its rents.[149] This category, containing those with holdings between 11 and (somewhat arbitrarily) 100 arouras, cannot be described as rich, but they almost certainly took in sufficient income from their land to be independent of the need for an occupation, although some were in imperial service. At Hermopolis they are about 35 percent of the landowners, at Antinoopolis, 49 percent. It is evident that the places in the distribution occupied by the smallholders and this group are reversed in the two cities. That may be taken to mean that Antinoites as a group were more likely to be an urban middle class living off rents than Hermopolites.

The large holders present a still more striking picture. Those with holdings larger than 100 arouras form about the same percentage of the landowning population in the two cities (10.8 percent at Hermopolis, 11.2 percent at Antinoopolis), but there the similarity ends. One glimpse of the difference comes from a simple table:

Arouras	Hermopolites	Antinoopolites
101-200	11	20
201-500	6	3
501-1,000	3	0
1,001+	6	0

The Antinoopolites are concentrated in the more modest reaches of the scale, with no individual holding more than 400 arouras. By contrast, concentration among Hermopolites is striking. And to it must be added the interrelatedness of the wealthy. In Hermopolis, for example, it appears that 38.8 percent of the *total* land is owned by six members of a single family, and another 17.5 percent is owned by two additional families.[150] Now this register represents only a quarter of the city, and the elite was not quite so narrow as this may appear to suggest; but it is an easy computation to reckon that every Hermo-

---

[149]The mean ownership figures can be misleading on this point. Cf. Lewuillon-Blume 1988, 280 n. 6, citing Bowman's computed means (51.37 ar. for all holders in F); it suffices to note that the *median* for Hermopolite holders is only ten, the mean being inflated by inclusion of the great landholders and thus essentially a meaningless figure.

[150]Lewuillon-Blume 1988, accepting the connection of the children of Aelianus to the family of Hyperechios' descendants. Her percentages, based on inaccurate totals, may be disregarded. It is, of course, possible that some of these families include still other landowners who cannot be identified with them given the information provided—husbands of women, for example. Eulalia daughter of Aelianus, for example, registers some of her land through a Hymnos, known from register G to be the son of D(e)ios. Is Dios the bishop (who owns nearly 500 ar.) their son?

politan male holding more than 100 arouras would have to belong to the council for that body to number as much as 100.

The very considerable concentration of wealth in the overall structure of landholding[151] has significant implications for the generation of surplus income after taxes. On the reasonable assumption that 10 arouras was sufficient to support the average household engaged in farming (as opposed to living on rents), 59 percent of the villagers' holdings were surplus to their personal subsistence requirements.[152] For the urban population, the concentration of surplus is of course even greater, some 88 percent for Hermopolites.[153] In all, the nome's landowners may have generated a surplus (*not* counting tax revenue) of some 380,000 artabas.[154] There is no ready means of computing how much of this was used to feed the nonlandowning population, much of which worked the land of the owners, and how much was exchanged for other purposes, but if all of it were used as wages for nonowners, it would have supported something like 16,000 households, or perhaps 80,000 persons. The figure of 16,000, however, is undoubtedly too high because not all surplus was spent on labor. All the same, it implies the practicability of a substantial urban population engaged in the production of other goods and services, for which there is other evidence (see below).

The way in which country estates were managed and the implications for city-country relationships are discussed in chapter 4. Here, two factors deserve mention. On the one hand, the holdings of most large landowners were located in multiple locations, usually in several different *pagi*.[155] There is no sign of any consolidation of ownership, leading to the creation of true "large estates" in the sense of a single large tract. On the other hand, there was still a sense in which any given person would be thought of as having a principal country seat. This perspective is visible in the minutes of a meeting of the council of Oxyrhynchos in the 270s, in which members agreeing to take on

[151]See Bagnall 1992b for the construction of this model, which depends on the Hermopolite and Karanidian material.

[152]This figure is derived by adding the holdings of those with more than 10 ar., subtracting the number of individuals multiplied by ten, and dividing the remainder by total holdings.

[153]Using eleven as a floor for urban residents because their net yield was no doubt lower than that of villagers who actually worked much more of their own land. Moreover, 10 ar. at Karanis is equivalent to 7 ar. of productive land, probably close to what it actually took to support a family.

[154]At a conservative figure of 2 art. per ar. The real return may have been higher, but land was more safe than it was lucrative. See Stone and Stone 1984, 11-12.

[155]Bowman 1985, 152-53.

liturgies are hailed by their peers with phrases like "Upright, faithful Horion, landlord at Nesmimis; upright, faithful Leonides, landlord at Dositheou."[156] And, in fact, most individuals do have a significant concentration within a single pagus; marriages within the landed elite—Horion's son and Leonides' daughter, for example—obviously would tend to produce subsequent generations with more dispersed holdings, but not enough to eliminate the sense of a principal base in the country.[157] The city was still their principal home, however; unlike the British landed elite, ancient magnates did not prefer country life.[158]

If the quarter represented in the Hermopolite land register is in fact representative,[159] then the city had about 450 landowners capable of being supported by the income from their country estates.[160] In a city of at least 7,000 households, that is about 6.5 percent of all households; even with broad allowances, the figure would not exceed 10 percent. The remainder of the city must have been supported by other means than revenues from their lands. The availability of a heavily concentrated surplus from the land offers part of the answer to the implicit question, but a more detailed response comes from a broader examination of the city economy (below, pp. 78ff.). For Antinoopolis, the situation is less clear. Hermopolite holdings by Antinoites are not likely to have given more than about 25 families the means necessary for council membership.[161] And a mere 125 families capable of being supported by landed revenues seems small for the physical splendor suggested by the remains still visible two centuries ago (cf. plate 1). Part of the answer here may lie in the constitution of Antinoopolis by Hadrian, which drew residents of nomes like the Arsinoite to citizenship there, attracted perhaps by citizen rights then unavailable in the nome metropoleis. How far Antinoite citizens of the fourth century still held extensive tracts in other nomes is impossible to say, although there are signs in the Arsinoite that some did.[162]

[156]*P.Oxy.* XII 1413 (*BL*) (270-275).

[157]A forthcoming study by Jane Rowlandson shows how the elite used dowries, sales and wills to avoid undue dispersion of landholdings.

[158]Cf. Stone and Stone 1984, 11-16, on the role of the country seat.

[159]There appears to be no means available of testing this hypothesis, but there are no contrary indications.

[160]The number might be somewhat higher if information about the 7th pagus were available, but probably not by a great deal.

[161]The 7th pagus is not likely to have been a factor here. As Bowman 1985, 152, notes, Antinoite holdings are heavily concentrated in the 5th pagus, no doubt that nearest Antinoopolis, and that pagus is included in the registers. Twenty-five is apparently the number by which the Antinoopolite council was *increased ca* 241-242: F. Hoogendijk and P. van Minnen, *Tyche* 2 (1987) 41-74 at 58-61.

[162]See p. 93.

The processes by which urban landholdings were formed and changed over time are obscure.[163] The main mechanisms for movement of land are clear enough: purchase and sale,[164] inheritance,[165] and transfer within families (gifts and dowries).[166] But it is difficult to tell either if concentration was increasing or at what speed change occurred. The two Hermopolite registers, written perhaps five or ten years apart, show approximately a 14 percent change in landholders between them. Short life expectancy would dictate considerable turnover: in the middle years (ages 30 to 45), the part of the population statistically likely to die in the coming five years rises from about 9 percent to about 12 percent. Death alone, then, would account for the visible changes between registers in little more than five years. But, strikingly, overall change in ownership during the interval is much higher, more than 35 percent.[167] This change, the result of changes in the holdings of those landowners who figure in both registers, indicates an active market in land.[168] This change was not unidirectional. There are several instances of sales by wealthy metropolitans to villagers, who may well be opportunists taking advantage of the urbanites' inability to manage some properties profitably.[169]

Apart from death and sales, of course, confiscation by the imperial government may account for some swings. Councillors, with the serious obligations placed on them by tax-collection liturgies, would be the most likely losers, and because they are the largest owners, changes in their condition would have a disproportionate effect on the totals. Even allowing for that, however, it appears that the market was

[163]See the study by Rowlandson cited above, n. 157.

[164]Examples: *CPR* VII 14 (Hermopolis, 305): one city resident to another; *SB* III 6612 (*BL*) (Oxyrhynchos, 365): metropolitan sells to villager; *P.Coll.Youtie* II 71-73 (Panopolis, 281): successive transactions.

[165]Examples: *CPR* V 9 (Hermopolis, 339); *P.Herm.* 26 (5c); *P.Vindob.Bosw.* 3 (*BL*; Drew-Bear 1979, 285) (Hermopolis, 279).

[166]*P.Michael.* 33 (*BL*; *Cd'E* 66 [1991] 284-87) (Oxyrhynchos, 367/8).

[167]Bowman 1985, 154, 161-63.

[168]Bowman 1985, 155: "The combined evidence for movement of land in the form of holdings which either disappear or increase or decrease in size certainly suggests a free market in land which was far from ossified." See J. Rowlandson, "Sales of Land in their Social Context," *Proc. XVI Congr. Pap.* 371-78, with a more constricted view in which sales are mainly adjustments to situations produced by other changes in ownership.

[169]*BGU* IV 1049 (*BL*) (Arsinoe, 342); *SB* III 6612 (*BL*) (Oxyrhynchos, 365); *SPP* XX 86 (= *CPR* I 19) (Hermopolis, 330); *P.Oxf.* 6 (Herakleopolis, 350). Cf. Keenan 1980 for the process in the sixth century. There are in fact few documented instances of the reverse, metropolitans' buying villagers' land. *CPR* XVIIA 17 = *SPP* XX 80 (Hermopolis, 321 [?]) is one.

active. Because the figures from the registers break holdings down only by pagus and category of land, they may even understate activity. (Selling one parcel of eight arouras in one village and buying one of seven arouras in another village in the same pagus would show up as a net change of one aroura.)

There was extensive wealth in the hands of urban residents other than land. Much of it was in cash or in staple commodities, principally wheat. The enormous number of surviving loan contracts and related documentation shows clearly that credit played a crucial role in the economy. Quantifying that role is made more difficult by the fact that the Roman administration made no attempt to keep records of liquid wealth after the fashion of the detailed documentation of real property that enables the kind of approximate understanding possible for land. Nor was wealth in cash or commodities taxed as such.[170] Short of any quantitative appreciation, however, much can be grasped from study of the documents that credit operations did generate.

Egyptian agriculture had a long history of reliance on some form of credit for working capital; for many centuries its principal form was seed loans extended at sowing time from the government to tenants of royal land, although private credit agreements, particularly loans in kind, are already plentiful in the Ptolemaic period.[171] In the fourth-century world of privatized land, the need for working capital from private sources can only have been larger and more diverse. It was a matter not only of seed but also of the ability to live, to pay laborers, to provide necessary tools and animals. Amounts range from very small to rather large. The documentation points to a long-term shift from loans in kind to loans in money, though a growing number of the latter are repayable in produce at the harvest.[172] It is possible that to some extent this reflects the dominance of the cities over the villages in the papyrus finds (cf. above, p. 5), and that at the village level loans of wheat payable in wheat continued as they had for centuries.[173] The choice of type of loan could have variable advantages for both parties, depending on circumstances.[174]

[170]Because there was no income tax as such, in fact, someone who lived purely by lending out money or grain might have escaped taxation except for the *chrysargyron* (below, p. 154).

[171]See Foraboschi-Gara 1981 and 1982.

[172]Foraboschi-Gara 1982, 70. Cf. generally Bagnall 1977b (too pessimistic) and Keenan 1981. For a labor-oriented analysis of loans repayable in kind, emphasizing the lender's interest in the goods supplied, see *P.Heid.* V, pp. 296-341.

[173]An example: *P.Oxy.* XXXVI 2775 (274/5), a loan of wheat for sowing.

[174]See Foraboschi-Gara 1981, 340-41, for hypothetical options.

Even allowing for this bias in the documentation, however, the overall pattern is clear: the cities were the source to which villagers went for their credit needs, in kind or in cash.[175] Because cash was far more portable, it had a certain advantage from the villager's point of view, and its compactness have made it easier for the urbanite to manage. Moreover, if sowing occupied a less prominent role relative to other needs of farmers, money's versatility for paying other expenses would have been attractive. Another development pointing in the same direction is the growing proportion of contracts that involve commodities other than wheat as the medium of repayment, a sign of the generalization of credit as a means of doing business.[176] Village craftsmen with urban markets used the same credit instruments that farmers did.[177] In one complex transaction, a landowner of high rank lent money for repayment in wine, with the jars to be provided by the lender.[178]

The lending of money and commodities was a private, not an institutional, business. The lenders tended, where anything is known of their identities, to be members of the same groups who own substantial amounts of land: the landed civic aristocracy with their offices and council membership;[179] soldiers and veterans;[180] and members of the civil service.[181] Only one transaction involving a banker turns up, and in that his identification as a banker may be incidental because the loan is in wheat and is made in a village where neither lender nor borrower resides.[182] The lenders are thus not professionals in providing credit. But they are people of some means, who in the absence of most modern vehicles for investment of their surplus funds, particularly publicly traded securities, habitually resorted to lending to individuals in order not to have their assets inert.[183] Some transac-

[175]See Keenan 1981, 484-85.

[176]Foraboschi-Gara 1982, 72, pointing out that noncereal products, the object of only 20 percent of contracts in the Roman period, are involved in 50 percent of those from the Byzantine period. Even allowing for structural changes in the documentation, that seems to be a decisive shift.

[177]P.Flor. III 314 (cf. BL 1.458) (Hermopolis, 428).

[178]P.Select. 2 (3/4c ed.; 4/5c is more likely).

[179]A few examples: P.Flor. III 313 (BL) (Hermopolis, 449), politeuomenos and riparius; P.Mert. I 36 (BL) (Oxyrhynchos, 360), former gymnasiarch and prytanis; P.Panop. 31 (ca 329), councillor.

[180]E.g., BGU XII 2140 (Hermopolis, 432); P.Oxy. VIII 1133 (BL) (396); P.Aberd. 180 (3/4c).

[181]E.g., P.Oxy. XIV 1711 (3c late); P.Oxy. XIV 1712 (394); P.Oxy. XIV 1716 (333).

[182]P.Vind.Sijp. 13 (BL) (Herakleopolite, 373).

[183]Which does not mean that hoarding did not go on; Foraboschi-Gara 1982 argue that it was one reason for a perennial shortage of capital in Egypt. That may be true, but Egypt was hardly unique in that regard, and it hardly explains a supposed differential in the shortage of capital.

tions are more complicated even than straightforward cash loans for repayment in produce. Loans of cash with monthly interest in produce rather than repayment of principal suggest strategies of asset management and even hedging against price fluctuations.[184]

Because agriculture was Egypt's largest economic sector, it is not surprising that so much documentation concerns loans to villagers. But city residents also borrowed money with great frequency. Most loans speak simply of "personal need" as the motive, which obscures rather than explains the phenomenon. In some cases one can discern specific business financing needs. A fruitseller bought a crop on credit and repaid the loan even though the lender lost the note—perhaps a sign that their relationship was ongoing.[185] Many retailers undoubtedly managed to stay in business on credit, and they may have had few assets to fall back on if things went bad.[186] Undoubtedly other business loans are not given the specificity of description found in one loan to a business-agent who borrowed 500 talents to be repaid at 24 percent interest "on account of business."[187]

Not only farmers, small businessmen, and needy people borrowed. Members of the council and former magistrates, though predominantly lenders, appear on occasion as borrowers of significant sums.[188] The reasons may have varied—short-term cash flow prob-

[184]For example, *BGU* XII 2140 (Hermopolis, 432), a loan of money by a soldier with annual interest of one artaba of wheat for each solidus lent (a low rate of interest, one would think; perhaps wheat was expensive at the time). Similarly, in *P.Rain.Cent.* 86 (*SPP* XX 103) (Herakleopolis, 381), a city resident lends money to the deacon of the catholic church of the village of Tamoro; in place of interest he is to pay five 5-mina bundles of tow each month, and he mortgages a silver cup. In *SB* XIV 12088 (Oxyrhynchos, 346), the borrower of a small sum is to supply edible greens for the household of an *officialis* of the office of the governor each month in place of interest. On strategies, see Foraboschi-Gara 1981.

[185]*P.Oxy.* VIII 1133 (cf. *BL* 1.466) (396), a singularly interesting text for geographical mobility. The borrower was an Arsinoite living in Oxyrhynchos, the lender an *ex-primipilaris* from Herakleopolis living in the *epoikion* of Nesos Limeniou.

[186]See the striking case of *P.Lond.* VI 1915 (*ca* 330-340): the creditors of a former wineseller who has failed have carried off his children, even though they are very young.

[187]*P.Coll.Youtie* II 82 = *P.Oxy.* XLV 3266 (337). The man is a *pragmateutes*, and the loan is "on account of *pragmateia*," a fairly vague description. He starts paying interest immediately, but principal is due only at the end, seven months later. It is interesting to see this contravention of the 12 percent limit, promulgated once again in *P.Select.* 9 (4c beginning), an edict of the *praeses Thebaidos* forbidding the charging of more than 1 percent (per month) interest. The loan is about the equivalent of 20 art. wheat.

[188]*P.Panop.* 21 (315), a former archon; *P.Charite* 33 (Hermopolis, 346/7) and 34 (348), in both of which the wealthy Charite borrows by mortgaging real property in the city. Cf. *P.Vind.Sal.* 7 (Oxyrhynchos, 293), in which all parties are of high rank

lems, the expenses of major offices—but the most important was evidently the burdens of tax-collection liturgies. Two examples show that even the wealthy might be short of cash or wheat at times. In one, a petition to the prefect, a former high priest of Arsinoe, who describes himself as a man of moderate means, complains that a former gymnasiarch has refused to repay two deposits totaling 22 talents, causing the petitioner great difficulty because he owes the treasury arrears from a tax collection office.[189] His surplus wealth for investment thus turns into a needed loan for another member of his class, but in turn he finds himself short of cash when his own liturgical obligations pinch him. In another, a councillor has to have someone else pay 60 artabas in taxes on his behalf, thus incurring a debt. That he does not simply have the wheat somewhere else is shown by his agreement to repay it over three months.[190]

The upper classes had access sometimes to credit from official sources, municipal or council funds. Where the system worked, it probably eased the burdens of public office with readily available funds at reasonable cost, enabling land-rich but perhaps sometimes cash-strapped magnates to ride out short-term shortages and repay them in better times.[191] But the system had its risks. The prefect of Egypt held the officials in charge of these funds, the *logistes* and the magistrates, liable for uncollectable loans, even though the borrowers were rendered insolvent by confiscation of their property by the imperial government.[192]

The entire tax collection system generated a significant volume of credit transactions at every level. The archive of Papnouthis and Dorotheos has shown what must have been a common phenomenon, small entrepreneurs borrowing to pay a tax due on a village or district, which they then proceeded to collect—at a profit, they hoped,

---

and the amount large.

[189] *P.Oxy.* I 71 (*BL*) (303). The sum is the equivalent of 90 artabas or so, a significant sum.

[190] *P.Vind.Sijp.* 15 (cf. H.C. Youtie, *TAPA* 95 [1964] 310-16 = *Scriptiunculae* I 410-16; *BL*) (Hermopolis, 4c). Because the payments are due at the end of Phaophi, Hathyr, and Choiak, long after the harvest, one wonders where he is going to find the wheat for repayment. Perhaps he is in turn the creditor for outstanding loans; or else he will sell some other crop (wine?) to buy wheat.

[191] *P.Oxy.* XII 1501 (3c late), a receipt for repayment by a councillor. See Bowman 1971, 41-42, for bouleutic funds.

[192] *P.Oxy.* XXXIII 2666 (308/9). The government was devoted to the principle of forcing others to bear all risks; this risk is particularly unpredictable, because a magistrate could hardly foresee this kind of catastrophe.

but that intention did not always work out.[193] This system was particularly suited to—almost inevitable in—situations where the tax was due in a form not readily collectible from smallholders, such as bullion or military garments; the collectors purchased what was owed to the government, then set out to collect their costs plus a surplus. Collectors lacking part of what was owed from them might have to borrow briefly to cover their obligations.[194]

Credit activity was not limited to the nome. The activities of imperial and military officials throughout the country and the workings of the tax system generated many needs for the flow of funds up and down the valley. Some of these were accomplished through loans made in one place for repayment in another, as in the case of an Alexandrian temporarily in Oxyrhynchos who borrowed 1,500 myriads on letter of credit from the imperial account and promised to an official to repay it in Alexandria. The crossing out of the document shows that he did so.[195] Alexandrian business agents also made loans in the smaller cities, perhaps recapitulating on a provincial level the pattern seen more commonly at the nome level.[196]

At the other extreme of the scale stands the humble enterprise of the pawnbroker, offering credit to those with no other means of borrowing. The occasional letter or account shows a variety of objects pledged for small loans, such as sacks (of hair and tow) and fine linenweavings.[197]

Other wealth in the hands of the rich is less well known. They certainly owned ships (cf. above, p. 37), urban residential real estate (see below, pp. 86, 97-98), and productive facilities like pottery works on their country estates (see below, p. 129). A mill and oil factory in

---

[193]The most illuminating documents, but not the only ones, are P.Oxy. XLVIII 3393 and 3394 (365 and ca 364-366, respectively), both petitions from the brothers. They had taken the position of assistant to a councillor to collect the taxes of a village, but he then interfered with their collection and sent others to collect instead, leaving them stuck with loans and no tax collections.

[194]A very brief term might be involved, as in P.Mich. IX 573 (Karanis, 316), where sitologoi "borrow" from the apodektai for six days, i.e. defer payment that long.

[195]P.Oxy. XLIII 3146 (347). Repayment is through the borrower's slave Polychronios when he arrives in the capital. The borrower himself probably remained in Oxyrhynchos, where the canceled document was found.

[196]P.Oxy. XVI 1880 and 1881 (427). In the first, a pragmateutes from Alexandria cancels a suit against another business agent from Alexandria who has settled a debt; in the second, he sues two residents of the Oxyrhynchite village of Senokomis for nonpayment of debt, and they swear to appear in court upon demand.

[197]P.Ryl. IV 606 (3c late), a business letter, evidently concerning a pawnbroking business; SB VIII 9834b, part of a pawnbroker's account. The editor's (TAPA 92 [1961] 253 ff.) suggested provenance (Philadelphia) and date (early 4c) both seem unlikely; the date must be earlier.

Oxyrhynchos belonged to a wealthy man who operated it through a dependent.[198] At a rather lower level, a future *systates* of the same city and his wife were involved in another mill-leasing transaction.[199] Such holdings may not have been uncommon. It is also possible that the rich invested in such things as much through lending as through equity ownership.[200]

Production, Distribution, and Services

From the preceding discussion it is clear that only a small minority of urban households could have depended directly on revenues from agriculture; a fair assessment would place the figure at about 6 to 10 percent of Hermopolitan households, although as many again owned some land. At the same time, it is evident that the concentration of land in the hands of an elite was sufficient to guarantee disposable surpluses of some magnitude, even after taxes. How far these surpluses were exported and thus exchanged for something else of value and how far they fed a local population not engaged in agriculture are figures impossible to compute. But feeding the other 90 to 95 percent of the urban population, along with the non-landowning population in the villages, must have been a first claim.

What the majority of the urban population did is then a critical question for understanding the very nature of these cities. This question is indeed central to most discussion of the ancient economy in general. The papyri offer, however, a level of documentation unique for ancient cities, even if it remains to be shown how far they were typical or atypical.[201] Above all the reader encounters a bewildering profusion of (male) occupational titles, literally hundreds of them. Analysis shows, however, that these can be unsurprisingly categorized under the headings of production, distribution, and services, particularly relating to food, textiles, and construction.[202] Per-

[198]*PSI* VIII 884 (*BL*; *P.Rain.Cent.*, p. 424 n. 13), of 390. See *P.Oxy.* LI 3639.4n. (below, p. 215 n. 33) for the still inadequate documentation of Fl. Limenius v.c.

[199]*P.Wash.Univ.* I 19 (cf. *P.Wash.Univ.* II, p. 242).

[200]On the controversial question of the involvement of the upper classes in industry and trade, see generally Pleket 1984 and van Minnen 1987, 35. The British elite preferred enterprises that involved developing their lands; cf. Stone and Stone 1984, 15. While that in part reflects an antiurban attitude foreign to antiquity, it may find its counterpart in clay and stone production on Roman country estates. See a forthcoming book by J.-J. Aubert.

[201]See Rathbone 1989 for a defense of the usability of the Egyptian evidence for study of the Roman Empire in general. Fikhman 1969, 150, suggests that what was true of Egypt was probably also true of other developed provinces in the East.

[202]For the analogous situation in Ottoman Aleppo, see Marcus 1989, 159: some 157 guilds are attested, but most "actually fell into one of three areas of production and trade: food, textiles, and construction." Women do not figure among the mem-

haps the most controversial is that of production.[203]

In broad terms, urban production of goods corresponds closely to the description of the material basis of life given in chapter 1. Food, shelter, clothing, and the main materials of technology dominate. The primary production of food was of course a matter for the country villages, where growing and harvesting took place, but the cities played an important role in processing (and securing; see p. 87) the food supply of its residents. One may indeed be surprised to hear of threshing and winnowing as urban occupations, but they do occur in the documentation.[204] The basic processing of grapes into wine was evidently a thoroughly estate- and village-based activity, but oil manufacture is well attested in the cities.[205] One attestation of the processing of honey is also found.[206]

Despite the presence of urban threshing floors, most wheat and other grains received their basic processing in the villages. Milling of grains into flour, however, was certainly (if not uniquely) an urban occupation.[207] Millers served the large baking trade, which enjoyed some differentiation. Along with the basic bakers of bread,[208] there

---

bers of Aleppo's guilds; their occupations were outside the range of those for which guilds existed.

[203]The bibliography, for Egypt and generally, is enormous. The most helpful items, each with documentation and bibliography, are Fikhman 1965 (summarized in Wipszycka 1971) and 1969 (summarizing 1965) and van Minnen 1986 and 1987 (the latter with particularly rich bibliography for both Egypt and the Roman Empire more broadly; for general issues, see also Pleket 1984). They (and the literature they list) are cited below only occasionally for specific points. Separating craft production from other production (as in Sodini 1979) is not helpful, and all such activities are brought together here.

[204]Winnowers, *koskineutai*, appear in *P.Genova* I 24 (4c: an 11th indiction), an account of *sticharia*, probably for the *anabolikon*, listing occupational groups; all seem to be urban. Threshing floors existed in Hermopolis (*P.Charite* 7.18).

[205]Examples: *P.Oxy.* LI 3639 (412), a lease of an oil factory owned by one Fl. Limenius v.c. to an oilmaker. The rent includes 120 sextarii of radish oil. Included are the necessary millstones, courtyards, well, and other appurtenances (see the editor's helpful notes); *P.Panop.* 15 (308-309) includes a receipt for a tax in gold imposed on the oilworkers of Panopolis, presumably as a guild; *P.Berl.Bork.*, p. 44. Panopolitan oil was proverbial: *Sancti Pachomii Vitae Graecae* (Subs.Hag. 19, Brussels 1932) 55 §82.

[206]*SB* XII 11003 (4/5c), *meliepsoi* (presumably processing by heating). Provenance is unknown, but the other occupations listed point to an urban source.

[207]*P.Oxy.* XLIII 3120 (310), a receipt for gold issued by a goldsmith to the mill of Leukadios via the master millers. *PSI* VIII 884 (*BL*) (390), a receipt for the *chrysargyron* (a tax on trade) paid by a dependent of a master miller on account of his mill. In *P.Oxy.* XLIX 3481 (442), the captain of a boat acknowledges receipt of wheat from a master miller.

[208]Despite numerous references, their numbers are hard to assess. In the list of payers of taxes on trades from Arsinoe in 276, nine *artokopoi* are listed in eight locations, only two of them in Bakers Street. (*BGU* I 9 [*BL*] + IV 1087 [*BL*] + XIII 2280; see

existed specialists in white bread and in cakes, both perhaps primarily
catering to the wealthy.[209]

Meat and fish, also important parts of the diet, employed residents of the metropolis in their production. Because of the proximity
of the Nile to most cities, fishermen were often based in them, and
cities controlled some of the more lucrative fishing grounds.[210]
Processing of meat is also well attested, with generalist butchers most
commonly mentioned,[211] but some specialists in particular animals
(goat, veal, pork) are also known and may have been fairly
numerous.[212]

Despite the relatively low proportion of processing outside the
home that may be supposed characteristic of the society, then, a few
basic trades carried out the main functions necessary for a city to be
something more than an overgrown village in its food supply. The
millers, bakers, butchers, and oilworkers were probably all relatively
numerous, as they served the main staple needs of the entire population, while other specialized workers produced smaller quantities of
expensive goods for the consumption of the wealthy. No Egyptian
city, to judge from the papyri, produced processed foods for shipping
beyond its own hinterland except for public bakeries and similar
establishments to process food for shipment to army units in other
parts of Egypt.[213] Egypt's main agricultural export, of course, was

---

Wilcken, *Archiv* 5 [1913] 273-75.) But it seems unlikely that nine bakers can have
served the bread needs of an entire metropolis, and the purpose of the papyrus is
not clear enough to support such a view. Bakers pay the lowest attested monthly
rate in this papyrus (8 dr.: 96 dr. a year when wheat was 200 dr. per artaba). A
female baker occurs in *P.Oxy.* VIII 1146 (*BL*) (early 4c). See generally for terminology Battaglia 1989, 131-206 (including pastry production).

[209]Cake and pastry makers: Cf. above, p. 31. White bread: above p. 24 and
P.Alex. 32 (*BL* 5.4 misreports Rémondon, who saw no basis for dating more closely
than to the 5c), a lease (addressed to the bishop) of a bakery owned by a catholic
church, to a *katharourgos*, of an establishment including two mills.

[210]E.g., *P.Oxy.* XLVI 3270 (309), a lease of fishing rights for the season of the current rise of the Nile at specified lock-gates; *P.Oxy.* XLVI 3300 (late 3c, prob. not long
after 271/2), an extract from a city property register, including two fishermen
among eighteen households; *P.Oxy.* XXIV 2421 (*ca* 312-323, *BL*).

[211]*P.Oxy.* XXIV 2421 (*ca* 312-323, *BL*); *P.Genova* I 24 (4c: 11th indiction), as an
occupational group; similarly in the Arsinoe list (above, n. 208): three butchers in
three locations.

[212]*SB* XII 11003 (4/5c), a list of occupations, includes *moschothutai* (veal
slaughterers) and *aigeothutai* (goat slaughterers); the former appear also in
P.Berl.Bork. (2: cf. p. 45), the latter in *P.Oxy.* VIII 1136 (420). *Choiromageiroi* (pork
butchers) appear as a guild in *PSI* III 202 (Oxyrhynchos, 338), making a price
declaration.

[213]*P.Oxy.* XLIII 3124 (*ca* 322?).

wheat, which received only the minimal processing necessary to reduce its bulk and purify it before shipping. Any other agricultural product with more than local significance remains unknown, with the possible exception of wine.

Construction also employed a significant number of urban residents.[214] The preparation of the raw materials apparently took place mainly in rural areas (see below, p. 129), for good reason: the materials were located there, whether stone outcroppings, clay beds for bricks, or trees for wood, the last of these being scarce in Egypt. Their users in the city, however, are well documented: master builders,[215] masons,[216] carpenters,[217] and joiners.[218] Among them they represented all the main groups necessary for the erection of most buildings in these cities, where brick was the staple material, wood used for framing and decoration, and stone mainly for foundations, door jambs, and facing (and occasionally otherwise in major public buildings). Decoration is less frequently represented, but plasterers[219] and painters[220] were certainly active, and the latter formed a guild.

Another type of construction was shipbuilding. As a timber-poor country, Egypt was certainly never a major factor in this field, and it is difficult to imagine anything larger than river craft for local use being built anywhere in the land. But there is nonetheless some evidence for

[214]See in general Sodini 1979, 72-80, with archaeological references. He does not (despite his avowed focus) sufficiently distinguish urban and rural activities.

[215]*Architekton*: *P.Berl.Bork.*, p. 44. They formed an occupational group or guild, as can be seen in *P.Genova* I 24 (4c).

[216]*Oikodomos*: Cf. *P.Oxy.* XLVI 3300 (late 3c, prob. soon after 271/2) and *P.Berl.Bork.* p. 44. They were an active and assertive guild, as can be seen in *P.Ryl.* IV 654 = *TAPA* 89 (1958) 398-99 (Youtie, *Scriptiunculae* I 308-9; *BL*) (Oxyrhynchos, before 354), an excerpt from judicial proceedings about a young man who had been apprenticed to the guild of linenweavers, but whom the guild of masons tried to grab for themselves. Masons also had an inspection function on behalf of the government when building safety or division was at issue: see *P.Oxy.* XLIII 3126 (328), concerning a division; *P.Oxy.* XLIV 3195 (331), a report from the meniarchs of the masons reporting on window-openings in a house; *PSI* V 456 (*BL*) (Oxyrhynchos, 276-282), a report on the condition of a house.

[217]*P.Berl.Bork.* p. 44; *P.Oxy.* XLVI 3300 (soon after 271/2); *P.Oslo* III 144 (Oxyrhynchos, 270-275); *P.Genova* I 24 (4c), as a group; inspection duties in *P.Oxy.* I 53 (316).

[218]*P.Oxy.* I 55 (= *WChr.* 196) (283), two Kasiotic joiners working on the beams in a colonnade along a street.

[219]*WO* II 1485 (*BL*) (Thebes, 3/4c), in an account.

[220]Most interestingly, *P.Oxy.* VI 896 i (*BL*; col. I = *W.Chr.* 48) (316), a report to a *logistes* from a *zographos*, who after inspecting the warm baths of Hadrian now under repair reports on what needs painting and offers an estimate of the cost. The *leukantai* (whitewashers?) appear in *P.Genova* I 24 (4c) and in *P.Mert.* II 95 (5c?), where as a guild they are responsible for a payment for a public service (see E. Wipszycka, *Byzantion* 39 [1969] 194-95 n.1).

construction of boats, and no doubt repairing both locally built and imported boats kept some shipyards busy.[221]

A major employer in some cities, and probably a significant factor in most, was the textile industry and related activities.[222] The various stages of production were in the hands of specialized workers, from washing, carding, dyeing, fulling, and weaving, on to tailoring and embroidery. There was also a division by the type of fiber used: wool was the most important, but linen (from flax) was also a large element in some places. The range of products was considerable, including clothing and a variety of such decorative items as rugs.[223] Related fiber products that involved weaving or plaiting included sacks,[224] mattresses,[225] nets,[226] ropes,[227] and baskets for sale. Some of these certainly were produced in villages, and monks seem, to judge from hagiographic literature, to have spent much of their time making baskets. But the cities remained the centers and largest producers of most textile products.

A unique glimpse of the quantities involved, and hence of the structural importance of the textile trade, comes from an Oxyrhynchos papyrus which appears to list quantities of chitons, *pallia*, and *lodikes*, with the chitons both for adults and children, destined for export.[228] It is probably of the third century,[229] but there is no reason to think that conditions differed greatly in the fourth century. A five-day period

[221]For example, see *P.Oxy.* XIV 1752 (378), an order to deliver wine to two *pristai* (sawyers) on account of the expense of the renewal of a boat. The shortage of wood might lead to tree-poaching; cf. *P.Lond.* II 214 (p. 161) = *W.Chr.* 177 (Memphite, 271-275), a petition from the steward of an estate owned by the treasury against a shipbuilder who, he says, invaded a vineyard of the estate and cut down two very large acacia trees. Four shipbuilders (*naupegoi*) appear in *P.Berl.Bork.*, cf. p. 44. For shipbuilding, see generally L. Casson, *BASP* 27 (1990) 15-19, and P. van Minnen and K. A. Worp, *ZPE* 78 (1989) 139-42.

[222]See particularly Wipszycka 1965 and van Minnen 1986; material from other areas is cited by Sodini 1979, 90-92. These make a full citation of the documents unnecessary here.

[223]No doubt encompassing a broad range of quality, up to what was evidently a special rug ordered for the visit of the *dux* (*P.Oxy.* XII 1431, 352) at a cost of 1500 T. Cf. also *P.Oxy.* XX 2275 (4c). See *Pap.Lugd.Bat.* XXV 62 for the guild of rugmakers.

[224]*P.Ross.Georg.* V 60 (Hermopolis, 390-400), a pay account that includes a sack-tailor. Sacks of hair and of tow (flax fiber) are mentioned in *P.Ryl.* IV 606 (3c late).

[225]With their own specialized guild, cf. *PSI* XII 1239 (cf. *BL* 3.229) (Antinoopolis, 430), in which an *epistates* of the mattressmakers appears.

[226]*SB* XII 11003 (4/5c).

[227]*P.Harr.* I 97 (*BL*) (4c middle?), payment to ropeweavers; *P.Berl.Bork.* p. 44.

[228]*P.Oxy.Hels.* 40; the discussion here depends on van Minnen 1986.

[229]The editor dates it second or third century, but prefers the third (*P.Oxy. Hels.*, p. 153). Although the interpretation of the values given in the papyrus is difficult, they seem clearly to support a date after the middle of the third century.

shows an export of almost 2,000 garments (almost 90 percent of them chitons, and the majority for children), and even conservative estimation would lead to a figure of over 80,000 garments per year, representing perhaps 12,000 to 15,000 large pieces of cloth from the loom.[230] Even with all the uncertainties involved, it is clear that Oxyrhynchos was a major producer for export and that many hands must have been involved. How typical Oxyrhynchos was, is hard to say. Panopolis was well known for linen production,[231] and references to members of the textile trade in the papyri are spread over the various provenances, though with a heavier concentration on Oxyrhynchos than its raw numbers of documents would predict.[232] Any large export business supposes regional specialization to some degree, of course, and other cities may have had extensive industries producing different types of textile products, without any surviving documentation.[233]

This extensive textile industry was based on Egypt's production of flax and on large flocks of sheep. By contrast, the relative silence of the papyri about cattle translates into little information about leather-working, which gives the impression of an industry with purely local significance.[234] Footwear—the making of shoes, sandals, and boots—is one necessary component.[235] Otherwise, the requisite equipment for transport animals, saddles, and other fittings employed a certain number of craftsmen.[236] But it is not surprising that in one taxation document (perhaps from Oxyrhynchos) the saddlemakers and bootmakers together pay less than one-sixth what the fullers do, or one-tenth what

[230]Van Minnen 1986, 92, cites Leiden in the second half of the fifteenth century as producing 20,000 pieces per year. His figures are trimmed somewhat here to allow for periods when transportation would have been suspended.

[231]See B. McGing, *ZPE* 82 (1990) 115-21 at 117.

[232]In Arsinoe, we find twelve dyers and seven fullers listed in 276 (cf. above, n. 208); it is otherwise the least well documented for textile production, and because these are only two of the specialties required, the total employed must be in the hundreds. It is telling that Fikhman 1969, 151, cites as cities known for textile production precisely all those from which there is significant fourth-century documentation!

[233]It is worth a moment's reflection that only in 1979 was quantifiable evidence for this large industry published for Oxyrhynchos. The silence of the rest proves nothing.

[234]See generally Sodini 1979, 89.

[235]Cobblers appear in *SB* XII 11003 (4/5c) and *WO* II 1485 (*BL*) (Thebes, 3/4c). Bootmakers appear in *P.Genova* I 24 (4c).

[236]The saddlemakers, *sagmatoraphoi*, appear among the occupational groups in *P.Genova* I 24 (4c). Other mentions are in *P.Harr.* I 100 (*BL*) (Oxyrhynchos?, 5c) and *P.Ross.Georg.* V 61 (Herakleopolite?, 4c). An *exartister*, probably a fitter of reins and the like, appears in *P.Ryl.* IV 641 (Hermopolis, *ca* 318-323).

the dyers do.[237] In the Delta, however, cattle raising may have been more important, thereby supporting a proportionately larger leather industry.[238]

Metalworking was more important.[239] There is abundant evidence for the importance of goldsmiths[240] and silversmiths,[241] and the other key metals of antiquity also were worked: bronze,[242] iron,[243] tin,[244] and lead.[245] Occupational division was essentially by material worked, not by product generated; as a result bronzeworkers produced anything in that metal, be it vessels, implements, or art. On the face of it, such a system should produce a low level of specialization. But it is in practice impossible to tell if such was the case; the use of a single term to cover craftsmen working in the same medium but specializing in different products is perfectly possible. Gold and goldsmiths appear more important than silver and silversmiths, an entirely credible situation in a country that possessed gold mines but no silver.[246]

The remaining materials-based crafts appear to have been of minor importance. Pottery, the most obvious,[247] was fundamentally—like bricks and tiles—a rural industry because of proximity to the clay beds, and large production of basic earthenware took place in the

[237]*P.Genova* I 24 (4c).

[238]A supposition based on names like Boukoloi and the Boukolikon mouth of the Nile mentioned by Herodotos (2.17.5), cf. Johnson 1936, 229, and Calderini-Daris, *Diz.* II 62-63.

[239]True generally: see Sodini 1979, 94-97 (precious metals) and 85-86 (nonprecious metals).

[240]Producing an imperial portrait: *P.Oxy.* LV 3791 (318); a gold "crown" for Licinius: *P.Oxy.* XLIII 3121 (*ca* 316-318); managing the guild's tax burdens: *ZPE* 59 (1985) 67-70; furnishing the medium for others' taxes or deliveries in gold: *P.Oxy.* XLIII 3120 (310).

[241]Price declaration by the guild: *P.Oxy.* LI 3624 (359); involvement in taxation: *P.Ross.Georg.* V 28 (Oxyrhynchos, 4c), *P.Oxy.* VIII 1146 (*BL*) (4c early); a slave of a silversmith: *P.Lond.* III 983 (p. 229) (4c).

[242]*SB* X 10257 (*BL*) (Antinoopolis, 300), declaration of prices by the guild; *P.Laur.* IV 155 (Oxyrhynchos, *ca* 282/3?), request for payment for work on the baths; *P.Genova* I 24 (4c), taxed; *P.Oslo* III 144 (Oxyrhynchos, 270-275), contributing to the association of *hieronikai*.

[243]*P.Oxy.* XXXIV 2718 (458), five ironsmiths are paid by the city for nails for the public baths; *P.Oxy.* I 84 (= *W.Chr.* 197) (316), the guild of *siderochalkeis* is paid by the city for iron for public works. For the ironworkers of Hermonthis, see Lajtar 1991.

[244]Four tinsmiths in Arsinoe in 276 (above, n. 208), paying 36 dr. a month, a relatively high rate.

[245]*P.Oxy.* XII 1517 (*BL*) (272 or 278); *P.Ross.Georg.* V 61 (Herakleopolite?, 4c); *WO* II 1485 (*BL*) (Thebes, 3/4c).

[246]Though it includes only a part of the city of Panopolis and may not be representative, *P.Berl.Bork.* (p. 44) shows seven goldsmiths with twelve properties and only one silversmith with one property.

[247]See Sodini 1979, 80-85.

villages and on country estates (see p. 129).[248] That does not exclude the urban production of pottery, probably in the main of fine wares, for which the transportation of the clay to the city would be less burdensome than in the case of bulky coarse wares.[249] There is in fact limited evidence for urban potters in the papyri.[250] Nor does the rural base exclude a key urban role of middlemen, like the dealer in pickled products who borrows cash for repayment in wine jars, which he will no doubt buy from a producer.[251] Woodworking is still less visible, apart from construction, although some lathe-turners are known.[252] Egypt's lack of extensive stands of high-quality wood (or any wood at all) obviously made this a craft of only marginal importance. Glass clearly occupied a small group of workers,[253] and luxury items like ivory still smaller.[254]

Assessing the economic and social role of urban production has obvious difficulties. The cities of Middle and Upper Egypt best known from the papyri all had flourishing textile industries (including rugs, an important business at Oxyrhynchos[255]), at least some of which produced on a substantial scale for export. No other industry can be shown on present evidence to have such a role; the remaining industries seem to have served local needs, including presumably those of the nome's villages not served by village production (which was probably rather limited, see below, p. 129). The Nile Valley saw other exports, of course, most importantly wheat, which were direct products of the countryside. Many of these may have passed through the cities, but they were not products of urban industry,[256] though

---

[248]See particularly Cockle 1981 (texts now *P.Oxy.* L 3595-3597) and *CPR* XVIIA 8 (Hermopolis, 317?), and cf. the sale of a village pottery in *PSI* IV 300 (cf. *BASP* 27 [1990] 86-89) (Oxyrhynchos, 324).

[249]See generally a forthcoming book by J.-J. Aubert, with bibliography.

[250]*P.Berl.Bork.*, p. 44; *P.Oxy.* LIV 3766 (329), declarations of the price paid for pitch by *kerameis*; *P.Oxy.* XXIV 2421 (*ca* 312-323, *BL*).

[251]*CPR* X 39 (Herakleopolis, 443). Given the role of wine vinegar in pickling, surely this (and not spice dealing) is the occupation of the *conditarius* in this papyrus.

[252]Sodini 1979, 86-88. For *torneutai*, see *P.Genova* I 24 (4c), where their payment is modest.

[253]Most interestingly, *P.Oxy.* XLV 3265 = *P.Coll.Youtie* II 81 (326), in which the guild of glassworkers estimates that 6,000 lbs. of glass will be needed for planned work on the warm baths. See Sodini 1979, 92-94.

[254]*P.Genova* I 24 (4c), with one of the smallest contributions. See Sodini 1979, 97, for minor crafts.

[255]See the large payment by the *tapetarii* in *P.Genova* I 24 (4c), and cf. *Pap.Lugd.Bat.* XXV 62.

[256]Stone from quarries no doubt was loaded onto boats at the nearest point to production, and the quarries were in any case under imperial control.

further processing may have occurred, as with wine.[257] The wholesale loss of evidence from the Delta should temper any sweeping conclusions; papyrus manufacture—an export business—may well have served in some cities there the role that textile production did for Oxyrhynchos.[258] Distinctive resources produced different patterns of production.

Estimating numbers of workers in these industries with any precision is impossible. The payers of taxes on crafts in public accounts may be listed as either individuals or heads of shops. And there is no way to know the workforce of the average establishment. It may be a fair guess that 15 to 20 percent of the heads of household were engaged in production, but that may not count their employees.[259] Despite the vagueness of such figures, they do suggest that far more of the urban population depended on such production than on revenues from land.[260] This productive group has often been described in rather bleak terms, as of low social status, locked in to hereditary obligations to stay with an occupation, heavily in debt, renting rather than owning, and under severe state pressure. It is now generally agreed that this picture is far too somber as far as state pressure and hereditary obligation go.[261] Nor should the use of debt or the existence of a rental market for workshops necessarily be taken negatively. Debt has no unequivocal meaning, for it may as easily be credit for the development and operation of productive enterprise as it is a burden. It played a large role in the operation of a complex agricultural system, and although it was no more problem-free than in

[257]Transfer to proper containers, performed by *katangistai* ("decanters"), was often necessary; cf. their appearance in *P.Genova* I 24 (4c). See below on *ekdocheis*.

[258]See N. Lewis, *Papyrus in Classical Antiquity* (Oxford 1974) and *Papyrus in Classical Antiquity: a Supplement* (Pap.Brux. 23, Brussels 1989) for papyrus manufacture.

[259]For the Arsinoite figures, cf. above n. 208; they seem very low, but it is impossible to tell if only a part of the city is represented (as seems likely). Van Minnen 1987, 37-38, offers very high figures for Oxyrhynchos, but they are simply invented on arbitrary premises. It is hardly safe to base computations on the percentages in *P.Berl.Bork.* (p. 43) as he does, because it is most unlikely (for example) that 7 to 8 percent of the households were headed by someone exercising a civic function (that would mean 500 to 550 such persons in Hermopolis). And the occupational titles there include much more than craft production workers (not just those exercising a "professional craft" as van Minnen says); about two-thirds are in fact production workers, indicating that perhaps 15 to 20 percent of the households were headed by such.

[260]There is nothing implausible about such a situation in a premodern city; cf. Marcus 1989, 155, for a view of Aleppo's economy as only modestly dependent on the surrounding rural districts.

[261]See Wipszycka 1971, summarizing (and to a large extent in agreement with) Fikhman 1965; Fikhman continues to see debt and rentals as negative factors.

a modern market economy, it made entrepreneurial activity possible. Rentals, too, are characteristic not only of misery but of urban existence in general; they were an essential part of middle-class life at imperial Rome,[262] and rental of both living and working space contributed greatly to the flexibility of the complicated population of smaller cities like Oxyrhynchos and Panopolis.[263] Nor were workers excluded from all the civic roles the landed held; though liturgies may have been a dubious honor, there is some evidence for craft and professional workers serving in them.[264]

To a large degree, production and marketing were united in the same establishments. Most craftsmen sold their own products, whether on a large scale to the city or a small scale to individuals. The cities did, however, serve as market centers for many things they did not produce, most importantly food and drink. In part, this function reflected the corporate concern of the city for an adequate food supply for its residents, expressed in specific regulations or agreements to ensure the availability of particular foods.[265] In part, it was no doubt simply a product of the demand of the urban market. A high degree of specialization is visible, as in the older quarters of Mediterranean cities today. Poultry is sold by one merchant (who may also carry eggs; but there are separate eggsellers too),[266] fish by another,[267] meat by the appropriate butchers. Vegetables are sold by one vender,[268] fruit by another.[269] Various sellers carried lentils and beans of various sorts.[270] Merchants in oil,[271] wine,[272] beer,[273] and condiments[274] complete the normal range,[275] though others can be found.

[262]See B. W. Frier, *Landlords and Tenants in Imperial Rome* (Princeton 1980).

[263]Tradesmen in Ottoman Aleppo normally rented working space: Marcus 1989, 180.

[264]*P.Cair.Preis.* 20 (15th indiction: 341/2?), a list of liturgists for Polis Apeliotes which includes a doctor, a butcher (*mageiros*), a carpenter, and a donkey driver.

[265]Three examples: *P.Lond.* III 974 (p. 115) = *W.Chr.* 429 (306) is a surety for a man to act as *karpones* (fruit-buyer) for Hermopolis, furnishing the various seasonal fruits. In *P.Oxy.* I 83 (= *W.Chr.* 430) (327), an eggseller declares under oath that he sells eggs only in the public market, and that he will not sell them secretly or in his own house; it is explicitly stated that the food-supply (*euthenia*) of the city is at stake. *P.Oxy.* XII 1455 (*BL*) (275) is a sworn undertaking by an olive-oil merchant to furnish oil daily in the shop which he has in the market.

[266]*P.Lond.* III 870 (p. 235) (*BL*) (Panopolis, 4c): an *ornithas*; one selling eggs, *P.Oxy.* XLII 3055 (285); for an eggseller, n. 265 supra.

[267]*P.Oxy.* LIV 3766 (329), price declaration.

[268]*Lachanopoles, lachanas* or *lachaneutes*: see *P.Oxy.* VIII 1139 (4c); *P.Oxy.* XLVI 3300 (soon after 271/2); *P.Oxy.* XXIV 2421 (*ca* 312-323, *BL*).

[269]See above, n. 265; also *P.Oxy.* VIII 1133 (*BL*) (396).

[270]*Phakinas* in Arsinoe, cf. n. 208 above; he pays 100 dr. a month, the highest figure by far.

[271]Cf. n. 265 above, and see also *PSI* XII 1239 (*BL*) (Antinoopolis, 430), house of

This commerce in foodstuffs was essentially local. There were also merchants in other basic commodities, not necessarily for local use. Rugsellers, linen merchants, and woolsellers were all closely tied to major export industries and probably served as conduits for those exports.[276] There is also evidence of regional animal markets, the best attested being that at Kynopolis, the source of many sales of donkeys,[277] but animal dealers existed elsewhere too.[278] Finally, there is a group of merchants described as *ekdocheis*,[279] "middlemen," who filed a declaration in which they listed the goods they dealt in and their prices; but the list of goods is lost.[280] They may have dealt in the local wheat and wine destined for export. The concentrated surpluses described earlier must have demanded considerable commercial expertise and activity for profitable disposition.

After production and distribution comes the third sector of the working urban population, services. A "service economy" is not a twentieth-century innovation; rather, it was until recently the natural consequence of the combination of a low level of technology, which provides few labor-saving options, with a wide gap between the minimum cost of labor and the income of those in whose hands wealth is concentrated. Probably the largest group of service workers was that in transportation. And among these, first place certainly went to Nile shipping. The transport of the grain taxes and exports by itself supported a large fleet of boats, about which there is extensive documentation thanks to the numerous receipts for loading tax grain

---

an oilseller; *SPP* VIII 758 (Hermopolis?, 4/5c), house rented by one; *P.Oxy.* VIII 1146 (*BL*) (4c early); *P.Oslo* III 144 (Oxyrhynchos, 270-275); *P.Berl.Bork.* p. 45; perhaps *P.Genova* I 24 (4c).

[272]Sold both by merchants (*oinoprates, oinopoles*) and in taverns (*kapeloi*). References are numerous.

[273]Five in Arsinoe in 276 (above, n. 208); *SB* XII 11003 (4/5c); beer was in decline in this period, cf. above, p. 32.

[274]Three *artumates* in Arsinoe in 276 (above n. 208); also *P.Oxy.* XII 1517 (*BL*) (272 or 278). The *myropolai* also carried spices, e.g., *P.Oxy.* LIV 3766 (329), price declarations.

[275]*P.Berl.Bork.* (p. 44) also records a breadseller, presumably not a baker; but most sales were evidently directly by bakers.

[276]*P.Berl.Bork.* (p. 44) includes linen merchants and clothing merchants. *P.Oxy.* XLIII 3141 (300), death of a woolseller; *P.Oxy.* XLI 2969 (323), linenseller; *P.Oxy.* X 1253 (4c), rug merchant.

[277]*P.Berl.Leihg.* I 21 (309); *P.Corn.* 13 (*BL*) (311), the one found at Hermopolis, the other at Oxyrhynchos.

[278]*P.Oxy.* XLIV 3192 (307) is the sworn declaration of a man who affirms that he has never engaged in the trade of donkeyseller.

[279]Contributing to the *hieronikai* fund in *P.Oslo* III 144 (Oxyrhynchos, 270-275).

[280]*P.Oxy.* LIV 3772 (*ca* 338).

onto boats.[281] Many of these boats, perhaps most, were owned by wealthy landowners and officials, for whom they were probably managed like any other asset. But the term *naukleros* sometimes appears in a context that suggests that owning ships was the primary occupation of the person.[282] In addition, several texts show ship-owners who doubled as the captains of their ships.[283] For the most part, however, ship captains were employees of the shipowners. The sailors who made up their crews must have been a significant multiple of their number.[284] The cities also (above, p. 37) supplied to the imperial post a number of rowers. Because the grain taxes alone may be estimated (above, p. 37) to have required something like nine hundred boats, when one adds commercial freight, passenger traffic, and government post, it is likely that the Nile carried several thousand boats in all. The average metropolis was thus probably home to several dozen at least, and probably several hundred of its residents were involved in river transportation. A certain number more operated ferry services across the Nile, a traffic still commonplace today.[285]

The transportation of tax wheat to the ports, the transportation of food to the metropolis, and a good deal of personal travel all used animals.[286] Many men who managed and drove these animals lived in the villages, of course, but some were urban residents along with their animals (see above, p. 50, for the extensive presence of animals in the cities). Donkey drivers were the most numerous group,[287] but camel-drivers were also present.[288]   And much transportation (at least between conveyance and destination) was carried out by unassisted humans, too, as the mentions of sack-carriers, porters, and the like

[281]See Meyer-Termeer 1978, with extensive documentation and bibliography.

[282]*P.Oxy.* VII 1071 (5c).

[283]For example, *SPP* II, p. 34 and *SB* XIV 11548 (both Hermopolite, 343).

[284]In the Panopolis list (*P.Berl.Bork.*), though it is not a random sample, it is interesting that sailors (*nautai*) are the most numerous single occupation listed, 8 of about 350 total persons.

[285]Examples of ferrymen: *P.Mert.* I 42 (5c); *P.Oxy.* XXIV 2421 (*ca* 312-323, *BL*); perhaps *P.Oxy.* VIII 1146 (*BL*) (4c early).

[286]See above, pp. 38-39 for details.

[287]One interesting example: *P.Oslo* III 135 (*BL*) (286-293), in which a gymnasiarch of Oxyrhynchos supplies animals with which an Alexandrian freedman residing in the city will carry out a liturgical duty of donkey-driving for a period of a year on his behalf. *Onelatai* routinely lived in the city, as can be seen from a tax receipt issued to one Oxyrhynchos resident giving that as his occupation, *P.Oxy.* XLIII 3142 (301). There were also supervisory positions like the *rhabdouchoi*.

[288]Their residence is often difficult to determine in the documents; *P.Ross.Georg.* V 61 (Herakleopolite?, 4c) looks like an example of an urban resident.

shows.[289] Some of these may have been only temporarily resident in the cities, others permanently. And, in the absence of a public postal service available for nongovernmental use, there were many private lettercarriers[290] and messsengers.[291] Virtually all of these workers are likely to have been at the bottom of the economic and social pyramid.

Not much better off were those who provided personal care services. Many, perhaps most, of these were part of the roughly 13 percent of the urban population who were slaves, about whom the documents generally reveal little (see below, pp. 209-10). But some were free: barbers and hairdressers,[292] bath attendants,[293] prostitutes,[294] undertakers,[295] wet-nurses,[296] hired domestic servants and companions, and, at the upper end of the scale, doctors and veterinarians.[297] The numbers of these groups are impossible to assess; they were probably not numerous, except for domestic servants and bath attendants, but in the aggregate it is hard to suppose that they did not number several hundred at least. The greatest unknown is the extent to which this slave-owning society also employed wage-earning domestic servants.

Another group in the lower reaches of society was the security personnel of public and private establishments. These include watchmen, guards, and doorkeepers. They are only occasionally mentioned and generated little paperwork. Many doorkeepers in private houses were no doubt slaves, but public offices, baths, and the like

---

[289]*P.Got.* 16 (4c) (porter); *SPP* XX 82 (*BL*) (4c) (transport-workers needed in the city); *BGU* I 286 (*BL*) (Arsinoite, 306) (villager sent to Alexandria for sack-carrying duty).

[290]E.g., *P.Oxy.* XII 1587 (late 3c).

[291]*Symmachoi*: *P.Ross.Georg.* V 61 (Herakleopolite?, 4c); they were probably vital in maintaining city-country links for large landowners, cf. chapter 4.

[292]*P.Berl.Bork.* p. 45; *O.Bodl.* 2143 (*BL*) (Thebes, 3/4c); *P.Oxy.* XII 1489 (*BL*) (3c late); *BGU* I 9 (Arsinoe, 276: above, n. 208), female barbers.

[293]Various types are attested; see, e.g., *P.Berl.Bork.* p. 45, bathmen; *SB* X 10555 (Oxyrhynchos, after 282), furnace attendants and water drawers; *P.Oxy.* VIII 1146 (*BL*) (4c early), furnace attendant; *P.Oxy.* XII 1499 (309), water pourers; *P.Oxy.* XLVI 3300 (soon after 271/2), *P.Oxy.* XXXVI 2798 (304/5), *P.Genova* I 24 (4c), all for *kapsarioi*, clothing attendants (on whom see *Tyche* 4 [1989] 115).

[294]See below, p. 197.

[295]Both male and female. See Derda 1991 for a comprehensive treatment. Fourth-century evidence is not abundant.

[296]*P.Grenf.* II 75 (*BL*) (Kysis, Great Oasis, 308); *P.Mert.* I 28 (3c late). See *CPGr.* I for a comprehensive corpus of contracts for their services, which disappear after the early 4c, although wet-nursing certainly did not.

[297]Known especially from reports of public physicians to officials who have ordered them to inspect someone, for example *P.Oxy.* XLV 3245 (297); *P.Rein.* II 92 (Oxyrhynchos, 392). See *CPR* XVIIA 23 for bibliography.

employed men for this function.[298] A partial list of the security guards of Oxyrhynchos lists about sixty men (or youths: the only age given is eighteen).[299]

Operations of documentation, recordkeeping, education and the law also occupied a significant group. The discussion of literacy in chapter 7 draws attention to the dependency even of the literate on a relatively small group of professional writers for most purposes. The handwriting of professional contract-writers is familiar to every papyrologist, and many of their names are known from their signatures.[300] They were mostly available to the general public. Where they were lacking (as, no doubt, in some villages), schoolteachers could prepare simple documents. Government offices and banks employed their own regular scribes.[301] When legal business required more than a competent contract-writer or petition-drafter, lawyers were available. Their usual title (*rhetor*) speaks to the rhetorical education they received, but it should not be assumed that they were ignorant of the law.[302] These and other literate people received at least their lower education locally, from teachers of letters.[303]

The literate also included two administrative groups. One is the imperial administration and the city government, described above. The permanent staff of both in most cities was probably not large, but it was not trivial. The other is the band of stewards, managers, and

[298]The doorkeeper of the *logisterion* appears as a surety in *P.Oxy.* L 3576 (341); he was thus not without means, probably one of the elite of his profession. Other *thyroroi* appear in *SB* IV 7336 (Oxyrhynchos, late 3c) and *P.Ross.Georg.* V 60 (Hermopolis, 390-400); in the latter, his *opsonion* for six months is eight artabas, just over a third of what a donkey-driver gets, but their compensation may have included other elements.

[299]*P.Oxy.* I 43 verso (*BL*; *W.Chr.* 474) (4c, certainly after 295). The occupational names in the list are almost all in the genitive (i.e., referring to the men's fathers); this suggests that these may indeed be mainly young men not yet in a permanent calling. See N. Lewis, *BASP* 18 (1981) 76-77, for arguments that these are not specifically night-watchmen, as they are often called.

[300]They are described by various terms and certainly ranged in status; some examples are the *synallagmatographos* of *P.Giss.* I 53 (*BL*) (Hermopolis?, 4c 2nd half) and the shorthand writer (*oxygraphos*) of *P.Ross.Georg.* V 61 (Herakleopolite?, 4c). See Diethart-Worp 1986 for a catalogue of those known from the entire Byzantine period.

[301]A bank's scribe in *P.Oxy.* XX 2287 (late 3c).

[302]Hiring a *rhetor* to plead one's case before the prefect: *P.Oxy.* XXII 2343 (*BL*) (*ca* 288). There are numerous reports of proceedings in which they appear. The various sorts of notaries also had some legal knowledge, but their exact nature in this period is not well documented.

[303]Poorly documented; cf. payments to them in *P.Oxy.* XXIV 2425 descr. (3/4c?), *P.Oxy.* XXIV 2421 (*ca* 312-323, *BL*). A letter addressed to a teacher, *SB* XIV 11532 (4c), mentions a woman teacher, probably in a Christian setting.

assistants retained by urban landowners to manage their country
properties. These are discussed in chapter 4. Many probably shuttled
between city and country with some regularity, but some would have
been in the city at any given time, and they were essential, out of
proportion to their numbers, to the viability of the landowning and
credit patterns described above.

Finally, the provision of public and private entertainment (see
below, pp. 101, 104-5) required entertainers. The best known group is
that connected with chariot-racing, which included charioteers, their
attendants, chariot-builders, trainers, starters, veterinarians, grooms,
and others.[304] Other athletic events, many of them more traditional
parts of Greek contests, such as boxing and the pankration, engaged
participants as well.[305] Athletics in turn were part of festivals involving other entertainments, and heralds, trumpeters, dancers, mimes,
flutists, reciters of Homer, comic actors, acrobats, and musicians all
were on hand.[306] How many of these actually were part of the regular
population of an upriver metropolis is hard to say, though
Hermopolis was famous for boxers. Many were no doubt migratory,
traveling from festival to festival.

Women

Most of the evidence for the activity of women in the cities concerns
their ownership of property, particularly rural agricultural property.
As such, it is one part of the larger phenomenon of urban ownership
of rural land, described in previous sections.[307] By the fourth century,
such ownership by both men and women was a well-entrenched pattern, and nothing suggests any significant change from the two
previous centuries.[308] Women's percentage of land owned by urban

[304]See particularly *O.Ashm.Shelton* 83-190, with ed.'s introduction, pp. 73-80,
discussing the various functions. *SB* XIV 12059 (3/4c) is an account of disbursements to persons connected with racing; cf. also *P.Oxy.* XLVII 3358 (4c).

[305]*CPR* VIII 44 (Hermopolite?, 4c), a boxer in an account; *SB* IV 7336 (Oxyrhynchos, 3c late), pankratiast in an account of festival expenses. A private letter
recounts the adventures of an athlete who chanced to be in Alexandria during an
emperor's visit: *SB* III 6222 (3c end).

[306]E.g., *SB* IV 7336 (Oxyrhynchos, late 3c), a list of expenses for festivals; *CPR*
XVIIA 19 (Hermopolis, 321), engagement of a flutist to appear in a village; *P.Oxy.*
VII 1025 = *W.Chr.* 493 (Euergetis =? Lykopolis, 3c late), engagement of mime and
homerist; *P.Ryl.* IV 641 (Hermopolis, *ca* 318-323), account with *akrobatai* and
charioteers; *P.Ryl.* IV 645 (Hermopolis, *ca* 318-323), account mentioning *mousikoi*.

[307]In keeping with Lawrence Stone's first commandment for the writing of
women's history: "Thou shalt not write about women except in relation to men and
children." *New York Review of Books*, 11 April 1985, 21.

[308]Cf. Pomeroy 1981 for the change from Ptolemaic to Roman periods in
women's ability to own land.

residents was low, only 8.5 percent in the Hermopolite Nome, half or less the rate for village women (see below, p. 130). This pattern seems to reflect an overlay of Roman preferences for private ownership on longstanding Egyptian willingness to see a significant part of family property in the hands of women. The lower urban percentage is perhaps to be attributed to Roman-style concentration of wealth, and it may suggest that estimates that women owned as much as one-fifth of Roman property are too high.[309]

A sense of the family character of most of this ownership of property can be had from a cluster of Karanis documents showing the connections of three generations of one Arsinoite metropolitan family to that village. The pivotal figure is one Serenilla, born to an Antinoite father named Ptolemaios, who owned about 19 arouras at Karanis. She married Apollonios, apparently a resident of Arsinoe, where the couple lived. If he is identical with the veteran Apollonios who also appears in the Karanis tax lists as a metropolitan, he owned about another 28.5 arouras of his own there.[310] At least some, if not all, of Serenilla's land was leased out, as shown by a lease to four Karanis villagers[311] and a rent receipt to Aurelius Isidoros, both dated to 300.[312] The receipt may have been written in her own hand,[313] but the

[309]See Champlin 1991, 46, 119, based on various rather rough indexes like the number of known wills. If, as it appears, individual female owners also owned less than individual male owners on average, the numbers of wills by females would give only an upper limit.

[310]For computation of their landholdings from wheat and barley taxes, cf. Bagnall 1991b and 1992b. Apollonios appears in *P.Cair.Isid.* 6.234 and Serenilla in *P.Cair.Isid.* 6.188, but in both cases the amounts held are lost. Their taxes appear in *P.Cair.Isid.* 9.32,55 (Serenilla), 9.35,48 (Apollonios). The argument for identity of the veteran with Serenilla's husband is based on the fact that his total payments of chaff in *P.Cair.Isid.* 10 amount to the equivalent of 1,200 lbs., or enough to cover 48 ar., while she does not figure in this text at all. Because his own holdings may be computed at 28.4 ar. from his wheat and barley taxes, and hers at 19, the combined payment covers their taxes exactly.

[311]*P.Cair.Isid.* 101. The editors take her to be the lessee there, but the entirety of the dossier shows that this is unlikely; and in fact line 14 describes her as lessor, which the editors must emend to preserve their interpretation. Problems remain in the formulation of the document, but mixups in references to the two parties are commonplace in leases.

[312]*P.Cair.Isid.* 112, for two years' rent totaling 11 art.

[313]Which is described by Boak as "a well-practised cursive with the letters written at times regularly and distinctly and at others in a crowded and hasty manner," *EtPap* 2 (1934) 15. But it is not clear that the end is preserved, and someone else's subscription could have stood there. Still, there are other examples of similar women writing for themselves, e.g., *P.Flor.* I 27 (*BL*) (Hermopolis?, 4-5c).

lease was executed through her son Zoilos. Serenilla's date of death is unknown, but she was still alive in 314.[314]

Her son Zoilos was certainly an adult when he represented her in 300, because he was active already as an assistant to the *prytanis* and *exegetes* in 296, when he leased 10 arouras near Karanis to Isidoros.[315] That lease relationship continued at least until 312, although Isidoros' lease seems to have diminished to 4.5 arouras in the latter part of the period.[316] Throughout this period Zoilos continues as an assistant to the *prytanis*. A business letter between the two shows that Isidoros kept a certain amount of wheat belonging to Zoilos, on which the latter could draw as needed.[317]

Zoilos' sister Ptolema also leased land to Isidoros, as we learn from receipts for rent paid for 313/4 and 314/5.[318] Because the amount of rent (and probably of land) is identical to that involved in Zoilos' transactions with Isidoros in the immediately preceding years, the land might well be the same, inherited by Ptolema from Zoilos. Just as likely, however, they might have shared equally a parcel belonging to one of their parents. Family members who operated their holdings jointly often paid taxes as a group, and precise ownership within the family may not always be clearly visible from such payments of taxes or rent.[319] Ptolema also appears in earlier receipts of 304 and 306, both times collecting 4.5 artabas from Isidoros—just half the amount of the later receipts. In both of these, her husband Ioannes, a former gymnasiarch, acts on her behalf,[320] while in the receipts from a decade later her son Serenos writes for her. He is the last documented member of the family.

The complexity and familial character of this dossier were no doubt as typical as any in this social class. These are not the very richest members of the municipal elite, but they are just below that stratum. The women own property of some substance—not equal to that of the men, certainly, but on the same order of magnitude. In

---

[314]As was Apollonios the veteran; both appear in *P.Cair.Isid.* 19, written after 313/4: probably not much after, though, given the closeness of the list to *P.Cair.Isid.* 9, dated to 309.

[315]*P.Cair.Isid.* 99.

[316]*P.Cair.Isid.* 117, 118, 120, 121 (309-312), all for 9 art., probably the rent on 4.5 ar., see *P.Cair.Isid.* 117 introd.

[317]*P.Cair.Isid.* 135 (undated).

[318]*P.Cair.Isid.* 122 (314 and 315). The form of the name there is Ptolemas, probably an erroneous genitive for nominative.

[319]See Bagnall 1977a for the way this worked in Isidoros' family.

[320]*P.Cair.Isid.* 114 and 115. Note that Ptolema is said to be illiterate in *P.Cair. Isid.* 122; but her husband apparently writes for himself in 114 and 115, as a man capable of the gymnasiarchy would be expected to be able to do.

some situations they act on their own, but more commonly husbands and sons represent them in daily business. This pattern was no doubt reinforced by the tendency for the male and female members of families to have adjacent property in country villages.[321] How far their ownership of property gave these women an important voice in family business matters is hard to say, for the documents present the outer rather than the inner face.

As always, widows and orphans, lacking a sufficiently close and able male relative, might find that this integrated system came undone.[322] One woman complains that she has not received a small parcel of land, bought for her by her father before his death, because the seller's brother has kept control of it, "despising my orphan condition."[323] Hiring a steward was a necessity, but not always a good substitute for relatives; a widow whose sons are away on imperial military service complains to the prefect that she has been cheated by two stewards in a row.[324] Tax collectors were more likely to try to collect twice from a widow, according to another petition.[325] Conversely, collecting from debtors became harder. A well-born woman, daughter of a now-dead city councillor of Hermopolis, wrote to the *praeses* to complain that a man who had bought wine from her on credit refused to pay when she sent her daughter to collect.[326]

That is not to say that family, particularly male relatives, were to be counted on in every case. One petition by a woman complains that she received only 1.5 arouras from her father's estate, while the other heirs got rich with land, slaves, animals, money and so on; now a brother of hers, who is a soldier, is taking away even that 1.5 arouras. One may suspect that she had received most of her share of the family fortune during her father's lifetime, perhaps as a dowry, because her real complaint seems to be about the small parcel her brother has usurped.[327]

Although the evidence overwhelmingly depicts women in the role of lessor to male tenants from the villages, the occasional role-reversal

---

[321]A good example is *P.Stras.* VI 555 and 556 (cf. 672) (Hermopolis, 289), a division of inherited property in Temenkyrkis Poimenon among three siblings (555) and then a swap by the two brothers (556). The women's husband owns some of the adjacent land, and the three siblings own much of the rest. The woman is literate and signs.

[322]This point is stressed by Pomeroy 1981, 309. Cf. below, p. 188, n. 43, on widowhood.

[323]*P.Oxy.* XII 1470 (336).

[324]*P.Oxy.* I 71 (303).

[325]*CPR* VII 15 (cf. D. Hagedorn, *Misc.Pap.* 107-108) (Hermopolis, *ca* 330).

[326]*SPP* I, p.2 (III) (Hermopolis, 4c).

[327]*P.Rain.Cent.* 85 (364-366).

presumably did occur. One such is a lease dated 321 in which Aurelia Kyrillous, a resident of Arsinoe, appears to lease twenty arouras of grainland from Sakaon, on the basis of half-shares, with Sakaon providing seed and animals as needed and paying the taxes.[328] It is difficult to imagine what the attraction of such a lease, in a struggling village at some distance from the metropolis, was for Kyrillous or how she could make it profitable. If one could just invert the parties in the opening of the lease, however, all would make sense. It is interesting that masculine forms are used throughout the lease for the lessee; perhaps in fact the lease was ineptly drafted.

Urban women also derived an income from their more portable and fungible assets, by lending money and commodities.[329] The best-known case is that of Koutina, a resident of Arsinoe who provided what might be described as a revolving credit facility to Tetoueis, a landowner in Karanis who was heavily dependent on these loans of wheat and money.[330] Other examples are again typically of the same sort, with a villager borrowing from an urban resident.[331] Women are in no way unusual in this role; loans made by them are closely paralleled by those made by other urban residents with liquid assets.[332]

Those residents, male and female, were a minority of the total, though they owned most of the wealth and generated most of the documentation.[333] It is unlikely that more than one-third of the urban population had sufficient wealth to be lessors or lenders for the rural population, and even that estimate may be too high. What of the rest of the women? Only rarely is there any evidence for them. As in early modern societies, it is likely enough that they helped run retail sales and service establishments of which their husbands, fathers, or sons were the legal proprietors. Occasionally one comes to notice, like an oilseller of Panopolis, known only because she so describes herself in the course of leasing the third floor of her house to another woman.[334] A particularly revealing document records a widow's lifetime division of her property between her two sons, in return for years of assistance

[328]P.Sakaon 67 (Theadelphia, 321).

[329]Cf. the prominent involvement of women in supplying credit in eighteenth-century Aleppo: Marcus 1989, 187.

[330]P.Col. VII 182, P.Mert. I 37, P.NYU 24, P.Oslo II 38 = SB VI 9311, all from the period 372-374. See P.Col. VII 182-184 introd. for bibliography. The name also appears in the form Kottine.

[331]P.Cair.Isid. 93 (Arsinoe, 282); P.Select. 7 (Oxyrhynchos, 314). For a seventh-eighth century example, see T. G. Wilfong, BASP 27 (1990) 169-81.

[332]See Keenan 1981, 484, for a list and brief discussion.

[333]See Bagnall 1992b for distribution of wealth. The same class, of course, owned most of the slaves, for whom see chapter 6.

[334]P.Panop. 11 (320).

from one: "Since you, Dionysios, have remained with me your mother for a long time since the death of your father and have carried on the dyer's craft and have not left me your mother, in gratitude I declare that I have transferred to both of you, my children, in equal shares and in common," the entire stock in trade of the business, which she is to continue to control while she lives.[335] Widows could thus carry on trades just as much as they could continue to lease land. But such businesses produced little paperwork and left few traces to posterity.

The same is undoubtedly true of women who worked for wages. The textile industries of the towns probably employed many such in small workshops. And, as in every age, women certainly worked in domestic service, whether for wages or, as in one Oxyrhynchite contract, to discharge the imputed interest on a loan.[336] The borrower is to live in the lender's household and perform whatever services he assigns; he can send her away at any time and demand back the two solidi he has advanced her, and she must repay them if she herself wishes to leave.

A complex picture emerges from the numerous documents concerning women and the urban real estate market. Just as they inherited, bought, and sold rural agricultural property, women inherited,[337] bought,[338] mortgaged,[339] and sold[340] urban houses or shares of houses. As a part of the active rental housing market of the metropoleis, women owned houses as investments and leased them, or parts of them, to tenants.[341] None of this is remarkable. More interesting, from a social point of view, are the leases in which women are the lessees, renting living quarters in someone else's house or renting entire houses.[342] These run the gamut economically, ranging from expensive houses costing the equivalent of a solidus or more down to

---

[335]*P.Coll.Youtie* II 83 (Oxyrhynchos, 353), following the editors' alternative punctuation in lines 8-9.

[336]*P.Köln* II 102 (418). A. Jördens, *P.Heid.* V, pp. 271-95, discusses such contracts.

[337]*P.Erl.* 76 (*BL*) (Oxyrhynchos, 4c): sale of inherited property; *CPR* I 227 (Arsinoite, 4c).

[338]*P.Sakaon* 59 (305) and 60 (306), sales by metropolitans to a female from Theadelphia of two houses in Arsinoe.

[339]*P.Charite* 33 (346/7, prob.) and 34 (348), a wealthy woman borrowing from a man of the same class.

[340]*SB* XIV 12021 (Oxyrhynchos, after 377); *SB* XVI 12289 (Arsinoe, 309); cf. also the previous notes.

[341]*P.Oxy.* VIII 1129 (*BL* [wrong]) (449): two rooms; *SB* VIII 9931 (*BL*) (Hermopolis, 405): two-story house; *P.Panop.* 12 (337): two rooms; *P.Panop.* 13 (339): part of a house.

[342]*SB* IV 7445 (*BL*) (Oxyrhynchos, 382): entire house; *PSI* V 467 (*BL*) (Oxyrhynchos, 360): a single room; *P.Oxy.* XVI 1957 (430): three rooms; *P.Genova* I 22 (*BL*) (Oxyrhynchos, 345): one underground room.

single rooms worth one-tenth of that.[343] The leases tell us nothing of the woman's life otherwise—was she alone or accompanied by children?—but they do suggest a significant population of urban women without husbands operating independent households, whether as a result of death, divorce, or other causes.[344]

Perhaps the most curious of all is a lease in which a woman offers to lease two rooms in a house, not for herself but for a soldier stationed in Hermopolis.[345] She gives no indication that she is any kin to the soldier. Is this the first female real-estate broker? There is one case known in which a member of the Hermopolite elite got so deep in debt to a woman that he surrendered a house and courtyard in the city to her for some additional cash and the cancellation of his principal and interest.[346] We know of village entrepreneurs who made their property grow through encouraging such strategic debt-dependence by their betters, and it was entirely possible for a woman to do the same.[347]

Women certainly were not shut away from the daily social life of the city, although it was clearly expected that those of high status would be more shielded from inappropriate situations than others.[348] A complainant alleges that a servant of a silversmith had come to his house and verbally assaulted his wife and unmarried daughter in a fashion "contrary to the laws and to our position in life."[349] If the beginning of the petition had been preserved, that position would be clearer, but it is obvious enough that one simply did not speak in certain ways to women of respectable station, especially if one was of servile status. The aggressors could be female just as well as the victim, to be sure; a petitioner complains that his wife was attacked in the house during the evening hours by one Tapesis and her slave Victoria. His primary concern appears to be the possibility that the assault might endanger her pregnancy.[350]

[343]See the first two texts cited in the previous note for these extremes.

[344]See Bagnall and Frier, forthcoming, for the low likelihood that a woman would not marry at all, and for figures on one-person urban households.

[345]P.Berl.Zill. 5 (BL) (417).

[346]CPR I 9 (271). The principal and interest total 4,200 dr., and another 3,000 dr. change hands, for a total of 1 talent 1,200 dr., the equivalent of at least 36 artabas of wheat and perhaps much more (a major episode of price rises was in course around this time).

[347]See Keenan 1980.

[348]There was nothing resembling the segregation practiced in Islamic society in the region later; cf. Marcus 1989, 53, on Aleppo, though even there the degree of separation of women from the outside world was very much a matter of economic and social standing.

[349]P.Lond. III 983 (p. 229) (4c).

[350]P.Oxy. LI 3620 (326).

Women, vulnerable to verbal and physical assault, might also be seen as open to deception. An affidavit reveals that a man (who has since vanished) somehow got access to the wife of the complainant and persuaded her to let him "borrow" a donkey, which has now disappeared with the man.[351] An interesting indication that a woman might prefer to trust other women may be found in a contract of deposit, whereby one woman entrusts a modest sum (but not trivial: a bit less than the value of a gold solidus) to two other women, to be handed back upon request.[352] There is little information in the text to clarify the situation, but the absence of family members recalls the independent women described as lessees earlier and perhaps their sense that other such women would be more trustworthy depositaries than an unrelated man.

Family, wealth, and social status: these were as ever the main determinants of a woman's position, all more important than her sex, decisive though that was in many respects. Parents of the upper strata took care to see that their daughters were registered with the right status,[353] and through all the trappings of a patriarchal system they transmitted property to daughters as well as sons.[354]

Greek Education and Culture

The cities of third-century Egypt, endowed at last with the institutions that allowed them to act as the equals of Greek cities anywhere, expressed their identity in cultural as well as political forms. The depth of this Hellenic culture is considered in chapter 7; it is easy enough to say that only the wealthy, the members of those families that supplied the ranks of liturgists and councillors, really participated in this culture, and there is some truth in that. There is also tautology, for success in athletics or letters might lead to fortune, and it is usually impossible to identify the origins of a wealthy retired athlete. Such a description also ignores the role of spectators in cultural life.

Those fortunate enough to receive an education began it with a profoundly traditional training in Greek, at the hands of an elementary-school teacher, the *grammatistes*, with whom they learned

[351]*P.Oxy.* XLVI 3304 (301).

[352]*P.Ryl.* IV 662 (Antinoopolis, 364). It is telling that the editors saw "no exceptional features" in this unusual document.

[353]*P.Oxy.* XLIII 3136 (292), registration of an eighteen-year-old daughter.

[354]*SB* X 10728 (Oxyrhynchos, 318), the sale of a house previously acquired and registered in the name of the seller's daughter, who is in his *patria potestas*.

and practiced letters, then syllables, words, and sentences.[355] There are numerous surviving examples of the various stages of this form of rote learning, in the course of which pupils' handwriting, vocabulary, and spelling developed more or less together.[356] Some students continued on to secondary education with a *grammatikos*, learning Greek more systematically and reading serious literature.[357]

Education in letters was largely a private matter, although there were publicly funded chairs for *grammatikoi* in some cities.[358] The public educational institution was the gymnasium, membership in which was a privilege limited to those certified as belonging to the hereditary group entitled to it.[359] Parents of this class registered their sons with elaborate declarations of their ancestry, to ensure the educational and social advantages gymnasium membership brought.[360] At fourteen, boys became ephebes, in a tradition reaching back to classical Greece, joining on graduation the gymnasium's alumni body, certified as part of the city's Hellenic elite. The gymnasium is best known, unfortunately, from the use of the title gymnasiarch as a status designation for those who had held that office, rather than from documents of its operations (see above). But the curriculum was clearly traditional in character, the Greek athletic training and contests originally aimed at preparing boys to be soldiers.[361] Gymnasia functioned also as cultural centers, and many probably had libraries.[362] Their social function was considerable, and news of a fracas in the gymnasium of Oxyrhynchos traveled quickly to Alexandria.[363]

Athletics served as the primary link between the world of the gymnasium and that of popular culture. An order of the *logistes*, dated to 323, exhorts the ephebes to do their best in the next day's per-

[355]A brief description is given in Clarysse and Wouters 1970, with extensive bibliography and examples. For teachers in Panopolis, see R. A. Kaster, *ZPE* 51 (1983) 132-34.

[356]See R. Cribiore, *Writing, Teachers and Students in Graeco-Roman Egypt* (Diss. Columbia Univ. 1993) for a comprehensive treatment.

[357]See Kaster 1988 for a comprehensive and illuminating survey of these men, generally found in relatively important cities; he discusses the relationship of *grammatikoi* to elementary teachers on 24.

[358]Kaster 1988, 114.

[359]Hereditary identity as "Hellenes" was the crucial factor, though by this time that identity was self-perpetuating and cultural, not (as originally) ethnic.

[360]Examples: *P.Mich.* XIV 676 (Oxyrhynchos, 272), with a list and bibliography; *P.Corn.* 18 (*BL*) (Oxyrhynchos, 291).

[361]See Turner 1952, 84, for a brief description.

[362]Krüger 1990, 158-61.

[363]*P.Oxy.* LV 3813 (3/4c.; the recipient is attested 283-292, cf. P. Pruneti, *YCS* 28 [1985] 277-81 and J.E.G. Whitehorne, *Aegyptus* 67 [1987] 118-19). A petition against some magistrates was submitted in consequence.

formance of an assault at arms for the pleasure of the audience.[364] The best youths emerged from the gymnasium with the title *hieronikes*, or victor in games, with "from the ephebate" added to distinguish it from the glory won later by participation in panhellenic festivals.[365] These international affairs (see below, p. 105) became an important part of civic life as the cities of Egypt entered the mainstream of the eastern Roman Empire in the third century and turned local contests into more ambitious undertakings.[366] In one striking example, Panopolis reestablished (apparently in the Roman period) games to Perseus Ouranios mentioned by Herodotos as being held by the partly Hellenic residents of that city in his time; the Panopolitans then expanded and refounded them again in 265, counting them in Pythiads (as at Delphi).[367]

In the same vein, the cities adopted the habit of their counterparts elsewhere in granting special privileges to their own citizens who won contests elsewhere, bringing glory to their home town by proclaiming it abroad.[368] Much of the surviving documentation of athletics consists of requests by victors for their privileges, which generally included exemption from liturgies and taxes, plus a public pension.[369] The proud victors, in turn, included titles like *hieronikes* and *paradoxos* ("astounding") in their self-identifications in ordinary contracts.[370] Athletic pursuits were not an isolated area, however. They formed part of entertainments that included dramatic presentations by the

[364]*P.Oxy.* I 42 = *W.Chr.* 154 (*BL*; for difficulties of interpreting the text, *P.Oxy.* XLVI 3297.9n.).

[365]An example in *P.Mil.* II 52 (*BL*) (Oxyrhynchos, 285), in which the lender holds this status. He is probably the son of the xystarch attested in *Pap.Agon.* 8 (273). Also *SB* X 10216 (Oxyrhynchos, 3/4c).

[366]The careful but pompous tone of *Pap.Agon.* 8 (= *P.Oslo* III 85) (Oxyrhynchos, 273) in dealing with preparations for the Capitoline games is striking.

[367]See *P.Oxy.* XXVII 2476 = *Pap.Agon.* 3 (288), with the essential commentary of W. van Rengen, "Les jeux de Panopolis," *Cd'E* 46 (1971) 136-41. The leather inscription he cites is probably to be dated to the third century on grounds of letter-forms. On the origins of Herodotos' statement, see S. Sauneron, *Villes et légendes d'Égypte*[2] (Bibl. d'Étude 90, Cairo 1983) 39-44, 89-90, opposed by A. Lloyd, *JHS* 89 (1969) 79-86.

[368]*P.Coll.Youtie* II 69 = *Pap.Agon.* 9 (272), in which the magistrates (and council?) of Antinoopolis write to their counterparts at Oxyrhynchos, announcing that Aur. Stephanos s. Achilleus has won the Dacian chariot contest in their penteteric games, and has "proclaimed your city publicly."

[369]The richest dossier is the Hermopolite material, for which see Drew-Bear forthcoming, with detailed commentary (cf. already Drew-Bear, "Ammonios et Asclépiadès, Alexandrins et Hermopolitains," *GRBS* 32 [1991] 203-213); cf. also *Pap.Agon.* 2 (Oxyrhynchos, 274); *P.Oxy.* I 59 (*BL*) (292: a *hieronikes* claims exemption from service at the prefect's court).

[370]As in (e.g.) *P.Hamb.* I 21 (Oxyrhynchos, 315) and *P.Lips.* 18 (*BL*) (Hermopolis, 308).

"artisans of Dionysos," musical performances, and horse and chariot races. The Dionysiac artists and other performers were, appropriately, given essentially the same privileges as athletes.[371] This ensemble of musical, dramatic, equestrian, and athletic entertainment was based in the theater, and its roots lie in the major panhellenic festivals of classical Greece and the traveling entertainers and athletes of the Hellenistic world. Although it reached full flower in Egypt only in the self-governing cities of the third century, its roots lay in the local festivals and contests of Hellenistic and earlier Roman Egypt.[372]

The trajectory of "high" culture is harder to plot. Direct evidence for libraries, for example, is extremely scarce.[373] One traditional approach is the counting of literary texts preserved on papyrus, but increasingly it is recognized that many factors other than the rise and fall of literary culture have affected the survival of such fragments.[374] More rewarding is the patient identification of individual authors, scholars, or scribes who are likely to have worked in a metropolis. The luck of the finds has combined with inherent significance to make Oxyrhynchos the best known and best studied city in this regard,[375] but it is unlikely to have been the only such city in Egypt. Panopolis was probably its equal (see below, p. 109), perhaps Hermopolis as well; and many cities simply lack evidence on which to form a judgment. Some of these cities—like cities elsewhere in the eastern empire—supported, presumably from public funds, full-time philosophers.[376] And men of high station, like ranking imperial officials,

[371]See the important dossier of *P.Oxy.* XXVII 2475-2477 (*BL*; 2476 = *Pap.Agon.* 3) (288); *Pap.Agon.* 1 and 2 (Oxyrhynchos, 273-274). In *P.Lips.* 44 = *M.Chr.* 381 (*BL*) = *CPLat.* 241 is the Dionysiac equivalent of the imperial decree on athletes' privileges set out in *CJ* 10.54; cf. R. Merkelbach, *ZPE* 14 (1974) 96.

[372]Cf. Bagnall, *Gnomon* 60 (1988) 44 on this point. Interesting is the very fragmentary *P.Oxy.* XXXI 2611 (192-193), perhaps a request of an athlete for privileges, dated 192 or early 193.

[373]Even the history of the great Alexandrian library is remarkably obscure, cf. M. El-Abbadi, *The Life and Fate of the Ancient Library of Alexandria* (Paris 1990). See Krüger 1990, 153-61, on the difficulties of assigning literary papyri to ancient institutions or individuals.

[374]For such figures see Cavallo 1974, 76 (insufficiently cautious), and the critical remarks of Treu 1986, 2, who points out that the chronological distribution mainly parallels that of documentation generally. See Parca 1991, 95-112, for a general assessment of literary culture in Roman Upper Egypt, with a list of finds on 100-103, in which the substantial share of the fourth century is notable.

[375]Above all studies by Turner 1952, 1956 and 1975; see also Krüger 1990.

[376]Oxyrhynchos: *P.Oxy.* XLII 3069 (3/4c), on which see the commentary of G. Horsley, *New Docs.* 4.18; Hypselis (?): *P.Lips.* 47 (cf. *BL* 1.208) (372), mentioning a foster-child of a *philosophos* who is required to appear in Alexandria.

sometimes can be seen to belong to self-consciously literary circles, the members of which use Greek with care, allusion, and affectation.[377]

The course of this literary culture in the century of the Christianization of Egypt is not easy to trace. Hellenic culture had never been a fixed body, despite tendencies in education toward a conservative canon; it was always creating new work and refining the canon of the past. Such tendencies are visible in the finds of literary papyri from the fourth and fifth centuries, and beyond, as the educated stratum of a Christian society continued to appropriate the classical heritage. Aeschylus disappears, for example, and there is less of Sophocles. Pindar, Sappho, and Theocritus are rare.[378] But it is hard to be sure that this is not partly just a matter of chance. The decline in quantity of many prose authors is counterbalanced by the first appearance of texts of Aeschines and more recent authors like Dio Chrysostom, Themistios, Philostratos, Himerius, Heliodoros, and Libanius. It is hardly to be supposed that Aeschines was in fact first read in Egypt in late antiquity, and other presences and absences may (apart from the late antique authors) be equally fortuitous. The recent appearance of three works of Isocrates on locally made wooden tablets excavated in the Dakleh Oasis is adequate warning against facile minimization of the role of chance survival.[379] It is doubtful that the audience for such authors exceeded a few thousands in all of Egypt at any period, after all, and the survival of their manuscripts out of many millions of papyri of all kinds is a very chancy affair.

The fourth century is in fact the source of some major finds of well-preserved books, among which must be included Christian scriptures and theological works. It seems likely that Panopolis was the source of a substantial body of surviving codices of both Christian and classical authors, most notably of the Bodmer collection, which includes Homer and Menander as well as Old and New Testament books, along with noncanonical works of the early church and school exercises.[380] If, as has been argued, the same library was the source of the Chester Beatty biblical papyri and the Barcelona codex containing both classical and Christian literature, and of the elaborate schoolbook in the Chester Beatty Collection,[381] as well as other texts, a picture

---

[377]The best example is that of Theophanes, the traveling Hermopolite of the early fourth century. See *P.Ryl.* IV 624 (*BL*) (*ca* 317-324), a showpiece from his sons, and the letters in *P.Herm.*

[378]Treu 1986, 3-4.

[379]A. J. Mills, *Archaeological Newsletter (Royal Ontario Museum)* 2 ser. 37 (March, 1990).

[380]Treu 1986, 1.

[381]Clarysse and Wouters 1970.

emerges of a library of considerable magnitude and breadth, possessing texts in Greek, Latin, and Coptic, and perhaps part of a school where both classical and Christian authors were read.[382] Such a milieu is a credible background for the numerous Panopolitan authors of the fourth and fifth centuries who achieved wider distinction (see below, p. 109).

Whatever the exact administrative form of such an institution, it was undoubtedly not the only such. Antinoopolis maintained in the fourth century its active intellectual life, with instruction in rhetoric and law, medicine and the sciences, and theology.[383] Despite rumblings of anti-classical thinking in some Christian authors, the upper class, which became largely Christian during the fourth century, had no intentions of giving up its classical inheritance.[384] And book production, even of non-Christian books, found its way into Christian hands before long.[385]

Literary culture, then, was to some degree transformed by the integration into it of Christian literature and by its conscious use as part of a Christian education. A transformation also touched popular entertainment and athletics. Far from disappearing,[386] traditional athletic, dramatic, and musical events were incorporated into the culture of the circus, which spread rapidly in the Greek East in the fourth century. There were certainly some changes, hard though they are to trace. The gymnasium remained in use in the later fourth century and into the fifth—and perhaps later, but the documentation is lacking.[387] In general, however, emphasis seems to shift to the professionally staged events of the circus, in which the characteristic racing of that setting is interspersed with other forms of entertainment historically associated with the theater.[388]

[382]On this view see most recently the persuasive arguments of J.-L. Fournet, *ZPE* 92 (1992) 253-66 and A. Blanchard, *Cd'E* 66 (1991) 211-20, both with extensive bibliographies of the controversy.

[383]Manfredi 1985, 284; Cauderlier 1978.

[384]Cf. Treu 1986, 5-6.

[385]A couple of specifically Christian references to books: *SB* XIV 11857 (4/5c; book used as security); *SB* XIV 11858 (4/5c; a priest receives a book for *kosmesis*, adornment). Treu (1986, 3) points out that Homer was copied at the Monastery of Epiphanios. Cavallo 1974, 75-76, makes a good argument for identifying some specific manuscripts as Christian professionally-made copies of classical authors.

[386]As claimed by Frisch, *Pap.Agon.* p. 12, who regards athletics as inextricably bound up with pagan cult.

[387]*SPP* XX 230 (*BL*), in which bricks for the boiler room of the baths in the gymnasium figure as an expense, is certainly to be placed after the currency changes of *ca* 351. For the gymnasiarchy, see above, p. 100.

[388]This transformation was demonstrated by Alan Cameron 1976, 193-229, who put it in the fifth century; cf. Roueché 1989, 218-19 for the material from Aphrodisias referred to by Cameron. For the circus in Egypt, mainly in later periods, the stan-

When did this happen in Egypt? It need not, of course, have been a simple conversion. The circus makes its earliest documented Egyptian appearance in 315, in Alexandria.[389] It was fully developed in Oxyrhynchos before midcentury, as an extensive archive of ostraka from Oxyrhynchos shows.[390] But that archive shows no signs of the integration of traditional athletics and entertainment into the circus; all the performers and other staff mentioned are from the world of chariot-racing. Suggestive evidence from Hermopolis, dated with near certainty to the period 320 to 324, points to just such integration. This is a cluster of orders for payment (similar to the Oxyrhynchite ones, but on papyrus), part of a larger archive of such orders connected with a wealthy household. Payments are made to a xystarch, the president of an athletic association, to a boxer and to a flute player.[391] But one is also made to a cellarmaster of the Blues, one of the circus organizations.[392] This combination of recipients probably signals the earliest stage of the combination of athletic, musical, and racing events into some sort of unified enterprise. That unification is thus present virtually from the introduction of the circus into one Upper Egyptian city.

Wider Horizons

The athletic displays of the upper class and the professional performances of the circus both transcended the scale of an Egyptian city. No city in Egypt, except Alexandria, had the volume of activity to justify the full-time residence of such artists. The world of the athlete was by nature international because excellence was defined, as has been seen above, by victories in major contests throughout the Empire, not only within Egypt.[393] An athlete away from home, even if not destined for some particular festival, would find opportunities. One letter describes the adventures of an athlete who happened to be

---

dard treatment is Gascou 1976b. A major addition is provided by *O.Ashm.Shelton* 83-190 (and add J. Shelton, *ZPE* 81 [1990] 265-66), an archive of ostraka from Oxyrhynchos with payments to performers.

[389]*P.Cair.Isid.* 57 and 58 (*BL*), receipts from Karanis for barley delivered to ships for transport to Alexandria to Hephaistion, *hippotrophos* and leader of the "Blues" in Alexandria, and for reimbursement for this paid requisition of 80 artabas.

[390]Cf. above n. 388. Shelton dates the archive before the currency changes of *ca* 351, probably rightly (though on slender evidence).

[391]*CPR* VI 41 (cf. p. 107) (xystarch), 47 (flute-player), and 50 (boxer).

[392]*CPR* VI 63, with the essential correction and discussion of Gascou 1983, 226-28.

[393]Important though the latter might be; for Naukratis, see *P.Oxy.* XXII 2338 in the reedition of R. A. Coles, *ZPE* 18 (1985) 199-204 (*BL*) (*ca* 290).

in Alexandria on business when the emperor was visiting, answered the call for athletes to gather, and won some prizes.[394]

Participation in such diversions was, of course, mainly the prerogative of the wealthy. The same is true of the links to Alexandria and even Rome that literature and scholarship generated.[395] Alexandria was the center where one could get books unavailable in a provincial city, whether through commercial circles or through copying friends' manuscripts.[396] The children of the wealthy would be sent to the capital for the continuation of their education beyond what an Oxyrhynchos or Panopolis could offer.[397]

This cultural traffic is several times linked to another upper-class phenomenon that is difficult to interpret, families with dual residence. The documents reveal a number of people who hold high civic offices both in Alexandria and elsewhere—mostly Oxyrhynchos, but that may be nothing more than a product of the Oxyrhynchite domination of the documentation from the third and early fourth centuries.[398] It is commonly assumed that these are Alexandrians who happen to own land in the countryside, whose sense of *noblesse oblige* prompts them to fulfill liturgies in the nome where they are propertyholders as well as in their main residence.[399] But the reverse is also possible and perhaps easier to understand: Oxyrhynchites, for example, of great wealth were attracted to life in Alexandria, just as some of the wealthiest aristocrats of the Empire were drawn to Rome, but they retained their land at home and either could not or did not wish to shed the liturgical obligations that went with it at home.[400] Under the Empire, after all, the exclusivity of citizenship that was the characteristic of the classical Greek city was long gone, and those in a position to bestow benefactions might be citizens of numerous cities (as well as of Rome,

[394]*SB* III 6222 (3c end).

[395]See Turner 1952, 1956, and 1975; Krüger 1990, 198-204.

[396]Turner 1952, 91-92.

[397]Krüger 1990, 208-212. On this traffic, see generally Kaster 1988, 21.

[398]*CPR* VI 81 (3/4c) may reveal an example of an Alexandrian *exegetes* originally from Hermopolis.

[399]Turner 1952, 85-86, gives a good (and typical) description of the phenomenon.

[400]This is not to say that there were not Alexandrians who acquired property upriver simply for investment purposes, without any necessary tie to the region. *SB* VI 9219 (*BL*) (Hermopolis, 319) probably documents such a case, in which an Alexandrian notable (life gymnasiarch and councillor) bought thirteen arouras at Thynis near Hermopolis, which his widow (herself daughter of a man who had been *neokoros* of Sarapis, *hypomnematographos*, high priest, and councillor) sold seven years later, after his death.

generally).[401]

Reflection about the nature of the surviving documents reinforces this hypothesis. What remains are papyri found in the cities of the valley, which in the main show the concerns and interests of those who lived in those provincial cities. Even the letters written from Alexandria are mainly the work of birds of passage, writing home to Oxyrhynchos or Arsinoe. They are thus prone to involve a unidirectional traffic, the concerns of outsiders in the *megalopolis*.[402] The letters an Alexandrian might have written home from Panopolis or the contracts benefiting an Alexandrian drawn up in Hermopolis hardly ever survive.[403] The loss of Alexandria's papyri, therefore, causes the great city to appear in an improbably passive role, as well as rendering invisible a considerable volume of traffic.

It is also in the nature of the documentation that government business figures rather more largely than it probably did in reality. Some of this has already been described: the flow of workers supplied by the cities for services and projects in Alexandria or on military bases; the constant shuttling of major and minor officials from provincial capitals to other cities; and the periodic movements of defendants or liturgists to appear before the governors (above). The largest flow to Alexandria, certainly, was the shipment downriver of grain for feeding Alexandria itself, for the food supply of Rome, and for general export. And of this flow, the tax grain has left most traces, because of the need to document it carefully and avoid loss.[404]

The tax grain, however, may have represented no more than half the wheat and barley traveling down the Nile. Probably as much was available for commercial export as was claimed for Rome through official channels. And wheat was only part of the story, the part that generated paperwork. The exports of Egypt filled a much broader spectrum, including beer, fish, textiles (especially linen), basketry, blank papyrus rolls, and other goods.[405] Not all of them went through

---

[401]Egypt reveals no Opramoas; but perhaps that is only the deficiency of the epigraphical record. An Oxyrhynchite with Athenian citizenship and the rank of *vir egregius* appears in *P.Oxy.* XIV 1643 (298); he had achieved the athletic distinction of *periodonikes*, victor in the cycle.

[402]As it is called in *P.Oxy.* XVI 1881 (427: translated in the edition by reflex as "metropolis"!); *P.Fouad* 74 (*BL*) (5c).

[403]An exception is *CPR* X 39 (443), a loan in which the borrower is an Alexandrian *conditarius* (see above) residing in Herakleopolis. He is to repay the funds in jars. He may well have remained in Herakleopolis, where the papyrus was no doubt found.

[404]See Meyer-Termeer 1978, 3-139, for a comprehensive description.

[405]For those exported to Palestine, see D. Sperber, "Objects of Trade between Palestine and Egypt in Roman Times," *JESHO* 19 (1976) 113-47.

Alexandria, of course; Pelusium probably was far more important than the surviving documents suggest.[406] But the flourishing development at Marea, on the lake which served as Alexandria's back door by water, points to vigorous commerce by this route in the late period.[407] Nor would the return trips have been made empty. Private commerce, however, is only occasionally and unsystematically recorded in the papyri. It is most often visible in the endless requests for various items, or announcement of their dispatch, in private letters, where, along with wishes for good health and greetings to and from family members, they form the staple subject of correspondence. Some letters or notes are virtual shopping lists, especially for Alexandria.[408]

If the steady stream of traffic between the cities of the valley and Alexandria is well documented only for a few activities of official interest, traffic with areas outside Egypt is still less extensively attested. Apart from predictable imperial service, however,[409] what does appear gives such an appearance of the absolutely routine that it would surely be wrong to measure its normality by its numbers. A few examples give us a sense of this daily commerce. An Oxyrhynchos papyrus of the early fourth century preserves a petition to the *praeses* of Aegyptus Herculia from a resident of the area around Eleutheropolis, evidently the Palestinian city not far from Jerusalem.[410] His adversary, who comes from the East Delta city of Boubastos, had lent money to a resident of Skenai ektos Gerous, also in the East Delta, a loan for which the petitioner Malchos had put up wine as security. A three-cornered financial transaction across provincial borders is treated as absolutely routine. The other appearance of Eleutheropolis in an Oxyrhynchite papyrus attests to a similarly diverse group of parties; this fragmentary agreement involves the *princeps* of the staff of the *praeses* of Aegyptus Herculia, a man from Eleutheropolis of Syria, an Alexandrian, and at least two other per-

---

[406]See the brief remarks of P. van Minnen, *Mnemosyne* 44 (1991) 167-70.

[407]See el-Fakharani 1983. A less encouraging picture of the situation around 300 is given by Schwartz 1983, but it rests on several very dubious lines of reasoning.

[408]*P.Fouad* 74 (*BL*) (5c).

[409]Like the famous case of Abinnaeus' trip with the Blemmyes to Constantinople: *P.Abinn.* 1.

[410]*P.Oxy.* L 3574 (*ca* 314-318). Eleutheropolis is described as "of the new Arabia," a phrase which has given rise to controversy. The editor, J. R. Rea, took it to refer to Eleutheropolis in Palestine. T. D. Barnes and G. W. Bowersock (see his *Roman Arabia* [Cambridge, Mass. 1983] 145-46) have claimed against Rea that this is an otherwise unknown city in a new province within Egypt, but P. Mayerson has argued persuasively in support of Rea that this is the known Eleutheropolis, not a hitherto unattested city: see *ZPE* 53 (1983) 251-58 and 69 (1987) 251-60, where he explores the administrative history.

sons, all temporarily in Oxyrhynchos.[411] Bostra, in the province of Arabia, was the home of the seller of a house in Oxyrhynchos in 321.[412] The purchaser was a woman from the latter city, the seller's guarantor a cavalry veteran now living in Hermopolis.

These people are undoubtedly typical of many members of middle strata of society, the propertied but probably not rich—veterans, merchants, traders, moneylenders, and the like, whose activities are only sporadically recorded for modern view. Far less typical but much more visible are those members of the local civic aristocracies who achieved prominence not only beyond their own home cities but on the larger imperial stage. Two members of such a family have become known from a still largely unpublished archive from Panopolis. One brother, Harpocration, was a panegyrist, who traveled with the imperial court; another, Apollon, was a poet. It is noteworthy that Harpocration had also served as an imperial procurator and as a *curator civitatis* in the course of his service to the emperor.[413] A third brother was a *scholasticus* remaining in Egypt.[414]

Panopolis produced other important literary figures who achieved prominence outside Egypt, including the poet and grammarian Horapollon, the poets Triphiodoros, Nonnos, Pamprepios and Cyrus, who reached the ordinary consulate in 441.[415] Nor was Panopolis alone, for Coptos produced Christodoros (though perhaps of a Panopolite family), Hermopolis Andronicus, and Thebes Olympiodoros.[416] The dense concentration of such figures in the period from the early fourth through the late fifth century is in striking contrast to the relative scarcity of such figures in earlier centuries, when only Alexandria was highly productive of scholars or literary eminences.

[411]*P.Oxy.* XIV 1722 (*BL*) (315-323).

[412]*PSI* VII 771 (*BL*).

[413]See *SB* XIV 11929 (Panopolis, 348) and the original commentary of G. M. Browne, "Harpocration Panegyrista," *ICS* 2 (1977) 184-96.

[414]For the family see also *P.XV Congr.* 22 and (for the previous generation) *P.Coll.Youtie* II 71-73 (281).

[415]See Alan Cameron 1982, especially 217-20.

[416]Alan Cameron 1982, 218; cf. his study "Wandering Poets," *Historia* 14 (1965) 470-509. For Antinoopolis, also lively in this period, see Cauderlier 1978.

CHAPTER 3

Country Villages

Land and Villages

If the cities were the outer face of Egypt, decorated with the universal trappings of Roman urban life, the villages were the inner being. There were some two thousand to twenty-five hundred of them; their residents farmed an average of around 1,000 hectares (3,630 arouras) gross, perhaps about 75 percent of them arable.[1] A fair estimate of the average population would be 1,270.[2] These averages, however, cover a wide range of actual sizes. An account of requisitions of military garments from Hermopolite villages shows a mean of about four items per village, but fifty of the seventy villages contributed fewer than four. A graph of contributions, in fact, shows a concentration in the range of one to three garments, smaller numbers at four to seven, and an average of one village each at figures from eight to fifteen. The largest village, then, contributed fifteen times as much as the smallest. The largest fifth of the villages contributed half the garments.[3] These figures imply that a large village, farming more than 4,000 ha., might have 5,000 inhabitants or more, while a small one, controlling only 250 to 300 ha., might have a few hundred inhabitants.

The actual sizes of the villages themselves should reflect this range. The scanty available information is all from the Fayum. Karanis, a large village, occupied at its peak about 80 ha.[4] Euhemeria extended to about 65 ha.[5] Narmouthis was only 17.5 ha.[6] Soknopaiou Nesos seems to have occupied only 15 ha.[7] For reasons already de-

---

[1]*P.Col.* IX 247 points to a total of about 100 villages for the Hermopolite, which occupied about 1,000 km[2] in this period (see App. 3). Extrapolating this figure of 10 km[2] (= 1,000 ha.) each to the total usable area of Egypt (estimated above, p. 20 at a little more than 23,000 km[2]) yields 2,300 villages. It is hard to say how large a margin of error is to be allowed.

[2]Based on second-century figures for Karanis and Theadelphia, which show about 0.35 inhabitant per aroura (for the figures involved, see Bagnall 1985a, 291-96). Various factors may make these numbers too conservative for the country as a whole. On population of villages and Egypt as a whole, see Rathbone 1990.

[3]These figures all come from *P.Col.* IX 247.

[4]Husselman 1979, 7.

[5]*EEF Arch.Rep.* 1898-99, 9.

[6]Bresciani 1968, 23.

[7]Estimated from the information in Boak 1935, 3.

scribed (p. 6), excavation of Egyptian villages of the Roman period has
been extremely limited. Even these few examples, however, suggest
that the size range of villages overlapped with that of the nome capitals. Karanis was almost as large as Thmouis, but it was only a third
the size of Arsinoe; and no city is likely to have been as small as
Soknopaiou Nesos.

The virtual limitation of village excavation to the Fayum also
makes it difficult to describe confidently the overall physical
appearance of an Egyptian village. The Fayum was, for one thing, the
site of a massive reclamation project under the early Ptolemies; many
villages have no history earlier than the third century B.C. Moreover,
the excavated villages were for the most part originally destined for
Greek and Macedonian military settlers. If they have a clear grid plan,
with wide streets and stone foundations, it is no cause for surprise.[8]
(See plate 3 for an example.) In the Roman period, as villages were
gradually rebuilt, the central authority imposed no such order. Here is
a description of the most flourishing level of Roman Karanis: "The
only main streets appear to have been the two thoroughfares that ran
from north to south . . . , with a possible third street providing communication between the south and north temples. There appear to
have been no through streets from east to west, and no other through
streets from south to north."[9] By the final rebuilding of the village, in
the late third century, even these through streets vanish; a plan of this
period (plate 4) suggests something close to chaos.[10] Karanis, it is true,
was in its final spasm of life, greatly reduced in size and prosperity
from a century and a half earlier; the lack of articulation of its public
space may reflect a declining village, not a normal, healthy one. It is,
however, equally possible that the transformation of Karanis reflects
the decline in its Greek element, that the villages of the Fayum in the
Roman period came to resemble typical Egyptian villages more than
they had under the Ptolemies. If so, it is late Karanis that informs us
best about villages throughout the country.

This poorly articulated space was mostly occupied by houses.[11]
What was said above (p. 49) about urban dwellings is even more true
for the villages. They were built of sun-dried bricks, constantly

[8]Cf. Viereck 1928, 7-9, for Philadelphia; Boak 1935, 20, for Soknopaiou Nesos.
[9]Husselman 1979, 29.
[10]Husselman 1979, Map 19.
[11]Unlike the cities, where leases of houses or rooms are common, villages show
little signs of any rental market (cf. Hobson 1985, 225). *P.Haun.* III 55 (Dinneos Koite,
Arsinoite, 325) and P.Mich.inv. 456 (in Gagos and van Minnen 1992) (Alabstrine,
425), however, offer examples of renting a single room.

refashioned according to the needs of the moment and repaired or reconstructed from their inevitable decline: an archaeologist's nightmare, offering few clearly definable "levels" for mapping.[12] As in cities, the size of houses varied considerably; an average of 120 m², of which about 90 m² was living space, appears typical for two-story houses.[13] And just as in cities, houses included space for the animal members of the family along with the human.[14] The usual cisterns for water storage were found.[15] Human and animal waste, along with other rubbish, was disposed of as best it could be. Vacant lots and abandoned houses were convenient, but a well-run village might emulate the urban practice of using dumps outside the town.[16]

Apart from houses, villages had a certain variety of other structures, though these were often adjuncts of private houses. Granaries are the best-attested of these,[17] and chaff-storehouses also occur.[18] Before the grain reached the granary, of course, it had to be threshed, and the threshing floor was a prominent public place.[19] Although much grain was no doubt ground and baked in the home courtyard,

[12]Lesquier 1911, 125-30, describes this phenomenon at Tehneh (Akoris) in terms reminiscent of Karanis. A well-built and well-maintained stone building, however, might continue in occupation almost indefinitely. Bresciani 1976, 3-10, describes a house at Narmouthis that she thinks was occupied from Ptolemaic to Byzantine times. A similar view seems by default to emerge from Viereck 1928, 16, on Philadelphia.

[13]See Hobson 1985, 214-16, and Maehler 1983, 122-24; Hobson's estimates are somewhat larger than Maehler's for the Roman period.

[14]*P.Abinn.* 62 (350) mentions a donkey stable that was part of a house in Philadelphia. The bones found at Karanis included pig, cow, horse, ass or mule, dog, sheep, and goat: Boak 1933, 88-92. Of course, we do not know how many of them came to town only after slaughter.

[15]*P.Cair.Goodsp.* 15 (*BL*) (Paploou, Hermopolite, 362) concerns *inter alia* the restoration of a cistern on a village property.

[16]Cf. Dixon 1972 for pharaonic parallels. At Deir el-Medina, the avoidance of generalized rubbish in the streets and houses helped prevent any rise in habitation level during 400 years of occupation. *PSI* III 184 (= *Doc.Eser.Rom.* 75) (Herakleopolite, 292) is a notice to a decurion from the komarch of the village of Bousiris, reporting a spontaneous fire in a refuse pile of chaff and filth in his yard on the west of the village.

[17] See Husselman 1979, 22-24, on third-century granaries at Karanis. *PSI* VI 711 (360) mentions construction of a new granary. There is no identified granary in the latest levels at Karanis, and it may not be fanciful to think that changes in the system of collecting grain taxes led to a decline in village granaries. Local consumption, however, will surely have meant a continued need for village granaries of some size.

[18]*P.Gen.* I 12 (*BL*) (Philadelphia, 383) mentions the use of a vaulted (probably basement) room as a storehouse for chaff.

[19]*P.Cair.Isid.* 124 (Karanis, 298) mentions a fire on one. Cf. *P.Cair.Isid.* 65-67, concerning the same incident. See also *CPR* VI 31 (Hermopolite, before 300/1).

there were also larger mills for public use[20] and bakeries.[21] Another characteristic structure, then as today, is the pigeonhouse.[22] Local pottery needs were normally met by local production, but a pottery works was potentially a substantial enterprise, with outside ownership.[23] Finally, often mentioned in the papyri are the villages' vacant lots, frequently produced by collapse of an older house.

The catalogue is short: houses, granaries, threshing floors, bakeries, dovecotes, pottery works. The defective character of village documentation (see Introduction) may be partly to blame, but it is hard to believe that all the responsibility lies there. Even in its most flourishing Roman level, the only identifiable public structures in Karanis were the two temples. In the latest period, they were buried, and there is no evidence for any secular public buildings at all.[24] Once again it is possible to incriminate the evidence: the center of the mound had been ruined by sebakh-diggers. There are some signs in the earlier centuries of Roman rule of large, well-constructed buildings in Soknopaiou Nesos and Narmouthis, edifices that the excavators considered "public."[25] In no case has it been possible to identify the function of such buildings with any confidence; indeed, in the case of Soknopaiou Nesos, the excavator rejected military use, grain storage, and religious activities for the large (315 m[2]) building he describes.

Military installations are easy to identify. For one thing, the members of the garrison tend to generate papyrus documentation attesting the existence of the unit in a particular place (see pp. 174-75). For another, their architecture and size are distinctive. Even where a temple was converted into a fort, the use is identifiable enough.[26] Dionysias has an extensive fortress, constructed perhaps around 258 by the Palmyrenes,[27] set outside the village itself. Similarly, temples are characteristic in form. They were a common feature of villages.

[20]P.Wisc. II 58 (298) describes a house in Philadelphia as a former mill.

[21]P.Cair.Isid. 136 (Karanis, early 4c), mentioning a share of one as part of an inheritance.

[22]P.Oxy. XIV 1700 (late 3c) mentions a pigeonhouse at Seryphis.

[23]PSI IV 300 (BL; BASP 27 [1990] 86-89) (Oxyrhynchos, 324) records the sale of a works in a village; the former owner is a councillor of Antinoopolis, the new one a cavalryman, but the price is about that of an ordinary house (see Bagnall 1985b, 71 n. 28).

[24]Husselman 1979, 55. It is true that one building in level C was claimed as a barracks, but this identification is very doubtful.

[25]Bresciani 1968, 47 (almost 300 m[2] in area), for Narmouthis, citing a similar construction at Theadelphia; Boak 1935, 13, for Soknopaiou Nesos.

[26]See Golvin et al. 1986 for Luxor.

[27]See Carrié 1974, 839.

Some were outside the area of the houses, in a separate zone; others were the center of the village.[28] Probably most of them were out of use by the fourth century (see pp. 262-68). The "public" buildings mentioned above bear no marks of temple character, nor any of such other religious practices as Christianity.

It is not surprising that excavators have by default been driven to suggest official use for these structures.[29] As will become clear, Egyptian villages of the fourth century, even more than earlier, lacked internal political and social structures as much as their villages lacked spatial articulation. There is no internal village purpose to be suggested. At all events, whatever such buildings existed earlier, there is no sign of them in the fourth century: no building remains found, no mentions of such buildings in the papyri. The varied texture of urban space finds no real counterpart in the villages.

Villages were surrounded with fields. The normal pattern of living in a village and working the fields around it posed little problem, becausee even the largest villages had a territory only about 6 to 7 km square.[30] Farmers might construct small buildings on their larger plots, to hold equipment and even provide a place to stay at times of most intense fieldwork.[31]

Independent Farmers

The rural world of these villages was almost by definition centered on farming. It is a truism that the economy of the ancient world was essentially agricultural, and Egypt was famed as the richest and most productive land of the ancient world. A papyrological documentation rich in mentions of wheat, barley, wine, oils, and other produce (see chapter 1) is therefore no surprise. Understanding the organization

[28]Cf. the comments in *P.Fay.*: Bacchias was centered on its temple, with the main streets running toward its walls and portal (p. 35); at Euhemeria, the temple was a few yards from town to the northwest (p. 45). At Theadelphia (p. 52), the temple was about thirty yards to the west of town: or so Grenfell and Hunt report. See, however, Breccia 1926, 87-131 (with Tav. LI), for a report indicating a central location reminiscent of the plan of Hermopolis.

[29]See, however, *EEF Arch.Rep.* 1898-99, 12, about a room at Theadelphia identified as the dining hall of the local weavers' group by an inscription of Trajanic date (now *I.Fayum* II 122). These villages had more communal institutions in the earlier empire than they reveal in late antiquity. But it seems unlikely that such associations can have been responsible for the large buildings in question.

[30]This is in line with findings that 4 km is a maximum radius around a village for intensive use of land; cf. Donald Engels, *Roman Corinth* (Chicago 1990) 24.

[31]In *P.Cair.Isid.* 141 (Karanis, early 4c), Isidoros petitions the eirenarch concerning a night raid by one Apynchis and a female slave of Atisis on a *mone* belonging to him, in the course of which they carried off grain and a hair sack.

and structure of the working of the land, however, is a difficult task. In other areas of the Roman Empire, it is easy to plead a lack of evidence, for neither ancient authors nor archaeological finds do much to distinguish the wealth and status of the large population of small farmers found in all parts of the empire.[32] For Egypt, with the papyri, it ought to be possible to do better; and so it is. But the matter is by no means as simple as it might be. The metropolitan origin and bias of the fourth-century papyri (see Introduction) makes the amplitude of the documentation deceptive. Virtually all the concentrated evidence for landholding and farming in villages of this period comes from just two archives, those of Isidoros and Sakaon.[33] In particular, Isidoros' papers dominate the picture. But it must not be forgotten that these are both from the Fayum, both from villages under great pressure from the decay of the irrigation system on the periphery of that region, and both from farmers well above the average in wealth for their villages. It is essential to look for evidence to corroborate or disprove the picture that emerges from these archives.

Recent scholarship has effectively demolished the view once prevalent that most independent farmers came under the domination of rich landlords in an arrangement usually referred to as the "colonate" and seen as the precursor of medieval feudalism.[34] Indeed, even the eventual feudalism to which this dependency was thought to lead is now being rejected, at least for the eastern part of the empire, in favor of an unchanging centrality of the small family farm.[35] It is possible to test this view by a study of the taxation records of Karanis dealing with the year 308/9 preserved in the Isidoros archive.[36] But an extremely difficult question must first be addressed: what size landholdings constituted an adequate family farm?

There can be no universal answer to this question.[37] Many aspects of the problem escape scrutiny entirely: family vegetable gardens, for

[32]See Garnsey and Saller 1987, 64-82, for a recent survey with bibliography.

[33]At a rough estimate, 70 percent of the documents that illuminate the life of the independent village farmer in the period 275-450 come from these two archives, and the other material is scattered enough to lack adequate context for evaluation.

[34]See Carrié 1982, 1983, 1984; Gascou 1985.

[35]Kaplan 1986, 198-99.

[36]These are not land registers but records of payments of wheat and barley taxes. Their conversion into landholdings is partly based on stated rates, partly on correction and normalization of data; a full description of the process is given in Bagnall 1992b.

[37]Bowman 1985, 150, thought there was no answer at all. Kaplan 1986 tries to derive one for a generalized Byzantine farmer, or rather for a range of possible situations.

example, certainly a key part of the nutrition of most if not all farm households, are never documented. Animals kept for milk and fowl kept for eggs are equally invisible if intended for domestic purposes. Such sources of nutrition may raise or lower the amount of staple cereal crops needed for a reasonable living. No helpful private agricultural accounts have been published from any village of this period. Still, a fair estimate might be that a family of four or five would need two artabas of wheat per month, or twenty-four per year.[38] Even with this figure, however, one must reckon with wide variation in the productivity of land. In at least the Fayum, there is the additional factor of crop rotation. Because valley land in Egypt was inundated each year not only with water but with fresh silt, rotation was apparently unnecessary in most of the country. In most of the Fayum, however, which was irrigated rather than flooded, there was no such deposit of fertilizing earth.[39] Most evidence for alternate planting in cereals and in nitrogen-fixing crops, thus, comes from the Fayum.[40] Such rotation could mean extremely high yields of cereals in the years when they were planted. In assessing the figures from fourth-century Karanis, however, a countervailing trend must be taken into account: the decline in the irrigation system, which made some of the land unproductive at least some of the time. Still, the village did manage to pay its taxes.

A small farmer might of course not rotate crops as faithfully as a richer one, thus trading yield for acreage base. Because tax rates fell on all land, the pressure at any time was no doubt to cultivate as much as possible of an owner's land. Assuming rotation but only average yields, each aroura planted might produce a gross yield of ten artabas,[41] of which about four would be paid in all taxes (because each bore the taxes of a fallow aroura) and one had to be retained for seed.[42] The net yield per planted aroura would then be about five

[38]Cf. Kaplan 1986, 211, for a similar calculation (his net 77 modii equal about 26 art. per year). Rathbone 1990, 139 n.18, takes the "wheat-equivalent" requirement to be about 8 art. per year per person, but only part of that nutrition would actually be provided by wheat.

[39]Indeed, the silt was deposited in the irrigation channels, thus becoming a nuisance, which had to be removed regularly and banked up to keep the channels usable.

[40]Although not all: see W. Bagnall 1974, 118-22, esp. 121 n. 18, for a discussion and evidence; there are a few examples from the Oxyrhynchite and Hermopolite Nomes.

[41]A commonly used figure, cf. Bowman 1985, 149; Rathbone 1991, 243 with n. 45.

[42]On tax rates, see Bagnall 1985a, 304.

artabas. It can be seen that a farm of ten arouras, half fallow each year, would barely suffice for the average Karanis family.[43]

Approximate as such a calculation must be, it may help to interpret the distribution of farm sizes suggested by the Karanis tax documents.[44]

Size (arouras)	Number of farmers
< 4	4
5-9	10
10-14	16
15-19	6
20-29	22
30-39	15
40-49	12
50-69	10
70-99	8
100-149	2
> 150	1

For four farmers the landholdings could not be estimated. Of the 106 landowners whose holdings can be computed, then, 59, or a bit more than half, held farms in the 10 to 39 aroura range, what one might call a farm sufficient for and manageable by a family. Another 14 landowners had less than a ten-aroura spread; for them some supplementary means of support must be supposed. A further 22 had more than 40 arouras but less than 70; holdings of this size could have been managed with only limited help from outside the nuclear family, perhaps with one or two additional hands. That leaves 11 farms larger than 70 arouras, for which other strategies would be needed: leasing, using slaves, hiring labor. These methods are examined in succeeding sections.[45]

[43]These calculations ignore the other expenses of farming, such as the amortization of the capital invested in livestock and equipment, or the renting of oxen for plowing; but equally they ignore the value of the grass or leguminous crops planted on the arouras not planted with wheat. Both are difficult to quantify, but probably they did not miss by much of balancing one another. The average rate of fallowing may also have been less than half.

[44]These include only the holdings of villagers, kometai, because metropolitan owners are likely to have held land elsewhere in addition, particularly the richer ones: cf. Bowman 1985, 153, who cites also P.Oxy. XLII 3047 from the middle of the third century.

[45]The tiny sample of farmers left in Theadelphia in 336—a dozen in all—break down as follows (P.Sakaon 4): 40+ ar., 3; 30, 1; 10 to 20, 4; 5 to 10, 1; less than 5, 3. No one has much over 60, so two-thirds have viable family farms, one-third smaller holdings. The distribution is thus much like that in more prosperous Karanis.

Even those who had smaller holdings, however, are not necessarily simple cases. Several factors of complexity enter in. For one
thing, landholdings were mostly not consolidated in one or two large
farms, but scattered through the area around the village, the result of
partible inheritance and an active land market. Declarations of landholdings help to give an idea of the results: in one, Isidoros declares
no fewer than eleven parcels of land in the territory dependent on
Karanis, ranging in size from less than 1 aroura to 5 arouras (not all
figures are preserved).[46] He also owned one parcel of 11/16 aroura in
the area of the village proper, which warranted a declaration bearing
ten signatures.[47] The modest size of village territories must generally
have made this fragmentation manageable, but no doubt some people
owned land at a distance greater than was convenient for farming,
even in other villages, or too small to be worth the required effort.
Such plots could be leased out.

As the study of family structure in chapter 5 shows, parents-
children families were the basic building block of Egyptian
households. But there were nonetheless close ties vertically and
horizontally, between parents and children and between brothers and
sisters. Households would be more or less extended at various points
in their natural cycle. In villages, extended family households, or at
least cooperation, were much more common than in the cities.
Isidoros, for example, was part of a considerable family, and he did
much of his farming and taxpaying in conjunction with his siblings.[48]
With them he formed a *pittakion*, a consortium for agricultural work;
the group was joined by various persons outside the family, as many
as a half-dozen of them at times, with the exact arrangements fluctuat-
ing from year to year.[49] Indeed, such family arrangements were considered normal; one petitioner, a widower whose children have died,
complains that he is harassed by tax collectors for the taxes due on his
father-in-law's land, even though he is not in partnership with him.
The governor, perhaps a bit sarcastically, replies, "the *praepositus* of the
pagus is not unaware from whom taxes must be collected in respect to
the sacred [= imperial] revenues of the land."[50] Because unmarried
relatives might well live in the household of married siblings,

[46]*P.Cair.Isid.* 5 (299).

[47]*P.Cair.Isid.* 4 (299).

[48]See Bagnall 1977a for an analysis of the family's holdings.

[49]*P.Cair.Isid.* 24-26; for *pittakia* see H. C. Youtie, *CP* 37 (1942) 142-44 = *Scriptiunculae* II 820-22 plus addenda on 828; *P.Berl.Leihg.* I 22 introd. Its origins apparently
lay in groups formed to farm public land, but by the fourth century the privatization
of land had made such groups less specifically related to any type of land.

[50]*P.Sakaon* 41 (Theadelphia, 322).

nephews, or the like, some families would be able to farm more land than they owned. Family labor beyond that of the householder, in fact, is a factor rarely documented in this period, but certainly to be reckoned with.

In short, the admittedly small body of evidence for village households in the fourth century suggests that the small to middle-sized family farm was the basic and most common unit in Egyptian agriculture. Villager-owned holdings between 10 and 99 arouras amount to three-quarters of all the land at Karanis. At the same time, it points also to great complexity in the remainder of the picture, where quite apart from metropolitan landholdings (discussed in chapter 4) there was a wide variety of sizes of farms, owned by many different people of all stations, offering opportunities for diverse approaches.

Leasing Land

Throughout the Roman world, letting land out to tenants was a basic strategy of estate management for owners who could not or did not find it desirable to farm a particular piece of land themselves. Leasing offered under the right conditions an attractive combination of stable yield, minimal risk, and efficient management of scattered property.[51] The use of leasing in this manner by metropolitan landholders in the fourth century is treated in chapter 4. Here, however, the focus is on the role of leasing inside the village.

It is clear from the analysis of Karanis landholdings in the previous section that some villagers owned more land than they could reasonably farm with any normal family. Leasing was one possible means of realizing an income from land beyond the capacity of a family to cultivate directly. A lessee could presumably cultivate as much land as an owner, more or less, and in a situation like that of Karanis, with a high probability of crop rotation, one lessee could handle 20 to 30 arouras on his own. Most larger owners at Karanis could thus have managed their lands with one or two lessees to help. The thinness of the documentation makes examples scarce, but in one very striking example Isidoros leases 25 arouras of grainland from two brothers from Karanis, Kastor and Ammonianos.[52] As he tells his story to the governor, he leased the land on half shares, for the sowing

> of the current year only, and I performed all the labors
> connected with the arouras up to the harvest, and the

[51]Cf. Kehoe 1988, with bibliography, and Foxhall 1990.
[52]*P.Cair.Isid.* 74 (315); another version in *P.Mert.* II 91.

seed was furnished by me, Isidoros, as an advance on
their share, that is, I supplied them for sowing with 20
(?) art. of wheat, 6 art. of barley, and 3 art. of phaselus
beans, but also fifteen talents in silver for sixty yoke-
days' work by oxen hired in the period of plowing, and
two talents as the price of . . . ; and they received in loan
from me in accordance with written and oral agreements
for their own use eight more talents in silver, one new
hair-sack, 22 more art. of wheat, 18 art. of phaselus
beans, and likewise 24 more art. of wheat which I
expended from my own resources as wages for the har-
vesters.

After all this, Kastor and Ammonianos seized the crop on the threshing floor and defrauded Isidoros.

The situation here is not quite what one would expect. Kastor and
Ammonianos lease the land to Isidoros, but the latter is not a poor,
landless peasant taking the leftover land in the estates of the wealthy.
Rather, he is a landowner of above average wealth (about 36 arouras
in the tax computation, but elsewhere holding 80 to 140 arouras, the
higher figures perhaps including some relatives' farms), with considerable capital, taking on the land of what were probably distressed
fellow villagers, lending them considerable sums, and himself advancing all the capital necessary for the farming of the land. It may
reasonably be estimated that the sums lent them equaled the totality
of their likely share of the produce of the land; even if all went well,
then, Isidoros would have kept the entire crop. The case is strikingly
reminiscent of the process whereby the sixth-century entrepreneur
Aurelius Phoibammon, of the village of Aphrodito, simultaneously
leased land from and lent money and grain to an absentee landowner,
a soldier, who sank ever deeper into debt, to the profit of Phoibammon.[53]

Had the papers of someone poorer than Isidoros survived, perhaps the other end of the spectrum would emerge more clearly.
Certainly women often let their land out to able-bodied male tenants
from the village.[54] Here too, however, expectation can be deceived. A
woman from the metropolis of the Arsinoite nome offers in one document to lease from (or to?) Sakaon twenty of his arouras in Theadelphia, on half shares, with Sakaon providing the seed and animals for
working the land, as well as paying the taxes.[55] It is unlikely that

[53]Keenan 1980 describes the process in detail.
[54]An example is *P.Col.* VII 185 (Karanis, 319).
[55]*P.Sakaon* 67 (321). See above, p. 96, on the possibility that the lease is mis-

Aurelia Kyrillous planned to cultivate the land herself, but she must have found interesting opportunities of some kind. There are, in fact, other examples of city residents leasing land from rather than to villagers; see chapter 4.

Examination of landholdings thus combines with some specific evidence to point to an enormously complex situation. Small landowners no doubt often leased additional parcels to bring themselves up to subsistence level, thus helping those with more land than they could farm to have it cultivated profitably. That much is predictable from the land ownership distribution. More striking and less predictable is the entrepreneurial element, in which prosperous landowners used their surplus for both loans and providing capital for further agricultural activities; the two were linked in some cases. Such activity might be found at relatively humble levels of society, where the farmer carried a permanent load of debt, owned little, and yet ran an active array of enterprises,[56] or as a sideline for a substantial landowner like Isidoros—or, probably, at intermediate levels of wealth. It is by no means clear just how such entrepreneurs, taking on more than they could do personally or even with the help of family, managed their lands, particularly in periods of peak work. The following three sections discuss sources of labor in the villages. But it must be kept in mind that above all the village was not a closed community. Metropolitans owned land and were both lessors and lessees to villagers. The villages were inextricably tied to the metropolitan economy and population. A view of the village in isolation, then, is only a partial one, which must be completed by its external relationships.

Hiring Labor

There is remarkably little information in the sources about persons working for steady wages in agriculture. The silence is so great, in fact, that one is tempted to suppose that it rests on reality: the bulk of the labor on the land through most of the year was not done by hired men. The strongest reason was probably that such labor was inefficient, in that it was needed only for small parts of the year: plowing, sowing, and harvesting of cereal crops, more continuously for cultivation of vines and trees. A landowner had no interest in paying wages throughout the year; but no one could live on the income from two or three months' work. For the fourth century few accounts are com-

---

drafted.

[56]Perhaps the most striking example is from the second century, the archive of Soterichos (*P.Soter.*); cf. Bagnall 1980.

parable to those from the Appianus estate in the third century, in which a core of permanent hired staff was supplemented by part-time workers.[57]

Full-time employment, on the model of the hired man on a modern dairy farm, for example, was thus not viable for most landowners. Casual labor, however, tends to leave few traces in the documents. Only if an agricultural expense book shows disbursements is there any hope of finding evidence of hired laborers. Such accounts do survive from other times: along with the third-century Appianus estate, one may mention the second-century archive of the descendants of Laches; they show that wealthy family employing an average of about eight men at a time in the period before the harvest.[58] For a family owning hundreds of arouras, that is not a large paid staff. For the fourth century, few similar accounts have been published, but the incident of Isidoros' tenancy discussed above (p. 119) shows him hiring teams for plowing and workers for harvesting.[59] The hiring of teams of men and oxen for plowing remained a constant for anyone who did not own the animals privately, as even quite wealthy landowners might not. A private letter shows that this could be a complicated business. The writer says that he had made an agreement with one man and got the workers ready; he then went to another man about another team, but he said that the owner had gone up to the city and nothing could be done until he returned. The writer then tried with yet another owner, but failed to reach agreement, because the team-owner was asking too much.[60]

For the most part, even surviving accounts help little because payments for workers tell nothing about their status. Two fifth-century papyri are emblematic. One orders a winemaker to pay out money; another is an account of amounts of wine owed by vineyard workers. There is no obvious way to tell if these are lessees, free hired labor, contractors,[61] or slaves.[62] Where status was not significant, it was not recorded; only function mattered. A striking case on a large scale is

---

[57]Rathbone 1991, 88-174.

[58]W. Bagnall 1974, 169-73, based on *P.Mil.Vogl.* II 69.

[59]It is possible that the large farm account book (on tablets) found in the Dakleh Oasis and as yet unpublished will offer evidence on this point. *P.Lips.* 97 seems to deal with permanent rather than casual staff. *CPR* XVIIA 9a (Hermopolite, *ca* 310-320) shows variable numbers (between one and twelve), perhaps casual laborers.

[60]*P.Gen.* I 76 (*BL*) (3c).

[61]Hiring an independent contractor to be responsible for the work, rather than leasing the property itself, was a realistic possibility. *PSI* XIII 1338 (Oxyrhynchos, 299) seems to be a contract of this sort. See *P.Heid.* V, pp. 222-32 for labor contracts; pp. 260-70 for work contracts in the context of lease.

[62]*P.Amst.* I 53 and 78.

the long account concerning an estate around Hermonthis, dated 338, discussed in the next section, in which numerous groups of special- ized workers are listed, with no indication of status.[63] But that account belongs to the world of metropolitan country estates.

At harvest time, once again, all hands turned out. It is likely that large numbers of men who did something else normally earned spare cash by helping at the peak season. Monks poured out of their desert monasteries into the Delta fields to work for a daily wage.[64] Given the relatively small distances, in fact, it is possible that the population of the nome capitals formed a significant pool of labor for the harvest in the nearby villages. Once again, only occasionally would such work leave written traces. Normally, cash changing hands at the end of the day was the end of the transaction; the story of the vineyard-owner who recruited throughout the day and paid all of his workers the same wage regardless of the hour of starting, told in the Gospel of Matthew (20: 1-16), describes the situation (even if not pay practices) with precision. It must be remembered that most country residents in antiquity (as still today) patched a living together from many sources, including working their own land, leasing, other occupations, and casual labor.[65]

Rural Slavery

From what has already been said, it will come as no surprise to learn that slave labor carried out only a small part of agricultural labor in Egypt.[66] That does not mean it did not have an important role. The limited evidence, though impossible to evaluate statistically,[67] speaks clearly to a structural place for rural slavery. A division of the inheritance[68] from one Psenamounis, who lived in a village in the western toparchy of the Oxyrhynchite Nome, among the members of his two families by different wives, seven persons in all, gave the older family a house, 3.5 arouras of grainland, and two-sevenths share

[63]*P.Lips.* 97, cf. below p. 126.

[64]Chitty 1966, 34 and 145, with references.

[65]Cf. Rathbone 1991, 209. My next-door neighbor in a poor upstate New York county raises horses, lets out pasture to a neighboring dairy farmer, sells real estate and insurance, and is the tax assessor for two towns!

[66]Biezunska-Malowist 1977, 83.

[67]The census declarations from the principate show that slaves were around 9 percent of the village populations (see Bagnall and Frier, forthcoming, for up-to-date documentation), but it is impossible to tell how many of these were agricultural workers. Interestingly, however, females outnumber males among the rural slaves by five to one.

[68]*P.Oxy.* XIV 1638 (282).

of four slaves; the remaining five heirs got the rest of the property and a five-sevenths share of the slaves. Of the slaves, one is apparently male, one undescribed, one an adult female aged twenty-five and one a child, her daughter aged ten. There is no sign of any actual assignment of slaves, merely shared ownership of the entire group. A village family of moderate means thus owned four slaves. The total amount of land owned by Psenamounis is not mentioned, but the older family's allotment of 3.5 arouras suggests a very modest total estate, perhaps no more than ten or fifteen arouras.

From the well-known archive of Aurelius Isidoros from Karanis, there is evidence that the wife of Isidorus' brother Heras, one Taesis, owned slaves. Her paternal inheritance, shared with her sister Kyrillous, included sixty-one sheep, forty goats, one grinding mill, six talents of silver, two art. wheat, and two slaves.[69] Each sister also inherited about ten or eleven arouras of grain-bearing land, for a paternal total of about twenty-two arouras; this is a very middle-range holding for a villager of moderate means.[70] About the slave holdings of the central figure of the archive, Aurelius Isidoros himself, we know nothing; because his and his siblings' landholdings far exceeded those of Taesis and Kyrillous, it seems hard to suppose that they did not include slaves. Another Isidoros papyrus[71] mentions the role of the female slave of another villager in carrying out a criminal raid. The one preserved census declaration by Isidoros[72] states that the household consists only of himself and his son. Similarly, in the census declaration of Sakaon, the central figure of the Theadelphian archives of this period, nine free persons are listed, but no slaves are mentioned.[73] Now Sakaon's return contains nine men and no women. Was this really such a bachelor establishment, even though five of the nine men were adults between thirty-five and fifty-five? It seems unlikely. It appears, in other words, as if these declarations of persons simply include only free males.[74]

Yet another small household with a few slaves is attested in a Hermopolite document,[75] in which two brothers divide up four slaves

[69]*P.Cair.Isid.* 64 (*ca* 298).

[70]The evidence for landholdings is found in or deduced from *P.Cair.Isid.* 6 and 9, using the methods of analysis from Bagnall 1977a, 330-31 n. 1. For the landholdings of village liturgists, who are the more prosperous part of village society, see Bagnall 1978a: twenty-two arouras is a very decent holding.

[71]*P.Cair.Isid.* 141.

[72]*P.Cair.Isid.* 8 (309).

[73]*P.Sakaon* 1 (310).

[74]It is hard to test this generalization: these are the only two declarations of persons known for the entire period from 275 to 450.

[75]*P.Lips.* 26 (early 4c).

in their inheritance: two farmers, a weaver and a donkey-driver, who were probably part of the family's rural estate.

In sum, the character of the evidence for slaves belonging to village families of moderate means suggests that ownership of a small number of slaves—one to four—was not remarkable. The economic importance of slavery in such households was not marginal. On a small family farm, say ten to twenty-five arouras, the presence of even one ablebodied adult agricultural worker alongside the family is not a trivial advantage. A farmer without a bunch of sons would find it hard to work his farm himself without help. The effects of such rural slaves, therefore, small though their numbers were, may have been pervasive and decisive in the structure of working the land.

That is not to say slavery was universal. The poorer families, with barely enough land to support themselves, would not have been able to afford a slave. The average slave represented a capital of perhaps twenty to thirty artabas of wheat; to own two such might be likened to having a year's income in human capital. And those metropolitan, absentee landowners who had small amounts of land or had it widely scattered normally leased it out to villagers; slaves probably had no role in the working of this land, either.[76]

In qualitative terms, the importance to the moderately prosperous of perhaps increasing by 50 or 100 percent the available labor force was significant. Because this middle class provided the villages with their rotating public officials of all sorts, it needed some means of freeing up time for these uncompensated duties. That precisely these men owned slaves can hardly be surprising. In terms of the economy and structure of the villages, then, the role of even a small number of slaves may well have been critical.

There is still the question of slavery on larger estates to be considered. Large estates in the fourth century are (see chapter 4) most elusive. The larger the landholdings of an individual, the greater the likelihood that they are spread over the nome rather than consolidated.[77] Great landowners certainly had staffs of some size, with stewards in charge, and there is abundant evidence for a constant flow of orders, information and goods between estates and the master or mistress in the city. But these orders normally show only the function, not the legal status, of the employees involved in these interchanges.[78]

[76]See the distribution of ownership in the Hermopolite land registers, as analyzed by Bowman 1985, with table on 158-59. Of the landowners listed (in Hermopolis and Antinoopolis combined), 62 percent held fewer than twenty arouras in the countryside.

[77]Bowman 1985, 154-55.

[78]There are occasional indications, apart from *P.Lips.* 97, to be discussed below,

The one item of useful evidence for slavery in the management of large agglomerations is the long account from an estate centered on Hermonthis, on the West Bank south of Thebes, dated to the first four months of 338.[79] Payments of wheat for salary, or at least subsistence, are made on a monthly or bimonthly basis to various groups of workers, whose numbers vary from month to month. Prominent are *organitai*, operators of irrigation machinery, of whom twenty-one are paid in Pharmouthi; staff for animal care (cowherds, shepherds, donkey rearers), who number eighteen; transport workers (wagon-eers, donkey drivers, camel drivers), totaling eleven at the peak; and gardeners, fourteen. But there are also some more undifferentiated groups: twenty *ergatai*, laborers; four *boethoi*, assistants; and fifteen *paidaria*, slaves. Occasionally some specific information is given about one of these: one *ergates* is identified as a *hypoboukolos*, subcowherd, and one slave is a breadmaker, another a weaver of rugs (*tarsikarios*). Most have no particular occupational identity. The identification of the *paidaria* as slaves seems certain. Not only does the term always mean this in the papyri of this period, but none of the people in question, with one exception, appears anywhere else in the long account in another capacity.[80] Moreover, that one exception, with the splendid slave name of Philokyrios, "master-loving,"[81] appears in another place with his name adjacent to that of a *doule*, a female slave.

It would be easier to interpret this information if the papyrus indicated to whom belonged the substantial properties connected with this account. The amounts are not small: wheat expenditures total almost 2,200 artabas in the four months; annualized that would come to 6,600 artabas, the income perhaps on 1,500-2,000 arouras, in line with the largest holdings found in the Hermopolite registers. The editor, Mitteis, argued that the estates could not belong to an

---

of rations paid to slaves; see *P.Harr.* II 233 (307), *P.Haun.* III 68 (402), and *BGU* I 34; cf. *P.Charite* 36 for a discussion of date and purpose, along with reedition of a small part of it. *SPP* XX 106, an account of payments by or for *paidaria* for contributions to the *vestis militaris* for the 14th indiction, seems to agree with this view also; it lists *paidaria* who are butcher, brickmaker, and pastry cook. The date seems likely to be 355/6 or later.

[79]*P.Lips.* 97. *P.Lond.* I 125 (p. 192), which is to be dated to July 336, seems to pertain to the same places and probably the same entity. It is interesting for Christian reading habits that the Leipzig roll has an extensive text of Psalms 30-55 on the back, while the London one has a magical text.

[80]Rathbone 1991, 89-91, argues that *paidarion* does not denote a slave in the Heroninos archive, but the evidence he cites is insufficient to support the argument. His demonstration that *oiketai* were free (106-116), however, is entirely convincing.

[81]Hardly found otherwise in the papyri. Solin, *Griech.Eigennamen* II 752, lists a fair number at Rome, none of them demonstrably freeborn.

individual; he preferred to think of them as held by a temple. For reasons given below (p. 267), this is not possible.[82] If the owner was an individual, what conclusions can be drawn about slavery in this context? The landholdings in question are distributed over several villages, and indeed given the preharvest season there is little evidence for the full extent of the property. Rather than think of an "estate," we should perhaps think of the "great house" that owned numerous properties and employed these people. But the conditions under which it employed them are obscure. The one obvious conclusion is that slaves coexisted with free labor in the pool of undifferentiated staff, those perhaps who filled multiple roles or who belonged to specialties whose members were not numerous enough to warrant their own heading in the account. The main groups of livestock and agricultural workers, however, were apparently not slaves but free.[83] Slaves make up about 15 percent of the payroll in this particular establishment. It is not even certain that these slaves were located in the countryside. The account could well have been drawn up at the urban headquarters of the great house, not at any of the rural locations mentioned, and the slaves could mainly have been located in the same place. The predominantly rural character of the free employees may speak against this possibility, but it does not quite exclude it. At all events, there is a significant slave component to the staff, but not any demonstrable role in agriculture or livestock-raising themselves.

Work Outside Agriculture

The two fourth-century villages best known to the modern scholar, Karanis and Theadelphia, give the impression that little except agriculture went on. The publications of the archives of Isidoros and Sakaon have no index for occupations, for the good reason that few are attested in their papyri. In the archive of Isidoros, the only

[82]Mitteis pointed out that the addressees of the account were *apo epitropon*, which he thought lent an official cast to things. But the term means that they are retired; such terms simply identify the persons by their status. Nor does the appearance of a couple of priests, *hiereis*, among the people with whom business is transacted (one of them as agent for the owners, it seems) mean much. Priests owned or leased land and engaged in normal economic transactions like other people. The term *ousia* (v.12) does not help much, either, as it may have a completely nontechnical meaning here. The term *phoros* can mean either rent or taxes and is thus unhelpful. An official government account would not be organized in this fashion. Overall, the accounts impress one as highly similar to other accounts of wealthy landowners in Roman Egypt, not to official accounting.

[83]This is deduced from the fact that they have occupational titles while *paidaria* are identified as such. It is of course possible that logic did not rule in the terminology of this account and that some of the others were in fact slaves.

livelihoods (other than that of farmer) mentioned that can be attributed to the village are shepherd and cowherd, bare extensions into animal husbandry. Moribund Theadelphia saw a few shepherds as well, but nothing more.[84]

Scattered evidence shows that more prosperous villages would have a bit more to offer. A request for the registration of a mill at Philadelphia suggests professional milling.[85] Probably some other food processing went on as well; Karanis 150 years earlier had also an oilmaker, a baker, and five men in retail trade, selling wine, vegetables, and fish.[86] That was in a population at least six times the size of that in the early fourth century, and these men are known from registers concerned with land tax; they thus had farm income as well as that derived from production or trade.

Second-century Karanis had also had some fourteen persons listed as involved in the fabric trade, from the shepherd through the woolseller, carder, weaver, dyer, purple-seller, cleaner, and sack-maker. That industry shows little trace there in the fourth century, but chance or a purely local decline may be responsible.[87] There were weavers in other villages, though nothing allows any estimation of their numbers or production.[88]

Villages needed a certain minimum of transport workers, like donkey drivers; but these were mobile, and small villages may have depended on those resident elsewhere (see above, pp. 38-39 for animal transport). A porter (sack-carrier) from Karanis agreed to go to Alexandria for two months to work in place of a resident of another village who had drawn compulsory duty carrying sacks of grain, as it appears.[89] Whether he was actually a professional at that menial trade, or an able-bodied farmer who thus earned some cash, is not clear. The building trades also were needed locally; although making huts of

[84]In the third century, numerous occupations appear in the Heroninos archive. These men were not full-time employees of the Appianus estate (Rathbone 1991, 174), but hired as needed. It is not clear, however, how many of these craftsmen—except the carpenters—were local in Theadelphia.

[85]*P.Mich.* XII 627 (Ptolemais Euergetis, 298).

[86]See Geremek 1969, 91-95.

[87]There is still mention in the late third century of practicing the weaver's trade in Karanis, but the weaver is a woman and she undertakes household duties as well: *SB* IV 7358 (*BL*) (277-282). She comes from another village and is to stay in Karanis working as payment for the interest on a loan for her father.

[88]See *P.Hib.* II 219 (Ankyrononpolis, 309), listing the linenweavers in that town with amounts of flax assigned to them. An account book from an Arsinoite village mentions several implements of the weaver's trade: *P.Lund.* IV 14 = *SB* VI 9350 (*BL*) (nr. Narmouthis, end of 3c).

[89]*BGU* I 286 (*BL*) (306).

mud brick was no great feat, making anything better required some professionalism. It is hard to imagine that there were not some carpenters, but they are not attested. A papyrus from Oxyrhynchos shows two men being paid for the production of 40,000 bricks: moonlighting farmers, however, not full-time brickmakers.[90] A stonecutter, by contrast, was a professional and might be detailed elsewhere when his craft was needed in a particular place by the authorities.[91]

Egyptian villages needed pottery as well, and no doubt most common ware was produced in the villages for not only local use but also the metropolis. Fine wares, however, were to some extent manufactured in the nome capital. Second-century Karanis had a potter, and potters are attested in later times in other villages. In a text from 428, a wineseller in Hermopolis pays in advance a potter in a village in that nome producing more than 1,200 wine jars for him.[92] Much of the village pottery production, and perhaps some other craft work as well, was conducted on the large properties of urban landowners.[93]

All this does not amount to a very diverse local economy for the villages. Apart from the low economic condition of the Arsinoite villages from which the main archives come, there is no reason to think that matters were much different later or elsewhere.[94] Prosperous Karanis in the second century had little more than what has already been mentioned: a goldsmith or jeweler, a trade found in one fifth-century Hermopolite village;[95] trades connected with care of the body, like doctor, barber, and undertakers of various sorts; and an occasional flutist for entertainment. (For priestly occupations, see below, p. 268.) A glance back at the Fayum villages in the third century B.C. suggests a far more diverse village economy, with many more trades.[96]

In second-century Karanis, the men working primarily at a trade other than agriculture amounted to no more than 6 percent of the adult male population.[97] Clearly at various times and places villages may have had a higher concentration of tradesmen, for example in the

[90]*PSI* VI 712 (*BL*) (295).

[91]*P.Oxy.* XLVI 3308 (373).

[92]*P.Flor.* III 314 (*BL*).

[93]See above, p. 84 and Wipszycka 1971, 231 ff.

[94]See van Minnen 1987, 39-40, for the limits to village production. Fikhman 1965 (cf. Wipszycka 1971, 218) and 1969, 151, has argued that there was no decline in craft production in the villages in Byzantine times. But his argument is based on Aphrodito and an assumption that it is typical, which is most unlikely.

[95]*P.Amst.* I 98 (Terton Kano).

[96]See the lists of *CPR* XIII and a forthcoming study of Ptolemaic census lists by W. Clarysse and D. J. Thompson.

[97]Geremek 1969, 94.

production of textiles. But in essence these villages were farmers' homes and agricultural centers. The dearth of other activity points all the more strongly to the critical place in the economy of the nomes occupied in the fourth century by the metropoleis, with their rich and varied markets (above, pp. 87-88).

Women in the Village Economy

The account of the village economy sketched so far, in which the actors are largely men, would suggest the exclusion of women from most economic activities. How far does this reflect reality? In a largely agricultural society, the answer must predominantly come from the land and its working. Women owned a significant portion of the land of Roman Egypt. The Karanis tax registers from the early fourth century indicate that about 17 percent of villager-owned land was held by women, and the figure is almost the same—18 percent—for metropolitan-owned land.[98] The surviving documentation for the shrunken arable land of fourth-century Theadelphia points to about 20 percent as the figure there.[99] Because these villages were struggling, they may not have been entirely typical. A study of women's property in Roman Egypt concluded that women owned about one-third of the real estate (village property, not arable land) at Soknopaiou Nesos and that second-century Karanis may have displayed a similar proportion.[100] That may be too high. It is based on the number of persons owning property, not on their holdings. At Philadelphia in 216/7 women owned about 25 percent of all land.[101]

Clearly such figures varied from place to place and time to time, but somewhere between one-sixth and one-quarter seems likely to be the normal range. These figures are all notably higher than women's share of land owned by city residents (cf. p. 92). Such holdings came to women mainly by inheritance of family wealth, both paternal and maternal.[102] That women owned one-quarter or less of the land certainly indicates that their shares in such property were not equal to

[98]Bagnall 1992b.

[99]*P.Sakaon* 4 (336) shows two women owning 56 arouras out of a total listed of about 270 ar. (About four entries, or perhaps a few more, are lost and left out of account here, but they probably amounted to no more than another 20 ar.)

[100]Hobson 1983.

[101]*P.Yale* III 145; cf. Bagnall 1992b.

[102]This is called into question by Gagos and van Minnen 1992, but (remarkably) on the basis of a papyrus in which it is explicitly stated that the land a woman is selling came to her by inheritance from her father!

those of male heirs,[103] whether because their inheritance came partly in movables or simply because males received larger shares of the total. Often enough, however, only female children survived to inherit.[104] That could be a vulnerable position, particularly if the orphaned girls were young. Male relatives sometimes moved in to grab anything they could, leading to later litigation.[105] Not only relatives: an employer might seize property under guise of recovering his own goods in the care of the decedent.[106] But the aggressiveness and ability of village women should not be underestimated. One petition tells a characteristic story from Theadelphia. Kaet and his sister Annous owned and farmed jointly some land inherited from their father. When Kaet died, leaving a widow and two minor children, Annous kept farming her share of the land but managed to stick the widow, Artemis, with the taxes on the whole estate.[107]

One way for a woman to manage landed property was to lease it out. The complexity of village lease arrangements has already been suggested above (pp. 119-21). Leasing was not necessarily a simple solution. An Oxyrhynchite petition records the travails of a village woman who had with much difficulty recovered (by petition) land misappropriated by others. After leasing it out, she now finds that her tenants have been beaten up by villagers, and she asks that the tenants be protected so that she will be able to pay the taxes.[108] The problems of being a woman surrounded by rapacious neighbors were not removed by having lessees. Still, no doubt most lease arrangements were more normal.[109]

Women were not, however, incapable of operating a farm themselves. The external character of the evidence generally makes it impossible to see just how this was done, whether with family help,[110]

[103]Unfortunately, wills from late Roman Egypt are too few in number to allow any systematic description of testamentary patterns; cf. my remarks in *Studies in Roman Law in Memory of A. Arthur Schiller*, ed. R. S. Bagnall and W. V. Harris (Leiden 1986) 1-3, for a list and discussion.

[104]For example, the case of Taesis and Kyrillous, the daughters of Kopres, described in *P.Cair.Isid.* 62-64 (Karanis, *ca* 296-298).

[105]Cf. previous note; see also *P.Cair.Isid.* 77 (*BL*) (Karanis, 320), where two generations of all-female heirs in one family are attested.

[106]E.g., *P.Sakaon* 36 (Theadelphia, *ca* 280), in which a wealthy man who had hired the late Kaet to take care of his flocks, seized Kaet's own sheep and goats after his death on pretense of recovering his own animals: or so Kaet's widow says, anyway.

[107]*P.Sakaon* 37 (284).

[108]*SB* III 6294 (*P.Freib.* 11; *BL*) (Oxyrhynchos, 336).

[109]Examples: *P.Col.* VII 179 (Karanis, 300), for an olive grove; *P.Michael.* 22 (*BL*) (Tebtunis, 291), for three cows.

[110]Perhaps the most likely case where suitable male relatives were around, as the frequent cases of men paying taxes or making declarations on behalf of mothers,

slaves, or hired labor. Loans of wheat in relatively large amounts, evidently destined for sowing, signal some such independent operations.[111] A woman barely making ends meet might find that tough to manage, as appears from a letter ordering that the interest on a widow's loan be forgiven, only the principal being collected.[112] Of course, a well-off woman might well be on the other end of the lending transaction, a position that also might expose her to violence. One woman, a landowner and daughter of a veteran, complains that, when she tried to collect a sum owing her, the debtor and his sister shut her up in his house and beat her severely.[113]

About the lives of women who were not among the possessors there is much less information. They did not generate much documentation. The kind of marginal life that these invisible women might have is visible in a loan contract from Karanis. Aurelia Taesis acknowledges to Aurelia Thaisarion that she owes three talents borrowed by her father. Taesis is to work off the interest—but not the principal—by weaving and doing household work in Thaisarion's house. She is not to be allowed to leave unless she can pay back the three talents, the equivalent of four years' income for many families at that time.[114] Her full-time services are valued here at something like the equivalent of eleven artabas of wheat per year, less than half of what one would need to support a family.[115] A combination of economic dependence and low valuation on women's work combines to put Taesis in a situation not much better than slavery. How much professional weaving, not for family use, went on in fourth-century villages is hard to say, given the lack of evidence.

Despite the tendency of the sources to obscure women's activities in the villages, it is clear that they extended over a large part of the

---

sisters, and wives would suggest (cf., e.g., *P.Cair.Isid.* 2 [Karanis, 298], in which Pankratios declares twenty-four olive trees for his mother Herois).

[111]See particularly the case of Aurelia Tetoueis (Bagnall 1977b with bibliography), who though heavily in debt seems to have been managing a significant estate in Karanis in the 370s. Her older sister Tamaleis was similarly occupied a half-century earlier: *P.Col.* VII 176 (Karanis, 325).

[112]*BGU* II 412 (*BL*) (provenance and date unknown).

[113]*P.Abinn.* 51 and 52 (*BL*) (Hermoupolis [Ars.], 346).

[114]*SB* IV 7358 (*BL*) (277).

[115]On a principal of three talents, at the normal interest rate of 12 percent, the annual interest would be 2,160 dr. Wheat at this time was about 200 dr. per artaba. It is interesting that one female slave sold around this time cost seven talents; Taesis was (at an effective price of three talents) a bargain! Cf. H.-J. Drexhage, "Zur Preisentwicklung im römischen Ägypten von ca. 260 n.Chr. bis zum Regierungsantritt Diokletians," *Münstersche Beiträge z. antiken Handelsgeschichte* 6.2 (1987) 30-45 at 36.

same range as men's, particularly in agriculture. Where a husband or adult son was at hand, women's property was managed with men's. But women found themselves more vulnerable than men on several fronts when they had to operate without the protection of a suitable male. Their problems, of debt, misappropriation, taxes, and violence, were not different in kind from those of men, but they were at times aggravated.

Government and Community

The documentation of fourth-century villages in large measure concerns or is generated by the abundant cadre of local officials, to the point that the reader of these papyri is inclined to see a manifestation of the bureaucracy so prominent in the stereotyped views of late antiquity and Byzantium. The reality, however, is very different and, in the end, suggests undergovernance rather than its reverse.

In the complex of obligations that may be described as "compulsory services,"[116] the village documents show three varieties. First come the metropolitan liturgies, nearly all tax collection offices. Villagers of the late third century encountered some of these collectors (for whom see below, pp. 157-60) or their agents at the local granaries, but for most of the fourth century they operated at the wholesale level, receiving shipments at the harbors and rarely present in the villages.[117] Far more important on the village scene were the village liturgies, numerous, burdensome, and frequent.[118] At the bottom of the pyramid—but correspondingly widespread—were the obligations for compulsory physical labor on public works of various sorts, to which practically every grown male was subject.

At the head of the village hierarchy stood the komarchs, varying in number. They had the important role of naming both their own successors[119] and the other liturgists for the village, and they had a key part in the distribution of tax burdens that fell on the village as an entity. Potential for abuse of these powers was considerable.[120] The komarchs were joined as supervisory officials by the *gnoster* and

[116]See Thomas 1983, 36, for terminology and typology. The basic reference works for this subject are Lewis 1982 and Lallemand 1964; this section also owes a good deal to work in progress by Jean-Jacques Aubert. Where no other references are given, the essential documentation may be found in Lallemand and Lewis.

[117]For the process see *P.Col.* VII, pp. 94-104.

[118]Lists may tend to exaggerate the number involved because of local or temporal variations in titles; the present account ignores the less significant of these.

[119]*SB* XVI 12829 (Philadelphia, 287).

[120]See, e.g., *P.Cair.Isid.* 71.

(rarely) an *ephoros*,[121] but their duties are much less well known. Although the office of the village secretary, the *komogrammateus*, had been abolished earlier in the third century, there certainly remained some recordkeeping function, and around 310 a secretary of the village is attested at Karanis[122] and elsewhere. In fact, the term *komogrammateus* reappears later in the fourth century.[123]

Much the best documented officeholders, however, are the tax collectors, with the *sitologoi* responsible for wheat and barley and *apaitetai* for many other things.[124] The obscure *tesserarius* and *quadrarius* also seem to be primarily concerned with taxes.[125] The principal collectors served in groups of numbers varying (apparently) according to the size of the village, so that even a village like Karanis with only 110 taxpayers might have a college of five *sitologoi*.

A further place in the collections system was occupied by a group of villagers appointed as *kephalaiotai*, "headmen." Karanis had ten or eleven of them—each in effect responsible for about ten landowners, probably.[126] They were responsible for ensuring and organizing the transportation of village grain taxes to the harbors and for distributing the compensation received from imperial authorities for compulsory deliveries outside the normal taxes. Their duties probably also extended to other, poorly-documented areas of tax collection and transportation, helping the tax collectors themselves to do their jobs. The burden of work was in this way spread around further.

Though rural security was to some degree in the hands of small detachments of the military, most routine police and surveillance duty was also in the hands of villagers appointed for this purpose. There was considerable local variation in the titles of these duties, and some may in fact have been a response to particular local conditions.[127] Changes over time intersect with these, to the point that identifying the relationship of offices like *eirenarchos* (a local peace officer) and

[121]Neither in Lewis 1982, perhaps for want of explicit attestation of a compulsory character, though that hardly seems doubtful. Cf. Lallemand 1964, 137 n.4, on the *gnoster*'s liturgical character, and *P.Charite* 15.52n. for further references.

[122]*P.Cair.Isid.* 68 (probably 309/310); not mentioned by Lewis 1982. Though Lallemand 1964, 137, seems to regard him as a paid employee, the context of the papyrus suggests otherwise.

[123]*CPR* VII 18 (prob. 379), cf. note to line 16.

[124]See now Palme 1989 for full documentation and discussion of the *apaitetai*.

[125]"A confusing variety of duties is attested in the documents," says Lewis 1982, 49, of the *tesserarius*.

[126]See Bagnall 1978b.

[127]The *agrophylax* is probably one such; see Bonneau 1988, who argues that this was the duty of guarding artificially irrigated land and its water-raising equipment, as distinct from inundated flood-plains.

archephodos (a chief of police) becomes difficult.[128] Such technical questions aside, however, the underlying principle remains the responsibility of the villagers to provide for their own security and, when asked, to be answerable to nome officials for such operations as delivering wanted men.

At the bottom of the pyramid, then, come the various forms of compulsory labor to which all adult men were liable. Local work on the irrigation system was probably the most important such obligation (see above, p. 23), but the village also met some particularly unattractive obligations. It was sometimes required to furnish one or two men for a specified period (a month or two, usually, sometimes longer) to work on major public or military works at a considerable distance from home. Such tasks included porterage of public grain in Alexandria,[129] canal work on a major watercourse,[130] serving as a sailor on the Nile,[131] quarrying and support operations at Alabastrine[132] and Alexandria,[133] baking bread at Memphis (probably for troops),[134] and no doubt many others from time to time. The villages usually dealt with such requisitions of personnel by distributing the cost among the taxpayers and hiring either a villager or someone from another village willing to perform the service for the money offered.

All these officials served without compensation, and probably none voluntarily, except perhaps on occasion the komarchs. The komarchs nominated all of them, first to the *strategos* and then, after the introduction of the *pagi*, to the *praepositus pagi*. Nomination was tantamount to appointment: protest was possible, but there is no evidence for successful protests of nomination to village liturgies in the fourth century.[135] Before Diocletian evidence was required of adequate means to undertake the financial risks of office, but this is no longer found in the fourth century.[136] That does not, however, mean that paupers were appointed; liturgists are on the whole men of

---

[128]See Lewis 1982, 21-22, for an example of the difficulty in making sense out of the pattern of attestations.

[129]Two months: *BGU* I 286 (*BL*) (Arsinoite, 306).

[130]"Trajan's River" (precursor of the Suez Canal): two months, cf. *P.Cair.Isid.* 81 (Karanis, 297).

[131]*P.Michael.* 28 (*BL*; *ZPE* 56 [1984] 128-29) (Herakleopolite, 313-314).

[132]Three months: *P.Sakaon* 22 and 24 (324 and 325).

[133]Two months: *P.Sakaon* 25 (327).

[134]*P.Sakaon* 23 (324).

[135]See Lewis 1982, 67.

[136]See Lewis 1982, 74. *CPR* VII 16 has been claimed to show a *poros* of 1,600 drachmas in 340, but as that figure was worth about a hundredth of an artaba of wheat at that date, it certainly cannot represent a *poros*.

moderate means or better.[137] Service in most village offices was for a year, but liability lasted until the last obligations resulting from the office were discharged, which might be several years. In a case like that of Aurelius Isidoros, the best known village liturgist of the century, ten liturgies in twenty years amounted to almost continuous service.[138]

In a small village, it is not difficult to imagine that a quarter or a third of the adult male population had some liturgical appointment, even without taking compulsory labor into account. When villagers met the bureaucracy, then, it was themselves. Estimating the time demands of these positions is difficult. They would be particularly significant around harvest-time, when taxes had to be exacted, but any given member of the college of *sitologoi* (probably the most burdensome appointment) probably had little official business during most of the remainder of the year. The series of appointments a man like Isidoros held was more likely to mean extra work at the busiest time of year than anything resembling a continuously absorbing job. The financial liability, should one fail to collect the full amount demanded by the government, may have been more threatening; but there is no evidence that would allow anything more definitive to be said.[139]

The supervisory officials, especially the komarchs, were also responsible for local expenditures on official business. There is no evidence to show how their annual budget, if there was one, was established, but several surviving accounts show their receipts and disbursements in some detail.[140] With their brief entries—readily comprehensible to those who made the accounts—they are often baffling to us, but they include many payments for gratuities to higher officials or to soldiers, seemingly acceptable entries in their reports to the nome officials. Supplying the wants of local military units, whether for food or for transportation, plays a considerable role.

The corollary of the wide distribution of state responsibilities among the landowners of a village was the absence of any real bureaucracy. In the archives of Karanis and Theadelphia, there is no

---

[137]See Bagnall 1978a for an analysis of the Karanis material, showing average holdings in the twenty to twenty-five aroura range for *sitologoi* and *apaitetai*.

[138]See *P.Cair.Isid.*, pp.11-17, for a list and analysis. The obligations of the chaff collectors of 310/311 were not extinguished until the summer of 314, or three years after their main period of collecting: see *P.Cair.Isid.* 13, introd.

[139]Despite the bleak picture painted by Boak and Youtie in *P.Cair.Isid.*, introduction.

[140]Examples: *P.Oxy.* VI 895 (*W.Chr.* 47) (305); *BGU* I 21 (*BL*) (Prektis, Hermopolite, 340); *SPP* XX 75 (*BL*) (Hermopolite, *ca* 338); perhaps *P.Oxy.* LVI 3874 (*ca* 345/6).

evidence for even a single regular resident employee of the imperial administration. Because such were scarce even at the city level (see above, p. 66), that should not be surprising. The villagers answered mainly to metropolitans who were themselves liturgists (see below, p. 157), and they in turn to the provincial administration. Imperial administration in the villages was characterized by its utter absence; only the military presence in the countryside gave any tangible sense that the central government existed.

That imperial absence, in the case of the cities, produced an extensive development of local institutions in the third and fourth centuries, as it had in the previous two centuries in cities throughout the Greek East. In the villages of Egypt, however, no such local political community and institutions came into being. There was no village council or assembly, not even any collective body of the current liturgical officials. Instead, virtually all governance was oriented toward the relationship with the metropolis, which had responsibility for the collection of the taxes from the village (see below, p. 157). That accountability was in turn passed on to the village, not in the form of even a limited autonomy—in the sense of self-management—but in the less beneficent form of collective responsibility for the village's obligations. Where a *koinon*, or "community," of a village appears,[141] it involves a community obligation for taxes on land; and where the term is used of smaller groups, they inevitably are rooted in profession or office, conferring joint or common responsibility for some function or sum.[142]

Only by verbal sleight-of-hand, then, can fourth-century villages be considered political communities. What the residents of a village had in common was answerability for a variety of demands from the state: taxes, physical labor, security, and local administration of all these. They satisfied these requirements as best they could and with as little time, money, effort, and produce as they could, by cooperating with each other to the extent necessary. The lack of any other political institution was exacerbated by the disintegration in the third century of the temples as a focus of community life (see below, p. 268), and the villages of the early fourth century give the impression of rudderless and captainless vessels.

[141]For example, *P.Abinn.* 66 and 67.
[142]Bonneau 1983 examines the evidence for what she calls "rural community" in late Roman Egypt and finds it lacking, all a matter of obligation imposed from above. Her conclusions are disputed by Gagos and van Minnen 1992, but their evidence—land registered to such a *koinon*—provides little support for their more optimistic views.

Some measure of leadership was ultimately provided by the development of the church. A striking example is offered by a papyrus from Karanis dated 439, the last dated document from that troubled village. In it, the twelve *presbyteroi* and five deacons of Karanis, together with "the rest, small and large, of those from the village," issue a statement forbidding the interception of water from a particular source and the cultivation of land around that source with the use of this water.[143] The clergy appear at the head of their people, forming them into a social contract in that they are giving orders to themselves more than to others.[144] The uniqueness of this document should restrain universal application of its pattern elsewhere. But it may be a sign that a re-creation of village community on a new basis was in progress, and a tale in Palladius offers a curious parallel. When the men of one village set out to attack another over the division of Nile water, a virgin warned by an angel asked the *presbyteroi* of the village to lead the resistance.[145]

Intervillage Links

Villages were thus connected to the larger world by their obligations to the imperial power for taxes and services.[146] They were connected to outsiders in many other ways. Economic and social ties to the cities will be examined in Chapter 4. But the nearest neighbors were generally other villages, the closest of which would on average be only a few kilometers away, an hour's walk. Although to an outside eye the Egyptian landscape may possess a certain uniformity, in reality it offered many local differences, the profitable exploitation of which was a longstanding economic habit of the rural population. A striking example is afforded by the temple center of Soknopaiou Nesos, on the north side of Lake Moeris, where religion and transit traffic from the desert were the mainstays of the economy, supple-

---

[143]*P.Haun.* III 58. See Bonneau 1979 for a detailed analysis, and see *ZPE* 28 (1978) 226 on the consular date.

[144]Karanis could not, obviously, legislate for other villages. The villagers' dual role of forbidding and being forbidden gives this the character of a *cheirographon*, a contract (cf. Bonneau 1979, 17), a fact that may help explain the confusion between nominative and dative in the enumeration of the parties.

[145]*HL* 31. As things turned out, they were too cowardly, and only her prayers stopped the invasion.

[146]This section owes much to Braunert 1964, although it diverges from his conclusions in many particulars. See also Keenan forthcoming (written in 1978), who points out that Braunert's conclusions for this period seem to owe more to traditional views of the late empire and less to his meticulous documentation than one would expect from the rest of the book.

mented by fishing in the lake.[147] The temple owned land in at least two nearby villages (Dionysias and Herakleia), and individuals in the village owned or farmed land in Herakleia, Apias, Nilopolis, Bacchias, and perhaps other villages. The virtual lack of arable land around Soknopaiou Nesos was thus for centuries made good by active use of the complementary resources of other villages.[148]

A shortage or surplus of agricultural labor in one village could be balanced by the needs of a neighboring village. To the extent that this market worked by hiring free laborers, as we have seen, it rarely generated documentation. The paper trail that survives is mainly from leases, which show both landowners leasing out to local residents parcels they owned in villages where they did not live and villagers leasing land in villages other than their own, presumably because these offered better opportunities than land in their own villages.[149] Though one would expect such transactions to involve closely neighboring villages, it was not always so. One lease application involves a lessee from Thraso, on the west side of the Fayum, and land in Boubastos, on the east side—a distance of some 55 km in a straight line.[150] In such a case, the lessee may well have moved for part or all of the growing season to the location of the land.

Such activity could also cross nome boundaries.[151] Philadelphia, on the northeast side of the Fayum, had since its founding had close ties to the Nile valley, which lay across a narrow (10 km) strip of desert from it.[152] A series of papyri shows residents of the Aphroditopolite Nome, on the east side of the Nile but accessible to Philadelphia in a day's journey, leasing several small parcels of land there.[153]

[147]Hobson 1984 gives a detailed analysis.

[148]"Soknopaiou Nesos was not the village to be in if you were a farmer, but it might not have been a bad place for a priest or a camel driver," says Hobson (1984, 108). Ultimately the village was abandoned by the middle of the third century; it is not clear why the complex act of the previous three centuries could no longer be sustained.

[149]Braunert 1964, 193 and 308, discusses this phenomenon. He believes that the balance between these two types of transaction swung drastically in the third century toward lessees taking land in other villages, but he sees a reversal in the fourth century. The small documentary base for the third century (he cites only nineteen leases pertinent to the question), however, makes this an exercise in pseudo-statistics.

[150]P.Sakaon 70 (338).

[151]Braunert 1964, 300 and 316, saw a decline in business trips and an increasing limitation of them to the boundaries of the intra-Egyptian provinces; the evidence seems insufficient to support such conclusions.

[152]Clarysse 1980, esp. 95-97; his map shows the situation clearly.

[153]BGU II 408 (312); I 349 and II 409 (BL) (313); P.Gen. I 13 (314). These largely concern a single person's activities, and it seems likely that this man cultivated a number of small parcels in Philadelphia, perhaps not large enough or good enough

Nor is such leasing merely a specialty of the Fayum. A parcel of land in the north Hermopolite village of Ibion Panektyreos, owned by a resident of the metropolis, was leased to a resident of another village.[154] Egyptian farmers were often enterprising in looking for and exploiting economic opportunities created by the complex patterns of land ownership and residence.[155]

Military camps in villages provided additional complexities. The cavalry camp at Dionysias, unique only in its documentation, naturally demanded goods and services from the surrounding villages, even at some distance.[156] Soldiers, a comparatively well-off group with fungible assets, made up an important source of loans. In a papyrus of 362, a resident of Andromachis acknowledges a loan of six artabas of wheat from a soldier from the camp at Dionysias; interestingly, the wheat is handed over neither in Dionysias nor at Andromachis, but in a third village, Pisais.[157] It may be that the soldier owned land near Pisais from which the surplus wheat was available, but other explanations are certainly possible. Loan relationships between civilians usually featured metropolites as lenders and villagers as borrowers, but intervillage lending—even across nome lines, once again—is known.[158]

All these individual activities involve short-range and short-term movement from village to village, in an intricate pattern of business trips, seasonal migration, daily commuting to work, and regular marketing. Together with the close links of villages and metropoleis, these ties bound villages together in a network of economic activity; social ties that generate no documents probably paralleled those of land, wheat, and money. There is little evidence that many people made more permanent moves from one village to another, actual changes of legal residence.[159] Such changes would properly require the consent of the authorities, but no such authorizations survive; in

---

to attract a local lessee.

[154]*P.Flor.* I 17 (*BL*) (Hermopolis, 341).

[155]A particularly interesting example, from an earlier period, is *P.Soter.*; cf. Bagnall 1980.

[156]Cf. *P.Fay.* O.21 (Euhemeria, 306), a receipt given to a resident of Taurinou for chaff delivered to the camp at Dionysias.

[157]*P.Flor.* I 30.

[158]Cf. *P.Oslo* II 37 (295), in which a man from Dimios (in the Memphite) borrows from a man of Philadelphia five art. of wheat; both loan and repayment are in Philadelphia.

[159]Cf. Keenan forthcoming, who points out that documents tend more often to attest temporary changes of residence from one nome to another than within a given nome; perhaps such internome moves were simply more important.

many cases, however, no one would care enough to object.[160] The very poor, who were not part of the land-based system of public obligations, could go. From a decaying village like Theadelphia, movement was attractive. Where people left without permission, however, their fellow villagers had every reason to try to get them back, because otherwise they were liable for the taxes on the land of the departed. The Theadelphians sought out their decamped compatriots in the Oxyrhynchite and Kynopolite nomes and asked the authorities to force them to return.[161] Karanis was visited by village officials from Bouto, in the Memphite Nome, looking for fugitives—successfully, as it happened; Aurelius Isidoros got a receipt for turning over two men to them.[162]

At the communal level, Fayum villages had a complex interdependence, growing out of the unique hydrological character of the area. Canal water, on its way from the Nile to Lake Moeris, passed by some villages before others. Those villages furthest along the canal network were dependent upon both the competence of dike and canal maintenance at the earlier villages and the good will—or at least absence of malevolence—of their neighbors.[163] The best-known case is that of Theadelphia, which not only failed to receive the water it needed but also left ample documentation of its vociferous attempts to remedy the problem. At various times they blamed the residents of Philagris, Andromachis, Narmouthis, Hermoupolis, and Theoxenis for their plight, at one point asking that Theadelphia be attached to Hermoupolis, "the rich village in the plain."[164] At the other extremity

[160]Braunert 1964, 311-14, discusses the question of villagers' changes of residences in some detail, concluding that there was in the fourth century no longer room in the system for free permanent movement, in large part because of the corporate responsibility of landowners in a village for its taxes and liturgical obligations. He notes that large landowners might well move to the cities; but it is equally true that those with little or no property could disappear without any impact on the system.

[161]P.Sakaon 44 = P.Turner 44 (331/2); cf. Braunert 1964, 310-12, who supposes that the request was—like most attempts to control the movements of peasants—ultimately unsuccessful.

[162]P.Cair.Isid. 128 (314). Cf. also P.Cair.Isid. 126 (?308/9), a letter of one praepositus to another, reminding him of the imperial edict that villagers residing elsewhere without permission are to be returned to their idia and asking his help in repatriating Karanidians now elsewhere. He offers in return help collaring those from his colleague's pagus.

[163]The authorities were well aware of the importance of a clear flow of water and invested resources in it. Cf., e.g., P.Stras. VI 538 (Narmouthis, after 281), a report from five public hydrophylakes to an aigialophylax, reporting on irrigation works on a long canal spanning several villages.

[164]See P.Sakaon 32, 33, 35, 42, and 45 for various stages of the struggle, ultimately unsuccessful, to keep Theadelphia watered. Cf. Braunert 1964, 316, on the

of the nome, Philadelphia blamed problems at Tanis for their own lack of drinking and irrigation water.[165] Such conflict between villages also occurred elsewhere over the control of floodwaters; the anecdote in Palladius mentioned above (p. 138) of an expeditionary force from one village that set out to attack another village gives as their motive the division of water from the inundation.

On the Margins

The villages of Egypt, as described so far, were essentially agricultural in a broad sense, growers of wheat, barley, grapes, olives, and other crops. But they had another productive dimension, the raising of animals, especially sheep. Individual farmers, to be sure, had their pigs and chickens, but sheep (and goats with them) were often a larger-scale enterprise, found in every part of Egypt for which we have documentation.[166] Shepherds occupy historically rather varying niches in agricultural societies, but they tend toward the edges even when they are not actually outsiders.[167] Egyptian shepherds were certainly marginal in the sense that they would lease land on the borders of the cultivable, such as the shores of Lake Moeris or the currently unirrigated land known as *chersos*, large quantities of which might be had for a low rent.[168] They were also marginal in a social sense, frequently coming into conflict with the landowners of their villages over the trampling or consumption of standing crops by their

---

absorption of weak villages by stronger ones.

[165]See *P.Wisc.* I 32 (*BL*) (Philadelphia, 305).

[166]See generally Keenan 1985b and Keenan 1989, with rich bibliography and many references. Keenan 1989 points out that it was once claimed that sheep raising was unimportant in Egypt, but that the papyri have demonstrated the contrary. He does, however, suggest that pastoralism is attested mainly for atypical topography (Arsinoite, Oxyrhynchite, Aphrodito) rather than "Nile bank villages." The evidence from the Herakleopolite and Hermopolite, however, points to greater universality: cf., e.g., sheep or shepherds in *CPR* I 40 (*BL*) (Herakleopolis, 300); *SB* XIV 12167 (*P.Erl.* 52) (Upper Egypt, 314); *P.Erl.* 107.4 and 110.19 (Upper Egypt, *ca* 314); *P.Lips.* 37 (*BL*) (Hermopolis, 389); *P.Ross.Georg.* V 60 (Hermopolis, end of 4c); *P.Lond.* V 1653 (Panopolite, 2nd half 4c)—to mention only some from our period.

[167]Models range from livestock raising as part of agriculture to nomadic pastoralism and long-distance transhumance. See Kehoe 1990, reviewing C. R. Whittaker, ed., *Pastoral Economies in Classical Antiquity* (Cambridge 1988). That volume, as Keenan has pointed out (*AJP* 110 [1989] 669 and 1989, 176), ignores not only Egypt but the eastern provinces of the Roman Empire as a whole.

[168]For the north shore of Lake Moeris, see D. Samuel, *ZPE* 33 (1979) 227-28; animal grazing can be seen on the south shore today. For leases of *chersos*, see, e.g., *CPR* I 40 (*BL*) (Herakleopolis, 300), a lease of fifty arouras at the village of Tokois to be sown with hay for grazing sheep. The rent of 250 dr. per aroura amounts in value to less than a half-artaba of wheat at this date.

animals.[169] The fourth-century papyri have their share of the usual complaints, such as a petition in which Isidoros complains to the *logistes* that Melas and shepherds employed by him have grazed sheep on one aroura of his land, which was sown with hay. After his first complaint, Melas and associates filed a countercomplaint. Isidoros makes it clear that this is habitual behavior for Melas.[170]

And yet the shepherds were not outsiders. With no high pastures to visit in the summer, Egypt's sheep stayed home, and the shepherds (with their dogs[171]) were part of the village population. Moreover, the raisers of sheep were in some cases not only lessees of village land[172] but also local landowners. Such most notably were Sakaon of Theadelphia and his family, who grew wheat and barley and raised sheep, both his own and those he took on lease from others.[173] The integration of agriculture and sheep raising offered many benefits, such as the use of the animals' manure as fertilizer and the ability to use productively green fodder from fields planted in nitrogen-fixing crops rotated with wheat. At the same time, milk, cheese, and meat from the flocks formed a welcome enrichment of the diet with high-quality protein.

The predominant use of the flocks, however, was for the production of wool, the main source of fabric for clothing, and owners of flocks can be observed choosing a "wool strategy" in many documents.[174] The use of marginal land is particularly well-suited to this strategy, and the importance of sheep in documentation from Theadelphia may well have something to do with its place on the edge of the cultivated area and the uncertainty of its irrigation in this period.[175] Particularly where land might be cultivable one year and not the next, animal husbandry could buffer the vicissitudes of agriculture. It could readily be expanded by hiring more shepherds. The documentation in fact comes mainly from middlemen—entre-

[169]Keenan 1985b and 1989 discusses much of the evidence and of strategies used to cope with the problem.

[170]*P.Cair.Isid.* 79 (Karanis, early 4c).

[171]See *P.Laur.* IV 189 (3/4c).

[172]As Keenan 1989 has described; they probably grew fodder crops in most cases.

[173]Compare *P.Sakaon* 46 and 47, petitions from 342 addressed to the *praepositus pagi* and to Abinnaeus, concerning the seizure of eighty-two sheep of his by another man, and *P.Sakaon* 39 (318), about sixteen goats leased by Sakaon from a retired *primipilaris*, which were pastured on the plain of Berenikis Aigialou, i.e., on marginal shore-land, and rustled by two men whom Sakaon identifies.

[174]See Keenan 1989 for a full discussion.

[175]Although sheep rearing was not new in late antiquity there; cf. for the middle of the third century J. Schwartz, "Une famille de chepteliers au IIIe S. p.C.," *RechPap* 3 (1964) 49-96.

preneurs who both owned and leased flocks but hired others to tend the sheep.

Marginal or integrated, sheepowners and shepherds belonged to the society of the "black land," green land reached by the Nile's water. But that green occupies only a small part of the expanse of northeast Africa. For all the valley, for the edges of the Delta, and for most of the Fayum, the desert lay always close at hand. The desert itself was diverse in character and served several purposes. The nearer portions, within ten km or so—or the "Outer Desert" as it is called in the monastic literature—had for ages served as a refuge. With numerous caves and wadis in many regions, this zone hid outlaws or fugitives from government demands for taxation or liturgies;[176] it was the escape valve for the sometimes tightly structured life of the cultivated land. Its nearest part, right on the sharp line between cultivation and desert, was the site of many villages, which did not waste cultivable land. And Egyptian cemeteries for thousands of years had regularly used nearby deserts, a practice that not only spared usable land but ensured better preservation of the bodies. But beyond that field-hugging zone, one did not live there regularly, and when Antony began to edge out into the desert, it was a novelty.[177]

It did not remain so, as numerous monasteries sprang up in the fourth and fifth centuries in this desert zone. It must be remembered that the desert of the monastic literature is mainly this strip of desert along the cultivated land; those who fled further into the "Inner Desert" were a much-discussed but small minority. The monastic sites along the valley have a paradoxical situation, at once close to the valley from which virtually every physical necessity comes, yet seeming to belong to another world, so drastic is the change in environment from black land to red land. This proximate remoteness from the activity of "Egypt" (as desert-dwellers referred to the cultivated land)[178] is an experience still readily accessible to visitors to monastic sites. Its practical consequences deserve further exploration (see below, p. 297).

The further reaches of the deserts had uses more commercial than the isolation demanded by the most ascetic monks. For one thing, they contained mines and quarries, sources of gold and of luxury building

[176] A long-lasting theme: see *HM* 14.5-6, where the wife of a man imprisoned for a 300 gold piece (solidi) debt to the treasury flees to the desert to avoid further harassment—her children have already been sold—by archons and *bouleutai*.

[177] See *VAnt* 3 (p. 7.6); the text represents the nearer desert as being on the edge of the village; he then moved further out: *VAnt* 8 (p. 14.9).

[178] *VAnt* 57 (p. 58.8).

stone, like the brilliant porphyry beloved of Roman imperial architects. There were certainly quarries in the nearer desert too, and it is often impossible to say which are meant by vague references in the papyri.[179] The logistical difficulties of operations in the desert between the Nile and the Red Sea were considerable, but the rewards obviously were sufficient to make the trouble worthwhile for the government. The bulk of the evidence for Roman exploitation of the Eastern Desert comes from the first century and a half of the empire, when roads were built or improved, numerous forts and way-stations constructed, significant forces deployed for security, and extensive quarrying and mining operations carried out.[180] There are, however, signs that the fourth century saw renewed (if not continued) efforts to control and exploit the quarries at Mons Porphyrites, the stone from which was at the zenith of its popularity.[181]

The same roads that led to these resources also led to ports on the Red Sea coast, vital terminals for sea trade with India.[182] That trade, given the difficulties and costs of transport, seems largely to have been in luxuries. There has been until now little to suggest that these roads were still in active use in the fourth century, but recent excavations near the supposed site of Myos Hormos, at Abu Sha'ar, have revealed the construction, or perhaps reconstruction, in 309-310 of a substantial fort, evidently the base of an *ala*.[183] The dedicatory inscription, mentioning merchants (*mercator[um]*), suggests that the commercial advantages of the region were not forgotten any more than its own resources.

[179]The best attested is the alabaster quarry near Alabastrine, for which see M. Drew-Bear 1979, 56-61, 213. It drew workers from at least as far away as the Fayum. References from the fourth century include *P.Flor.* I 3 = *W.Chr.* 391 (Hermopolis, 301); *P.Sakaon* 22 (324) and 24 (325).

[180]The introduction to *O.Florida* gives a general description and bibliography. See also R. E. Zitterkopf and S. E. Sidebotham, "Stations and Towers on the Quseir-Nile Road," *JEA* 75 (1989) 155-89; S. E. Sidebotham et al., "Fieldwork on the Red Sea Coast: The 1987 Season," *JARCE* 26 (1989) 127-66 (both with extensive bibliography); J. Bingen, "Première campagne de fouille au Mons Claudianus, rapport préliminaire," *BIFAO* 87 (1987) 45-52; M. J. Klein, *Untersuchungen zu den kaiserlichen Steinbrüchen an Mons Porphyrites und Mons Claudianus in der östlichen Wüste Ägyptens* (Bonn 1988). See Isaac 1990, esp. 102-103, for the army's role in controlling lines of communication. For quarries see also above, p. 42 n. 199.

[181]*SB* V 8162 (*SEG* 13.604) is the fourth-century dedicatory inscription of a catholic church of Melitios at Mons Porphyrites, renewed by the *eparchikos* and the chief stonecutters and the rest of the craftsmen. See also the fourth-century ostrakon published by H. Cuvigny in *Mélanges Étienne Bernand* (Paris 1991) 193-96.

[182]Apart from the works cited in n. 180, see for the Indian trade Lionel Casson, *The Periplus Maris Erythraei* (Princeton 1989), with rich commentary.

[183]Unpublished inscriptions, to be published by Bagnall and Sheridan. For the similar tetrarchic activity in the Syro-Palestinian area, see Isaac 1990, 164.

In the other direction from the Nile lay the oases of the western desert.[184] The Great Oasis, in the south, was closely tied to the Thebaid, with road links to the major valley centers between Syene and Lykopolis.[185] The Small Oasis, further north, depended above all on the Oxyrhynchite Nome, but roads also connected it with the Hermopolite and the edges of the Fayum. There was a steady traffic between the oases and the valley, of a less exotic sort than on the way to India; the Oases were more integrated into Egyptian life than was the Eastern Desert. The economy of the oases depended, unlike that in the valley, on irrigation from wells. Though wheat was grown, barley seems to have been more common, and there is ample evidence for import of wheat into the oases (especially the Small Oasis, from the Fayum). There is also evidence for the growing of cotton.[186] The unique contribution of the oases, however, was the exploitation of their alum deposits, from which this substance essential for tanning and dyeing was extracted and exported.[187] The Small Oasis also produced and exported natron (cf. above, p. 44).[188] There is also reason to think that areas so dependent on transportation by camel and donkey raised these animals and exported them to the valley.[189]

The desert was not always a source of benefits. The characteristics that made it a good refuge made it a good hideout, easy to burst out of and fade back into. The extensive traffic and government control of roads and desert areas, both east and west of the Nile, kept any desert-based brigandage at a minimum during most of the Roman period. But insecurity could strike if that control slackened. And, during the imperial turmoil of the middle of the third century, it did. Nubian desert tribes, generally referred to by the sources as Blemmyes, moved north and began to menace Upper Egypt with their raids.[190] From that time through the fifth century they and other tribes

[184]See above all Wagner 1987, a monumental compilation and analysis on which what follows largely depends.

[185]Wagner 1987, 152, summarizes the road network; connections to the Theban region and to Tentyra seem to be particularly close.

[186]See *O.Douch* 51; Wagner 1987, 291-93.

[187]Wagner 1987, 306-9.

[188]In *P.Abinn.* 9 an officer of the natron monopoly reminds Abinnaeus that any natron imported is to be impounded, and the persons importing it, together with their beasts (presumably camels) detained. Cf. Wagner 1987, 130 n.11.

[189]See the remarkable *P.Genova* II App. 1 (319) and *P.Genova* I 21 (cf. *P.Genova* II App. 2) with Wagner 1987, 319-20 and 327-28: two contracts in succeeding years concerning a partnership to buy animals in the Oasis and take them to Egypt for sale.

[190]Demicheli 1976 provides an exhaustive analysis of the very inadequate sources, more literary than documentary and often not inspiring very much confidence. For the background, see R. Updegraff-L. Török, "The Blemmyes I," *ANRW*

periodically renewed their attacks on the valley, although threats to Middle Egypt were exceptional. The relationship of these tribes to Egyptian civilization and religion was complex, and it was in part their support of Philai's temple that made it one of the last bastions of pagan worship in Egypt. This is perhaps the one area where the Egyptian "frontier" zone displayed some of the characteristics of frontiers elsewhere in the empire.[191] At times these peoples were in diplomatic contact with the court at Constantinople; the military commander Abinnaeus accompanied a Blemmyite mission to the capital and back, spending three years in all with the representatives of the nomads.[192] At times they were simply the unpredictable enemy of settled life—even occasionally of the ascetic desert-dwellers.[193] Other tribes, too, occasionally caused trouble on the margins.[194] Their importance, however, should not be exaggerated. Despite the army activity directed to controlling desert roads, military units were mainly stationed not in the desert but where they could be easily supplied, in the valley.[195]

10.1 (Berlin-New York 1988) 44-106; L. Török, *Late Antique Nubia* (Antaeus 16, Budapest 1988). Cf. also D. Feissel-K. A. Worp, *OMRO* 68 (1988) 97-111; V. Christides, "Ethnic Movements in Southern Egypt and Northern Sudan," *LF* 103 (1980) 129-43 (ignorant of Demicheli). See Isaac 1990, 100, for the lack of evidence of trouble with nomads in the Levant until the fourth century.

[191]As described by, e.g., C. R. Whittaker, "Trade and Frontiers of the Roman Empire," *Trade and Famine in Classical Antiquity*, ed. P. Garnsey and C. R. Whittaker (Cambridge Philological Society, Suppl. vol. 8, Cambridge 1983) 110-27.

[192]*P.Abinn.* 1.

[193]For the complex relationship between raiding tribes and settled communities, cf. P. Mayerson, "Saracens and Romans: Micro-Macro Relationships," *BASOR* 274 (1989) 71-79.

[194]Isaac 1990, 76 (with nn.102 and 103) on Berber migrations around 410.

[195]Isaac 1990, 133, points out a similar situation in the East more generally, but his explanation (problems in controlling the urban population) need not be correct, at least for Egypt.

CHAPTER 4

City and Country

Managing the Land

Many aspects of the interaction of the cities and their rural surroundings have already been considered separately in the two preceding
chapters. But several subjects cut across the physical organization of
the nomes and demand a more coordinated treatment. As always, the
most basic is land. Both metropolitans and villagers owned agricultural land. Fragments of the pattern by which they exploited their
property have emerged from the separate discussions in the two
preceding chapters. Because agriculture was the most important
single area in which city and village residents encountered one
another, it is critical to attempt a description, however incomplete, of
how the fragmentary pieces fit together.

Villagers owned somewhere between two-thirds and three-
quarters of the land in the average village, although the actual percentage may have been lower or higher in particular cases.[1] Within the
village landowning class a relatively large middle group had enough
land to support a family, and the overall degree of inequality of distribution was lower than among city residents. The latter included
some great magnates with holdings greater than a thousand arouras, a
larger group of the very wealthy, and still larger groups of those with
an adequate base for support and those with very small holdings. The
major distinction is that the group of moderate landholders with
enough to support a family, those in the 10 to 50 aroura range,
amounted to 67 percent of village owners, but only 38 percent of
Antinoite and 30 percent of Hermopolite metropolitan owners. The
extremes mainly belonged to the city residents, although three villagers of Karanis held more than 100 arouras.

The evidence does not show clearly whether any substantial
change in this situation had occurred in the two hundred years before

[1]For the analysis underlying these remarks, see Bagnall 1992b; at Karanis in 309
the figure was as high as 86 percent (in a situation unattractive to outside investment), while in the Hermopolite Nome it was apparently overall as low as 65 to 70
percent. The Aphrodito records (Gascou and MacCoull 1987) show about 26 percent
as *astika*, "citizen accounts." Though that cannot be taken to reflect the status of
owners at the time of these registers, it probably does reflect that at an earlier period.

the fourth-century documentation; nor is it obvious that it altered much in the next two hundred. There is at least as much indication of villagers acquiring land from metropolitans as the reverse in the fourth-century papyri, and similar patterns can still be observed in the sixth century.[2] Despite persistent belief among scholars that the fourth century is the scene of a massive change in agricultural landholding in the direction of concentration of land into "large estates," the attachment of peasants to the land, and a growing importance of protection—patronage—by the powerful, there is little to support such notions.[3] Reality was far more complex, and basic patterns inherited from the past more tenacious.

The structure of land ownership in the villages strongly suggests the seemingly obvious: the bulk of the land was farmed directly by members of the family that owned it. Some more detailed support for that proposition has been given in chapter 3, but it is in the nature of the documentation that most such activity escapes modern scrutiny. Small holders farming their own fields need no leases, no rent receipts, no applications for parts of machinery—that is, none of the paper generated by more complicated arrangements.[4] Even their tax receipts may reveal nothing about how they farmed their land. It is harder to say for certain if a similar pattern existed among urban residents with landholdings in the zone around the cities, particularly given the absence of the section of the Hermopolite register dealing with that zone. But all that zone was certainly within a two-hour walk or donkey ride from the center of the city; indeed, much more than that one pagus was within an easy walk. There may have been a concentration of orchards and gardens, rather than grainland, near the city, but there seems no reason not to suppose that city residents were a part of those who cultivated the orchards and gardens. Moreover, the concentration of Hermopolite and Antinoopolite holdings in the other pagi nearest those cities suggests an active rather than passive role for the owners.[5]

[2] Well analyzed by Keenan 1980 on the basis of one fairly well-documented case at Aphrodito.

[3] Lewuillon-Blume 1979, 177, assumes that these propositions are "sans conteste."

[4] Even in more complex situations, of course, paperwork may be lacking; cf. Keenan 1985a, 138 n.6: "For Byzantine Egypt, it is impossible to gauge the documentary loss, or to estimate the (possible) importance of oral agreements at certain levels of these arrangements."

[5] See Bowman 1985, 160, for a table. The 6th and 8th pagi had notably large amounts of Hermopolite ownership, the 5th and 6th of Antinoite. Bowman points out (152) that the large Hermopolite holdings in the 15th pagus result almost entirely from four very large holdings.

For urban landowners with very small holdings—remember that 53 percent of Hermopolite and 40 percent of Antinoite landowners have listed holdings smaller than ten arouras—there were essentially two options: direct farming, where the property was near enough, and leasing. Estates of such small size did not warrant the use of middlemen and agents, and leases were normally executed directly by tenants with the owner or a family member; even with holdings in the fifty-aroura range, such direct dealings were normal enough.[6] Some of the abundant surviving leases undoubtedly record such relationships, although too few lessors are otherwise known to allow many such cases to be described. Leasing, though providing some stability and perhaps in many cases the highest profit, had its problems; tenants might refuse either to pay rent or to leave, especially when they had held the land for a long time and a new owner inherited it.[7]

The large owners, the "honorables" (*euschemones*), however—the top 10 percent of the urban landowning population and the top 1 percent of the entire urban population—offer the most complex and interesting picture.[8] With holdings of 100 arouras and more, they could not even with some hired help farm the land themselves. Nor, no doubt, did they wish to; the purpose of such wealth was to allow its possessor to live in the city free from just such work. Much surviving documentation from the third, fourth, and fifth centuries concerns these men and women and the operations of their estates, and the same remains true in the sixth century. A description of how the system worked in that period is equally applicable to the fourth century: "The prototypical (secular) landlord in mind here is the middle-level absentee who, owning land in more than one venue, operates locally through agents. . . . The agents stand responsible to their landlord for collecting yearly rents and dues. They rent out the landlord's land to local middlemen. In their turn, the middlemen oversee, and may even assist in, the land's farming, but the land is principally worked by sub-lessees and by work-contract and day-labor hirelings."[9]

[6]See the case of Serenilla and her family, above, pp. 93-94. For sixth-century analogues, Keenan 1985a, 141.

[7]*CPR* V 9 (Hermopolis, 339), a petition in which the complainant, whose mother had recently inherited the land, describes the lessee's behavior as "rustic audacity." See Foxhall 1990, 100-104, on the attractions—both economic and social—from the landlord's point of view of lease arrangements.

[8]In the sixth century, they have been joined by institutional owners, all religious, which are absent in the fourth century.

[9]Keenan 1985a, 137-38. He points out that subleasing and hired labor are the poorest-documented features of the system, as is true also in the fourth century.

That system, in all its complexity and responsiveness to local conditions, was a logical solution for medium-sized holdings or for the smaller, less concentrated parts of large holdings.[10] Such arrangements might be stable for generations and they involved an efficient use—from the owners' point of view—of the rural work force.[11] It was also a sensible method for soldiers or officials to manage their land if they moved around.[12] But it was not the only possible method. There were also larger, more concentrated estates, directly operated and managed by staff hired or owned by the landowners, country seats of a kind known two centuries and more earlier and with which the possessors were identified (see above, p. 70).[13] These are sometimes described as *epoikia*, "hamlets."[14] They were not necessarily fully consolidated holdings stretching unbroken over large tracts, but they required at least large holdings within a small enough radius to support a central establishment, with facilities allowing some degree of self-sufficiency. Although undoubtedly no two were alike, typical features included a mill, pottery works, water storage, storehouses, presses for oil and wine, dwellings, and a variety of plantings of vines and trees as well as ordinary farmland.[15] Elaborate construction projects continued the improvement of such properties.[16] No doubt some properties with many of these features were leased out as an entity, particularly if the lessor had other such estates.[17] A large estate

[10]*SB* XVI 13035 (Oxyrhynchos, 341), with its variety of holdings and crops, probably is an example. Part of Aurelia Charite's holdings were handled this way, as the numerous leases in *P.Charite* show.

[11]*P.Oxy.* XXXIV 2712 (*BL*) (292/3) shows us such a long-term relationship only at the point of its apparent disintegration. See Foxhall 1990 for tenancy patterns in Greece and Italy.

[12]One instance is Fl. Taurinos, a soldier in the *numerus Maurorum*, stationed in Lykopolis in 426 (*BGU* XII 2137 [426]), but later in Hermopolis (*BGU* XII 2138 ff.). By 446 he had risen to the status of *centenarius* (*BGU* XII 2141).

[13]Keenan 1985a, 168-69, notes the absence of such in Aphrodito in the sixth century, contrary to the Oxyrhynchite picture, whatever the reason.

[14]Though that word may refer to other settlements too. See Lewuillon-Blume 1979 for a good description of the *epoikia* and some of the clearest documents, though her view (184) that they are a new phenomenon in the fourth century is contradicted by evidence she cites (182) from the third century.

[15]Lewuillon-Blume 1979, 182.

[16]E.g., *P.Ant.* I 46 (*ca* 337-348? [*BL*]), an account of construction costs.

[17]An example may be the *ktema* of *P.Herm.* 26 (5c), which included a cistern, palm trees, acacias, mulberry trees, a house, and other appurtenances. The rent of 140 art. of wheat, 13 art. of barley, and 2 solidi + 18 carats of gold is enough to suggest a property of 35 ar. or so. Another is the 30.75 ar. property, irrigated by a waterwheel, of *P.Mich.* XI 611 (*BL*) (Plelo, Oxyrhynchite, 412). The rent includes 120 art. of wheat, 40 art. of barley, and smaller amounts of vegetables and hay, a total equivalent to about 150 art. of wheat.

possessed transport animals and a boat or two to facilitate the constant traffic in people and goods between country and city.[18]

The best known case of this sort is the "estate" of Aurelius Appianus, a third-century Alexandrian notable whose extensive holdings in the Fayum were concentrated around nuclei in as many as forty villages.[19] Each unit had its own manager and some permanent staff, but they were supplemented by part-time workers and lessees in an effort to exploit the unit's land in the most cost-effective fashion. Given that the units differed greatly in the kinds of land they included, the exact pattern of labor deployment also varied by unit. Transportation services and most marketing of cash crops were centralized in a management center in the nome metropolis. The estate sought and obtained a considerable degree of self-sufficiency in providing its operating needs, but this good was always subservient to the pressure to keep costs low and profits high.

The exploitation of such an estate was certainly a complicated matter. Some land was leased to tenants, of varying degrees of dependency.[20] Other parts were farmed by hired labor, perhaps even by slaves, though there is little evidence for them.[21] Even lease contracts themselves sometimes seem ambiguous, covering a relationship in which lease of facilities and hiring of labor seem to be the same act.[22] Managing the whole enterprise was a group of business agents, variously titled; the most important were uniformly free, evidently salaried men, the *pronoetai*, who acted as general agents.[23] They handled a wide variety of transactions with lessees, hired hands, buyers, sellers, and borrowers. They were also the key figures in the enormous tide of correspondence that passed from the Great House in the city to the country estate; some of it was written by the landlords

[18]E.g., *P.Oxy.* L 3598 (4c early), an account of boat transportation of grain from Berky to Oxyrhynchos; *P.Oxy.* XLVIII 3406 (2nd half 4c), a letter from a female landlord to her *pronoetes* at Sadalou about sending various goods to the city by boat.

[19]The Appianus estate is known through the Heroninus archive, a mass of papers concerning mainly the unit at Theadelphia. A comprehensive description of the texts published to date (many more are unpublished) and the workings of the Appianus estate is given by Rathbone 1991, on which the following remarks are based.

[20]For example, *SB* VIII 9907 (Hermopolis, 388); *P.Mert.* I 36 (*BL*; Lewuillon-Blume 1979, 179-80 n.4) (Oxyrhynchos, 360), both discussed by Lewuillon-Blume 1979. On dependent relations, with their complexities, see more generally Keenan 1981, Foxhall 1990, and Rathbone 1991, 175-211.

[21]See above, pp. 123-27.

[22]Cf. the pottery leases in Cockle 1981 (*P.Oxy.* L 3595-3597), and more generally A. Jördens, *P.Heid.* V, pp. 222-70.

[23]Managers of particular estates are often called *phrontistai*, as in *PSI* V 472 (*BL*) (Oxyrhynchos, 295) and the Appianus estate (Rathbone 1991).

themselves, but much of it was intrastaff. Receipts and orders for payment or delivery figure largely in these notes, which regulated daily
receipts and expenses of every conceivable substance or good.[24]
Through this staff and their activities, the great owners were, though
hardly freed from involvement in the daily affairs of their estates
(indeed, they were often very active in them), at least given enough
leisure to discharge their public duties.[25]

Taxation

All taxation systems are selective in their choice of economic activities
to tax and discriminatory in their effects on different types of activity.
Hardly any direct evidence of the reasons underlying the Roman
government's policies of taxation has survived, but the pattern of the
evidence is so distinctive and striking that it cannot reflect merely
accidents of survival. The preceding chapters have shown that
agriculture was the foundation of the Egyptian economy, as of
virtually every other ancient economy, and it is therefore no surprise
to find that the burden of taxation fell principally on the land. What is
less expected is the very light taxation of urban economic activity.
Although late antiquity has acquired (along with its undeserved
reputation for bureaucracy) a high-tax profile, the reality is very different.[26]

First, there was no income tax in fourth-century Egypt (or
elsewhere in the Empire).[27] There was, moreover, no tax on urban
property. In fact, the sole regular tax to affect the urban population in
this period was the tax on trades and businesses called the
chrysargyron, supposedly instituted by Constantine, that is, in 324 or
later in the case of Egypt.[28] It fell upon craftsmen, traders, merchants,
and even moneylenders, though it is not known if its application was

[24]See Gallazzi-Wagner 1983 for a small archive on ostraka of such correspondence. *P.Lips.* 97 (cf. pp. 126-27) shows the accounting of such an estate on a
large scale.

[25]Cf. *CPR* VI 12-71 (Hermopolis, 4c early) for an example of a dossier of
landlord-estate correspondence.

[26]There is no recent published study of taxation in this period. Michael Ford's
unpublished thesis, *Taxation in Fourth Century Egypt* (Diss. Birmingham 1986) has
been useful for references but is not cited in detail below, and it would not really fill
the gap.

[27]For general remarks on how the Romans taxed their empire, see Duncan-
Jones 1990, 187-98.

[28]See *P.Rain.Cent.* 122 introd.; Karayannopulos 1958, 129-37, for general discussions. Constantine may well have introduced it earlier elsewhere in provinces under
his control. In some sense it certainly replaced earlier taxes on trades attested in the
third and previous centuries.

this wide from the start or gradually expanded. It was originally assessed on a four-year cycle, but in practice it seems to have been collected by indiction year and in monthly installments.[29] Next to nothing is known of how it was assessed, but one indication is the monthly quota of goldsmiths, 200 myriads, in a text from 426.[30] That comes to 16,000 talents per year, or a little more than a half-solidus, the value of about five artabas of wheat. Although the *chrysargyron* is said to have been a much-hated tax, its value in fact comes to significantly less than the normal capitation taxes of the principate and equals roughly what a farmer might have paid on two to three arouras. Because goldsmiths were a relatively well-off group, it is likely that this is near the top of the range for the tax.[31] The yield from the tax, all the same, was certainly substantial, perhaps as much as 100,000 solidi or 1,400 pounds of gold a year.[32]

Only one other urban tax is known from the fourth century, the enigmatic *epikephalaion*, or "head-tax," known only at Oxyrhynchos from about 297/8 to 319/320.[33] It began, apparently, at 1,200 drachmas, rising to 1,600 dr. in 306/7 and 2,400 in 312/3. It thus never exceeded the value of about two artabas of wheat per year. The population liable for it is unclear. One suggestion is that only villagers residing in Oxyrhynchos, that is, those without Oxyrhynchite "citizenship," were liable for the tax. Many receipts, however, give the occupation of the payer, which might suggest that this tax served a function similar to that of the later *chrysargyron* (not attested until after the disappearance of the *epikephalaion*).[34]

It is clear, then, that taxation of city residents cannot have provided the means for the support of cities and their amenities, the more so in that the few taxes known benefited the imperial rather than civic treasury. The bulk of civic expenses was evidently borne by

[29]See Bagnall 1992c.

[30]*PSI* XII 1265 (Oxyrhynchos); see *P.Rain.Cent.* 122 introd.; *Aegyptus* 62 (1982) 65-68 = *SB* XVI 12260 (421); and *ZPE* 59 (1985) 67-70.

[31]Karayannopulos 1958 notes the evidence of a hagiographic source that Edessa paid 140 lbs. of gold every four years for *chrysargyron*. If true, it would imply 35 lbs. per year, and applying the Oxyrhynchite goldsmiths' rate of about 0.57 solidus per year, one gets 4,421 persons paying the tax, with a population of some 20,000 to 25,000 thus dependent on the taxed activities. That seems perfectly credible.

[32]*If*, at a rough guess, 60 percent of the urban population (including Alexandria) was supported by activity hit by the *chrysargyron*, and *if* that population totaled 1.2 million, and *if* each taxable person supported three others, and *if* the average payer was liable for 0.57 solidus: All plausible assumptions, none likely to be exactly right.

[33]See most recently *P.Oxy.* LV 3789, introd., with evidence and discussion.

[34]Rea adduces *P.Oxy.* LV 3787 in support of the villager hypothesis, but it could as well simply concern that part of the liable population that came from villages.

other city revenues (from land and other property) and by liturgists.[35] These liturgists in turn, however, drew their wealth in the main not from city activities but from the ownership and management of land. Agriculture, therefore, and not urban production or commerce, bore the cost of supporting the public splendor of the cities.

Given the ancient world's enormous ideological preference for agriculture as a livelihood and for land as a repository of wealth, it may seem paradoxical that precisely the purveyors of this ideology, the upper class, should have decided to tax what it valued as secure and proper and let off what it despised as volatile and degrading. Why not institute a significant income tax on all urban incomes? An economically rational answer can be given: If the natural preference for land were not counterbalanced by weighty obligations, too much wealth would chase the fixed supply of land, drive its price up and diminish economic activity of other types. But that may not be the real answer. There is also an administrative one: Taxing land, at least as it was done in the fourth century, was an administratively straightforward matter and provided stable revenues. In a society with the borderline levels of literacy this one had (see chapter 7), administering complex, essentially self-declared taxes of a modern kind would have been extraordinarily difficult, and the revenues from them would have been most variable, as modern governments regularly discover.

A third answer, though to modern minds less compelling, may have still more to do with ancient decisions. Modern taxation is a fundamentally democratic institution, melting all contributions into a single pot and dissociating them from the names of individuals. A public building constructed with tax revenues owes nothing to anyone in particular and does nothing to enhance any taxpayer's public recognition. A low-tax liturgical system, in contrast, keeps both power and visibility in the hands of the individuals who are the community's benefactors, for they are anything but anonymous contributors to a larger pool. The governing class of the empire kept taxes on their lands as low as they could precisely to maximize their own prestige and power, for the state had to turn to them, with their concentrated wealth, to achieve more than minimal survival. The by-product of that willingness to accept expenditure in return for power and recognition was a low-tax environment for others.

That taxes were low for city residents—lower, in fact, than in previous centuries—has been argued above. The land taxes are somewhat more complex, though probably more straightforward than they

[35]See Millar 1983, 81, on the conceptual basis.

appear at first sight.[36] Diocletian introduced a system, maintained by his successors for centuries despite various changes in terminology and methods of collection, in which taxes in kind on the land were kept at low flat rates on a limited number of classes of land. At the imperial level, rates were set each year on a gross scale, per unit of approximately 100 arouras or even on multiples of that, and communicated to the provincial offices. There they were translated into nome-by-nome quotas and dispatched as such to the individual cities, which then had the responsibility of collecting them. The overall burden was apparently fairly constant, but the precise distribution between "private" and "public" land (all, in reality, now in private ownership) and between wheat and barley varied from place to place and time to time. Good evidence indicates that the overall total of these taxes in grain amounted to an average of around 1.6 artabas per aroura.[37] The government's need for wheat for the populations of Rome, then Constantinople, as well as military use, kept wheat a useful commodity for tax collecting purposes, and two centuries later the total tax rate in grains was much the same.[38]

For most of the fourth century, the balance of the taxes on land was assessed in gold. That did not happen overnight. Diocletian had found a monetary system mainly dependent on billon, bronze with an admixture of silver, and set out to replace it with one in which gold was the key element, a policy continued by Constantine. Diocletian had first to get the vast quantities of gold hoarded by individuals around the empire back into circulation, a goal largely accomplished by requiring landowners to deliver gold (and silver) to the government each year in return for reimbursement in billon coinage at a government-set price significantly below the market value.[39] This compulsory purchase scheme was accompanied by several minor taxes collected in currency (probably then recycled into "paying" for the gold and silver) and a complex system for acquiring military uniforms by requisitions, reimbursed like the gold and silver at a fixed rate that represented a declining percentage of the true cost of the garments.[40] The aggregate worth of all these exactions is difficult to estimate.

[36]The following discussion is based on Bagnall 1985a and Carrié forthcoming. See also Palme 1989, 69-70, for a brief summary.

[37]At least in some places, there was also a levy in chaff, but its value was low.

[38]Bagnall 1985a, 303. See Carrié forthcoming for a convincing demolition of the view that more and more of the grain taxes were converted into cash in the fourth century and later.

[39]See Bagnall 1977a and 1985b.

[40]See J. Sheridan, *P.Col.* IX, forthcoming.

After Constantine's victory over Licinius and his takeover of Egypt in 324, all this was regularized into a more straightforward system. The compulsory delivery of gold for purchase was eliminated, as was the reimbursement system for military garments; the latter was turned into a true tax, and the other minor taxes along with it were all levied in gold. Each year, therefore, the government issued a schedule of these minor taxes in the form of a rate on a large unit like 2,000 or 3,000 arouras. As with taxes in kind, these were translated downward by officials into levies per aroura or per so many arouras. The amounts clearly varied annually and taxpayers might in time of need (a major war, for example) be hit with surcharges. But a reasonable estimate is that these taxes in the aggregate amounted to about 0.2 gram (one-twentieth of a solidus, or 1.2 carats) per aroura, or the equivalent in wheat of about a half-artaba.[41] There may have been some additional charges not included in this, but they were probably not material.[42] The overall burden on the land would thus have been something like 2.1 artabas per aroura in a normal year.[43]

The responsibility for the collection of all these taxes lay on each city for its nome. A multitiered liturgical system, parts of which have been described above (pp. 57, 133-34), was put in place early in the fourth century to handle the task. At the village level were annual officials, the *sitologoi* (for the main wheat and barley taxes) and a variety of *apaitetai* for other charges.[44] They were responsible for seeing that the taxes were collected and delivered to the "receivers" (*apodektai* or *hypodektai*) appointed by the city. These receivers in turn would, under the overall supervision of the superintendents (*epimeletai*), see the tax revenues either loaded on boats to head down the Nile, handed over to distributors (*diadotai*) who conveyed them to the military, or sent in to the provincial authorities by other official channels. Along with this nomewide structure existed (from 307/8 on) the *praepositi pagi*, responsible for supervision of the village liturgists in their circumscriptions (on average, about six or seven villages each) and the

[41]See Carrié 1977, 383, extended now by Carrié forthcoming.

[42]Carrié (forthcoming) also makes a good case that this figure represents a higher than normal level of taxation which was lowered by a third a few years later; with that level and a higher wheat price (such as is found in much of the fourth century), these taxes might have been as little as a quarter-artaba.

[43]Bagnall 1985a, 304, with the same result by a different computation. See Carrié forthcoming on extraordinary levies, which might as much as double the money taxes, pushing the total tax on land to an equivalent of 2.6 art. The tax rates were generally set irrespective of the actual use of the land. There were, however, some poorly-documented taxes on such activities as beekeeping, for which see Chouliara-Raïos 1989, 85-89 and 167-70.

[44]See Palme 1989, 78-89, on these collectors.

integral collection of the amounts due from them. And the major civic officials had the overall care of appointing liturgists and seeing that they did their jobs properly; the *exactor* was most directly involved in the whole process, but the city council was corporately liable for any default by the members it had chosen for specific tasks.

So things were organized on paper. The village liturgists no doubt did a fair amount of the direct work of collection themselves, though certainly not all of it. But it is impossible to imagine the members of the top 100 families of Oxyrhynchos or Hermopolis, who held most city liturgies connected with taxes and would have to pay up if they were not delivered in full to the imperial government, going about the dusty countryside collecting a few artabas here, a few grains of gold there, from their social inferiors. And the average peasant, required to pay tiny fractions of a gram of gold for particular taxes, can hardly have done so.[45] The practicalities of tax collection must have been quite different.

In reality, most of the work was done by assistants, *boethoi*, hired by the liturgists responsible for collection. Their role, though indirectly seen in many documents, has come into sharp relief from the archive of Papnouthis and Dorotheos, brothers who worked as assistants to Oxyrhynchite nobs in the middle part and second half of the fourth century, with their main documented activity falling in the period 360-375.[46] Their employer hired them for particular tasks, like the taxes of a particular village or group of villages, or for a specific tax in the city (Dorotheos at one stage was involved in collecting the *chrysargyron*[47]). They were themselves city residents and came from a propertied (though presumably not wealthy) family; both "wrote fluently, though with a striking disregard for rules of spelling and grammar," as the editor put it.[48]

Apart from the sheer administrative detail of receiving and paying, Dorotheos and Papnouthis document the practice that made the whole system of money taxes work but which was only dimly known from other texts. They collected all the gold taxes in billon currency from smallholders and then converted it into gold by buying solidi on the open market.[49] This complicated procedure required sig-

[45]See Carrié forthcoming for a good description of the difficulties involved in a gold-based system.

[46]The bulk is published in *P.Oxy.* XLVIII 3384-3430; a few other texts are scattered elsewhere (some listed in the editor's introduction, p. 76; others are *P.Oxy.* IX 1223 and XLIX 3480). On paid service in liturgical offices and assisting liturgists, see generally A. Jördens, *P.Heid.* V, pp. 185-221.

[47]*P.Oxy.* XLIX 3480 (undated).

[48]*P.Oxy.* XLVIII, p. 74.

[49]A good description of the operations is given by Carrié forthcoming.

nificant financial acumen. Gold fluctuated substantially in nominal price through the year,[50] and if one became involved in silver a three-way fluctuation of still larger magnitude was possible. The expenses of collection and transport had to be reckoned. And collectors at least at times borrowed to pay the taxes in advance, recovering the funds only later and thus incurring considerable risk. It was no doubt worth a good deal to a liturgist to be able to shift some of the risk of his office in this way to his entrepreneurial employees. There must have been substantial possibility of profit in such a situation, too. At the same time, if the collectors set the equivalent in billon coins too high, there might be repercussions. A remarkable sense of alertness and even sharp dealing pervades the archive, and care was clearly needed; one's own employer might try to cheat one.[51]

One other aspect of this archive provides a significant bridge to the developments of the fifth century, but it is not easy to interpret. The brothers are not only tax assistants; sometimes Papnouthis is described as a *pronoetes*, business manager.[52] The term has, up to this time, had a purely private connotation; such men managed the property of their employers. In the sixth century, however, the *pronoetai* of the Great Houses can be seen in what are clearly transactions of a public nature, managing tax collection.[53] And even when engaged in tax collection, Papnouthis and Dorotheos often refer to their employers as landlords, *geouchoi*. This term is, strictly, irrelevant—or so it seems from the perspective of the earlier fourth century.[54] From the perspective of the sixth century, however, the view is different, and a brief excursus will show the significance of the development to which this archive witnesses.

The Great Houses[55] of the sixth century, what historians have often called "large estates," were to a considerable degree public, rath-

---

[50]A range of about 4 percent at Oxyrhynchos in one well-documented year: see Bagnall 1989b, 70-72.

[51]See *P.Oxy.* XLVIII 3393 (365), a petition against a councillor who had hired the brothers and then, after they had advanced the funds, prevented them from collecting the taxes.

[52]"Caretaker," as the editor translates the term in *P.Oxy.* XLVIII 3388, 3406, and 3407, is misleading; the position was more like that of a bailiff or in some cases a steward.

[53]See Gascou 1985, 13-18, pointing out that such involvement seems to go back to the fourth century.

[54]See Carrié forthcoming, n.78, arguing that Sarapammon (one of the brothers' employers) was involved in a purely private capacity (rather than as, e.g., *praepositus pagi*) in tax matters. That is in one sense true, but it ignores the evolution of private responsibility for public business.

[55]Meaning here the ecclesiastical and family establishments called "pious" and "glorious" houses, respectively.

er than private, entities.[56] The cities allocated to wealthy landowners a share of the responsibility for collecting the taxes owed not merely on their own land but on much else; this represented a permanent institutionalization of the liturgical role that these families played in the fourth century. They collected taxes, paid expenses, and transmitted the amount due the government. They performed various compulsory services on behalf of the city and, in effect, were departments of the city government.[57]

The documentation of the Great Houses, however, includes some transactions comprehensible only in the context of a private economy.[58] And clearly their public role was possible only if substantial private wealth remained to sustain the whole enterprise.[59] In effect, the wealthy landowners came to form a college sharing public responsibilities, in such a fashion that it is very difficult to disentangle public from private functions—hence the temptation for scholars to try to describe the Great Houses as one or the other. The two aspects were probably kept separate in the accounting, but what the papers of Papnouthis and Dorotheos suggest is that the unification of management of the two aspects was becoming a reality in the middle of the fourth century. In this way, the management of the landholdings of the wealthy city residents and the carrying out of their civic responsibilities formed a single, complex enterprise with a substantial staff. This part-public, part-private model also avoids the need to suppose a vast concentration of land in the ownership of the Great Houses, such as is almost universally thought to have taken place,[60] but of which no evidence can be found.[61]

[56]This has been shown by Gascou 1985, the brilliant and original article to which this section is heavily indebted.

[57]It follows that the relationship of the Great Houses to the farmers, the so-called *coloni*, was primarily one of public law rather than private contract; see Gascou 1985, 20-27, with Carrié 1982, 1983, and 1984.

[58]Gascou 1985, 28-35, discusses some of these, but his main thesis about the public character of much of the Great Houses' activities leads him to frame the matter too much in an either/or fashion.

[59]Gascou 1985, 36-37, discusses accounts showing roughly equal income and expenditures for public purposes; he suggests that this shows the harshness of fiscal pressure. If, however, this is an account dealing only with the public role of the Great House, it provides no information about the private economy of the enterprise. It is indeed clearly impossible that it should have continued if it had to pay out to the government everything that it took in on all accounts!

[60]Even by Gascou 1985, 30. This is not to say that the Great Houses were not large landowners, of course.

[61]See Bowman 1985; Bagnall 1992b. The phenomenon of concentration of ownership seems little changed from Roman times to the sixth century and tends to retreat into the future whenever confronted with evidence for any particular period.

Order, Disorder, and Justice

Among the responsibilities placed in the hands of the city administration by the reorganization of the early fourth century (above, p. 59) was the maintenance of order and security in the entire nome. A complicated network of legal relationships linking city and country has already appeared in the context of ordinary business: leases, loans, sales, and other documents involve every possible combination of persons and residences. Disputes are as sure to arise from business transactions as from taxation, and the means by which they are handled help reveal the society. In the case of Roman Egypt, such disputes—civil matters, in modern legal parlance—were treated in the same way as personal conflicts or misdeeds classified today as criminal. From the standpoint of neither the plaintiff nor official procedure was any distinction drawn, although the seriousness of a matter could lead to its being handled at a higher or lower administrative level.

It is by no means any easier to form general judgments from the analytic documentation of conflict than from the papyrological record of many other areas of life.[62] For example, one may wonder if this was a litigious society. The record-office registers of first-century Tebtunis show that documents classifiable as petitions of some sort made up about 6.7 percent of the total documents registered in a sixteen-month period, but that number does not interpret itself.[63] Nor is it easy to decide if Roman Egypt was a lawless or violent society, as upper-class Romans who had never been there seem to have thought.[64] Even the least crime-ridden of complex modern societies would readily produce registers of litigation or anecdotes of crime to match anything in the papyri, but with no means of measuring the incidence, reported or otherwise, of any type of conflict or misdeed, the historian is hard put to assess its societal significance.

Certainly most conflict did not result in litigation. Petitioners, often alluding to an earlier history of conflict with their adversaries, indicate attempts to reconcile differences on their own or even a willingness to absorb a certain amount of hurt. That is very much in line with anthropological observation that actual litigation is only the tip of the iceberg; most disputes were handled (not necessarily "settled" or "resolved") in other ways. From this one might conclude that the amount of actual conflict was therefore many times what the papyri report, and this may well be correct. But almost all litigation concerns

[62]See Bagnall 1989a, 202-203, citing divergent opinions.
[63]Hobson 1993.
[64]Cf. Hobson 1993 and Bagnall 1989a for the following remarks.

persons known to and identified by the plaintiff; only 6.6 percent of
petitions from Roman Egypt concern acts by unknown strangers.[65]
Few conflicts with known persons, usually neighbors or family members, are likely to be without prehistories. Is one to be more impressed
by their prevalence or by the ability of the society to resolve them
without a resort to outside authority?

The judicial process itself remained relatively constant from the
principate to the fourth century, but there was a substantial change in
the identity of the officials handling cases.[66] Petitions of the first three
centuries of Roman rule are addressed to a variety of levels of
officialdom, from local military officers functioning as police officers
and magistrates to the prefect of Egypt. The officers (centurions and
beneficiarii, for the most part) were resorted to almost exclusively by
villagers, but the higher officials were used by all. The bulk of the petitions went to the *strategoi* of the nomes.[67] Diocletian's reforms aimed
at producing a much greater direct involvement by governors in the
judicial business of their provinces.[68] Petitions addressed to the *praeses*
or prefect thus increase greatly in number.[69] The governor did not
handle most cases himself. In all but a handful of instances, the petition was returned to the sender with a brief reply, usually directing
him to submit his petition to the appropriate local official who would
examine the facts. These replies often judge the question of law, if
there was one, but are framed conditionally. "The *exactor*, having
adjudged between you according to the laws in the presence of the
party wronging you, will cause that to be done which justice
demands, provided always that no other petition takes precedence."[70]
The petitioner then submitted a copy of his original petition, with the
governor's subscription and his own cover letter, to the designated
official, asking for assistance.[71]

The governor might also write directly to a local official with
instructions, of stereotyped character: "Take care then, if you observe

[65]Hobson 1993: Of her base of 182 petitions, only 12 involved acts by unknown
perpetrators, or 16.2 percent of the 74 petitions occasioned "by what one might call a
criminal act" (as she puts it).

[66]The following account is based heavily on Lallemand 1964, 139-67.

[67]See Hobson 1993 for an analysis.

[68]Lallemand 1964, 147. The entire structure of legal protection in Egypt and the
standard rhetoric of petitions show that protection of the population was seen as
part of the governor's task, despite the sweeping assertions of Isaac 1990, 393, that
the Romans had no interest in the safety of their subjects.

[69]See B. Kramer, *ZPE* 69 (1987) 155-61, for a list of petitions dating from 284 to
the end of the fourth century; the mix of officials is clearly visible.

[70]*P.Mert.* II 91 (316). For a collection of such subscriptions from the fourth
century, see *CPR* XVIIA, pp. 79-80.

[71]See P. J. Sijpesteijn and K. A. Worp, *Tyche* 2 (1987) 178.

that he is telling the truth, to compel those who are detaining (?) the lands and farming (them) to make (?) restitution (?) of the rents which are owed."[72] "Eudaimon approached me claiming that he has debtors acknowledged as such, as you will learn from the copy of the petition he submitted. Take care, if you find he is telling the truth, to protect him from loss."[73]

Important matters, however, might be tried directly before the governor. Where a petitioner had a rescript from the emperor, this was natural enough.[74] In other cases, persistence might be needed (cf. above, p. 64). "I have presented applications to our lord the prefect, and no decision has been subscribed for me so far. Your opponent is tireless in making petitions, and so am I in making counter-petitions; so that I have heeded (your instruction): 'Stay close to the prefect's office, and whenever you are cited, enter an objection.'"[75] Because the prefect was about to leave town for a while, however, proceedings threatened to stretch out for a while. The courts of the regional governors were probably more available than the Alexandrian prefect's, but even so local officials had to take care of most actual hearings.

One way to reduce the burden of litigation on the governors and even on local officials was to encourage arbitration and reconciliation, a preference of considerable antiquity and persistence. The high proportion of conflicts between parties familiar to one another must have made this a yet more logical procedure than in modern societies with a higher incidence of strangers in conflict or of anonymous crime. Informal mediation[76] and formal delegation of arbitrators to hear cases[77] are both recorded, usually in the context of written settlements. Cases that had not yet proceeded to the point of formal litigation normally did not need such documents to record the outcome of successful mediation or arbitration.

Arbitration, for whatever reason, continued to gain in popularity as the centuries went on.[78] That might seem a turn toward amateurism

---

[72]P.Oxy. L 3579 (341-343).

[73]P.Oxy. XLIII 3129 (cf. P.Oxy. LV, pp. xviii-xix) (335: prefect to *syndikos*).

[74]P.Oxy. LV 3820 (*ca* 340?) describes the actions of a man in Alexandria on business, who presented an imperial rescript concerning some property to Philagrios, presumably the prefect, and minutes were compiled. Then he was passed on to the department of the *magister*, he got into court, and a second set of proceedings was made.

[75]P.Oxy. XXXI 2597 (*BL*) (prob. 4c).

[76]Intervention of friends just before trial: P.Haun. III 57 (412-415?), a case involving a former governor and one of his subordinates.

[77]P.Oxy LIV 3764 (*ca* 326).

[78]Indeed, it has been argued that civil process essentially disappeared by the sixth century: A. A. Schiller, "The Courts are No More," *Studi in onore di Edoardo Volterra* I (Milan 1969 [1971]) 469-502.

in conflict resolution. But the fourth century saw as well a continuation of the third century's trend toward greater legal professionalism.
A growth in the collection and citation of imperial legislation of all
sorts, including both rescripts and general laws, was characteristic of
the third century.[79] In reports of fourth-century trials lawyers play a
substantial role, and they display both rhetorical skills and a considerable knowledge of imperial law.[80]

The forces of law and order must have looked substantially different to urbanites and villagers. The most obvious difference was
perhaps that cities had public security forces. These were hardly sufficient to produce order in case of a major riot, but that was true even in
the great cities.[81] These were largely amateur, liturgists like most other
public officials. At the head of the apparatus were the *nyktostrategoi*,
"night-generals," who, despite the title, had responsibility for twenty-
four-hour surveillance.[82] They normally disposed of a considerable
cadre of guards assigned to particular locations,[83] but apparently on
occasion the city failed to provide them with the required forces.[84]
Little is known about the details of their responsibilities, but they
received petitions about what might be termed petty crime.[85] They

[79]See Ranon Katzoff, "On the Intended Use of P.Col. 123," *Proc. XVI Congr. Pap.*,
559-73; cf. also his ""Responsa Prudentium" in Roman Egypt," *Studi in onore di
Arnaldo Biscardi* II (Milan 1982) 523-35, on the role of jurisprudence in the period.

[80]Among the reports of proceedings, see particularly *P.Col.* VII 175 = *SB* XVI
12692 (cf. *ZPE* 45 [1982] 229-41). The still-enigmatic memoranda and speeches of
advocates headed with an "N" are also emblematic. See the discussion of all six by
H. C. Youtie, "Pragmata meteora: Unfinished Business," *Scriptiunculae Posteriores* I 1-
15, though his own solution is not entirely persuasive: cf. N. Lewis, *P.Rain.Cent.*, pp.
121-26.

[81]Cf. T. E. Gregory, "Urban Violence in Late Antiquity," *Aspects of Graeco-Roman
Urbanism*, ed. R. T. Marchese (BAR Int. Ser. 188, Oxford 1983) 138-61. Evidence for
such disturbances is, on his account, mainly limited to places like Rome, Alexandria,
Antioch, Constantinople, and Thessalonica. Isaac 1990, esp. 56, 140, 209, stresses the
need to control city populations as a motive for stationing troops in them, but there
is no evidence that this was generally true; his focus on Judaea certainly distorts the
picture.

[82]Lallemand 1964, 164-65. The *archephodoi* in charge of quarters of Hermopolis
(*CPR* XVIIA 3 [314]) are probably similar.

[83]See particularly *P.Oxy.* I 43 verso (*BL; W.Chr.* 474) (after 295, date of the
account on the recto: perhaps as late as the 320s), a list of guards (cf. N. Lewis, *BASP*
18 [1981] 76-77).

[84]*P.Oxy.* VII 1033 = *W.Chr.* 476 (392) records a complaint that they have no help
at all and are in great danger.

[85]E.g., *P.Herm.* 52 (*BL*) (398); *P.Oxy.* LI 3620 (326). Despite the statement of J. D.
Thomas, *Cd'E* 44 (1969) 352, that these officials were "of only minor importance" in
the later fourth century, it is notable that in *P.Herm.* 52 the *nyktostrategos* is a
politeuomenos.

were not a wholly new creation in the fourth century, but they may have been extended to most cities only in the tetrarchic period.[86]

The development of a yet higher security apparatus in the cities is still not entirely clear. Oxyrhynchos, at least, experimented briefly in 341-342 with an "overseer of the peace," but that office, attested only for about thirteen months, was apparently not a success.[87] More lasting was the institution of the *riparius*, sometimes single and sometimes a college, who first appears in 346 and is attested for hundreds of years. The office was held by high-ranking members of the curial class and disposed of paid assistants.[88] The *riparius* tended to receive petitions about matters of public order and acts against persons or property, ranging from assault to theft of hay,[89] as well as being the superior of the *nyktostrategoi*.

The exact articulation of responsibilities among civic officials is also somewhat obscure. The *syndikos* (or *ekdikos*[90]), generally a very senior member of the local aristocracy, handled particularly cases concerning property in a broad sense, but the limits of his competence are unclear.[91] An office of this name had existed in the third and early fourth centuries,[92] but it was transformed into something quite different around 331.[93] The differentiation of his powers as a delegated judge from those of the *logistes* is particularly unclear, and the two occasionally appear together.[94]

[86]They are attested in Antinoopolis and Alexandria much earlier, but the earliest secure evidence for a metropolis is *P.Oxy.* L 3571; cf. note to lines 12-13 with earlier bibliography.

[87]*P.Oxy.* L 3575 (341) introd. and note to lines 3-4 for references and discussion. Even if present evidence is deceptive, it cannot have lasted more than another few years.

[88]Not well-paid, perhaps. See *P.NYU* 4 (*BL*) (Karanis, probably 353/4, not earlier), in which the amount paid would buy little more than an artaba of wheat per month.

[89]E.g., *P.Cair.Goodsp.* 15 (*BL*) (Hermopolis, 362); *P.Lips.* 37 (*BL*) (Hermopolis, 389); *P.Select.* 8 (Oxyrhynchos, 421). For bibliography about the office, see *P.Harr.* II 218 introd.

[90]The variation may have been local; both are renderings of the *defensor civitatis*. See B. Kramer, "Syndikoi, Ekdikoi und Defensores," *Pap.Flor.* XIX, 305-329, for a complete list and discussion.

[91]One might think that personal matters were at stake in *P.Oxy.* LIV 3770 (334), but in fact the petitioner's request is lost.

[92]Bowman 1971, 46-52. His duties are not easy to define but include concerns with elections, naming of liturgists, and external representation of the council. The last example of the "old" *syndikos* is *P.Stras.* IV 296 (Hermopolis, 326; cf. B. Kramer, *ZPE* 69 [1987] 143-61), although the (plural) *syndikoi* there seem in some respects to prefigure the new office.

[93]*P.Oxy.* XLIV 3195 (June 331) is the earliest example known to date.

[94]The dossier of documents concerning the *logistes* in *P.Oxy.* LIV, such as 3756-3759, 3767, and 3775, has added much to the picture but not yet resolved this matter.

How did all of this look to a villager? The papers of Isidoros and Sakaon, the two really well-known village residents of the time, certainly suggest men unafraid to use the system of justice. Petitions, drafts of petitions, and court documents make up a significant part of these two archives. And not only the protagonists petitioned. One cluster of Isidoros papyri concerns the attempts by his sister-in-law Taesis and her sister Kyrillous to reverse their uncle Chairemon's misappropriation of their inheritance, or at least the movables in it.[95] They petition not only the local military police officer, the *beneficiarius*, but also the *strategos* and threaten to appeal to the governor. In 298, Isidoros' grain on the threshing floor was set afire, leading to a petition to the *strategos*, a verification visit from that official's assistant two days later, and a subsequent complaint in which the culprits are named. He then (probably early in 299) petitioned the prefect and "betook myself to your Magnificence in order to make this complaint."[96] His opponents had also appeared, and he asked that they be compelled to furnish security or be instructed to remain. The outcome is (as so often) unknown.

A further round of litigation, a decade later, concerned what Isidoros regarded as abusive nominations to liturgy, whereby he in effect bore the cost of the local komarchs' protection of their friends from such nomination. Not long after this abuse came attempts to collect taxes from him on land that he did not own and to apportion those taxes idiosyncratically.[97]

Perhaps the most interesting litigation is the protracted affair of Kastor and Ammonianos.[98] In 314/5, Isidoros leased twenty-five arouras of grainland from these brothers on half-shares, with Isidoros to do the work. He paid all the costs and even lent money to his landlords. Instead of paying, however, the brothers seized the crop. Isidoros petitioned the *strategos* and *praepositus pagi* and finally (at the end of 315) the governor. The latter referred the matter to the *exactor*, the new title for the *strategos*. Isidoros petitioned him on 30 January 316. A settlement was reached a month or so later, in which the brothers paid off Isidoros except for an amount, recorded as a loan

[95]*P.Cair.Isid.* 62-64 (*ca* 297-298).

[96]The pertinent documents are *P.Cair.Isid.* 65-67 and 124.

[97]The opening salvo is *P.Cair.Isid.* 68 (prob. 309/310), followed by *P.Cair.Isid.* 69 (*BL*) (310) and 70 (*ca* 310). There is then a break until *P.Cair.Isid.* 71-73 (*BL*) (314), although other documents not preserved may have covered developments in the intervening years.

[98]*P.Cair.Isid.* 74 (315) and 76 (318); *P.Mert.* II 91 and *P.Col.* VII 169-170 (318). For property management aspects see above, p. 119.

due that summer, of thirty-two artabas of wheat and eighteen of beans, secured by three oxen and a surety. Subsequently, after no payment was made, one brother died, another fled, and their successors would not pay. Isidoros once again (on 13 April 318) petitioned the *praeses*, who ordered him to apply to the *praepositus*, which he did on 16 July. At that point the documents stop.

Another set of complaints, which closes Isidoros' recorded career, concerns animals invading his land and trampling his growing crops. Both cattle and sheep are implicated, and some of the owners did not hesitate to beat up Isidoros, now an old man by local standards, in his middle to late fifties.[99] This accounting does not quite exhaust the record of Isidoros' litigation, but the other items are scattered or undated.[100]

In the Sakaon archive, by contrast, the most significant documents, those that have dominated discussion of the archive as a whole, concern the collapse of the local irrigation system and the villagers' struggle to cope with land taxes and taxpayer flight in its aftermath.[101] But there is also a string of family fights. One petition by a woman complains about her late husband's sister, who is not paying her share of the taxes due on their common father's inheritance; the petitioner and her children thus must pay more than their fair share.[102] In another complex case, a man complains that he betrothed his son to an infant girl, whose mother then died. He took the girl into his house and eventually married the children off. The girl's father Sakaon then objected that he had not received any marriage gifts, and he "abducted" the girl. Mediation produced a decision that the petitioner should pay a certain amount, which he had to borrow, but Sakaon still kept the girl. The prefect, probably wary of getting involved in an Egyptian family dispute, replied, "If the girl is pleased with living with her husband, this is to be made plain to the *logistes* according to the laws."[103]

Before the villages are seen as hotbeds of litigation, however, and as veritable cauldrons of conflict, some caution is in order. Most important, Isidoros and Sakaon both belonged to the upper crust of

---

[99]*P.Cair.Isid.* 78 and *P.Mert.* II 92; *P.Col.* VII 171 (all 324); *P.Cair.Isid.* 79 (no date).

[100]Notable are *P.Mert.* II 89 (300), about an assault on Isidoros when he was a field guard; *P.Cair.Isid.* 75 (316), about a drunken raid on his house when he was not home; and *P.Cair.Isid.* 77 (*BL*) (320), perhaps by Isidoros' wife about the inheritance of her sister's children.

[101]*P.Sakaon* 32 (late 3c); 33 (320); 34 (321); 35 (332); 42 (*ca* 323); 44 = *P.Turner* 44 (331/2); 45 (334); 46 and 47 (342).

[102]*P.Sakaon* 37 (284).

[103]*P.Sakaon* 38 (312).

village society. For all their complaints, they were relatively well-off landowners with diverse economic interests and, obviously, the means to pay petition writers (both were illiterate) and even to travel to the prefect's court on occasion. A survey of other preserved petitions originating with villagers confirms the impression that they come from the propertied class.[104] This group was a substantial part of the village population (above, p. 117), but it certainly omitted a considerable portion, especially the landless laborers, a group even less visible in the fourth century than earlier, thanks to the virtual disappearance of taxes not based on land ownership.

Parallels from other societies suggest strongly that village residents are likely to have preferred to avoid recourse to outside authority in managing conflicts. Self-help, mediation, or acceptance are all more likely responses than litigation.[105] On the whole, villages in Roman Egypt seem to follow this pattern; they both prefer to deal with violence by internal processes rather than legal processes and see the problem primarily as reintegration and restoration of status and property rather than as punishment.[106] The extensive body of petitions, however, despite the evidence that they were often a last resort, points to at least the wealthier parts of village society as being (unsurprisingly) more ready to use formal structures of the government to accomplish restoration of social stability than are most village societies studied by anthropologists or social historians. Whether this is more true in the fourth century than in earlier periods is hard to say.

The village situation can also be seen from a reverse perspective, that of the recipient of petitions. This vantage point is offered by the archive of the military commander Abinnaeus, which has raised the general question of military competition with civil authorities in the area of jurisdiction. In principle, the jurisdiction of military commanders, as subordinates of the *dux*, was supposed to be limited to cases involving military personnel as defendants in criminal cases.[107] An edict of 367-370 apparently widened this competence slightly to include civil cases in which one party is military.[108] Even in the Abinnaeus archive, the source of nearly all documentary evidence for military jurisdiction, most cases do in fact involve active or retired

[104]In many if not most cases, of course, nothing is known about the petitioners. Some examples of the landed: *SB* III 6294 (*P.Freib.* 11) (*BL*) (Oxyrhynchos, 336); *P.Oxy.* XLVI 3302 (300/1); LIV 3769 (334); L 3575 (341); XLIII 3140 (3/4c).

[105]See Bagnall 1989a.

[106]See Hobson 1993 on this point.

[107]Lallemand 1964, 148; the key text is *CTh* 2.1.2 (355), admittedly dating after the Abinnaeus archive.

[108]*P.Oxy.* VIII 1101 (*BL*).

military personnel. In the others, it is difficult to say whether military status of one party simply is not mentioned[109] or whether there is an abuse of the rules in order to get help from someone with great local power.[110] At least one clear case of the latter is apparently documented in a pair of petitions by Sakaon, concerning an incident of seizure of sheep by a fellow villager, submitted simultaneously to Abinnaeus and to the *praepositus pagi*.[111] These papyri, however, are evidently copies retained by Sakaon, and nothing is known of the outcome. In other instances of apparent civilian appeals to Abinnaeus against other civilians, once again nothing is known of the outcome. Although there is some evidence—or at least claims—of direct abuse by Abinnaeus of his powers of protection (below, p. 180), there is no real evidence that he heard and decided cases outside his competence. The fact that local residents tried to invoke his power shows only that they thought it was worth a try.

If anything, in fact, there was a decline in the military role in rural justice. It is probably significant that the system of military officers, centurions or *beneficiarii*, described as *statizontes*, or in charge of a local military police station, disappears from the documentation after the first decade of the fourth century. Petitions that until this time[112] would have gone to such officers now are sent to the *praepositus pagi*, a civilian liturgical official from the metropolitan bouleutic class.[113]

For all those who used the system of official justice, the key question was certainly its effectiveness. This has sometimes been rated rather low: "One is struck forcefully by the improbability of an individual ever actually receiving a satisfactory resolution of his difficulty."[114] And yet the evidence suggests a more complex evaluation. For one thing, the persistent use of the petition process by the propertied suggests that they expected some result from this expenditure of time and money. In fact, responses were generally fairly swift,

[109]In many cases the information about status is not preserved. Cases where it is and there is no indication of any military connection are *P.Abinn.* 53 (346); 55 (351); 56 (*BL*) (no date); *SB* XIV 11380 (346).

[110]Cf. Lallemand 1964, 149. For the role of the military in policing see also Isaac 1990, 136-38, with an exaggerated description of such activities in the Abinnaeus archive.

[111]*P.Sakaon* 46 and 47 (342).

[112]The last dated instance is from 304: *P.Oxy.* XVIII 2187. The appearance of the term in *P.Berl.Zill.* 4 (349) does not obviously pertain to the same institution. See *P.Cair.Isid.* 63 introd. for the terminology and practice.

[113]There are a few, rather late, instances of appeals to a *tribunus*, probably an active military officer, although they provide little information on the exact context. One at least (*P.Rain.Cent.* 91 [419]) is from a veteran. The tribune in *P.Oxy.* L 3581 (4/5c) has an additional (and unparalleled) title ending in "peace" that is partly lost.

[114]Hobson 1993.

considerably faster than any modern judicial system, as the case of
Isidoros vs. Kastor and Ammonianos shows. The first stage of that
litigation, up to partial payment and an agreement to pay the rest,
occurred entirely between harvest (early summer) and February of the
following year and probably occupied no more than three months.
Given the time required for communication with Alexandria, that is
an impressive performance. Isidoros probably got about two-thirds of
what was due in the settlement and some expectation of receiving the
rest in a few months.

Nor is this case unique. There are many references to legal settlements worked out as the result of litigation, involving the restitution
of land and the repayment of money, precisely the outcomes most
often desired.[115] The many extracts from legal proceedings are
probably all evidence for successful litigation on someone's part, as
they were certainly kept to provide proof of title to property or of
exemption from some obligation.[116] Similarly, the threat of judgment
was almost certainly responsible for some settlements before trial.[117]
That is not to say that all relief was lasting. Just as litigation largely
emerges from a context of preexisting conflict, so it is sometimes only
a stage in the continuation of this conflict, and cases settled by mediation or compromise probably[118] were less likely to recur. The use of
the courts as one means of pursuing social conflicts, rather than of settling them, is nothing new in ancient society—it is abundantly attested
in classical Athens, for example—and it is a modern prejudice to see
this as abnormal.[119] But it was evidently an effective means of pursuit.

One reason was surely fear. Petitions and other texts sometimes
refer to "the fear of your Highness" or similar thoughts,[120] a fear not
entirely rhetorical in character. Though documentary evidence for

[115]Examples: *SB* III 6294 (*BL*) (Oxyrhynchos, 336); *P.Oxy.* LIV 3756-3758 (325);
3767 (329 or 330).

[116]This must be the case with *P.Col.* VII 175 = *SB* XVI 12692 (Karanis, 339).

[117]Above, p. 163; cf. also *P.Lips.* 14 (*BL*) (Hermopolis, 391); *P.Oxy.* XXXVI 2768
(3c late); XVI 1880 (*BL*) (427).

[118]Though not always: cf. the late example of the Patermouthis archive, for
which see J. J. Farber, "Family Disputes in the Patermouthis Archive," *BASP* 27
(1990) 111-22.

[119]See Bagnall 1989a for the difficulties produced by scholarly preference for
dispute settlement as a conceptual category.

[120]E.g., *M.Chr.* 77 (*BL*) (Great Oasis, 376 or 378); *P.Oxy.* LIV 3757 (325): "keeping
in my heart the fear of the Nobility of so great an official." In the first case the writer
is a *politeuomenos*, in the second the *logistes*. Even the locally mighty feared the truly
important. This fear was not unwelcome to the powerful, however, who cite it with
approval, cf. *P.Select.* 8 (Oxyrhynchos, 421): "In such a time, with peace ruling
("prytanizing") everywhere because of fear of the power of the most eminent
governor." See MacMullen 1988, 84-96, on the uses of fear in the Roman system.

official violence is relatively scarce, it is not nonexistent. Slaves could be tortured,[121] of course, even if flogging them was officially discouraged, and despite official disapproval,[122] violent treatment of free men by officials is often mentioned in literary sources. Even if it is exaggerated by them, it was surely something to worry about.[123] Moreover, despite the prevalence of self-help and the relatively low number of officials, the latter were quite capable of executing their decisions. The curt orders from officials to village liturgists, ordering them to send a defendant up to the metropolis, are witnesses to the state's machinery.[124]

That apparatus served, unsurprisingly, the interests of the powerful. For the urban residents with rural property, it was a means of securing the effectiveness of their contractual relationships with villagers, of whose bold, obstinate character they sometimes complained.[125] But it also was widely used by urbanites against others of their own standing, particularly the rich against the rich. And it was clearly used by the relatively well-off among the village population against their neighbors. Because most petitions request remedies involving land or money, whether they seek immunities, cash payments, restoration of land, or recovery of movables, it is not surprising that few if any are from the really destitute. Their conflicts could not be settled by a system that depended on property-based remedies. They lacked the resources to pursue justice against the better-endowed, and their conflicts were probably in any case mainly with those of similar standing, the judgment-proof. The Roman system did not generally jail criminals, certainly not as punishment, though serious offenders might be sent to work in the mines or quarries. Unless an offense was serious enough to warrant capital punishment, it could not be dealt with effectively. And the government probably did not care; no vital state interest was threatened if such conflict was regulated by informal mechanisms rather than the state. Gross violence, which would threaten the public order in a larger sense, was

[121]*P.Lips.* 40 (Hermopolis, 4/5c, in any case after 368).

[122]*P.Oxy.* IX 1186 (4c): It is an injustice for free men to suffer such an outrage.

[123]See MacMullen 1986; cf. Bagnall 1989a for the limited documentary evidence on this point and the reasons for its scarcity.

[124]See *P.Mich.* X 589-591 introd. for a general discussion with list; cf. U. Hagedorn, *BASP* 16 (1979) 61-74 and H. Drexhage in *Migratio et Commutatio. Studien zur alten Geschichte und deren Nachleben* (St. Katharinen 1989) 102-118.

[125]"Kometike authadeia," as in *CPR* V 9 (Hermopolis, 339), a petition to the *defensor civitatis* by a resident of Hermopolis, complaining about a tenant who will neither pay the rent nor leave the land; likewise *CPR* XVIIA 9b (Hermopolis, 320) concerns villagers' interference with crops. Similar situations underlie, e.g., *P.Lips.* 37 (*BL*) (Hermopolis, 389); *P.Köln* V 234 (Oxyrhynchos, 431).

always a concern,[126] but petty violence was not. Routine force used by the powerful against the weak was, likely as not, seen as acceptable behavior.[127] The system thus did not so much privilege city over country as provide for all a protection of those interests the state found it important to defend. For that purpose, the system worked well enough.

The Military in Society

The still-widespread image of late antiquity as a time of militarization is a product of many factors.[128] When these are broken down into components and looked at with care, many prove not to be what they once seemed. The earlier examination of the taxation system of the fourth century shows that far from being crushing and steadily increasing, it was moderate, fairly proportioned to normal productivity of land, and stable over a period of more than 250 years. For some classes of activity, in fact, it was if anything rather light. It is hard in the absence of high-level financial documents to say what proportion of the total tax burden was taken up by military expenditures, but it seems unlikely to have been more than about a quarter to a third of the total.[129] And because the tax burden as a whole is unlikely to have amounted to more than half of the total concentrated *surplus* production, the military's share of the total economic output of Egypt was certainly under 10 percent. That is not to say that it was trivial, but neither was it the all-devouring consumer sometimes pictured. Its propensity for generation of paperwork makes it appear rather larger in the papyri than it probably was in reality.

The regular taxes, even allowing for the periodic extra levies, were certainly not the whole burden. There are many references in the documents to what look like special costs created by a passing military unit or individual officer.[130] Because they appear mainly in the form of entries in expenditure ledgers, their role in the overall budget is obscure. Some of them are clearly distributions by the regular liturgical officials from the store of accumulated taxes, like the chaff handed

[126]Cf. *W.Chr.* 23 = *BGU* IV 1035 (*BL*) (Arsinoite, 5c).

[127]See Bagnall 1989a. The notion that the wealthy developed private, feudal military forces as a systemic form of coercion was, however, demolished by J. Gascou's study of the *bucellarii* in *BIFAO* 76 (1976) 143-56.

[128]See Carrié 1986, 449-55, on this historiographic problem, with many good observations and criticisms.

[129]See Carrié 1977, 383-86, for some incomplete estimates (he does not reckon the total tax revenues); cf. M. El-Abbadi, *Proc. XVI Congr.* 516.

[130]*SB* XIV 11591-11593 (cf. Bagnall 1985b, 34, 39), from *ca* 325-330, are good examples of the genre.

out in Oxyrhynchos in 295 for various officers, troops, and their animals.[131] But when the village officials of Prektis in the Hermopolite Nome report to the *praepositus pagi* that they have paid 300 talents for hire of a camel for carrying arrow poison for the recruits, was that a disbursement of normal tax revenues or an extra burden for the village?[132] In all likelihood, most of such spending constituted the use of regular tax revenues, not all of which were simply gathered in to central coffers. But exceptions would not be easy to identify.

More irregular, though probably not in most cases formally improper, were exactions of personal services. The ever-unpopular billeting of soldiers in private homes, for example, seems to be exceptional but not particularly remarkable.[133] Providing transport for the military was a commonplace, indeed normal, obligation for villages.[134] And local officials were expected to assist military officers in their duties, whether strictly military or involved in more purely administrative matters.[135]

Two other areas of military involvement in civilian life similarly tend to evaporate under bright light. One of them is justice, treated above; for the most part, military officers are seen in judicial situations only in the officially specified circumstances, when a party is a soldier.[136] The introduction (apparently around 346[137]) of the *riparius* as a civic official in charge of security, in fact, may have led to a decline in the military involvement in petty policework and judging at the local level. And that problematic activity called "patronage," which is treated in chapter 6, proves to differ little from the behavior of other local notables like members of the bouleutic class.

The possibilities of quantification allow some confidence in conclusions about the burdensomeness of taxation for military purposes, while in the areas of justice and patronage the evidence is episodic and thus harder to assess for typicality and broad impact.[138] Something similar may be said of the questions to which the discussion must now turn. The pattern of stationing of troops, the effects of the army on manpower, and (to a lesser degree) the economic power of

[131]*P.Oxy.* I 43 recto (*BL*).

[132]*BGU* I 21 ii.14 (*BL*) (340).

[133]Cf. *P.Oxy.* L 3581 (4/5c), where the plaintiff alleges that her "husband" stole from the soldiers and then decamped, leaving her to face the music.

[134]E.g., *BGU* III 899 (*BL*) (Philadelphia, 4c).

[135]*P.Oxy.* XII 1428 (4c).

[136]Carrié 1986, 482, also rejects the notion of a military usurpation of justice.

[137]Lallemand 1964, 163; there is still no secure example before that date.

[138]On the difficulties of the "analytic" character of documentation, see Carrié 1986, 450.

the military all lend themselves to global assessment, even though the evidence is incomplete. The social behavior of soldiers and their effect on the tone of civil society are harder to assess. As so often, documentation follows trouble.

The garrison of Egypt in the Roman period has been estimated at about twenty thousand men, probably a bit higher in the fourth century.[139] It is somewhat easier to identify new units arriving in an area or being created than to finger those departing, and any picture is thus incomplete.[140] The highest quality troops were mainly held in central forts or in key border locations: Babylon, Memphis, Philai. Smaller and less experienced units were stationed in a variety of posts throughout the valley and the Delta.[141] The third century had seen some concentration on the desert edges, largely in response to difficulties with the Blemmyes and other nomadic groups. The best-known such witness is the fort at Dionysias, on the edge of the Fayum, probably constructed around 260 and in use until the later fourth century.[142] In the early fourth century, there was a renewed effort to secure control over the commercial routes to the Red Sea and, presumably, through its ports (above, pp. 145-47). The decline in nomadic threats after Diocletian, however, may have allowed the better part of a century in which the desert needed only modest attention, allowing troops to be stationed mainly in the valley towns.[143]

The Arsinoite had other troops besides the *ala* at Dionysias: a cohort at Narmouthis (also on the desert edge), evidently withdrawn by 346, and a cavalry detachment placed at Arsinoe itself by 319.[144] Later a *numerus* of Transtigritani appear in the Arsinoite.[145] A legionary vexillation was evidently at Oxyrhynchos under Diocletian,[146] and there was an *ala* in the nome in 324.[147] In the Hermopolite appears a

---

[139]Cf. Carrié 1977, 385. See on the Egyptian garrison also A. K. Bowman, *BASP* 15 (1978) 25-38; K. A. Worp, *ZPE* 87 (1991) 291-95.

[140]See Rémondon 1965, 132-36.

[141]The picture rests in part on the *Notitia Dignitatum*, but Carrié (1986, 459) has shown that much of what it treats as "central" army units were in fact stationed throughout the country. Any mobile army in Egypt is thus largely notional.

[142]Schwartz et al. 1969; Carrié 1974; Rémondon 1965, 132-34.

[143]So Rémondon 1955, 26; 1965, 137. He probably overestimates fluctuations in both needs and responses.

[144]Rémondon 1965, 132-34. For the *cataphractarii* at Arsinoe, see *M.Chr.* 271 (= *BGU* I 316, *FIRA* III 135) (*BL*), the well-known slave sale from Ascalon dated 359. The purchaser is Fl. Vitalianus, *biarchos* of the *vexillatio* of cavalry *cataphractarii* now based in Arsinoe under the tribune Dorotheos.

[145]*SB* XIV 11574 (Oxyrhynchos, 406) and *SB* XIV 12129 (Arsinoite?, 4/5c).

[146]See *P.Oxy.* XLI 2950, probably the cartoon for a dedication to Diocletian and Maximian, in Latin, by a *vexillatio* of Leg. V Maced.

[147]*PSI* IV 300 (*BL*; *BASP* 27 [1990] 86-89), in which a cavalryman purchases a pottery works in an Oxyrhynchite village from a councillor of Antinoopolis.

numerus of Mauri, stationed there by 340, at least part of which was stationed at Lykopolis still in 426 and in Hermopolis in 446.[148] Lykopolis had had at least part of the Sixth Legion in 354.[149] Under the tetrarchs, an *ala* was stationed just upriver from Panopolis.[150] And more such could be cited. Clearly some units remained in a particular locale for an extended period, while others came and went. Overall, units appear both at major population centers and at strategic places in their nomes, guarding key points on the river or the desert fringes.

These units were in general not large, and in a total provincial garrison in the range of twenty to thirty thousand, no one nome is likely to have had more than one thousand to fifteen hundred men at any given time, apart perhaps from major encampments in the areas of Alexandria and Memphis. The number is proportionately small, and the garrison as a whole will have amounted to somewhere between 0.5 percent and 0.8 percent of the population of the country.[151] That is not a lot different from the empire as a whole, where a reasonable guess is 0.8 percent.[152] A garrison that size probably needed around two thousand recruits per year, or perhaps forty to fifty from a typical nome.[153] A typical village might thus contribute a recruit in alternate years. That is not a large drain, and it is difficult to see any large impact of army recruitment on the total labor supply. Nor would the annual class of veterans reentering civil society be large, perhaps a third of the number of recruits.[154]

Enlistment was not, however, very popular, and even those already in the army would look for excuses to get away for personal business or simply to avoid active service altogether.[155] Rather than

---

[148]See Rémondon 1965, 136; *BGU* XII 2137 (426); 2141 (446).

[149]*PSI* IX 1077 (Oxyrhynchos), two soldiers selling building lots.

[150]*P.Oxy.* XLI 2953 (293-305): the Ala I Hiberorum Diocletianae Max. Const. Max., stationed in Thmou.

[151]Using a figure of 4.2 million.

[152]See Carrié 1986, 470-76, using the lower estimates for both population and army size, and the middle option for mortality. He sees Egypt as proportionately undergarrisoned (1977, 385), but that is in part a result of his use of a traditional but excessive figure of 7 million for the population of Egypt.

[153]Carrié 1986, 473, estimates that (on the middle demographic model) about 7 percent of the total strength needed to be recruited each year, amounting to perhaps 5.6 percent of the available men in an age cohort each year in the empire at large.

[154]Cf. Duncan-Jones 1981, 81; Shaw 1983, 139-40 (probably something of an underestimate).

[155]See (e.g.) *P.Herm.* 7 = *Naldini* 82 (4c), the writer of which says, "And I never go on active service, being unfit; since I have a complete excuse for this by reason of my finger; it has not festered nor has it healed either." See generally Rémondon 1965, 136, on problems like desertion and shirking. But it must not be forgotten that ill-health was a reality; see Rea 1984 for some instances of retirement for disability.

face the possible difficulties of conscription, particularly when such a small percentage of the available males would be taken, the government shifted the burden to the cities, and they to the villages, which had to come up with recruits when ordered. They had at their disposal a powerful persuader, an enlistment bonus of thirty solidi, capital sufficient to support a family.[156] Recruits naturally tried to milk their enlistment for all they could, while local authorities tried to keep their entitlements down to the amount prescribed; in one case the recruits complained to the military commander of all Egypt, the *dux*, but after examining the accounts he backed up the local officials.[157] The recruit's ideal, to be sure, was to keep the cash and somehow escape the actual service, and some tried to do just that. The existence of the army, however, bears witness that most did not, or at least did not succeed.[158]

As all of this implies, recruitment for the army was by this period mostly local. The surviving partial rosters of military units in Egypt bear out this supposition, for their onomastic repertory is for the most part exactly that of contemporary Egyptian civil society, except for the official name prefixed to the real one—that is, Valerius under Licinius and Flavius under Constantine and his successors.[159] It is certainly true that some units recruited outside Egypt were transferred there; the *cataphractarii* stationed at Arsinoe had come there from Palestine, for example, and it is generally thought that Fl. Abinnaeus, the commander at Dionysias whose papers figure so largely in this domain, first came to Egypt as part of a Syrian unit stationed in Upper Egypt.[160] And Egyptian recruits were sent abroad, both for particular campaigns in the eastern theater of operations and to prevent an excessive concentration of Goths in the imperial army elsewhere.[161] Sailors for the fleets were also recruited in time of need.[162]

[156]See the receipt *W.Chr.* 466 (*P.Lond.* III 985) (Herakleopolite, 4c). In *P.Michael.* 28 (*BL; ZPE* 56 [1984] 128-29) (Herakleopolite, 313-314) seven villages agree with a man on his service as the sailor demanded from them.

[157]*P.Oxy.* VIII 1103 = *W.Chr.* 465 (360).

[158]Rémondon 1965, 136, makes much of the known cases. But the authorities had to be careful; see *W.Chr.* 469 with Rémondon 1955, 27.

[159]See Rea 1984, 84-85; *P.Oxy.* L 3580 (post 324); *P.Mich.* X 592 (311-324); *P.Mich.* X 593 (312: more Roman names than the others).

[160]See *P.Abinn.*, p. 7, though the argument is hardly conclusive; Abinnaeus was sufficiently at home in Egypt to marry an Alexandrian woman. For Abinnaeus' career, see Barnes 1985.

[161]See Rémondon 1955, 27-32, on this "exchange" program and its consequences.

[162]*CPR* V 10 (*ca* 339-341).

This local army may not have been militarily very impressive; there is no evidence that some of these units ever engaged in battle. But their local recruitment, from both villages and cities, should have made them fit fairly easily into the society they guarded.[163] By no stretch of the imagination was this either the advance guard of a Roman civilizing mission, nor yet was it an alien body, recruited elsewhere and at odds with its subject population.[164] If its impact through taxation, justice, recruitment, public works, collective economic activity and "patronage" was more modest than has generally been supposed,[165] was there an area in which it affected society more heavily? An affirmative answer is suggested by Libanius' oration on patronage, which has been shown to be in reality an outcry against the wealth, and particularly the landed wealth, of the officer class, which was perceived by the curial class as harming their interests.[166] But that speech concerns Antioch at a particular time (around 390), and it is not immediately obvious that the chronology or severity of the problem was comparable in Egypt.

The career of Abinnaeus has been offered as the primary evidence that this problem was equally visible in Egypt, and the years between 350 and 380 or so claimed as the high point of the rise of the wealth of military officers.[167] There is an initial chronological embarassment from both ends, however, for Libanius must be seen as complaining about a phenomenon already on the wane,[168] and Abinnaeus is last attested in 351, just as the problem is supposedly on the rise. But the foundations of this view are still more insecure than a problem of timing. The documents supposed to show Abinnaeus' holdings are for the most part by no means securely private in character and in fact

[163]They even had birthday parties for their children: *P.Oxy.* IX 1214 (= *Sel.Pap.* I 175) (5c).

[164]See Shaw 1983 on the Roman garrison of Numidia for a striking contrast: soldiers recruited in the municipalities of the province of Africa and from the camps themselves, controlling an area which did not contribute to the composition of its garrison. Similarly see Isaac 1990, esp. 116-17, on Palestine as a province controlled by an army of outsiders.

[165]On the marginality of military economic activity and public works, see Carrié 1977, 374-75.

[166]See Carrié 1976 for an exposé of Libanius' ideological and economic agenda underlying the rhetorical strategies he uses.

[167]For this argument, see Carrié 1976, 169 and 176; earlier, Rémondon 1965, 140. Both also cite the case of Fl. Vitalianus, whose economic activities appear in *P.Grenf.* I 54 (378, lease) and *P.Lond.* V 1656 (4c, loan for repayment in winejars). But it is worth noting that the land leased in 378 produced a rather poor return, and that Vitalianus is there only a middleman, leasing the land himself from a member of the curial class.

[168]As Carrié 1976, 175, does.

seem unlikely to be so.[169] And the only source that provides any possibility of quantification for the 350s, the Hermopolite land registers, offers no support at all. In the Hermopolite list, less than 1.8 percent of the land is owned by present or deceased men who *could* be military;[170] it is in fact at least as likely that they are civil servants, many of whose titles in this period are military ranks (see above, p. 66). The Antinoite list, as noted above, shows much larger percentages of official holders, with 7.7 percent of the land in the hands of active and 9.4 percent in the hands of retired or deceased persons designated by titles which may be military or civil. Because the Antinoite holdings are much smaller than the Hermopolite, however, taking a weighted average of the two nomes[171] would indicate that active officers owned 1.2 percent of land owned by city residents, and retired or deceased owned just 0.5 percent. Because the wealthy are disproportionately likely to live in the cities, adding into the calculation land owned by village residents would only reduce these percentages.

This unimpressive showing is not the result of impoverishment on the part of either retired or active officers, even if the wealth of the latter is often overestimated.[172] There is in fact considerable evidence that military men owned land, which because they were otherwise occupied they rented out to tenants.[173] Having as they did considerable liquid resources as well, they figure also as lenders in a fair number of surviving loans,[174] including those that constitute working capital for repayment in goods.[175] Their methods of investing their surplus thus parallel those of members of the curial class, and although they were not liable to liturgical offices, they did have other

[169]They are enumerated by Carrié 1976, 176. See Bagnall 1992a for a detailed version of what follows.

[170]The following titles are included in the figures used here: *quaestonarius, beneficiarius, primipilarius, speculator, librarius, ducenarius*, soldier, veteran.

[171]Multiplying the Hermopolite figures by four to account for the other three quarters of the city, and assuming that the military were half of the official ranks cited (probably too high a percentage).

[172]Carrié 1986, 484, argues that military service was, overall, profitable only if one lasted to retirement. This was probably true for enlisted men, but it is questionable for officers.

[173]The papers of Fl. Taurinos in *BGU* XII are the most extensive dossier. Another interesting instance: *SB* IV 7445 (*BL*) (Oxyrhynchos, 382), a lease of a house by a former *praepositus*, now a landlord in the Oxyrhynchite.

[174]E.g., *P.Coll.Youtie* II 82 = *P.Oxy.* XLV 3266 (337), a loan by a *protector*; perhaps *P.Oxy.* XIV 1711 (late 3c), loan by a *ducenarius* of equestrian rank; *P.Flor.* I 30 (362), loan of six artabas of wheat from a soldier stationed at Dionysias.

[175]Even sheep's fleeces, see *P.Lund.* VI 10 = *SB* VI 9359 (*BL*) (Arsinoite, 400), in which an Arsinoite resident acknowledges to Fl. Sarapammon, soldier of the camp of Skenai Mandron in the Memphite Nome the price of five fleeced adult sheep, which he promises to deliver.

normal burdens on the land.[176] The similarity extends also to the occasional investment in productive facilities of other sorts, whether in villages or cities.[177] And they certainly did not form any sort of separate caste. In one case the veteran son of a deceased veteran leases to yet another veteran a quarter of a house in a Herakleopolite village, which he owns jointly with the heirs of a deceased councillor of Naukratis and those of a deceased soldier.[178] And in some cases officers came from well-off families and inherited land; not all their wealth was acquired from military service.[179]

Numbers were decisive. Probably no more than one soldier in a hundred at any given time had attained both the rank and the seniority to be able to compete economically with the councillors; even that estimate, which means five men in a five-hundred-man auxiliary unit, is probably high. But it yields just three hundred men in all of Egypt, even on a high estimate of the total garrison. If each acquired two hundred arouras, their total holdings would come to less than 1 percent of the country's land. In reality, the average holding of the rank-holders in the Hermopolite and Antinoite registers is about seventy-five arouras. Obviously in some situations a particular high-ranking military officer was in a position to compete vigorously with curial landlords in a particular place, enough no doubt to irritate the occasional Egyptian equivalent of Libanius. But it is simply not arithmetically possible for this to have been more than a very exceptional case. Nor, it should be noted, is landholding by active soldiers a new phenomenon in the fourth century.[180]

One ugly aspect remains, probably inescapable in a society with an underdeveloped civil state and any military at all, the abuse by individual members of the military of its near-monopoly on force.

[176]Including paying taxes on land compulsorily leased to them, as in *W.Chr.* 380 (*P.Gen.* I 70) (Philadelphia, 381).

[177]E.g., *P.Oxy.* XIV 1705 = *Sel.Pap.* I 36 (298), sale of a loom; *P.Oxy.* XLII 3079 (4c), ship owned by *speculator*; cf. above n. 147 for purchase of a pottery works.

[178]*P.Gen.* I 10 (*BL*) (316).

[179]A case in point is *SB* XII 10989 (*ca* 325), in which the deceased father of a *beneficiarius* and brother of an *ex-protector* had acquired and improved land, about which they are now in litigation. The father is not accorded any official title and seems simply to have been an industrious (and perhaps not wholly scrupulous) landowner.

[180]See for the third century, e.g., *P.Cair.Isid.* 110 (280 or 281), a rent receipt from a soldier; *P.Oxy.* XXII 2346 (2nd half of 3c), a register including two soldiers; *P.Flor.* I 83 (Oxyrhynchos, 3/4c), an order for soldiers in the nome for the sowing to present themselves, rather suggesting that many of them were away from their posts in order to sow their land. Imperial prohibitions of owning land in the province where a soldier was serving (*Digest* 49.16.9, 49.16.13) were thus not very effective.

Even apart from the "protection" discussed in chapter 6, not to speak of the use of violence in the maintenance of order, there are some reports or threats of illegitimate use of coercion. Probably the most common was the use of force to collect debts, which a civilian would have had to take to court. The most graphic instance may be a memorandum of a *ducenarius* to his "tentmate" Geladios, asking him to look in the Arsinoite for a barber who lives there, having fled from Lykopolis, and try to collect from him on a surety agreement. If he refuses to pay, Geladios is to ask an officer of the local vexillation to have him put in irons and handed over on the charge of having sold stolen camels.[181] There are other instances.[182] A woman complains that her brother, a soldier, is depriving her of her meager inheritance; does his military status play a role?[183] A sailor is described as a drunkard and a bad character.[184] A more imaginative abuse is protested by a very high-ranking citizen of Hermopolis, who complains that a man of "military appearance" whom he names forced him to draw up a bogus acknowledgment of loan.[185] It is surprising to find a man who presumably had slaves and other staff to protect him sounding so vulnerable. Here as with the other cases, it is hard to know how typical such incidents were. But power rarely exists without abuses.

Even such abuse, however, hardly constitutes a militarization of society in the sense of systemic oppression.[186] Nor is it militarization in the sense that military personnel become dominant forces in civil society, either socially or economically. That clearly was not the case.[187] Instead, the military was one more element in the complex series of links that made city and country into a single, closely connected, society, with many forms of interdependence.

---

[181]*P.Abinn.* 42 (*BL*) (probably after 351).

[182]*P.Fay.* 135 (Euhemeria, 4c), a letter threatening a man with imprisonment at the hands of soldiers if he doesn't pay up 1.5 art. of vegetable seed owing since last year; *P.Coll.Youtie* II 88 (4c). *P.Oxy.* XII 1588 (late 3c) may not be illegitimate; the context is unclear. See generally MacMullen 1988, 122-70, *passim*.

[183]*P.Rain.Cent.* 85 (364-366).

[184]*P.Laur.* II 42 (Oxyrhynchite, later 4c).

[185]*P.Stras.* VI 560 (*BL*; Index to *P.Stras.* 501-800, p. 108) (Hermopolis, *ca* 325). See below, p. 227 on this incident.

[186]See Carrié 1986, 481, making the point that this is propaganda.

[187]Despite the remarks of Rémondon 1965, 142-43.

Plate 1
Antinoopolis, triumphal arch (*Description de l'Égypte* IV, pl. 57)

Plate 2
Hermopolis, reconstruction of Komasterion area
(*Excavations at el-Ashmunein* IV, pl. 23, courtesy of Trustees of
the British Museum, British Museum Press)

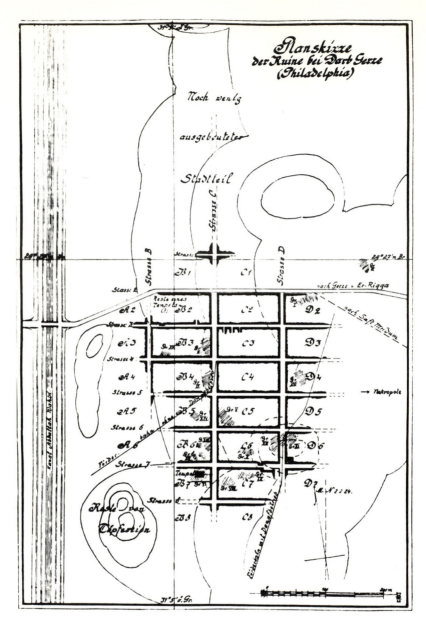

Plate 3
Philadelphia, plan (*BGU* VII, pl. I)

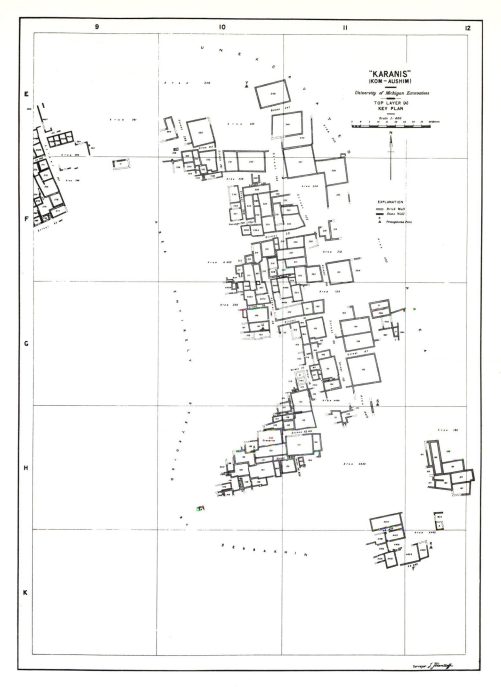

Plate 4
Karanis, plan in the last phases (Courtesy of
Kelsey Museum Photo Archives,
University of Michigan [Photograph 8.1046])

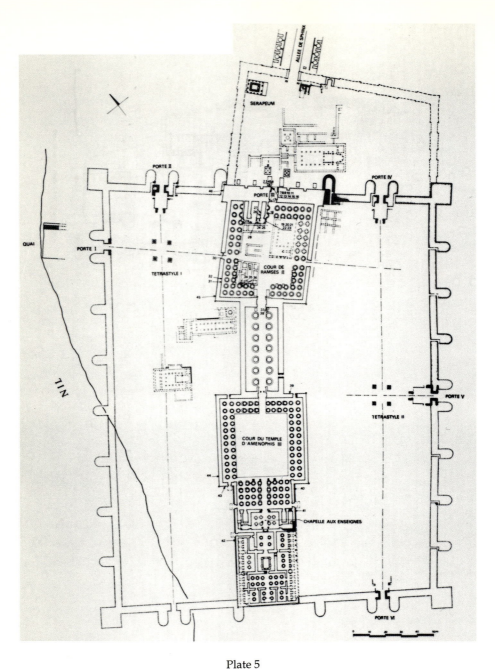

Plate 5
Thebes, plan of temple converted into army camp (Golvin et al.,
Le camp romain de Louqsor, pl. I, courtesy of the
Institut Français d'Archéologie Orientale)

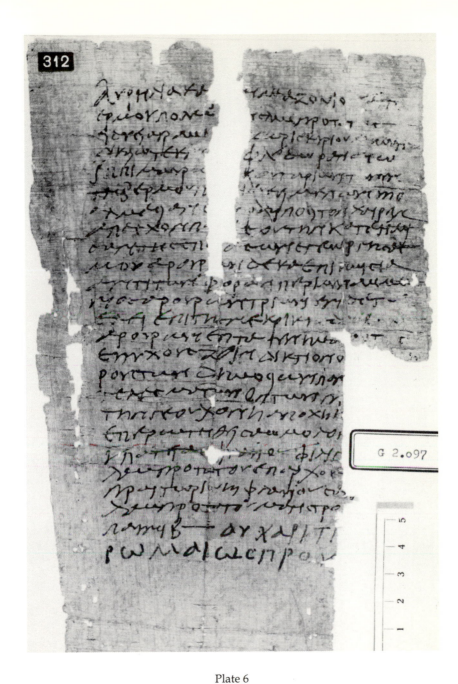

Plate 6

P.Charite 8 (Greek papyrus with woman's hand)

(P.Vindob. G.2097, courtesy of the Österreichische Nationalbibliothek)

Plate 7
P.Lond. VI 1922 (Coptic letter)
(By permission of the British Library)

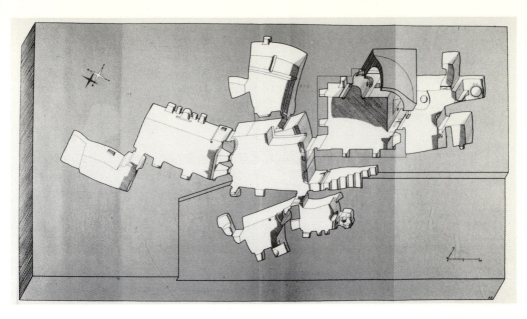

Plate 8

Esna, axonometric plan of an atrium hermitage (S. Sauneron and
J. Jacquet, *Les ermitages chrétiens du désert d'Esna* II, pl. CLXXX, courtesy of the
Institut Français d'Archéologie Orientale)

Plate 9

Naqlun, view from monastery to cultivated land
(Original photograph, courtesy of Dr. W. Godlewski)

Plate 10
Naqlun, view of a monk's cell
(Original photograph, courtesy of Dr. W. Godlewski)

Plate 11
Monastery of St. Simeon at Aswan, storage magazines
(Original photograph, courtesy of Dr. A. K. Bowman)

CHAPTER 5

People and Families

It is in the nature of the heavily official surviving documentation that what is sometimes (but misleadingly) called "private" life should be less easily described and understood than other aspects of society. And the reticence of private letters, often written for their senders by slaves or scribes, makes it particularly hard to recover the values and attitudes underlying institutions and behavior. The real difficulty, however, lies not in recording what the documents tell us but in putting the fragmentary information in a context. Borrowing from what is known of earlier periods creates an exaggerated version of the usual risks (above, p. 13). It is, to be sure, most unlikely that the basic pattern of mortality discernible from the second- and third-century census declarations had changed significantly in the fourth century. But one cannot be confident that the associated behavioral patterns of the earlier centuries continued along with the demographic continuum, as the disappearance of evidence for brother-sister marriage shows.

Understanding Egypt in the larger context of the Roman Empire is even more problematic. The "Roman family" has been one of the liveliest areas of historical research in the past two decades, and the central questions are framed with far more sophistication today than even a few years ago. But nearly every one of them remains highly controversial; there is little acquired agreement. Much of this scholarship, moreover, takes the late third century as its terminus, cutting off just too soon to be optimally illuminating for the fourth century. Most difficult of all, though the meaning of "family" is almost always described in all its complexity,[1] the other half of the phrase, "Roman," is treated as though a self-evident category. Sometimes Rome itself is the standard, sometimes Italy, but at other times the western provinces are included; though the other eastern provinces rarely form part of the discussion, Egypt is at times invoked thanks to the papyri. In truth, family history is scarcely even in its infancy for the Greek East under Roman rule—the context in which one would really like to place Egypt. Nor, once again, should social and economic standing be

---

[1]See, e.g., Dixon 1992, 1-11, and Bradley 1991, 3-5; such discussions are virtually a ritual requirement of the literature on the history of families.

forgotten. Although students of Roman families have scrupulously noted the limitations of their data, so many subjects are approachable only for the highest stratum of society that the reader may at times be excused for thinking that these are the real Romans.

Given all these constraints, it is useful to start with the most external and quantifiable elements of the situation, the demographic regime. It seems likely that in this respect, at least, Egypt is fairly representative of the Mediterranean world of antiquity and the middle ages. Demography sets the context in which the more culturally determined characteristics of family life operated. Although it is difficult, if not impossible, to assign all these to any particular source in the complex background of late Roman Egypt, recent work on Roman families usefully frames some of the remaining questions.

Demography: The Shape of the Population

By modern standards, the population of Roman Egypt was young and short-lived.[2] For one thing, infant mortality was high; nearly one-third of all children died before their first birthday and more than two-fifths by the age of five.[3] This high rate of early death caused the life expectancy at birth to be low by modern standards, around twenty-two for women and twenty-five for men. Those figures, however, combine high early mortality with a very different sort of experience for those who survived early childhood. A child who survived to age five could expect on average to die in his or her middle forties. Five of six such five-year-olds would make it to the childbearing years, but after age twenty the death rate rose steadily. Of the twenty-year-olds, nearly two-thirds would live long enough to raise a family, surviving to forty-five or older, but less than half of these would then live to age sixty-five.

There is virtually no direct evidence for change in demographic trends between the second and fourth centuries. Census declarations

[2]The bibliography on life expectancy and related issues in antiquity is enormous. Statements here are provisional and largely based on Bagnall and Frier forthcoming; see already Frier (1982 and 1983), who gives extensive bibliography and analysis for the Roman Empire more generally.

[3]Infant mortality is perhaps the most difficult aspect of the subject; this part of the population is very sketchily documented and somewhat underrepresented in the census declarations because they were filed the year after the year being reported on and virtually always omitted infants who had died in the intervening year. The figures quoted here depend in part on the use of model life tables for modern populations whose adult members have mortality rates similar to those prevalent in antiquity.

of persons virtually disappear: After a hiatus since 257/8, there are two in 309-310 and then no more,[4] probably as the result of changes in the taxation system (see above, pp. 153-55) which eliminated the taxes that the original census was designed to help collect. There is no reason to suppose, however, that mortality in Egypt was much different in the fourth century than in the first to third centuries, and the assembled evidence of the census declarations from Augustus to the third century agrees very closely with the general picture for the Roman Empire, being perhaps just a shade more favorable.[5] The picture was no doubt better for some elements of society than others, especially once past the mortality of infancy, but the differences were probably just matters of degree.[6]

The death rate and age structure of any population have a profound impact on every area of social relations; some of these are hidden by the objective and analytic character of most of the evidence, but others emerge in connection with points in this chapter and elsewhere. One important area is the subjective concept of age. A minor orphan's petition to a provincial governor complains about the proceedings launched against him (that is, against his inherited property) by his paternal grandfather's sister, alleging that "believing, obviously, that the death of my father (against whom she had presented no claims nor raised any action about anything during his lifetime) was a windfall, she proceeds against me for the first time now, when she has reached a very old age; for she appears to have lived more than sixty years, during which (until now at least) she lived inoffensively."[7] Other evidence suggests that this age estimate was about right,[8] but most striking is the petitioner's assumption that a person over sixty would be considered old by anyone; because the boy's guardian is presumably responsible for the statement, this can-

[4]*P.Cair.Isid.* 8 (309), *P.Sakaon* 1 (310), from the same census.

[5]Cf. the articles of Frier cited in n. 2 above. The then-known data were set out in M. Hombert and C. Préaux, *Pap.Lugd.Bat.* V (1952), with limited analysis. An updated list of census declarations, with a tabulation of the data, appears in Bagnall and Frier, forthcoming.

[6]Cf. Frier 1982, 228 with n.36, quoting P. R. Cox: "Class differences [in mortality] are small when mortality is very high." Considerably more pessimistic figures emerged from a study of the Theban tax receipts in *Death and Taxes*; these were questioned by P. S. Derow and E. O. Derow, *Phoenix* 27 (1973) 80-88, and more comprehensively by T. G. Parkin, *Demography and Roman Society* (Baltimore 1992) 22-27, who attacks the statistical basis of that study. Even with these reservations, however, it is probable that the Theban peasantry had a shorter life expectancy than more affluent groups.

[7]*P.Sakaon* 40 (318-320).

[8]Bagnall 1982b, 40-42; the child was petitioning through his guardian, who was the husband of his aunt.

not be dismissed as merely a child's perspective. In Roman Egypt, sixty was the end of poll-tax liability; in classical Athens, sixty was the end of the obligation for military and other public service. A fragmentary fourth-century papyrus cites an edict exempting those over sixty from some public burden.[9] It was, in effect, a kind of retirement age for the tenth of all births who lived that long; a hardy few might live to extreme old age, but anyone over sixty could be classified as "old."[10] Indeed, the category probably included almost anyone past the average age of death for those who survived early childhood, the early to middle forties; in the Renaissance, men in their forties and fifties were routinely termed old, both by themselves and by others.[11]

Another critical point underlying family relations was the need for a high level of reproduction to continue merely to maintain the numbers of the population. Without an average production of six live births per woman, the forces of mortality would wear away the populace. Even though there is little ancient sign of population policy in the modern sense, society could not be indifferent to its own continuation.[12]

Disease, Injury, and Death

The Egyptians of late antiquity, like other people of the ancient world, knew that life was mostly short. And like others, when death came for one of them the survivors were sure to say to one another such commonplaces as "it is necessary to bear mortality. Therefore put off your grief for this mortal event and consider that no one among men is immortal except God,"[13] or "I know that you, being mortal and being one who has had experience of many matters, will be able to master yourself."[14] They did not, however, actually feel death less keenly than

---

[9]*SB* XVI 12306 (324), very fragmentary, an edict of Constantine with an appended petition from a man seeking to avoid some liturgy or other burden because of old age; after quoting from an edict exempting those over sixty from something he remarks that he, at seventy-three, is both old and ill.

[10]Cf. Dixon 1992, 150 (with 235 n.85).

[11]See the extensive collection of information and analysis by C. Gilbert, "When did a Man in the Renaissance Grow Old?" *Studies in the Renaissance* 14 (1967) 7-32.

[12]This pressure is well evoked by Brown 1988, 6.

[13]*P.Princ.* II 102 = Naldini 34 (3/4c); despite the latter's attempt to dignify the sentiments of this letter as a "pensiero di conforto così altamente religioso" of Christian origin, there is nothing distinctively Christian about it. See *P.Oxy.* LV 3819 (early 4c) for similar sentiments.

[14]*CPR* VI 81 (cf. J. R. Rea, *ZPE* 62 [1986] 75-78) (3/4c). Such sentiments are not actually much help for grief, cf. Ira Nerken, "Making it Safe to Grieve," *Christian Century* 105 no. 36 (30 November 1988) 1091-94.

anyone else;[15] though private letters were in many cases written with some restraint because they were dictated to slaves or public scribes, they show signs of normal difficulty in dealing with death. One correspondent writes to his brother, "Put all things aside and come immediately to us because our mother has died and we badly need your presence. . . . Do not neglect it and feel repentance afterwards."[16]

Death came soon, and it came swiftly; sometimes also without any explanation.[17] Inundation time seems to have been particularly risky to the health.[18] Medicine's ability to control infections or degenerative diseases was practically nil, and any illness might be swiftly fatal. "For if anyone among us in the village falls sick, they do not rise," wrote one correspondent.[19] A public official in the Oxyrhynchite Nome, faced with the sudden death of the chief peace officer of the village of Teis in 392, asked the logistes to have a public physician examine the body for signs of foul play. The doctor's report says that he found no trace of a blow or contusion; rather, the eirenarch had died of a "rapid illness."[20] Unlike the modern belief (reasonable enough today) that most infections are either self-limiting or curable, the ancient expectation was that any illness might end in death without much warning.[21] Probably for this reason ancient letter writers are obsessed with wishes for health, reports on the sender's health, and inquiries after the health of the recipient.[22] A modern reader might be tempted to dismiss as so much polite formula the phrases like "above all else, I pray for your health," or "please write to me about your health," or assurances of the writer's health. But that would be quite wrong. There are many very strong statements reproaching correspondents

[15]On the controversial question of parental grief for the death of young children, cf. below, p. 202.

[16]*P.Wisc.* II 74 (3/4c).

[17]Cf. *P.Sakaon* 50 (317), a report of death, broken at the top: "as he was pasturing his sheep. As I was unable to carry his body, even with difficulty, or to ascertain the cause of his death (for I do not know how he passed away) without official certification, I submit this report to you to safeguard myself regarding the matter and so that you may take cognizance."

[18]*HL* 35.4.

[19]*P.Oxy.* LV 3817 (3/4c). G. Casanova, *Atti XVII Congr.Pap.* III 949-56, argues for a fourth-century outbreak of plague, but both date and plague are refuted by J. Bingen, *Studia varia Bruxellensia* (Brussels 1987) 3-14.

[20]*P.Rein.* II 92.

[21]Thus one would make a will on becoming sick, as in *P.Col.* VII 188 (320), in which the writer refers to the possibility of his death in the course of the "very terrible" disease which has attacked him. For the commonness of such actions, see Champlin 1991, 64-65.

[22]A good analysis can be found in Koskenniemi 1956, 71-75, 130-39, with many typical examples.

for not writing about their health, like "I am astonished that so far you have not written me about your health."[23]

These are universals in Roman Egypt, hardly peculiar to the fourth century. But a noticeable change in the tenor of mentions of disease is discernible. Letters written[24] by Christians not only seem somewhat more likely to refer to illness than other letters, but they also go into far greater detail in describing diseases.[25] Christians also ask for and offer prayers for the healing of the sick with some frequency.[26] Pagans believed that many diseases came from divine agency,[27] and illness is included among the evils from which magic could help to protect one.[28] But where for a pagan the ritual of the *proskynema* before the local god on behalf of others was a general means of propitiating the god on their behalf, for a Christian prayer was a more specific means of asking divine help in dispelling a particular illness.

Most references to disease in the papyri are fairly vague, but several more specific ones can be found, such as chronic pulmonary coughing,[29] infection of the feet,[30] difficulty in breathing (asthma?),[31] a white spot in the cornea,[32] and pus and granulation in the eye.[33] The inability to rise from the sickbed and travel is often mentioned, frequently coupled with exhortations to the recipient to come and visit the sick person.[34] In some cases, illness dragged on for months,[35] but

[23]*P.Iand.* VI 100 = Naldini 87 (4c); there are many examples throughout the Roman period, cf. Koskenniemi 1956, 71.

[24]The term here includes those dictated.

[25]See R.J.S. Barrett-Lennard, *NewDocs* 4, 123 commentary (pp. 247-50), who notes that the Christian letters are full of rare words in such contexts.

[26]E.g., *P.Lond.* VI 1926 and 1929 (Herakleopolite, mid 4c).

[27]Cf. *P.Herm.* 2 (*BL*) (4c), where the writer says "for it was one of the gods who in malice sent these [his daughter's illnesses] upon me, and may he yet bring them to an end!"

[28]Cf. *SB* XVI 12222 (3/4c), where illness figures along with poverty, disgrace, slavery, outrage, and other physical and moral problems. For an amulet against various types of fevers, see *SB* XIV 11493 (3/4c).

[29]*P.Oxy.* XII 1414 (*BL*) (270-275), a *prytanis.*

[30]*P.Oxy.* LV 3816 (3/4c).

[31]*P.Lond.* VI 1926.

[32]*P.Oxy.* XXXI 2601 = Naldini 35 (early 4c), about a *leukoma.* A miraculous cure of *leukomata*: *HM* 1.12.

[33]*Sel.Pap.* I 158 = Naldini 8 (end of 3c); other parts of this sufferer's body were also afflicted.

[34]E.g., *Sel.Pap.* I 158 = Naldini 8 (3c end); *P.Oxy.* VIII 1161 = Naldini 60 (4c); *SB* XIV 11437 (4/5c).

[35]Over two months in *P.Oxy.* X 1299 (*BL*; = Naldini 76) (4c); eight months in *P.Herm.* 19 (392). The champion invalid is the plaintive mother in Naldini 93 = *BGU* III 948 (*BL*) (prob. mid 5c, Herakleopolis).

whether swift or lingering, it produced acute anxiety on the part of both the victim and nearby family members. Still worse than the situation of the relatives at hand, perhaps, was the plight of those at a distance, who might be kept in suspense and anxiety when they were unable to rush to the bedside. One letter, sent to the absent master of a household by a dependent, speaks for what must have been a commonplace situation: "As on many other occasions, so now even more plainly than ever has the regard of the Lord God for you been revealed to us all by the recovery of my mistress from the sickness which overtook her, and may it be granted us to continue for ever to acknowledge our thanks to him because he was gracious to us and inclined his ear to our prayers by preserving for us our mistress." He seeks pardon for any anxiety his earlier letters may have caused: "I wrote the first letter when she was in much pain." He would have sent his son along with his messenger except that the son was sick then too. "Her condition seems, as I have said, to be more tolerable, as she has sat up, but she nevertheless remains rather ill. We comfort her by hourly expecting your arrival."[36]

One's health might also be endangered by accidents. The official descriptions of parties to contracts generally include their distinctive disfigurements, mostly scars.[37] A differentiation by class can be found: the poor—villagers, mostly—almost without exception were scarred,[38] while the wealthy had a better chance of having made it to adulthood uninjured. Petitions and the reports of public physicians indicate that many scars were the result of violence, assaults, or brawls.[39] Presumably those acquired in more innocent pursuits—perhaps the majority—are not identifiable. The better-endowed, however, were by no means immune from accident. Those symbols of wealth, horses, could give trouble through riding accidents[40] or a swift kick.[41]

Death was perhaps the end of troubles for the decedent, but not for the survivors. Until the early fourth century, a declaration had to be filed with the government before the end of the current half-year, in order to get the dead man off the tax rolls.[42] That minor burden

---

[36]P.Oxy. VI 939 = Naldini 61 (4c).

[37]The standard works are J. Hasebroek, *Das Signalement in den Papyrusurkunden* (Schriften Papyrusinstitut Heidelberg 3, Berlin 1921) and A. Caldara, *L'indicazione dei connotati nei documenti papiracei dell'Egitto greco-romano* (Studî 4.2, Milano 1924).

[38]Cf. *P.Abinn.* 67 verso, with a summary of persons from whom amounts were owed; all have scars.

[39]E.g., *P.Oxy.* XLV 3245 (297); *SB* III 6003 (*P.Oxy.* VI 983 [316]); *P.Oxy.* XLIV 3195 (331); *P.Lips.* 42 (*BL*) (late 4c).

[40]P.Oxy. XLVI 3314 (4c).

[41]P.Abinn. 37 (*BL*): "I suffer in my side, having received a kick from a horse."

[42]The latest is *P.Oxy.* XII 1551 (*BL*), of 304. For a discussion of these declara-

brought some compensation. But quite apart from the emotional problems of grief, women surviving their male kin, whether father, husband, or son, often found themselves newly unprotected, vulnerable to a bold raid on the family movables.[43] Nor were older men safe after the death of their sons. Unscrupulous officials could press unwarranted tax claims.[44] And the costs of preparation and burial of the body, along with a tombstone, were significant.[45]

Sex, Marriage, Divorce

The residents of Roman Egypt were inheritors of a complex set of laws, traditional values, and customs concerning the relationships of the sexes. The early Greek settlers certainly brought with them a view of marriage conditioned by the culture of shame and honor prevalent in classical Greece and indeed (in varying forms) in much of the Mediterranean over all of recorded history up to the present.[46] A woman's behavior affected the honor of the men connected with her—father, husband, and brothers. Not only adultery but all sorts of laxity were potential sources of trouble. Greek women were given in marriage by their fathers, and they were tightly laced in by the law. Men were not expected to be faithful, but they were supposed to avoid public and expensive involvements like a concubine.[47] Along with these attitudes went a highly restrictive body of law, in which women had little legal independence.

The legal disabilities of Greek women came with them to Egypt. Once there, however, the Greeks encountered a very different legal and moral tradition. As early as the sixth century B.C., the Egyptian woman's own consent was necessary for marriage. There were no requirements of ceremony, written document, or consummation, but

---

tions, with bibliography, see W. M. Brashear, *BASP* 14 (1977) 1-10.

[43]*P.Sakaon* 36 (ca 280); *P.Oxy.* VIII 1121 (*BL*) (295). On widowhood, see G. Tibiletti, *Atti XVII Congr. Pap.* III 985-94, and J. Beauchamp, *Pallas* 32 (1985) 149-57.

[44]*P.Sakaon* 41 (322).

[45]See *P.Grenf.* II 77 (= *W.Chr.* 498, *Sel.Pap.* I 157; *BL*), from the Great Oasis, ?ca 260-270 (a date suggested in *P.Stras.* 233, commentary, on the basis of prices compared to *P.Gron.* 16). This letter reproaches a man for collecting his dead brother's effects but not the body. The total cost of preparation and transport amounts to the equivalent of about 13 art. of wheat, several months' income for an ordinary person. Burial expenses may also be involved in *BGU* I 34 (*BL*; cf. *P.Charite* 36 introd.).

[46]A convenient summary can be found in D. Cohen, "The Augustan Law on Adultery," in Kertzer and Saller 1991, 109-26 at 112-23. A good, brief analysis of the limitations of the use of such generalized Mediterranean patterns can be found in Cohen's *Law, Sexuality and Society* (Cambridge 1991) 38-41.

[47]For a general treatment of the Hellenistic background, see Sarah B. Pomeroy, *Women in Hellenistic Egypt from Alexander to Cleopatra* (New York 1984) 89-98.

cohabitation was the normal sign of a marriage. Married women suffered from no legal disabilities and were not in their husband's control. Legal documents came into play only to regulate and attest specific arrangements involving property, such as a dowry or undertaking of support. Either party could end the marriage with or without grounds, unilaterally or by mutual consent. Where agreements so specified, certain conduct (usually adultery) could exempt the innocent party from paying back a dowry or gift.[48]

This much freer legal regime does not necessarily point to any particular set of values governing relations between the sexes. Egyptian literature and documents suggest a far less strict attitude toward the sexual activity of the unmarried (and of married men with unmarried women), but strong hostility toward adultery with married women.[49] The themes of honor and shame do not play any crucial role, and, though injured husbands could pursue a wife's lover at law, there is little indication that such actions generally led to much result. In general, then, Egyptian sentiment placed a high value on harmonious and faithful marriage, but showed little of the regard for male rights in women visible among the Greeks.

The early Greek settlers in Egypt, deprived of the milieu of the Greek city and the social sanctions of a settled Greek society, and often marrying Egyptian women, tended over time to assimilate their behavior and expectations to those prevalent on the local scene. Both the generally more open society of the colonial setting and the absence of societal pressure probably played a part. As a result, Greek marriage contracts increasingly resembled Egyptian ones in tone and content. By the late Roman period, however, the possible influence of Roman institutions, habits, and attitudes must also be taken into account in assessing the behavior recorded by the papyri, as must any possible effects of the spread of Christianity.

One dominant factor in the character of marriages is the age at which people usually marry. The age of Egyptian women at first marriage was most commonly in the years between sixteen and twenty, although perhaps 30 percent married earlier, and about 70 percent of all women married by twenty, 90 percent by twenty-four. Men, of whom about 40 percent married in their teens, were still mostly unmarried at twenty; they, by contrast, reached the 70 percent mark only at twenty-eight.[50] A husband-wife age gap of three to ten years

---

[48]See Pestman 1961.

[49]See C. J. Eyre, "Crime and Adultery in Ancient Egypt," *JEA* 70 (1984) 92-105.

[50]Bagnall and Frier, forthcoming. Cf. Brown 1988, 191, first suggesting that Christian parents may have married their daughters rather later than others, then citing evidence that very early (i.e., fourteen or under) marriage may in fact have

was thus typical, but in some cases—second marriages, particularly—it was two or three decades.[51] The age of women at first marriage certainly is young, though on average by no means as low as it would be if protection of teenage virginity were a high priority.

Early marriage is often taken as a sign that first marriages, at least, were arranged by families.[52] It is difficult, however, to be certain how far Egyptian parents actually controlled children's marriage choices. The phenomenon was no doubt most prevalent among the wealthy, where family connections involved the future transmission of property,[53] and among those who married very young. It was, however, by no means restricted to the wealthy.[54] But the formula of commonly used love charms (see below, p. 274) certainly suggests individual choices on the basis of desire by those free to make such decisions, and in a society with high mortality and relatively free divorce, second and later marriages were no doubt numerous and less parentally controlled, if only because many parents were no longer alive. Even at first marriage, for that matter, many young people had no living parents, though other relatives may have expected to take their place in arranging marriages. At all events, marriage was hardly the private, individual business moderns may tend to expect.

There is, interestingly, no evidence for the use of matchmakers, an institution known in the rest of the Greek world.[55] Written agreements, however, were made in many cases, especially when large amounts of property were involved.[56] Weddings are mentioned in several texts; they were obviously as now social occasions of importance, with elaborate preparations and invitations.[57] They could also

---

been rare anyway.

[51]Giving rise to the usual stock situations and themes, as in the man of sixty with an unfaithful younger wife in *HL* 22.

[52]Dixon 1992, 63-64.

[53]Brown 1988, 260, portrays parental control as virtually absolute, but this view is dependent on the upper-class origin of his sources. Studies of Roman marriage (Dixon 1992, 61-97, gives a good survey) tend to generalize from wealthy exemplars.

[54]See the expectations expressed in the petition from the Sakaon archive quoted above, p. 167.

[55]D. Noy, "Matchmakers and Marriage-Markets," *EMC/CV* 34 (1990) 375-400 at 385 n.49.

[56]*P.Vind.Bosw.* 5 (Hermopolis, 304) is perhaps the most striking, coming from a very upper-class background. Attiaina's marriage to Paulos (*P.Oxy.* L 3581, cf. below) was put into written form only after some cohabitation. Dowry lists are sometimes found, as in *BGU* XIII 2328 (mid 5c).

[57]See *P.Oxy.* XII 1486-1487 for invitations; *P.Oxy.* LI 3646 (3/4c) includes the instruction "write to Ailouras about ten Saite jars of wine, because they are needed for my son's wedding."

be sources of trouble: in one papyrus[58] the *exactor* of the Lykopolite Nome writes to the provincial governor, acknowledging receipt of instructions to local officials "concerning taking care that nothing improper or contrary to public order shall occur in connection with the wedding of Apollonia." Who was the bride that her wedding should elicit such instructions? There is one text in which a brawl is said to have broken out after a wedding, outside the house in which it was held.[59]

The affective character of Roman marriage has been a matter of sharp controversy,[60] and the papyri are only ambiguous evidence on the matter. Even about the harmony of the average marriage they tell us little.[61] Successful marriages, of course, generated little documentation. Normal letters of husband to wife and vice-versa are businesslike, occasionally mildly affectionate; there is one letter in which a soldier orders the addressee (his mother-in-law?) to send his wife to him; he is getting impatient.[62] One prospective groom writes his mother-in-law-to-be a very affectionate letter, which, to be sure, stands out in our documentation by its rarity.[63] At all events, there is something to support and little to contradict the view that affectionate companionship was expected, particularly in the propertied classes, as a part of marriage.

As is perhaps natural, information about what went on in marriages surfaces mainly in cases where things went wrong. In one text,[64] a man complains that while he was away on business, his wife took advantage of his absence to carry off all the contents of the house, including business papers. She has refused to give anything back,

---

[58]*P.Oxy.* XLIII 3123 (322).

[59]*BGU* III 909 = *W.Chr.* 382 (Arsinoite, 359), a petition in which the victim asks for redress.

[60]"Affective expectations in Roman marriage had to be low"—Bradley 1991, 8, representative of many views (cf. also his remarks on 128-30). For a more optimistic view, see Dixon 1992, 83-90, arguing "that these matches . . . were expected to yield affectionate companionate relationships and that this happened in numerous cases" (90). Cf. also Brown 1988, 13-14.

[61]Bradley 1991, 6-8, rather scorns the *concordia* he discerns as the cardinal virtue of a good Roman marriage. (7: "But think how odd it would seem if you were to describe a successful marriage today by saying that it was full of concord or harmony between husband and wife.") This seems a curious comment on a society with a high divorce rate!

[62]*P.Oxy.* XXXIV 2731 (4/5c). Maximus writes to his "mother" Zenobia. After greeting his wife Salamaei, he writes, "Once, twice, three times I have told you to send my wife, and you have refused. Well now exert yourself night and day to send my wife."

[63]*P.Ant.* II 93 = Naldini 80 (Antinoopolis, 4c).

[64]*P.Lond.* V 1651 (Hermopolis, 363).

especially the documents from sales of his house lots. He asks her to be brought before the *strategos* and held until the *praeses* Cerealius Telephius Hierocles comes around and he can bring her before him. In another instance,[65] a petitioner alleges that six years earlier he married a woman named Tamounis and gave her marriage gifts. He carried out all the legal and normal duties and lived with her three years. But her mother took her away and gave her to another man in marriage while the complainant was away on private business trying to make enough to live on. Parental meddling turns up also in the petition from the Sakaon archive quoted above (p. 167).

When marriages went sour, money was often the trouble, which can come as no surprise. A wife's complaint[66] against her husband tells us that she was married to him as a young virgin. She is of excellent family, she says, respectable folk of good reputation. He changed his behavior toward her, used up her money, behaved as is not fitting for the well-born, and so on. It is all remarkably vague, but he seems to have kicked her out. One is left with the impression that wasting her money was the most specific bit of bad behavior of which this unsuitable husband was guilty.

A similar complaint occurs in a petition to a provincial governor filed by a man on behalf of his daughter.[67] Twelve years ago, she married from maidenhood a man named Paniskos; they had children, with now only a son surviving. Then she was cast out a year ago, and she and the son are being supported by her father the petitioner. Worse still, the former husband used the dowry as security for a loan from a moneylender and has not redeemed the items. And then he recently kidnapped the boy. The father asks for the redemption of the dowry and its return to him and that he not be troubled about the debt of the husband. He says nothing about the boy.

Yet another striking case[68] is the story of a woman orphaned of both parents. Her guardian was asked by a former military officer for agreement for him to marry her on the basis of certain marriage gifts. The bride was willing, and the guardian accepted the proposal (without any written contract), and agreed. The groom was unable to provide the gifts in cash at that time, so he gave the bride a promissory note for them. At length, after the marriage had been in existence for some short time, and the guardian and wife demanded the gifts, the husband up and left, taking his stuff and some of hers. If he will

---

[65]*P.Cair.Preis.* 2 (Hermopolis, 362; *BL*).
[66]*PSI* I 41 (Antinoopolis, 4c).
[67]*P.Panop.* 28 (Panopolis, 329).
[68]*P.Lips.* 41 (Hermopolis, 4c).

pay up and restore what he took, the harmony of the marriage will be complete, the guardian says.

Often enough, though, harmony could not be restored. Traditionally, Egyptian law had, like Roman law, allowed divorce either by mutual consent or by repudiation, with no penalties for either party unless some had been established in a contract concerning property.[69] In Roman Egypt up to the fourth century, these compatible traditions produced a consistent habit of divorce agreements by mutual consent, in which both parties are freed of liability.[70] The first of the fourth-century documents[71] shows the expected pattern: Herakles and Maria[72] agree that they are divorced, that both have their own property, and that they have no claims against each other. There are no children; each is able to remarry at will. From the following year comes another such text.[73] It begins, "Since, as a result of some evil demon's having come upon us, we have agreed to be divorced from one another with respect to our common marriage," and again proceeds to declare that neither party has any obligations to the other.

In 331, Constantine introduced legislation limiting unilateral divorce by repudiation, a law apparently canceled by Julian.[74] Documents concerning divorce, however, are lacking for the period when it was valid. The next such document, similar in all respects to those mentioned already, is found only in 391.[75] Regrettably, there are no actual divorce documents from the fifth century with which to compare the complicated history of imperial legislation and church teaching, but sixth-century documents are very similar to those of the earlier period.[76] There is, in fact, significant continuity, in substance and

[69]See Pestman 1961 for a comprehensive treatment; see also the interesting article by S. Allam, *JEA* 67 (1981), 116-35, stressing practical deterrents to behavior as free as theory would allow.

[70]The standard list is O. Montevecchi, *Aegyptus* 16 (1936) 20, with additions in her *La papirologia* (Turin 1973) 206. A comprehensive treatment of divorce in the later period can be found in Andreas Merklein, *Das Ehescheidungsrecht nach den Papyri der byzantinischen Zeit* (Diss. Erlangen-Nürnberg 1967).

[71]*P.Oxy.* XXXVI 2770 (304). Similar is *P.Oxy.* XLIII 3139 (3/4c).

[72]Despite the editor's preference for seeing her as pagan (rather than, on Tcherikover's criteria, as Jewish), in a fourth-century context a Christian identity is more likely.

[73]*M.Chr.* 295 (= *P.Grenf.* II 76 = *Jur.Pap.* 21; Great Oasis, 305/6).

[74]For the history of imperial legislation on divorce and a detailed treatment of the subject generally, see Bagnall 1987a.

[75]*P.Stras.* III 142 (Arsinoite). A similar document seems to be referred to in *P.Lips.* 39 (390), a petition in which a woman states that she sent her former husband a *repudium* after a *dialysis*, a mutual dissolution of the marriage, executed between them. (Her current complaint concerns his subsequent assault on her.)

[76]*P.Herm.* 29 (586), executed between two Samaritans, is a good example. See also, from 569, *P.Flor.* I 93 = *M.Chr.* 297. A unilateral father's declaration appears in

phraseology, from the time before Constantine to the late sixth century, through numerous changes in imperial laws.[77]

This continuity of Egyptian practice, little affected by either church or state, is the background of a petition[78] from one Aurelia Attiaina to Flavius Marcellus, tribune and officer in charge of the peace. She recounts that "a certain Paul, coming from the same city, behaving recklessly carried me off by force and compulsion and cohabited with me in marriage." She had a female child by him and lived with him in her house. He behaved badly (the context is damaged) and cohabited with another woman.

> After some time again he beguiled me through priests until I should again take him into our house, agreeing in writing that the marriage was abiding and that if he wished to indulge in the same vile behaviour he would forfeit two ounces of gold, and his father stood surety for him. I took him into our house, and he tried to behave in a way that was worse than his first misdeeds, scorning my orphan state, not only in that he ravaged my house but when soldiers were billeted in my house he robbed them and fled, and I endured insults and punishments to within an inch of my life. So taking care lest I again run such risks on account of him, I sent him through the tabularius a deed of divorce through the tabularius of the city, in accordance with imperial law. Once more behaving recklessly, and having his woman in his house, he brought with him a crowd of lawless men and carried me off and shut me up in his house for not a few days. When I became pregnant, he abandoned me once more and cohabited with his same so-called wife and now tells me he will stir up malice against me. Wherefore I appeal to my lord's staunchness to order him to appear in court and have exacted from him the

M.Chr. 296; translation in Select Papyri I 9.

[77]It is true that we have no divorce documents from the period between Constantine and Julian, nor from the fifth century, although P.Cair.Masp. II 67154 from the reign of Justinian (which year, we cannot tell) does provide an example of divorce by mutual consent in the first half of the sixth century. It is sworn to by the Holy Trinity and the emperor, thus breaking impartially Jesus' bans on divorce and oaths in one breath.

[78]P.Oxy. L 3581, dated to the 4th or 5th century on the basis of the handwriting. The reference to priests, presbyteroi, guarantees in any case a date after the church in Egypt came above ground in the second decade of the fourth century, after the edict of toleration of 313.

two ounces of gold in accordance with his written agreement together with such damages as I suffered on his
account and that he should be punished for his outrages
against me.

Another undated fourth-century affidavit[79] provides an interesting glimpse of a similar marital conflict and of the church's involvement in these marriages. The couple in question lived together
without any written documents; both were evidently well-off
slaveowners. There were disputes over property, with the man
suspecting theft by the staff. "He shut up his own slaves and mine
with my foster-daughters and his overseer and son for seven whole
days in his cellars, having insulted his slaves and my slave Zoe and
half killed them with blows, and he applied fire to my foster-
daughters, having stripped them quite naked, which is contrary to the
laws." Other insults are recounted. Then there was an agreement, in
the presence of the bishops: "Henceforward I [the husband] will not
hide all my keys from her (he trusted his slaves but he would not trust
me); I will stop and not insult her." Whereupon a marriage contract
was drawn up, and after these agreements and the oaths he again hid
his keys." She went to church on the sabbath, and he asked her why.
He did not pay the 100 artabas of wheat due on her land and
prevented her from doing so. His assistant was taken to prison. And
so on. He ordered her to send away her slave Anilla. He said, "After a
month I will take a courtesan for myself." "God knows these things,"
concludes the woman.

The role of the bishops (perhaps of Oxyrhynchos and
Antinoopolis) here is that of reconciler, witness, or guarantor of the
reconciliation. This is, of course, the same role that the presbyters,
priests, exercised in the case of Attiaina, although in retrospect it
looked to her like being "deceived" by the man through the priests.
There is not in either document any indication of any disciplinary
attempts or coercion by the clergy; rather, so far as we can see, these
texts are evidence for a reconciling pastoral role.

There is very little evidence in the papyri of any sexual activity
not involving married persons. This obviously does not mean that
such activity did not exist, but it did not generate documentation.
There is, for example, no certain reference to homosexual behavior in
the documents.[80] And yet references in the monastic literature show

---

[79]*P.Oxy.* VI 903.

[80]There is one doubtful reference, *P.Oxy.* VIII 1160 (3/4c), a letter by a son at
Alexandria to his father; the son is evidently in Alexandria for a trial, waiting for
documents. After various unremarkable statements, he says, "You wrote me "You
are staying at Alexandria with your muchos." Write me, who is my muchos?" The

that homosexual activity among monks was, though sternly forbidden, a persistent problem.[81] One might infer that such activity went on
simply because the monks in question had no access to women; tales
of monks' fornication with women are even commoner in the
monastic literature, in fact. But whether there existed any group of
Egyptians whose normal sexual activity was with others of the same
sex, there is no evidence to say.[82] Within the walls of the house,
among the better-off, men had ready access to slave women, with only
the internal dynamics of the household to restrain their freedom.[83] It
appears that in general society took little official interest in the sexual
activity of unmarried men and women.

This is not to say, of course, that parents were unconcerned about
what their offspring were up to. A famous papyrus letter gives some
sense of popular standards of behavior:[84] Artemis writes to her husband, a soldier, enclosing a note for him to read to its recipient,
Sarapion alias Isidoros. Written in what Wilcken calls "such obscure
Greek that it simply isn't clear what all of it means," it runs something
like the following: "You write to us as to amaze us, saying that the
hegemon does not want house-corrupters. If you want to put up with
the whorings of your daughters, do not examine me, but the priests of
the church, how the two (girls) have jumped out saying "We want
men!" and how Lucra was found with her lover (*moichos*)." The context is Christian—priests are mentioned—but that fact seems to
influence social institutions more than moral attitudes. Pregnancy out
of wedlock is the motif of a story about the monk Makarios the Great,
who was forced into a shotgun marriage by a false accusation.[85]

Prostitution, however, and extramarital sexual activity in general,
are a central theme in one key text, a Berlin codex from Hermopolis of
the later fourth century.[86] It includes a collection of a governor's

---

editor interprets this as *moichos*, "paramour," and it is taken over into LSJ as the sole
example of homosexual usage of this word. This seems dubious, because all cita-
tions of this word and its cognates refer to adultery specifically.

[81]Cf. Brown 1988, 246. For example, see *ApPatr* Isaac 5 and Poemen 176.

[82]This question is still a matter of lively controversy at more general levels, of
course, including the question whether homosexuality itself as a category is of
modern construction or existed already in antiquity. Cf. John Thorp, "The Social
Construction of Homosexuality," *Phoenix* 46 (1992) 54-61, with bibliography.

[83]Cf. Brown 1988, 21-23.

[84]*P.Grenf.* I 53 = *W.Chr.* 131 = Naldini 56 (4c).

[85]*ApPatr* Macarius 1.

[86]*BGU* IV 1024. The codex in its original form, only part of which is now
preserved, included receipts of officials who conveyed supplies collected as taxes to
the army units to which they were destined, two magical texts, an official letter of
the governor Fl. Domitius Asclepiades to the magistrates and council of Hermopolis,
complaining about their failure to deliver the supplies due to the army, and

sentences on capital crimes, in only one of which is a woman not demonstrably the victim.[87] The second case concerns a woman taken by her husband with an adulterer; the husband kills her. The case is fragmentary, and the sentence is missing. In the fourth case a man who found his mistress with another man and killed her with a sword is sent to the mines. The fifth case concerns a soldier who seems to have been guilty of incest involving a mother and daughter. The seventh case concerns "a certain city councillor called Diodemos of Alexandria, who loved a public prostitute," whom he frequented in the evening. Diodemos murdered the prostitute and was imprisoned as a result. The next day, the councillors of Alexandria asked for Diodemos' release, which was agreed to but not carried out.

The case then went to trial. "The mother of the prostitute, a certain Theodora, being an old woman and poor, asked that Diodemos be compelled to provide her on account of sustenance some small consolation of her life. For she said, "It was for this reason that I gave my daughter to the pimp, that I might be supported. Since then my daughter having died I am deprived of means of support, for this reason I ask that I be given a little modest woman's portion for my support." The governor says,

> Diodemos, you have basely killed a woman who re-
> proached her fate among men. . . . And I have taken pity
> on the unfortunate woman, because while alive she was
> offered to all those who wished her, like a corpse. For
> the poverty of her fate pressed down on her excessively,
> selling her body to a dishonoring rank and encountering
> the reputation of a prostitute, full of constant labors. . . .
> I order, as purifying the order of the city and of the
> council chamber, that you be struck with the sword as a
> murderer. Theodora, the poor and elderly mother of the

---

accounts concerning meat, chaff, and wine. See G. Poethke, "Der Papyrus-Kodex BGU 1024-1027 aus Hermupolis Magna," *Proc. XVI Int. Congr. Pap.* 457-62, for a general description, and J. G. Keenan, "Roman Criminal Law in a Berlin Papyrus Codex," *Archiv* 35 (1989) 15-23.

[87]The papyrus resembles others that appear to be judicial decisions extracted with a view to some similar trial. J. E. G. Whitehorne, "Sex and Society in Greco-Roman Egypt," *Actes XVᵉ Congr.* IV 245, considers this text's connection to reality to be suspect, on the grounds of the bizarre and detailed character of the cases and the rhetorical nature of the text. He suggests that "at best the records may have been manipulated to juxtapose cases of a particular type, at worst they may have been embroidered in order to highlight the crimes' more sensational aspects." This is a curious view: collecting precedents for sentences in a particular type of crime is not "manipulating the records" but carrying out a standard lawyer's procedure.

dead woman, who because of her constant poverty
deprived her own daughter of modesty, and through
which also she killed her, will inherit a tenth part of the
belongings of Diodemos, the laws suggesting this to me
and magnanimity supporting the power of the laws.

Despite all the obscurities of these texts, they show us a
society—Alexandrian, probably—in which there is both free con-
sensual sexual activity and prostitution,[88] along with infidelity, and
where this is not all taken lightly. Obviously if one were gathering
cases with violence against women, one would not be making a
representative picture of society. But violent passion is obviously
neither absent nor accepted: the men involved are all sent to the mines
or executed, and the crowd is outraged by a big-shot's murder of a
poor girl put out to whoring by her poverty-stricken mother. The
peculiar character of the papyrus and its Alexandrian reference
should deter facile conclusions about the life of upcountry towns, let
alone the villages, but the other texts quoted above show a society
with a well-defined set of traditional standards for relationships
between men and women and a normal assortment of the standard
human failures that mark such relationships. The government intervened only to deal with complaints of violence or the breaking of
property agreements.

The church appears in these situations mainly in a pastoral role,
with limited power over its members. That position was probably
fairly typical. The fourth century produced an enormous church
literature on the body, sexuality, and relations between men and
women, but the impact of all these currents of thought on the lives of
ordinary men and women was probably limited. For one thing, even if
the hearers of a preacher like John Chrysostom, with all his attempts
to undermine the longstanding relationship of sexuality and the city,
paid any heed to what he said, they were only a small upper crust on
society.[89] For another, the monastic movement in some ways quar-
antined sexual abstinence to a well-defined group, leaving the remainder of society free to consider it irrelevant.[90] The main body of the
church continued to support marriage without either laying down

[88]On prostitution generally, see S. Leontsini, *Das Prostitution im frühen Byzanz*
(Vienna 1989).

[89]See Brown 1988, 308-19, for John Chrysostom's preaching on sex and marriage; and cf. MacMullen 1989 for the audience.

[90]Brown 1988, 208.

elaborate rules for the conduct of sex within it[91] or challenging the social structures that underlay the character of the institution. If, as has been claimed, there was a move toward stricter codes of sexual behavior during this period, it may be quite independent of Christianity. And it remains unclear how far such strictness is so bound to characteristics of class and geography in the sources as to be irrelevant for any particular region, particularly one with the distinctive heritage in such matters that Egypt had.[92]

Parents, Children, and Families

Quantifiable evidence for the structure of the Egyptian family in the fourth century is almost nonexistent because of the disappearance of census returns early in the period. Once again, however, there is no reason to think that any substantial change from the practice of the earlier empire occurred, and the composition of the family in Roman Egypt is fairly well known.[93] Rather than a single pattern for Egyptian families, the census declarations display several.[94] (See p. 200 for the family tree of Aurelius Isidoros.) Most families were made up of parents (or one surviving parent) and a child or children. In many cases, the same household might have three generations, older parents of the family living with a couple and their young children. After the older generation died, the household would for a time be a nuclear family, then perhaps adding the children's spouses and, eventually, their children. Through this life-course, then, a given household could exhibit several types.[95] It has increasingly been recognized that these family types—widely attested elsewhere in the Mediterranean—are not alternatives but different stages in a single type.[96] There are also some instances—mainly in the villages—of horizontally extended families, with siblings remaining under the same roof along with their spouses and children, but they are proportionately fewer. The living

[91]Brown 1988, 255; in this it rejected the path chosen by Clement (Brown 1988, 133-38) and eventually by the western church of the sixth century and later; it is doubtful that the scenario of married life sketched by Brown (1988, 149) on the basis of Clement ever had much relationship to reality.

[92]See Brown 1988, 206-7 (the supposedly puritanical developments) and 251 (possibly non-Christian origins of the same), but in neither case with sufficient distinctions drawn.

[93]For a valuable bibliographic essay on family history, ranging from antiquity to modern times, see Hareven 1991; limited references for antiquity at 97 n.5.

[94]For this and following generalizations, based on the census returns, see Bagnall and Frier, forthcoming; Hombert and Préaux, *Pap.Lugd.Bat.* V, pp. 154-55, with earlier bibliography.

[95]See Hareven 1991, 100-102, for such cyclical development in western Europe.

[96]Cf. Dixon 1992, 7-11, for a good summary.

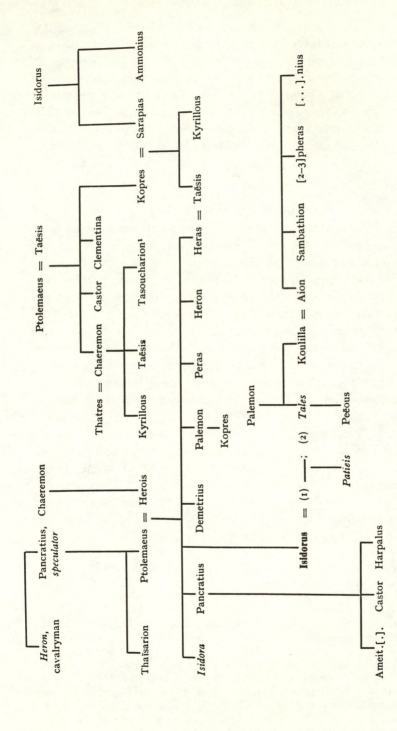

Family tree of Aurelius Isidoros
(from *The Archive of Aurelius Isidorus*, p. 6)

1 The name of another daughter of Chaeremon has been almost obliterated: T.[.].

conditions of the cities may well have favored the smaller households characteristic of them.[97]

This combination of constantly changing vertically extended families with some horizontally extended ones is essentially identical with what is coming to be accepted as the standard family arrangement of the Roman world, apart from a few "deep rural" areas not closely tied to urban society.[98] This family is the central institution, with lateral ties beyond direct ones to siblings of fairly minor importance. Lodgers and slaves, however, also formed a part of many households and no doubt played a significant role in forming the character of the household and the way in which children were reared.[99]

There is evidence that in the western part of the empire this pattern remained dominant in late antiquity.[100] If anything, the dominance of the Egyptian countryside by the city increases in intensity in the fourth century, and it would be paradoxical indeed if a family pattern closely associated with the ancient city and well entrenched in Roman Egypt should decline in such a time. Despite a want of quantitative data to verify this logical supposition, it serves as a useful working hypothesis. The patterns of behavior and expression visible in less quantifiable documentation like letters and petitions in fact turn out to be just those one would predict on the basis of such a model of family structure. The papyri show us a picture quite different in many other respects, however, from that visible in Roman Africa in this period.[101]

The most striking testimony to the centrality of the life-course family is simply the dominance of various aspects of the parent-child

---

[97]Cf. B. Shaw in Kertzer and Saller 1991, 72. The same thing was true of eighteenth-century Aleppo; cf. Marcus 1989, 197.

[98]A relatively simple version of this view was argued in R. P. Saller and B. D. Shaw, "Tombstones and Roman Family Relations in the Principate: Civilians, Soldiers and Slaves," *JRS* 74 (1984) 124-56. Tombstones, however, are not wholly representative of the population (cf., e.g., J. C. Mann, "Epigraphic Consciousness," *JRS* 75 [1985] 204-6; W. Eck, "Aussagefähigkeit epigraphischer Statistik und die Bestattung von Sklaven im kaiserzeitlichen Rom," *Alte Geschichte und Wissenschaftsgeschichte: Festschrift für Karl Christ* [Darmstadt 1988] 130-39), and Shaw (in Kertzer and Saller 1991, 66-90) has shown how much time, place, and religion affect the testimony of the tombstones.

[99]See Bradley 1991, 93-95, and Dixon 1992, 8-9, for the role of nonkin and more distant relations. Cf. also Hareven 1991, 105, for this common pattern in other societies.

[100]See Shaw 1984 for a full analysis, rejecting the view of E. Patlegean and others that extended kin networks reemerged into prominence in late antiquity.

[101]See Brent Shaw, "The Family in Late Antiquity: The Experience of Augustine," *Past and Present* 115 (1987) 3-51.

relationship. In a time lacking a census of persons, the birth of children produced little documentation,[102] and their early rearing hardly any.[103] But those who survived childhood figure more extensively. A major debate in family history in recent decades has concerned the thesis that parents reacted to high infant mortality by avoiding emotional "investment" in very young children.[104] There is little direct evidence on this question in the papyri, not surprisingly. If the 2:1 sex ratio of females to males in the slave population documented in the census declarations is evidence for differential rates of infant exposure and enslavement (it can hardly be the natural result of slave births), it is at least arguable that the bonds were not so strong at birth as to preclude exposure of unwanted children. On the other hand, the rate at which young children were commemorated with tombstones—perhaps an indicator of valuation—in the western empire correlates positively with urban centers, with later antiquity, and with Christian commemorators.[105] If the same was true in the East, the urban societies of fourth century Egypt may have come to place a higher value on infants.

Once the children survived the early years, parents, as always, fretted over their offspring's behavior, especially sexual.[106] They meddled in their children's marriages, to the point of removing daughters from husbands considered unsuitable.[107] They complained endlessly about the younger generation's failure to write often enough (a complaint by no means limited to parents!). Fathers worried about

---

[102]A birth declaration occurs in *P.Köln* II 87 (Oxyrhynchos, 271), and a registration in *P.Oxy.* LIV 3754 (320). Childbirth itself is referred to in *P.Mil.* II 84 (*BL*) (4c), *P.Oxy.* VI 992 (413) and *PSI* VIII 895 = Naldini 27 (3/4c), miscarriage in *P.Wash.Univ.* I 36 (cf. *P.Wash.Univ.* II, p.244) (428 or 429).

[103]There are occasional references to nursing, most clearly and interestingly *P.Lond.* III 951 verso (p. 213) (*BL*) (late 3c), a fragment of letter from a man to his son-in-law: "I heard that you are forcing her to nurse. If you wish, let the baby have a nurse; for I do not allow my daughter to nurse." But most of the papyrological documentation of nursing concerns wet-nursing for hire, which virtually disappears from the documents in the third century, cf. M. Manca Masciadri and O. Montevecchi, *I contratti di Baliatico* (*C.P.Gr.* 1), 1984. They suppose (p. 4) that fourth-century (i.e., Christian) disapproval of exposure of infants is the cause, but in fact there is almost no third-century evidence either.

[104]Most students of the Roman family would offer a qualifiedly negative response to this thesis; see P. Garnsey, "Child Rearing in Ancient Italy," in Kertzer and Saller 1991, 48-65, and more briefly Dixon 1991, 98-99.

[105]See B. Shaw in Kertzer and Saller 1991, 66-90.

[106]Especially interesting are two texts discussed in the previous section, *P.Oxy.* VIII 1160 and *P.Grenf.* I 53 = *W.Chr.* 131 = Naldini 56.

[107]*P.Cair.Preis.* 2, discussed above, p. 192.

protecting their wives and daughters from unsuitable behavior by others.[108]

Despite all the trouble they created, children were indispensable for providing care in old age and illness, "what is owing from children to parents," as one woman put it after nursing her mother through her final illness.[109] One letter pleads for an exemption from military duty for a young man "since his mother is a widow and has none but him."[110] Failure to discharge this duty of attention to the parents results in reproaches.[111] A widow executes a deed transferring her property to her two sons by her deceased husband, effective on her own death, in gratitude for the fact that one of them has stayed with her ever since their father's death and worked in the family dry-cleaning business.[112] Indeed, the rather extensive documentation of inheritance is overwhelmingly a matter of transmission from parents to their children. This turns up in legal cases mainly when someone interferes with it,[113] particularly when the children are minors, but the uneventful and amicable passage of property was no doubt the normal objective.[114] Parents expected respect and affection, and despite the reserve characteristic of most papyrus letters, there are some with strong expressions of filial sentiments.[115]

Grandparents played a certain protective role, particularly where parents had died or were absent. A grandmother registers a new child because the father is away being examined for military service.[116] A grandfather tries to protect the land of his grandchildren from double taxation.[117] When an uncle adopts the orphan child of his late brother, it is the child's grandmother (and uncle's mother) who acts on the

---

[108]*P.Flor.* III 309 (*BL*) (4c), a petition complaining about outrageous language (*iniuria*).

[109]*P.Oxy.* VIII 1121 (*BL*) (295). Cf. Dixon 1992, 108-11, on parental expectations about their children's support in old age.

[110]*P.Abinn.* 19 (*BL*) (*ca* 342-351). One should not take this too literally; the writer is the husband of the widow's daughter.

[111]Most vividly in the querulous Naldini 93 (5c).

[112]*P.Coll.Youtie* II 83 (Oxyrhynchos, 353).

[113]*M.Chr. 55* = *P.Lips.* 33 (Hermopolis, 368) is perhaps the best example of many.

[114]Cf. *P.Princ.* II 79 (Philadelphia, 326), a division of paternal inheritance by three brothers, explicitly carried out in order to avoid strife: a recognition of the potential for trouble almost always present.

[115]To be sure, these might be set pieces designed to show off the results of a tutor's work, as probably in *P.Ryl.* IV 624 (*BL*), from the Theophanes archive (*ca* 317-324). Something less affected is found in a Christian letter, *P.Oxy.* XIV 1680 = Naldini 32 = *Sel.Pap.* I 153 (3/4c).

[116]*P.Oxy.* LIV 3754 (320).

[117]*P.Oxy.* XIX 2235 (*ca* 346).

child's behalf.[118] If such cases are not more common, it is simply that early death claimed more than half of the population before their grandchildren's birth, leaving relatively few to cope with the situation when the young parents died.

There are many indications that brothers and sisters had close relationships as adults.[119] Brother-sister marriage is no longer documented in this period,[120] but siblings were held together, for good or ill, by their inherited property. A parental house might be divided or simply shared. A widow in a Hermopolite village tells the *praepositus pagi* that she had for long shared a house with her full brother and his wife, until one day without any quarrel or warning they fell upon her and beat her to within an inch of her life.[121] Struggles over inheritance were common and unpleasant; a commonplace instance shows a woman who has been shut out of the family property by her brothers trying to recover at least the trivial share (1.5 arouras) she was originally allocated.[122] Certainly in villages, where brothers and sisters would often have contiguous land even if they did not share a house, common interests existed along with causes for quarrels. It is impossible to say how typical households like that of Sakaon in Theadelphia in 310 were: he housed two brothers, two sons, one nephew, and two adult male relatives whose exact connection is not specified.[123] In fact, relations less close than uncle or nephew are hardly ever identified with any exactitude in the few cases where they are even mentioned. The papers of Aurelius Isidoros contain numerous documents pertinent to his brothers and their wives, including tax receipts in their names and various texts concerning the inheritance of his brother's wife and her sister.[124] It is clear that he was deeply involved in joint farming enterprises and in his siblings' legal business.[125] Isidoros' own census return, however, shows him living with a son and no one else.[126]

[118]*M.Chr.* 363 = *P.Lips.* 28 (Hermopolis, 381).

[119]These (in part) emotional connections do not necessarily (despite Bradley 1991, 125-26) depend on any particular view about the centrality of the parents-children family.

[120]There are no documentable instances after the early third century. Cf. Bagnall and Frier, forthcoming.

[121]*P.Amh.* II 141 = *M.Chr.* 126 (350).

[122]*P.Rain.Cent.* 85 (364-366). Cf. the fraternal strife in *M.Chr.* 55 = *P.Lips.* 33 (Hermopolis, 368).

[123]*P.Sakaon* 1 (310).

[124]See for this inheritance particularly *P.Cair.Isid.* 62-64, 105.

[125]See Boak and Youtie's introduction to *P.Cair.Isid.* (pp. 5-6); they note that the archive gives "the impression that he acted as head of the family."

[126]*P.Cair.Isid.* 8 (309). The mother of his son may have died by this time. But there are no women in either this return or in Sakaon's, indicating perhaps only that

"Brothers" and "sisters" turn up in great numbers in letters as well; many are addressed to them, and still more mention them for greeting. It has long been known that Egyptians used these terms not only for siblings but also for their spouses, and to some extent for more distant relatives or for close friends as well. As a result papyrologists have developed a deeply skeptical attitude toward any literal interpretation of the terms in the letters.[127] All the same, many of these letters deal with what looks like family business, and some of these occurrences no doubt actually do refer to brothers and sisters.

Neither relatives by marriage nor more distant blood relatives play much of a role in the papyrus documentation. One of the few direct pieces of evidence for relationships with a spouse's relatives is found in a highly affectionate letter written by a man to the mother of his fiancée shortly before the wedding.[128] Kin mattered more. A man writes his "brother" (probably really his brother) in one letter, "I would have you know, brother, that on the 10th of the present month of Thoth I received your son safe and sound in every respect. I shall take care of him as if he were my own son. I shall not neglect to make him attend to his work."[129] But such relationships might be left unattended for a long time and resuscitated only when need interposed; an example is a letter from a woman currently in Apamea in Syria to her aunt in Koptos: "Know, my lady, that since Easter my mother, your sister, has been dead. When I had my mother with me, she was my whole family. Since she died, I have remained alone, having no one in a foreign land. Remember then, aunt, as if my mother were living, to write to me if you find someone (to bring the letter)."[130] Though the quantity of evidence is not large, it is striking that all these are letters of Christians.

Trouble about family property was a more common strand in relationships with more distant relatives. Such themes as the inheritance-gobbling uncle[131] or the rapacious great-aunt swooping down on the orphan child[132] recur. But generally it seems that little of the intensity of ties between brother and sister survived to the connection between kin of different generations or a degree of relation even

---

women were not included in these declarations.

[127]See Naldini, pp. 15-16, for a brief statement with bibliography, and cf. *P.Oxy.* LV 3813-3815 introd.

[128]*P.Ant.* II 93 = Naldini 80 (Antinoopolis, 4c).

[129]*P.Oxy.* XII 1493 = Naldini 33 (3/4c), again a Christian letter. Cf. also *P.Oxy.* LV 3815 (3/4c).

[130]*P.Bour.* 25 = Naldini 78 (4c).

[131]*P.Oxy.* XVII 2133 (*ca* 308; *BL*).

[132]*P.Sakaon* 40 (318-320).

so close as first cousin. This void, taken with the evidence centered on parents and children first and siblings second, provides an impressionistic but significant confirmation of the hypothesis that family relations were dominated by the nuclear family and its immediate vertical and horizontal lines just as much in late antique Egypt as they had been in the three preceding centuries.

Key aspects of the dynamics of family life evidently result from the mortality rate. The most salient are certainly the numerous mentions of orphans. The chances were poor that a child would reach the age of eighteen with both parents still living, and for many both parents would have died. Guardianship inevitably resulted,[133] at least for those under fourteen, and with it opportunities for misappropriation of the orphans' assets by the relatives entrusted with them.[134] No doubt even a fairly honest guardian might wind up in a disagreement with the children later about what was reasonable management. Those who were left little or no property by their parents became burdens for the relatives who had to support them.[135] Third parties would almost inevitably seek to take advantage of the weakness of orphans, a vicious attitude often offered as a motive for injustices complained of in petitions to authority.[136]

The high death rate for children, however, sometimes produced the reverse situation—older adults all of whose children had died before them.[137] Such people, particularly widows, were increasingly vulnerable as they grew older, easy marks for anyone stronger or more active who did not hesitate to abuse relative power.[138] There are occasional exceptions, such as a creditor who instructs his agent to collect nothing more than the principal on a loan due from a widow who had appealed to him.[139] But ancient society generally provided little protection to the weak beyond the generosity and forbearance of the strong.

Mortality also joined with the ease of divorce described above to make it likely that many adults, especially men, would marry more

---

[133]Even appointing guardians sometimes posed problems, witness the complaint in a prefect's edict: "whereas at present much business concerning orphans and depending upon their guardians is delayed because the orphans are unattended by tutors or curators" (*P.Oxy.* VI 888 = *M.Chr.* 329; *BL*: not long after 287).

[134]Examples are *P.Cair.Isid.* 64 (*ca* 298) and *Pap.Flor.* XIX, 507-9 (319).

[135]*SB* XIV 11881 (4c) complains that the writer, because she is a woman, is having trouble supporting the children of her deceased brother.

[136]*P.Oxy.* XII 1470 (336): "despising my orphan condition."

[137]*CPR* V 9 (Hermopolis, 339) and *P.Oxy.Hels.* 44 (322-324) are examples of childless, intestate death.

[138]E.g., *P.Sakaon* 36 (*ca* 280).

[139]See below, p. 216.

than once and have surviving children by more than one wife or husband. Such multiple families are a natural breeding ground for strife over people and property, particularly because men, who owned most of the property, remarried more consistently than women.[140] Some incidents resulting from divorces are recounted in the previous section. One of the most colorful petitions from the fourth century has already been quoted (p. 167), that about Sakaon's daughter Kamoution, her upbringing by her uncle and her father's renewed involvement at her marriage. Of course, things might be arranged amicably; we have one settlement in which a man's estate is divided among the children of two marriages, seemingly without incident.[141]

[140]The percentage of women ever married gradually falls well below that of women currently married, while the two percentages for men remain close. Some widowed and divorced women did not remarry, despite an apparent shortage of marriageable women.

[141]*P.Oxy.* XIV 1638 (282).

CHAPTER 6

Power and Dependence

The description of urban and rural societies and economies in chapters 2 and 3 revealed a substantial concentration of agricultural surplus in the hands of a small group of urban landowners, along with a lesser concentration of surplus in the hands of a much broader band of village landholders. Nonagricultural economic activity was concentrated in the cities. The specific administrative, political, and juridical institutions described in those chapters and in chapter 4 showed the degree to which city and country were integrated in the fourth century into a single unit, one in which the city, and particularly its upper crust, consolidated its power in particular social and political forms. There are, however, a number of types of relationships of power and dependence involving individuals or families rather than larger social structures. Some of these are rather informal, but the most readily visible is also the most formal and radical. Slavery deserves a place of primacy in this discussion.

Slavery

Although slavery had a significant place in the structure of village society (see pp. 123-27), its natural habitat was the city. That is not to say that slaves formed a large part of the population. We do not know how numerous they were, but the census declarations of the Roman period suggest about 13.5 percent of the population in the cities compared to 9 to 10 percent in the villages.[1] Nor is that to say that slaves supplied a substantial labor force to urban economic activities;[2] rather, their importance lay in their central role of support to the social structures of the city.

The slaves occurring in the papyri are almost all household slaves or personal assistants for their masters' business dealings. It is there-

[1] See Bagnall and Frier, forthcoming. It is often asserted that slave numbers declined in late antique Egypt, but there is no good evidence for the claim. See Bagnall 1993 for a detailed treatment.

[2] There are only a few examples of slaves or freedmen in such activities: *P.XV Congr.* 22 (slave girls working in an Alexandrian inn); *P.Lips.* 97 (a *tarsikarios* weaver); *P.Mich.* IX 574 (freedman employed in an unspecified workshop). Cf. Bagnall 1993 for discussion.

fore hardly suprising that most evidence for urban slaves is connected with owners belonging to the upper stratum of society: members of the bouleutic class, the military, and the imperial civil service. The use of slaves in households for domestic purposes, with their number in proportion to the grandeur of the household, is so universal a fact of life in the Roman world as to need no comment.[3] The slave as confidential personal agent of the master in business dealings is also a common phenomenon;[4] it has been observed that the master's complete control over the slaves and ability to torture them made slaves far more suitable than free persons for such positions. Even though production was hardly affected at all by slave labor, then, the importance of slave assistance for the ability of a small elite to manage business, civic, and military affairs should not be underrated.[5] The urban elite was as dependent as the village elite on the use of slaves as support for their own activities.

It is, however, at the social level that the effects of slavery are more determinative for the character of life. First, the papyri give an unfavorable impression of master-slave relations. Slaves ran away when they could,[6] even those working for important people in, probably, responsible posts, like Magnus, a slave of an *officialis* in the office of the prefect of Egypt, who fled to Hermopolis. His owner gave another *officialis* an authorization to arrest Magnus and bring him back.[7] An Oxyrhynchite who had won many prizes and high rank as an athlete and consequently been awarded Athenian citizenship had a slave run away to Alexandria; he authorized his representative to imprison the slave, accuse him, beat him, pursue those harboring him, and bring him back.[8] The correspondence of a nome *strategos* in the Panopolis rolls in the Chester Beatty collection includes an acknowledgment of instructions from the *magister rei privatae* to send up to him an absconding slave.[9] A letter from a slave to his master

---

[3]Some examples from the papyri: *P.Ross.Georg.* III 9 = Naldini 77 (house servants in Memphis receiving goods); *P.Stras.* IV 296 (Hermopolis); *P.Oxy.* VI 903 (both members of a couple own slaves in the house).

[4]Some examples from the papyri: *P.Oxy.* XLIII 3146 (347: *pais* is surely "slave" here; a business transaction); *P.Oxy.* XLIX 3480 (ca 360-390; the staff of a tax collector); *P.Abinn.* 36 (general agent of a *praepositus*).

[5]Even so minor a witness as the slave of a *praepositus* in *O.Bodl.* 2152 helps show such usage.

[6]See for the general problem D. Daube, "Slave-Catching," *Juridical Review* 64 (1952) 12-28.

[7]*P.Oxy.* XII 1423 (mid-late 4c, according to the ed.).

[8]*P.Oxy.* XIV 1643 (298).

[9]*P.Panop.Beatty* 1.149 (Panopolis, 298).

remarks, "I am again your slave and don't secede from you as I did before."[10]

If slaves did not run away, they tried to get their freedom legally. Few manumissions and freedmen are attested from this period, but the nature of the human relationships involved is made clear by one salient case. A female petitioner alleges that some slaves came to her and to her brother Eustochios by inheritance from their parents and that they owned them jointly and equally. Without effecting any written division of ownership, they divided them in practice (evidently two for each). The two slaves of her brother have persuaded him to manumit them, along with their child, but without the petitioner's consent. She objects and asks that the slaves be prevented from escaping the bonds of slavery.[11] Legally speaking she was probably correct, but it is obvious that her brother behaved as if a division of the property had left him free to do as he pleased with his slaves. Another Oxyrhynchite petition concerns a jointly owned slave (the petitioner's sister is the other owner) who, since the death of their parents, has paid them an *apophora*; but now he refuses to pay it. It appears, despite the petitioner's terminology, that the slave had been manumitted by the father in his will and that *apophora* is his due to them as patrons of a freedman. The owner's attitude—and perhaps the reality of being a freedman—is made clear enough by her request that the former slave be compelled to pay the *apophora* and remain in their service.[12] In another family, the patron apparently sought to assert his rights to the estate of his deceased freedman, against the claim of the latter's son.[13]

Those who remained in slavery often did not behave as their owners would like. The Roman law of slavery regards theft by slaves as a vice which could be warranted against; there is confirmation in a complaint by a member of the council of Hermopolis that his slave has been "kidnapped"—corrupted, it sounds like—by another person. Last night, he says, the slave opened the door of the house while he was asleep and stole some of his goods. He caught the slave with the goods in the house of the other man. He asks to recover his property; curiously enough, he does not ask specifically for any punishment for the corrupter.[14] In an affidavit of a wife against her husband (above, p. 195), the ultimate insult on his part in household matters is that he

[10]*P.Abinn.* 36.

[11]*PSI* V 452. Biezunska-Malowist 1977, 125 n. 78, thinks that there were originally four slaves, two of whom had a child after the division.

[12]*P.Oxy.Hels.* 26 (296).

[13]*P.Oxy.* LV 3813 (3/4c).

[14]*P.Stras.* IV 296 (326); see B. Kramer, *ZPE* 69 (1987) 143-61.

trusts his slaves, but not his wife, with his keys.[15] Later on, he ordered his wife to send her slave Anilla away. Slaves, in short, could not always be trusted.

Moreover, slaves talked back both to their owners and to other free persons. The writer of a rather obscurely written Christian letter complains to the recipient that he has been unable to bear the constant *hybreis*, outrageous remarks, of the addressee's *oiketes* Agathos.[16] The complaint about a female slave who had inflicted *hybreis* on the complainant's wife and virgin daughter in a way contrary to the laws and to their station in life has been mentioned earlier (p. 98). He requests that she be punished for what she shouted at them.[17] Ulpian says that the praetor's edict expressly provides the grounds for these complaints: "One who is said to have loudly shouted at someone contrary to sound morals (*adversus bonos mores*) or one through whose efforts such shouting is effected contrary to sound morals, against him I will give an action."[18] That particular remark has to do with the shouting of crowds, but individual utterances are also punished if said for the sake of insulting someone. The jurists quoted in the Digest make it quite clear that the relative status of the parties involved contributed to defining how contumelious such remarks were, and the petitioners mentioned make it clear that their station in life makes such insults particularly reprehensible. It hardly needed to be said that a slave's insults of a free person were punishable; the jurists were more concerned to deal with the less obvious cases, as where a slave insults another slave—as a result the slave is taken to have insulted the other slave's master.[19]

It appears in general that though slaves provided much of life's comforts to the slave-owning class, they also posed much of its trouble and even danger. Apart from insults and theft from their masters, slaves appear to have been sources of violence for others. This is true most obviously when they beat someone on their master's behalf, as someone complains happened to him at the hands of a tax collector and his slaves.[20] But there are also complaints such as that to the police magistrates at Oxyrhynchos by a man whose wife was attacked

---

[15]*P.Oxy.* VI 903.

[16]*P.Select.* 18 = Naldini 81 (provenance unknown; Bingen, *Cd'E* 41 [1966] 191 suggests the Hermopolite; 4c).

[17]*P.Lond.* III 983 (p. 229) (no provenance or date). The discussion makes it clear that *hybreis* here (and elsewhere) means verbal, rather than physical, attacks.

[18]*D.* 47.15.2, from *ad edictum* 77. The entirety of Book 47 of the Digest is devoted to contumelious action.

[19]*D.* 47.18.1.

[20]*P.Oxy.* XLIX 3480.

in their house during the evening hours by one Tapesis and the latter's slave Victoria; it seems (the text is fragmentary) that a theft of gold was also involved. He asks that a midwife be sent to check his wife, who was thus evidently pregnant, and that the culprits provide guarantees in the event anything happens to her.[21]

The prize document of this sort, however, is a report of proceedings before the governor of the Thebaid.[22] The accuser, one Philammon, reports that his son had been attacked, beaten to within an inch of his life, and robbed of a substantial sum in public funds that he was carrying (ten to twelve gold solidi), by a party of four slaves. Philammon says that one of them held the victim's hands, one knocked him to the ground, and the other two beat and robbed him. Only two slaves are in court, Acholius and a young boy. Acholius claims that the supposed victim actually attacked them; that there were only two of them until a third joined them after the incident was over. Acholius is tortured but sticks to his story. His master Sergius was and is out of town. A neighbor who came out, with his own slaves, when he heard the noise of the scuffle, says that there were two or three of them, thus incidentally supporting the story of the defendants more than that of the plaintiff, though he seems to imply that the slaves were the aggressors. Because the neighbor happens to be the highest ranking official in town, the *logistes*, his testimony carries some weight.

All these accounts convey an impression of town life as involving for the upper class significant risks, not merely of verbal abuse but also of theft by their own slaves who were suborned by others, of assaults by free persons assisted by slaves, and of physical violence in the streets at the hands of unsupervised slaves. Like all crime reports, this one no doubt gives such incidents more prominence than they occupy in normal daily life, but their contribution to the tone of urban existence is nonetheless unmistakable. Slaves no doubt usually helped protect their own masters in violent situations, but they could not be relied upon.

There is little information about how people became slaves in this period. A few were acquired abroad;[23] most were no doubt born slaves, and there are explicit attestations of such origin.[24] A slave of a

[21]*P.Oxy.* LI 3620 (326).

[22]*P.Lips.* 40 (Hermopolis, 4/5c).

[23]*BGU* I 316 (Askalon, 359) is the best known; but the power of attorney in *P.Oxy.* XXXVI 2771 (323), whereby a husband in Cos is authorized to sell a slave on behalf of his wife, presumably traveled with the slave to Oxyrhynchos as part of the title papers.

[24]E.g., *P.Lips.* 26 specifies that two of the four slaves are house-born; the origin of the other two is not specified.

military officer describes himself as *threptos*, exposed as an infant, rescued and brought up by the owner.[25] It was also possible to fall into slavery through debt. For example, one letter complains that the addressee has taken the writer's money in order to get him released but has failed to do so. "Now then [he says], do not neglect this, master, for God's sake; for you have already given my children as securities to the money-lender on account of the gold."[26] In another letter, the writer recounts (to his wife) his seizure in Alexandria by a creditor; because he has nothing to pay him with, he asks her to put their little *paidion* Artemidoros in hypothec and send him the proceeds.[27] One supposes that the luckless Artemidoros is already a slave and not their child, but the seizure of the writer himself suggests that the insolvent could wind up in indefinite bondage.[28]

Emancipation, however, was always a possibility. It may, in fact, have been a virtual certainty for those who survived to mature age. The census declarations of the Roman period show no male slaves older than thirty-two years, and no female slaves older than forty-four, except for one sixty-eight-year-old fugitive. It is exceedingly unlikely that such a pattern could have been produced by natural causes, and the only plausible explanation is that men were manumitted by their early thirties and women toward the end of their childbearing years.[29]

Roman society contained plenty of people whose exact status may have been unclear to those around them, as well as those who moved from free to slave and slave to free. There are two graphic illustrations of the difficulties that could ensue. A papyrus from Hermopolis reports proceedings about the status of one Patricius, evidently because his owner had sold him and the purchaser wanted to register the sale. The slave himself is asked if he is free or slave; he answers that he is a slave. He then answers questions about where he was bought, from whom, who his mother was, what her status was (slave), whether he has siblings (one, a slave); and on the basis of all this the registrars agree to register the sale, but at the purchaser's risk if the facts turn out to be wrong.[30]

The reverse case is found in a petition to the prefect, in which the complainant alleges that his wife and children were carried off by

[25]*P.Abinn.* 36.

[26]*P.Herm.* 7.

[27]*P.Amh.* II 144 (no provenance, 5c).

[28]Another example of creditors seizing children occurs in *P.Lond.* VI 1915 (*ca* 330-340).

[29]See Bagnall and Frier, forthcoming.

[30]*P.Herm.* 18 (323?).

another couple (the husband in which seems to be a *prytanis*), on the grounds that they were their slaves. The petitioner claims that his wife is of free descent and married to him and that her brothers are free; he claims that her parents were also free. The case was probably not quite so clear, we may think, but it is striking just how much one might have to prove simply not to be enslaved.[31] As with social relations, so with status: what is important about slavery is not the number of slaves but the cast the permanent prospect of enslavement lends to the existence of all but the most protected.

Patronage and Dependency

It is in the nature of papyrological documents to show the economic relationship of urban landowners and rural tenants in an analytic fashion, such that in one text A is the lessee of B, in another A borrows grain from B, and in yet a third A writes to B asking for some favor. Rarely do all these types (and others) survive for any particular relationship. But it can hardly be doubted that these individual documents form part of a larger pattern. Where they survive in clusters as part of a villager's papers, as with Aurelius Isidoros or his sixth-century counterparts at Aphrodito, the connections of leasing, credit, sales, and indeed litigation become clearer. They were clearly not always to the disadvantage of the village entrepreneur who built on a secure local base to provide needed services to others on terms beneficial to himself. It is not necessary to see Isidoros as a rarity—he probably was not—to recognize him as a minority. The substantial numbers of villagers with no land at all, or with only tiny holdings, became lessees of urban owners or of their village middlemen on very different terms. Their leverage was far less and their lot undoubtedly much worse. Illiterate and not paper collectors, their voice is mostly mute.

Occasionally reports to the city show that those voices have been raised in unison for some reason. One interesting example is a letter written by a rural steward of an urban landowner to his employer.[32] Ammonios, the steward, tells Limenios that "everybody from Paomis" (a village in the 8th pagus of the Oxyrhynchite) had gone to the *epoikion* of Psankerma, under the mistaken impression that Limenios was there. They were intending to ask Limenios for a loan and had with them the contract (already drawn up, apparently) and the inter-

---

[31]*P.Grenf.* II 78 (Great Oasis, 307, cf. *RFBE* 31).

[32]*PSI* IX 1081 (cf. *P.Oxy.* LI 3639.4n.) (Oxyrhynchos, late 4c? The editor dated this earlier, but connections discussed below make the later date probable.)

est. Ammonios advises Limenios to grant the request because these people are reasonable, always do what they are told, and have always repaid their loans in the past. Psankerma was no doubt an *epoikion* of the type described earlier, the country estate and center of operations for a major landholder, in this case Limenios.[33] It seems to have been one of the larger such establishments.[34] Limenios presumably also had substantial holdings at the nearby Paomis, but it was a village, and no doubt "everybody" means "all your tenants."[35]

The dependent relationship of the tenants is clear. They are in no position to borrow on their own, in either village or city. Their only recourse is to approach their landlord, *geouchos*, and ask him for credit. His roles as landlord and creditor become blurred, and in both he becomes a kind of absent and distant figure, to be approached through the mediation of the steward. Ammonios, pleading on their behalf, argues that they are good credit risks and obedient; that is, their performance as tenants guarantees their performance as borrowers. They are frozen in dependency, outside the flux of the lively market of the city.[36]

Another collective relationship can be seen in a curious acknowledgment addressed to Dorotheos, a councillor of Hermopolis, by fifteen villagers of Sesiu.[37] They state that collectively they owe him the damage from the burning of his wheat crops at Sesiu, namely 300 artabas wheat and 300 baskets of chaff. The date is 376, presumably late in the year, and they are to pay from the harvest of 377. The wheat for the harvest of 377 can hardly have been of a height or dryness to be burnable even at the very end of 376, which suggests that the event must have taken place the previous spring; this instrument is thus probably the result of months of litigation. Neither the relationship of the villagers to Dorotheos nor their connection with the burning is stated. One may imagine that they are independent farmers and guilty

[33]See Rea's note, *P.Oxy.* LI 3639.4n., on the probable identity of the Limenios of *PSI* VIII 884, where he owns a mill, in *P.Oxy.* XIV 1752 (an order for payment), in *PSI* IX 1081, and in 3639 itself, in which he leases an oil-factory and is addressed as *lamprotatos*, i.e., *vir clarissimus*, a very high rank.

[34]Psankerma was also in the 8th pagus, cf. Pruneti 1981, 221. Other than here it appears only in *P.Oxy.* XII 1448 and XLVI 3307, both early 4c. In 3307 it is listed under the village of Souis, with the largest assessment of the *epoikia* in the list.

[35]Fikhman 1979, 192, cites this is a case of a dependent village, but the text is far from supporting such a sweeping conclusion, and he admits that the large landowner will have owned only part of the land in such villages.

[36]This kind of debt is perhaps characteristic of hierarchical, traditional societies. Cf. Wood 1992, 68, on colonial America: "Such credits and debts more often worked to tie local people together and to define and stabilize communal relationships."

[37]*P.Flor.* I 52 (*BL*) (376).

of starting the fire; that they are the most substantial villagers and being held collectively responsible for some unknown party's misdeed or accident; or that they are Dorotheos' tenants settling up for lease obligations they would have had to pay anyway. In any case, an average indebtedness of 20 artabas was a substantial burden, almost a year's income for many families, and one may well wonder how successful these men were in escaping permanent indebtedness to Dorotheos and his family, and thus permanent dependency. The settlement itself shows how effective the machinery of "justice" was in enforcing the claims of urban landowners in the village setting.

Power can, of course, be used beneficially or detrimentally. Economic and political power can be used to maintain a poor, dependent, and disciplined labor force that is useful for producing high profits from rural landholdings;[38] it can also be used charitably, as it seems to have been in one letter of a lender to an assistant:[39] "Since Launous, who is a widow, has come to me with her son, and has confirmed that she is having exacted from her the thirds [i.e., the interest] on what she owes to our account, exact only the principal due from them and do not take from them anything beyond." Even in this case, however, the charitable action maintains dependency; only interest is forgiven, and one type of dependency is substituted for another. Donors, too, have power.

This kind of ascendancy is part of what is generally meant by patronage, a term to which it is difficult to assign exact meaning, whether in ancient sources or modern discussions: "the diffuse and sometimes delicate webs of paternalistic obligation inherent in a hierarchical society" may do.[40] The various parts are intertwined, but there is some benefit in disentangling them. The basic phenomenon is that of economic dependency in various forms, some of which have been described above. Ancient terminology does not help very much.[41] *Patron*, for example, comes into use in the papyri (apart from some technical usage) only in the late third century, vanishing again by the early to middle fifth.[42] It carries no discernible specific content,

[38]See Foxhall 1990, 100-101, with references to modern third-world exploitative situations and suggestions (102-4) that less scrupulous Roman landlords may have taken advantage of similar possibilities.

[39]*BGU* II 412 (*BL*).

[40]Wood 1992, 57 (on colonial America).

[41]See Fikhman 1979 for a discussion and extensive bibliography. He concludes, among other things, that study of the key vocabulary does not advance the subject very much.

[42]*PSI* VII 835 is assigned by M. Manfredi in *PSI Corr.* I, pp. 11-26, to the 6c on inadequate palaeographical grounds. The hand resembles many late fourth century ones as much as the late sixth century parallel he mentions. Fikhman 1979, 191, cites

expressing rather deference and a generally subordinate relationship that can usually not be determined in any detail from the text and that no doubt varied in its precise form from case to case.

Any competition for landed property inevitably brought with it competition for labor and for the upper hand in these relationships of dependency. There were certainly some local pockets of such competition between high-ranking military officers and the local aristocracy, but it is argued in chapter 4 (above, pp. 177-79) that these have been much exaggerated by both Libanius and modern commentators. In the fourth century, the competition was primarily still within the curial class and between them and leading villagers. Despite all attempts to tie peasants to land, they naturally sought out more lucrative opportunities. The flight of six workers (and their families) from a struggling village like Theadelphia to the *epoikion* of a wealthy Oxyrhynchite offered benefits to both workers and landlord, who forcibly defended them from recapture by their fellow villagers.[43]

One significant novelty in the complex web of relationships was the church. Members of the clergy begin to play an important role in protecting the powerless, probably both for good and ill; this development is treated in the following section. But at some point the church also began to occupy the role of landowner, of detainer of economic power (see below, pp. 289-93 for this development). In the fourth century the ecclesiastical acquisition of land was still in its infancy and played little part in the competition. But by the sixth century, churches, monasteries, and the like owned substantial amounts of land, even as much as 46 percent of one category at Aphrodito.[44] This land was farmed by tenants, some on permanent leases. What is striking, however, is the control exercised over some of these establishments, and thus over the church itself, by the wealthy families that had been the source of the ecclesiastical endowments.[45] The church as landed patron, then, became another means for the wealthy to play out their competition.

The extent to which the wealthy acquired an economically patronal relationship to entire villages is much debated.[46] To the extent that *epoikia* formed little villages within villages, of course, they

---

this text for the "protection" of peasants (see the next section), but from Manfredi's improved text it can be seen to be a fairly straightforward request for grain, with no trace of patronage in the sense of protection.

[43]*P.Turner* 44 (= *P.Sakaon* 44) (331-332). *Hybreis* are almost certainly acts of physical rather than verbal violence in this context.

[44]Gascou and MacCoull 1987.

[45]MacCoull 1989, 498-502, describes this development.

[46]Summary in Fikhman 1979.

were dependent on their owners, and some of them evolved into villages over time.[47] How far, or if, the dependency was attenuated as they grew into villages is impossible to say. And true collective dependency is rarely attested in the documents.[48] Perhaps the clearest example is a letter addressed by eight named individuals and "everybody" from the Arsinoite village of Euhemeria to their "patron" Necho.[49] The occasion of the letter is unknown, but the villagers show the durability of the links by saying that "neither in your father's time nor in that of Your Beneficence did we hand over our bodies. But since we pay the taxes ordered yearly, we furnish ourselves to no one. There is no outsider in our village; there are two watchtowers, and no one can enter riding or on foot (without notice). But if your household needs something, we'll not refuse you; if you think it necessary to act, do so." The connection is thus multigenerational.[50] It is not clear what request for personal service they are responding to. Despite the note of pride, the deference at the end is unmistakable, in keeping with the tone throughout.[51]

All this, of course, is quite apart from the more direct and personal dependence of individual free employees on their employers. The personal and household staffs of the rich were not all, or perhaps even in majority, slaves. Their activities do not, except at the upper echelons of managerial employees, leave much written evidence. A few work contracts, however, suggest the relationship; one telling document is an undertaking addressed to a councillor of Oxyrhynchos from a man who undertakes to attend him, travel abroad with him, and obey all of his commands, in return for food, clothing, and other compensation lost in the breaking of the papyrus.[52]

[47]A development not always easy to see with confidence, given the tendency to interchange the terms *epoikion* and *kome* in later centuries; cf. Drew-Bear 1979, 42. Of her list, Demetriou, Hermitariou, Isidorou, Paploou, and Chairephanous all seem to have undergone the change. In the Oxyrhynchite, see Pruneti 1981 s.vv. Dositheou, Episemou, Herakleidou, Lenonos, Nomou, and Sarapionos Chairemonos, to cite only the clearer instances.

[48]Cf. Fikhman 1979, 194, a leap of faith in collective patronage after several pages showing virtually no evidence for the phenomenon. His prime exhibit, in fact, is *PSI* 1081, discussed above, n. 32; a lumping together of villages and *epoikia* confuses the result.

[49]*P.Ross.Georg.* III 8 (4c).

[50]The villagers address Necho as "O best child," which suggests that he is a young man at most.

[51]"We will never comprehend the distinctiveness of that premodern world until we appreciate the extent to which many ordinary people still accepted their own lowliness." Wood 1992, 30.

[52]*P.Oxy.* VIII 1122 (407). See A. Jördens, *P.Heid.* V, pp. 130-84, on such contracts.

Even those at the top of the staff hierarchy were very much subject to the power of their employers. One letter to a business agent, ordering him to collect some money that the employer needed to pay to the *strategos*, threatens that "if you throw this note aside, I'll have you brought in and squeezed; I've got enough troubles."[53] Those lower in the economic hierarchy in turn imitated their betters and sought on a smaller scale to acquire their own dependents from those still less well-off. Urban craftsmen would use their liquid capital to acquire immobile workers, by making loans the interest on which was worked off in the establishment of the lender, leaving the borrower indebted for the capital and thus unable to leave.[54] In some of these, the lender retained the power to dismiss the worker and ask for the capital back without notice, a powerful sword over the head of someone who had probably borrowed the capital to meet some urgent family need and had no way of repaying it.

Perhaps the most interesting such small-scale dependency is a marriage contract, whereby a landowner marries his daughter to a penniless worker he has taken on. The groom will not be allowed to leave his wife for any reason, and if he does he must pay the prohibitive sum of ten solidi.[55] The scribe for this contract of marital servitude is the local priest.

Protection

It is natural enough that a tenant economically dependent on a landlord would turn to the patron for forms of assistance other than loans. Although the apparatus of the state could function with some effectiveness where and when it chose, it was a minimal day-to-day presence in the villages, where its representatives were one's fellow villagers serving as liturgists. Nor did horizontal structures, other than kin, offer most villagers much support. By the early fourth century, few visible forms of social organization were left in the villages (above, p. 137). Though the better-off and more entrepreneurial villagers show every sign of confidence in using the system of justice to protect themselves, there is little sign that the landless, the truly dependent peasants, felt capable of doing so. It is thus hardly surpris-

[53]*P.Oxy.* XLVII 3358 (4c).

[54]*P.Rein.* II 105 (432), a loan of three solidi to a weaver; *P.Köln* II 102 (418), two solidi to a village woman, both texts from Oxyrhynchos. In the latter case, the lender, Chairemon son of Serenos, is to be identified with the important goldsmith of *P.Rain. Cent.* 122, *SB* XVI 12260, and *PSI* XII 1265, all from the 420s. See A. Jördens, *P.Heid.* V, pp. 271-95.

[55]*P.Ross.Georg.* III 28 (Arsinoite, 358).

ing that the vertical axis of social organization acquired considerable importance in the tenant's search for protection; nor was there anything inherently deplorable, from the viewpoint of a highly stratified society, about protection extended to dependents. Indeed, an ideology of benevolence toward those lower on the social and economic scale was deeply embedded in the hierarchical self-consciousness of the ruling elites of the Roman world.[56]

The potential for abuse of this protection, however, is obvious. It had been obvious for centuries, in fact, and there is substantial evidence for abusive protection in the Ptolemaic and Roman periods.[57] Although documentation of abuses like illegal protection against liturgies and taxes is not abundant, it is widely enough distributed to dispel any doubt that it was a perennial problem. An often-cited letter of a centurion to a *praepositus pagi* is emblematic:

> Ph. . . , the bearer of my letter, is my tenant. He states that he has been appointed to a public office at the village of Dositheou, namely the collectorship of tunics and cloaks, but has not yet undertaken the collection. Accordingly use all your efforts, brother, to rescue him from the office, and also to give him your favorable consideration, thereby conferring a great favor upon me, and further not to allow the people of the village in the future to injure him in other respects or appoint him to other offices, but let him testify to me to the benefits gained by your goodwill.[58]

The addressee was a senior member of the curial class of Oxyrhynchos.[59] He is, on the face of it, asked for a blatant violation of the law, the exemption from liturgical service of a man otherwise liable to it. That is actually only one of two possibilities. The tenant may be a true dependant, a landless (or virtually landless) farmer leasing the centurion's land; and in this case he would in fact not be liable for liturgical service, which was based on land ownership. Or he may be an Aurelius Isidoros type, a village landowner who served as a wholesale lessee for the centurion and sublet the land to others, in

---

[56]Cf. Brown 1988, 11, for a good summary and Kaster 1988, 69, on the moral acceptability of mutual favors.

[57]M. Piatkowska, *La skepe dans l'Égypte ptolémaïque* (Wroclaw 1975); Crawford 1974. See Fikhman 1979 for general bibliography. It is a major theme of MacMullen 1988, esp. 89-95 and chapter 3.

[58]*P.Oxy.* XII 1424 (*ca* 316-318, Heras' term of office).

[59]In *P.Oxy.* XVII 2232 he is identified as former magistrate and councillor as well as *praepositus pagi*; he is probably the grandson of the Herakleides alias Dionysios, councillor and *dekaprotos* (248-249), in *P.Oxy.* XII 1444.

which case he was indeed liable to serve, and the request is abusive.[60] The interpretation of this text as the latter is based on the fact that the centurion (the chief centurion of a legion, a man of importance himself) offers no arguments for exemption except the man's relationship to himself. That is not conclusive. Nor is it known if the *praepositus* in fact did what he was asked to, but that is probably less important than the centurion's assumption that this was a plausible request to make.[61]

A similar situation might seem to underlie a letter from the Sakaon archive, written by Posidonios, who may be a former *praepositus pagi*,[62] to the current *praepositus*.[63] The inhabitants of Theadelphia had approached Posidonios because Silvanos was proceeding against them on account of a debt, even though they did not owe him anything. He writes to ask for help, but damage to the pertinent passage makes it hard to say if he offers any substantiation of their claim or merely repeats it. This may then be an instance of benevolent intervention, an important patron getting the attention of an official to the legitimate claims of oppressed villagers. Or it could be an exercise in influence peddling.

Most people, of course, were not eager to write letters asking for blatantly illegal acts. And private letters are usually written with mutual knowledge of context, making it possible to omit precisely the information the modern reader wants. For example, a man writes to two of his father's assistants that his father has written to them ordering them not to bother "our man" Loios concerning dike work for himself and his land. If they have left him alone, he says, good; if they have forced him to do the work, then they are to give him the father's letter so that he will know that they acted against instructions.[64] It is unclear if this is a purely private matter within the writer's properties—someone else is to do the work instead of Loios, for example—or if the local agents are supposed to get Loios off his legal obligations. Or a cryptic letter in which Herakleides writes to Sarapion: "Demetrios the *gnoster* asked me to tell you that he is to be free from concern over previous years. For he says you helped him greatly in the *annona*. He says that the *annona* is now being claimed. If then you can again get him off by yourself, good luck; if not, tell me what preparations you want made. . . . If you are strong enough to get

---

[60]On this text see Lewis 1982, 155-59, esp. 158. He very improbably takes "brother" in the greeting literally (*contra* see Fikhman 1979, 190 n.5). The term means something like "colleague" in such contexts.

[61]*CPR* XVIIA 39 (Hermopolis, 4c) probably concerns a similar request.

[62]Cf. *P.Sakaon* 35.

[63]*P.Sakaon* 56.

[64]*W.Chr.* 390 = *P.Rein.* I 57 (4c).

him off, it will be a great achievement, since I have no cattle or pigs."[65]
The correspondents certainly knew what this meant, but too little is
known for the situation to be clear now.

Military protection of illegal behavior by civilian dependants, as
in the centurion's letter, has also been identified in the Abinnaeus
archive, but once again interpretation is problematic. A magistrate of
the metropolis of the Arsinoite writes to Abinnaeus to complain that
he has behaved badly.

> You sent the [. . .] under you to Theoxenis and you
> dragged them away, though so many crimes have
> occurred in the village. For you know that the house of
> Hatres was looted, when he had other people's property
> on deposit; and there have been cattle-rustling incidents,
> and you did not permit an inquiry but carried them off
> as if there were no laws. By God, either send them so
> that we can investigate what they have done or the
> entire council will report to my lord the duke about it.
> The residents of the epoikion of Ktesis have submitted
> written complaints to me and to Alammon (?) the
> praepositus of their pagus against you.[66]

The short lacuna at the start looms large. The editors restored
"soldiers" there, making this an instance of lawless behavior by
military personnel, but it has been argued that these men were in fact
civilian dependants of Abinnaeus whom he is protecting from justice.[67] That is most unlikely, however, for "under" in this construction
always refers to an official relationship, either military or administrative.[68]

A great deal of illegitimate "protection" at the expense of someone
else did not require extensive vertical networks. The village was a sufficient context. One group of petitions to Abinnaeus exemplifies the
problem. In one, a resident of the village of Hermoupolis complains

[65]*P.Oxy.* XII 1490. The editors dated to the late third century, but the office of
village *gnoster* does not appear until the 320s. The translation depends on taking
ophelesa (line 4) to be for *ophelesas*; otherwise, "again" makes no sense.

[66]*P.Abinn.* 18 (BL). See MacMullen 1988, 161 ff. on Abinnaeus' supposed corrupt
behavior.

[67]Carrié 1976, 172-73.

[68]Carrié 1976, 173 n.32, admits that *hupo* generally refers to soldiers. It is used in
fact also with reference to public offices, the staff of such offices, nomes, and pagi.
Carrié's notion that the writer is indulging in a clever metaphor of Abinnaeus'
dependants as a second army is fanciful. The letter, though vigorous, is hardly subtle.

about the pillaging of his house.[69] He had complained to the previous village eirenarch, but the sons of the current one (probably nominated by his predecessor) did the deed. The same villain is accused in two other petitions,[70] and the preceding eirenarch was also a malefactor with a delinquent son. Though a soldier was accused along with the villagers in one crime, there is no suggestion of protection of the offenders by Abinnaeus himself, to whom the victim turns for justice. Rather, the internal network of the village has caused the reign of lawlessness, in which those responsible for controlling crime cause it.

Similar is the string of complaints from Isidoros mentioned earlier (p. 166), first about the attempts by a neighbor (and longtime foe[71]) to shunt off onto Isidoros the taxes for some land owned by a councillor and cultivated by the neighbor,[72] and second against the komarchs for misallocation of taxes, allegedly with the connivance of the *praepositus pagi*, use of tax funds for private purposes, use of public animals for private purposes, and illegal trading in animals.[73] It is not necessary to believe Isidoros to be a wholly innocent party, or his opponents wholly guilty, to see that such accusations were likely to be normal and plausible.

None of this was new in the fourth century, not even the military involvement of which so much was made by Libanius and many moderns. A century earlier, much the same story is heard at Soknopaiou Nesos, on the north shore of Lake Moeris: "Aion, the representative of the *kolletion*, both has not allowed anyone else to approach the decurion and he has four brothers. He protects these, and others. And he demands special emoluments from the villages and though farming in other villages he pays no taxes on these lands."[74] The *kolletion* was evidently a military officer with tax and policing functions. Other documents from the same dossier show that the combination of village power with military and official connections enabled some villagers to usurp land, escape taxes, and transfer their burdens to less powerful fellow villagers.

A new center of protective power appears in the Christian church, evidently well in advance of the church's corporate acquisition of

[69]*SB* XIV 11380 (*ca* 346).

[70]*P.Abinn.* 48 and 51.

[71]This was an old feud, because in *P.Cair.Isid.* 65-67 the same man is accused along with two others of arson; cf. also *P.Cair.Isid.* 127, where this man reports that Isidoros son of Pemmeis (probably an error for Ptolemaios) was cultivating 4 ar. of grainland formerly owned by Horion.

[72]*P.Cair.Isid.* 69 (*BL*) (310); cf. 70.

[73]*P.Cair.Isid.* 71-73 (*BL*) (314).

[74]Crawford 1974, 170. Cf. P. J. Sijpesteijn, *Cd'E* 66 (1991) 279-80.

landed property. The limited evidence for this activity tends to give it
a pastoral character. The priest of the village of Hermoupolis writes to
Abinnaeus asking him to forgive a soldier named Paulos for going
AWOL, just this once; if he does it again, then regular discipline is in
Abinnaeus' hands. It appears that Abinnaeus had asked the priest to
come see him about the case, but the latter says that he cannot come
that day.[75] A letter from the Nag Hammadi finds is addressed to
Sansnos, a monk or priest (or perhaps both): "Make Peter, who is
harassing our brother Appianos through Papnoutios' people in the
matter of the rents, hold off for a few more days until they find an
opportunity to come to you and settle their problem." He appeals to
his love in Christ, and asks him further, if it is not burdensome, to get
him ten loads of chaff and let him know the cost.[76]

That is not to say that all acts of priests were beneficial interven-
tions on behalf of others. They owned property and had private affairs
like anyone else. A petition of two brothers from the village of Paneuei
to a *politeuomenos* says, "Because of your splendid administration we
returned from flight to our homes and found the *presbyteros* of the
catholic church of the village possessing them and the land. We therefore with good reason ordered him to hand this over to us, and he
would not."[77] The power acquired by the pastoral office has always
been susceptible to abuse, and by the time two generations of official
recognition had gone by, priests were undoubtedly well enough
entrenched in villages to be significant factors in local matters.[78]

That position of authority no doubt made them suitable
arbitrators in private disputes, and what was true of any priest was
particularly true of bishops. In a couple of cases, there is evidence for
disputes brought before bishops, and in one of them a decision is
preserved. It concerns some Christian books left behind by a deceased
man named Besarion, about which the heirs have disputed whether
they were removed from the premises and by whom. The bishop's
judgment is that either the nun Thaesis is to be shown by witnesses to
have taken them, in which case she must then bring them back, or else
she is to give an oath that no such removal took place and that she has
had her half share of the estate.[79] In another case (discussed above, p.

---

[75]*P.Abinn.* 32 = Naldini 40.

[76]*P.Nag Hamm.* 68; cf. Shelton's introduction, pp. 7-8, on the identity of Sansnos.

[77]*P.Wash.Univ.* 20 (Oxyrhynchos, 4c, perhaps around 370 if Makrobios, the
recipient, is the *riparius* mentioned in *P.Oxy.* XVII 2110; cf. *P.Wash.Univ.* II 83 with p.
242).

[78]Cf. MacCoull 1989, 499, on a situation in which a man entrusted his property
and family affairs to a priest for a period of a year.

[79]*P.Lips.* 43 (= *M.Chr.* 98); cf. *Aegyptus* 13 (1933) 199 ff. (4c). The use of an oath
has deep historical roots in Egypt; see U. Kaplony-Heckel, *Die Demotischen Tempel-*

195), bishops served as neutral parties attempting to reconcile feuding spouses—successfully for the moment, but not permanently.[80]

These papyri, taken with some dubious passages in the legal sources, have spawned extensive theories of episcopal jurisdiction. These rest on very little. There is in fact no reason to think that bishops had any formal powers of civil adjudication, enforced by the state.[81] They did, however, have a very real authority deriving from religious and social position, an urban, upper-class equivalent of the intercessor's and arbitrator's roles visible for the village priests.

A Sense of Class

It is worth asking at this point if a class structure can be identified in this society, with all its relationships of dependency, and if so, whether the people of fourth-century Egypt were conscious of such classes. Provided that "class" is understood in a sense not dependent on any particular theory of social relations or production, the answer to the first question is certainly affirmative.[82] That is not to say that some neat dichotomy can be established or that the edges of classes were not blurred. But a broad tripartite division certainly included most of Egyptian society.[83] At its top comes a very small group of those urban residents (though normally with country seats as well) wealthy enough to live from the income of their property. In broad terms this group coincides with the councillors and their families, but it also includes some people of equivalent economic power who were in public service, such as high-ranking civil servants and military officers. Few male members of this group, in fact, were without some public function, whether remunerated or liturgical. It is doubtful that

---

eide (Ägypt.Abh. 6, Wiesbaden 1963).

[80]*P.Oxy.* VI 903.

[81]Lallemand 1964, 150-52, with bibliography, is decisive, although that has not stopped proponents of the legal powers of bishops from continuing to make unsupportable claims, such as in Giulio Vismara, "La giurisdizione dei vescovi nelle controversie private dai laici (sec. IV)," *Orlandis 70: Estudios de derecho privado y penal romano, feudal y burgues*, 59-82 (*Boletín semestral de Derecho privado especial, histórico y comparado del Archivo de la Biblioteca Ferran Valls i Taberner* 1/2 [1988]), where the medieval role of the papacy is retrojected to the fourth-century empire.

[82]For a persuasive defense of such a nontechnical usage of the term, see Harris 1988, with a selective bibliography and criticism of earlier discussions. Wood 1992, 21, rejects the terminology for colonial American society, but on the grounds that distinctions of that time "did not resemble our modern conception of 'class,' " which is true enough.

[83]See Harris 1988, 605, for such a scheme, derived from Aristotle, which Harris does not develop in any detail.

in most cities more than a hundred or so families belonged to this class.

A significant middle group should perhaps be subdivided. Its members had in common the possession of some property, using which they made an adequate living. A part of these were participants in the urban economy of production, distribution, and services, owners of establishments of one sort or another rather than workers for others. There may have been as many as several thousand of these in the larger metropoleis. The other principal subgroup in this middle ground was made up of the village landowners who had enough land to live on, though that did not prevent them from engaging in various entrepreneurial activities. Their numbers are more conjectural still, but an average village might have had between 50 and 100 such owners, a nome perhaps 5,000 to 10,000. They were the backbone of village administration, those with enough property to make accountable liturgists.

This middle group, with its families, may well have accounted for something rather less than half the total population, urban and rural. The remainder existed in various forms of dependency. Of their number, something like 25 to 30 percent were slaves, the remainder free. The free were in the main rural tenants, who must have made up something like half the village population, urban wage-earners, and employees of the great houses. All of these had in common dependency on those with greater resources, many on the half of one percent of the population in whom a large share of the wealth was concentrated, but many also on the people of more middling means who owned shops and small factories or the village landowners who leased out part of their properties to fellow villagers or hired them as casual labor.

One should not claim too much for a model of this sort. It does not take into account the bulk of the military population or the middle-level officials, who probably have not only more in common with the middle group than with anyone else but also some significant differences with it. But it does give a reasonably accurate sense of where people stood in hierarchical terms, and neither the military nor the officials were numerous. A more serious problem with it is that class in fourth-century Egypt was not a matter only of belonging to a group; it was conceived rather differently, in fact, with a combination of group identification and a relational sense, combining in a consciousness of one's standing in the world.[84]

[84]A more purely horizontal self-consciousness may be identified in the church; cf. Averil Cameron 1991, 186.

This self-consciousness is harder to define than the objective economic groupings. Perhaps most elusive is the middle ground, so commonly referred to in the papyri (above all in petitions) by *metrios* and its derivatives: moderate, modest, neither wealthy nor poor. The term might be more persuasive if it were not so often used by people who are clearly members of the tiny curial elite.[85] Its vagueness of reference made it rhetorically attractive, because it might be used of anyone in the vast range above true poverty and below the equestrian order.[86] One's opponent, of course, was powerful, while one was oneself of modest means.

A concept of the upper crust is perhaps easier to identify. "Land-lord" (*geouchos* or the participle *geouchon*) is one distinguishing word, which comes over time to be ever more sharply a reference to the urban magnates. But in the fourth century it is still found referring to members of the middle class, village residents of middling means. "Patron," which has been discussed earlier, is usefully relational but unhelpfully vague. Perhaps more definitive is *euschemon*, "honorable" or "noble" in its documentary usage, found throughout the Roman period to refer to members of the curial aristocracy of the Greek cities and the metropoleis.[87] "The *euschemon*" was usually sufficient to identify such a person, like the neokoros of Sarapis, former strategos and current councillor of Alexandria referred to as such in the middle of a lease of sheep and goats addressed to him.[88] Joseph of Arimathea, who was able to obtain an audience with the governor, is described by Mark (15:43) as an *euschemon bouleutes*.

The upper class's view of the lower echelons has a split character. On the one hand, those who offend them in some way are described with telling epithets. One of the highest-ranking citizens of Hermopolis in the middle to late 320s, Aurelius Nilammon alias Hierax, who had held every local office including that of *logistes* and now had the rank of *vir egregius*, complained to the prefect of Egypt that he had been coerced by one Asklepiades, "with a soldierly appearance about him," into signing a bogus loan note.[89] He describes

[85]Like the former high priest of Arsinoe who submitted *P.Oxy.* I 71 (*BL*) (303), or the daughter of a former magistrate who filed *P.Panop.* 27 (323).

[86]It was, fundamentally, a relative term. See the sound remarks of Kaster 1988, 133, concerning *mediocritas*.

[87]The word still retained other usages, of course, but this one becomes almost a technical term.

[88]*P.Alex.Giss.* 5 (215).

[89]*P.Stras.* VI 560 (*BL*; Index to *P.Stras.* 501-800, p. 108; R. Coles, *BASP* 22 [1985] 25-27) (Hermopolis, *ca* 325). This is a rather messy draft. The value of the loan was not great. Nilammon was not a young man; he was already a councillor in 289 (*P.Stras.* 555, 557 intro.), and *syndikos* and former magistrate in 326 (IV 296).

his inability to bear the *banausotes*, "meanness" or "vulgarity," of the man; the word is a neologism derived from a favorite classical adjective for the working class. "Rustic churlishness" was a sufficiently disdainful term for an urban petitioner complaining about a tenant of land inherited from his mother who will neither pay rent nor leave.[90]

More interesting perhaps are terms that refer to the dependency of another person from the patron's point of view. One of these is the verb *diaphero*, in the broad sense "to be connected to." The verb, and its participle used as noun, express connection in a general way, and only the context allows recovery of the more precise connection intended.[91] For example, a letter to Abinnaeus tells him that one of his lower-ranking officers "is connected" to the writer and also to Paulos, the *cornicularius* of the camp.[92] He explains the latter connection: "For he is the father-in-law of Timotheos the veteran, who owns land at ———, being brother of Paulos." But he does not explain the connection to himself, although he is asking Abinnaeus to let the man go look after family affairs. In a letter of around the same time, the *diapherontes* of an official are presumably members of his staff, employees of the administration.[93] In another order, a landlord elsewhere attested serving as a *praepositus pagi* writes to a member of his staff to furnish to his *diapherontes*—not otherwise identified—six spathia of wine.[94] The term evidently might cover a considerable range, from officials who would be regarded as important figures by the average person right down to a dependent relative or even a slave. Legal status, kinship, and economic standing all went into the making of the relationship, but none of them needed to be identified; it was sufficient to describe someone as a dependant. The relationship itself was the crucial element.

Similar, though less common, is the word *idios*, which appears in a tax receipt of 390 to describe a miller in the service of the same Limenios who figures in the discussion of dependent peasants (above, p. 215). Sarapion is described as "*idios* of Limenios."[95] The same ambi-

[90]*Kometike authadeia*: CPR V 9 (Hermopolis, 339), CPR XVIIA 96 (Hermopolis, 320): no doubt a rhetorical commonplace. Cf. above, p. 171.

[91]Preisigke, WB I 367, defines this usage (his no. 7) as "Familienmitglied, Hausgenosse, Bediensteter, Höriger, zur Familie oder Hausgenossenschaft gehörend"—a remarkable flurry of words in an attempt to get at a term that eludes simple definition. WB IV 562 gives "Angehöriger (Anhänger, Familienmitglied, Hausgenosse, Bediensteter, Höriger)." This usage seems to appear in the papyri only in the second half of the third century, cf. Rathbone 1991, 133-34.

[92]*P.Abinn.* 33.

[93]*SPP* XX 111 (*ca* 340s; cf. Bagnall 1992c).

[94]*P.Oxy.* LVI 3875 (360).

[95]*PSI* VIII 884 (*BL*; *P.Rain.Cent.* p. 424 n. 13) (Oxyrhynchos, 390).

guity of denotation is present as with *diaphero*; the relationship of dependence is the key point.[96] Sarapion could well be a slave, but nothing authorizes such an identification, and the legal status is not important. Only as a dependant, a representative of the house, is he identified.

Class was thus relational in this hierarchical world with its "long train of dependence."[97] Even very important men, of course, lived with some measure of terror of those above them and the brutality they could inflict.[98] But in everyday life, the tiny urban elite could see village entrepreneurs, city tradesmen, tenant farmers, hired staff, and slaves as being in one important sense all on one level: not theirs. For those in the middle, matters were more complex; they had their dependants, but they might be one also.[99] This relativity thus cut across the broad lines of economic class both to simplify and to complicate them.

[96]Preisigke, *WB* I 685 (4) resorts to similar definition: "Familienmitglied, Angehöriger, Hausbediensteter, Vertrauter."

[97]Hume, quoted by Wood 1992, 19.

[98]See MacMullen 1986 for a rather lurid characterization.

[99]For a sense of superiority to slaves, see Naldini 56 = *P.Grenf.* I 53 (*BL*).

CHAPTER 7

Languages, Literacy, and Ethnicity

Languages, Names, and Ethnicity

Ethnicity in late antique Egypt, as in much of the Mediterranean world, was a complex matter. Modern writing, even scholarly, displays a range of opinion from one extreme to another: at one, a naive belief in the existence of discrete groups called "Copts" and "Greeks";[1] at the other, a confidence that all ethnicity had been melted down into one mixed civilization over a thousand years of contact. The problem goes back to the idea of the Hellenistic, which came into the languages of scholarship by analogy. Language was "hellenistic" in mixing foreign elements with Greek; as the *Oxford English Dictionary* puts it, the word was "applied to the modified form of the Greek language, with many foreign elements, current in Egypt, Syria, and other countries, after the time of Alexander the Great." The extension of this concept to history and more broadly to culture thus carried with it an agenda of interpretation: the age was named by a term that itself denoted mixture. It is hardly surprising, then, that the question of mixture has so dominated modern scholarly discourse on the period, and in its train has followed the question of maintaining or submerging ethnic and cultural identity. It must not be forgotten that the original sense embraced the early centuries of the common era as well as the three centuries following Alexander that are now commonly termed Hellenistic.

So far as Egypt was concerned, it was somewhat more than a century ago, with the beginning of large-scale discovery and publication of Greek papyri, that these questions began to be able to be treated in some depth. At first, the massive documentation of the papyri seemed only to confirm the understanding evoked by the word Hellenistic, and the period up to the end of the Second World War was dominated by the idea of fusion, or mixture, of cultures and peoples. But this consensus came unglued so rapidly that by 1968 it was possible to describe as a "truism" the statement that "we cannot

---

[1] In fact, the term "Copt" is nowhere found in the ancient sources; it is an Arabic term for the native Egyptians who remained true to Christianity.

speak of a mixed Greco-Egyptian civilization."[2] And in the past two decades the concept of juxtaposition has become the new orthodoxy. Culture and ethnicity are terms carrying a heavy freight, the subjects of interminable and complex debate. Many aspects of them emerge from other chapters; here, however, the focus is on language, perhaps the one indisputable factor, a vehicle of culture as well as a part of it.

Egypt in the fourth century had at least three languages in wide use, Egyptian, Greek, and Latin. Given the thousands of published papyri and a society with more than one language in common use, the documents are less forthcoming with information about their relationship than might be expected. Perhaps the most straightforward case is that of Latin. Its position in Roman Egypt before Diocletian has been summarized as follows: "The edicts and decrees of the central government were Latin, when they concerned the Roman army, Roman magistrates, or Roman individuals; the correspondence between Roman magistrates was mainly written in Latin; the official language of the Roman army was Latin and the documents of Roman citizens inside the sphere of *ius civile* had to be originally written in Latin. Furthermore, Latin literature, especially juridical, historical and political prose works, were [sic] to a small extent copied and read in Egypt and a small part of the private correspondence of soldiers, veterans and other Romans was in Latin."[3] In short, Latin occupied a marginal position, fulfilling some official functions but relatively little used between individuals and not the dominant language in any community in Egypt, even the army.[4]

Certainly more Latin was used in the fourth century than earlier, to judge from the papyri. Latin plays a larger role in court proceedings before high officials;[5] some correspondence from high officials has a token Latin framework, but still the main text is in Greek.[6] Otherwise, the documents in Latin, or partly in Latin, fall almost entirely into the categories listed for earlier centuries. A couple of letters in Greek with

[2]Naphtali Lewis, "'Greco-Roman Egypt': Fact or Fiction?" *Proc. XII Int. Congr. Pap.* 4, quoting J. Bingen in *Cd'E* 40 (1965) 512; it should be noted, however, that Bingen is there only summarizing Claire Préaux's summation at the Warsaw Congress of 1961 (*Actes X Congr. Int. Pap.* 233).

[3]Kaimio 1979, 27, citing already Stein 1915, 132-86, for the main outlines.

[4]As Kaimio 1979, 28, points out.

[5]As John Rea has put it (*P.Oxy.* LI 3619 introd.), "the formal framework is given in Latin while the words of the participants are given mostly in Greek. The judge in these cases usually speaks Greek, but he may address his staff in Latin." Rea lists thirty-nine examples of such texts from *ca* 298 to the 6th century; it is thus a Diocletianic innovation.

[6]E.g., *P.Oxy.* L 3577 (342) and 3579 (*ca* 341-343), both from Herakleopolis; *SB* XVI 12580 (late 4c, perhaps written in Alexandria).

Latin greetings at the end in the sender's own hand are known, but at least one of them comes from an archive connected with the military.[7] Sociologically perhaps more interesting are the bilingual or trilingual glossaries, tools of those trying to use at least a little Latin. One of them gives the Latin words in Greek transliteration, with declensions and cases often altered from the original.[8] A sixth-century conversation manual includes Greek, Latin, and Coptic.[9] Clearly Latin had its importance for a career in the imperial civil service or the army, where the higher one climbed the more one needed some Latin.[10]

In the trickier problem of understanding the use of Greek and Egyptian, and of ethnic identity as Greek or Egyptian, there are many obstacles. First, the Romans did not officially classify people in this way; by the time of Diocletian, such a division had been officially obsolete for 300 years. Instead, the Romans initially divided the population into the citizens of the Greek *cities*, meaning only Alexandria, Ptolemais, Naukratis, and Antinoopolis, and Egyptians, the latter term including all "Greeks" who were not citizens of one of these cities.[11] Within the "Egyptian" population, however, there was a distinction between the privileged metropolitan residents and the villagers, who paid different rates of tax. That distinction, though no longer linked to the rates of money taxes, persisted—if anything, reinforced—in late antiquity, even though all were Roman citizens.

It might be supposed that personal names offer one approach to identifying those who thought of themselves as Greeks or Egyptians. In the aggregate this is probably true, at least in the villages, where

[7]*P.Abinn.* 16; the other example is *P.Mert.* III 115 (early 4c), closing "opto te fili bene valere."

[8]*P.Lond.* II 481 (p. 321) (*BL*) (4c); the principles on which the words were chosen are obscure: they include heavenly bodies, animals, plants, and weather phenomena. See the corpus of J. Kramer, *Glossaria bilinguia in papyris et membranis reperta* (Pap.Texte Abh. 30, Bonn 1983) and the survey of glossaries by A. Wouters, *The Chester Beatty Codex Ac 1499. A Graeco-Latin Lexicon of the Pauline Epistles and a Greek Grammar* (Chester Beatty Monographs 12, Leuven 1988) 101-106.

[9]Pack² 3009: P.Berol. 10582, text in *Klio* 13 (1913) 27-38; *CPLat.* 281.

[10]For the view of Latin's limited gains in the fourth century set out here, cf. E. G. Turner, "Latin versus Greek as a Universal Language: the Attitude of Diocletian," *Language and Culture: Essays Presented to A.M. Jensen* (Copenhagen 1961) 165-68, who stresses the "narrow limits within which Diocletian sought to impose by authority the use of Latin in its place." An interesting essay by A. D. Leeman in the same volume ("Latin and Greek," 91-97) argues the superiority of Greek for most purposes, perhaps the best reason why Latin did not make greater inroads. For the juristic side, the classic treatment is H. Zilliacus, *Zum Kampf der Weltsprachen im oströmischen Reich* (Helsinki 1935) 86-97, who considers Egypt the province least affected by Romanization under Diocletian and Constantine. Dioskoros of Aphrodito knew a little Latin; cf. MacCoull 1988, 149.

[11]See Bagnall 1988 for a summary with bibliography.

characteristic assemblages of the old Egyptian theophoric names survive into the fourth century.[12] But from Constantine on, the impact of
Christianization is seen in the growing use of identifiably Christian
names, from the scriptures, saints, virtues, and heroes of the faith.[13] If
it is not immediately obvious what language a man named Sarapion
spoke, it is still more obscure what is to be expected from an Isaac, a
Thomas, a Gennadios, a Paul, a John. Even before this change, however, the situation is unclear. An example from what would generally
be regarded as a clearly hellenophone milieu makes this point. One
Marcus Aurelius Apion, son of Philippos, and his wife Apias, who
bears the Alexandrian demotic Althaieus, asks to have his four
children enrolled in the appropriate class of their agemates in the official records; these are, he says, children of his deceased and former
wife Tisois, the daughter of Sarapammon the son of Eutychides alias
Sarapion and of his wife Thatoes, who was from Oxyrhynchos. The
children are named Philippos, Gaios, Melaina alias Anoubiaina, and
Taeous.[14] This family, in 291, clearly belongs to a privileged milieu,
with Alexandrian citizenship on one side and Oxyrhynchite
metropolitan (and indeed gymnasial) status on the other. Apion's
father has a Graeco-Macedonian name, but his own name and that of
his mother are derived from the Egyptian god Apis: Greek names of
an Egyptian milieu. His deceased wife has an Egyptian name; her
father a Greek name derived from Egyptian gods; her mother an
Egyptian one; her grandfather twin names, one Greek and the other
derived from Sarapis. Of the children, one has the grandfather's name
Philippos, one a Roman praenomen, one dual names—one Greek, the
other based on Anoubis—, and the last one purely Egyptian. Nothing
is simple.

In a society with three languages in use, and two of them of daily
importance to large numbers, one might expect to find translating and
interpreting to be important activities. But interpreting and interpreters—*hermeneia* and *hermeneis* in Greek—are precisely a good
example of the reticence of the documents.[15] The terms are not terribly
common, and most instances fall into a few groups. Some documents
indicate that they are or contain a translation into Greek; all thirteen
not only involve translation from Latin into Greek but also fall in the

[12]A small Memphite example is found in *SB* I 5272 (*BL*), from 304.
[13]See below, pp. 280-81 on this phenomenon.
[14]*P.Corn.* 18 (*BL*) (Oxyrhynchos, 291).
[15]There is an extensive but unsatisfactory treatment in W. Peremans, "Les
hermeneis dans l'Égypte gréco-romaine," *Das römisch-byzantinische Ägypten* (Mainz
1983) 11-17. Cf. also Hanson 1991, 176.

century and a half between about 150 and 300.[16] Ten records of court proceedings indicate that a party spoke through a *hermeneus*, an interpreter; all ten fall between 180 and 340, and in only one case is the other language indicated: there it is Latin, in the rendering of the sentence of a governor.[17] It seems likely that translation from Egyptian to Greek is meant in most of the other cases, but there is something stylized about the whole genre.[18] Some villages in the Arsinoite Nome, and only there, had a six-choinix grain measure called "the interpreter's," attested in ten or eleven texts; neither evidence nor the scholarly speculation about a broker's role for the *hermeneus* really helps very much.[19]

Only two texts, in fact, seem to provide the kind of information needed. The first is a letter of the second century A.D., prefaced with "You who read the letter, whoever you may be, make a little effort and translate what is written in the following letter for the women and inform them."[20] The letter following, addressed to two women called mother and sister, is a typical family letter from a man named Ptolemaios, rebutting the women's accusations of misbehavior and in turn castigating them for not inquiring after him when he had been severely injured by being kicked by a horse. The women have Greek names—Zosime, Rhodous—and the editor resisted taking the text at face value because "it is difficult to think of a man with a Greek name writing in Greek to his mother and sister who, while they also have Greek names, are not only illiterate in Greek but do not understand it when it is read to them."[21]

[16]*P.Harr.* I 67 (*ca* 150, guardianship); *PSI* XIII 1325 = *SB* V 7630 (176-180, registration of inheritance); *BGU* I 326 (194, Roman will); *Pap.Lugd.Bat.* XIII 14 (2c, Roman will; restored); *P.Oxy.* XIX 2231 (241, claim to succession of an inheritance); *P.Oxy.* XII 1466 (245, request for a guardian); *SB* VI 9298 (249, *agnitio bonorum possessionis*; a fuller version of *SB* I 1010); *P.Oxf.* 7 (256-257, Roman will); *P.Oxy.* IX 1201 (258, *agnitio bonorum petitio*); *P.Oxy.* XXXIV 2710 (261, request for a guardian); *CPR* VI 78 (*ca* 265, release from patria potestas); *P.Oxy.* IX 1205 (291, manumission *inter amicos*); *P.Oxy.* XX 2276 (3/4c).

[17]*P.Sakaon* 34 (321).

[18]*PSI* XIII 1326 (181-183, *epistrategos*); *P.Oxy.* II 237 (186, *epistrategos*); *SB* XIV 11391 (2/3c); *P.Stras.* I 41 (*ca* 250); *P.Oxy.* XLII 3074 (3c, *strategos*); *P.Ant.* II 87 (late 3c); *P.Sakaon* 32 (late 3c, *strategos*); *P.Vind.Tandem* 8 (3/4c); *P.Col.* VII 175 = *SB* XVI 12692 (339, *defensor civitatis*).

[19]There is a tax on *hermeneia*, but we cannot tell its purpose. Payments to or for *hermeneis* occur in a half-dozen or so papyri and ostraka, but the context tells nothing useful about the motive. A few other references are enigmatic. References can be found in the article of Peremans cited above, n. 15. Interpreting also appears in monastic literature, as in *HL* 21.15, where Kronios interprets Antony's Egyptian for a Greek-speaking Alexandrian. Cf. below, p. 245.

[20]*ZPE* 58 (1985) 71-79.

[21]*P.Haun.* I 14 introd.

That sentence is laden with unnecessary assumptions. But it raises an issue of great importance. As the editor says, this is a man with a Greek name writing a letter in Greek. He had, as emerges below (p. 237), no choice. No form of written Egyptian was in everyday use in the second century. In these circumstances, then, the author of this letter (who no doubt dictated rather than wrote it), who certainly did know Greek, had no choice but to write a letter in Greek which could be translated back into Egyptian for the benefit of his female family members. It is difficult to know whether to be more struck by the situation or by the absence of any parallel in the large body of papyrus letters.[22] Was it typical for women to be able to speak only Egyptian, while men learned Greek for their activities in the outside world? Some small confirmation of the scene comes from a property sale of the end of the sixth century:[23] toward the end, the sellers, who are two women, assert that the whole contract was read to them and translated into Egyptian for them. Once again, the situation is unique.[24] The clause in the letter is strongly reminiscent of Egyptian letters of the pharaonic period addressed to men but written to women. Even where language was not a barrier, therefore, the man was often expected to be the intermediary.[25]

At least there are obvious clues that already in the earlier Roman period the spoken use of Greek and Egyptian was as complex as the written, affected by residence, social and economic class, sex, and contingent personal factors. After a brief description of the use of the different forms of Egyptian in the Roman period, it is most convenient to divide the discussion once again by place—villages first and then towns.[26]

The Decline of Demotic and Rise of Coptic

To ancient observers and modern visitors alike, the hieroglyphic writing of the Egyptians was a distinctive characteristic. For the most part, the Greeks and Romans offered fantastic explanations of this pictorial script, which by the Hellenistic period was used only for inscrip-

[22]*P.Wash.Univ.* II 107 may refer to a similar situation.

[23]*P.Monac.* 13 (594).

[24]The clause is paralleled however (*ca* 600) in the will of Bishop Abraham, *P.Lond.* I 77 (p. 232), where of course it is a *man* who has given his instructions in Egyptian (and who does *not* say explicitly that he does not understand Greek).

[25]See Wente 1990, 9.

[26]An extended bibliographical essay by G. Horsley in *NewDocs* 5, 5-40, on "The Fiction of 'Jewish Greek,'" has many useful observations and references for bilingualism and literacy, both in Egypt and elsewhere.

tions.[27] Although the Egyptian temples kept some knowledge of the traditional script alive for many centuries, it had been replaced for most practical purposes first by a more cursive form called "hieratic"; this, in turn, had given way (except for some literary uses) by the Hellenistic period to a derivative and more cursive script usually referred to as "Demotic." Demotic, like its ancestors, was an Egyptian script, not a separate language. Whether in epigraphic or cursive form, the signs included alphabetic, syllabic, and ideogrammatic representation, and though the development of scripts ran chronologically parallel to that of the language, one could transcribe texts of quite different periods into the same script.

These scripts have in common not only the repertory of signs but also a high level of difficulty.[28] Their traditional users were the royal administration and the temples; being a scribe was a comfortable, well-paid, and distinctive profession, and few outside it seem to have needed to be able to write. The coming of the Ptolemies dealt one serious blow to the currency of Demotic, for though the Egyptian script continued to be used by some local officials, it was replaced by Greek as the medium of higher- and middle-level administration.[29] Nonetheless, the flourishing state of the native temples under the earlier Ptolemies enabled Demotic to hold its own for at least the first two centuries of Ptolemaic rule; as a vehicle for Late Egyptian literature, in fact, Demotic blossomed, and it was used for private letters. But already in the later Ptolemaic period (the first century B.C.) there are signs that Egyptians increasingly preferred to use Greek for practical purposes. This was no doubt particularly true of the propertied classes.[30] The coming of Roman rule led in time to pressure on the temples (for which see chapter 8); the results for Demotic were not long in following.

The one official use of Demotic still known in the Roman period is the issuance of tax receipts on ostraka. Their numbers decline rapidly; after falling by about 85 percent from the first to second half of the first century A.D., they hold steady until the middle of the second century, after which there is only a handful, with the last ones from

[27]Cf. Gardiner 1957, 8-9. Gardiner gives (11-18) a lively survey of the equally remarkable early modern interpretations and of Champollion's decipherment and its aftermath. Baines 1983 gives a survey of the uses of writing in pharaonic Egypt.

[28]Though Baines 1983, 581, thinks them "not particularly difficult to learn."

[29]For much of the preceding two centuries, of course, it had already lost this function to Aramaic, under Persian rule.

[30]A similar phenomenon can be seen in Palestine and the Provincia Arabia; cf. *P.Babatha* 18 introd.

around 235.[31] Private documents are not much better: though not as few as their publication would seem to indicate, they occupy a narrow niche. Apart from the tax receipts, there is little more than sales, accounts of money or commodities (little studied to date because of their difficulty and relatively low interest), and priestly agreements concerning their rights and duties. Compared to the riches of the Ptolemaic record, this is strikingly feeble. The range is also geographically narrow: after Augustus not a single published Demotic documentary papyrus comes from anywhere except Tebtunis or Soknopaiou Nesos, both in the Fayum. Religious and literary texts, equally dominated by the temples, fare somewhat better, with the first and second centuries the high point of literary production; but once again, only a few magical texts continue in the third century. Otherwise, the third century has little to offer but mummy tags (produced by a semi-priestly group); in the fourth and fifth centuries, Demotic is increasingly a relic preserved in a few temples.[32]

It is fair to say that after about A.D. 50 there was for most Egyptians only one means of recording things in writing: Greek. A narrow priestly cadre clung to Demotic for their literature, which had no other means of being recorded in its own language, and for occasional other texts. The small base of persons literate in Demotic was its undoing in the face of adverse circumstances.[33] For two centuries or so, until the middle of the third century, Egypt witnessed the striking phenomenon of a majority population with no way of recording anything in its own language in writing. Most of the population had always been illiterate, but they had at least had scribes to whom they could go to have things written down. Now, except for perhaps a few hundred priests (at a very optimistic assessment), there was no such facility.[34]

[31]For the Theban ostraka, see the list of money-tax receipts dated after A.D. 40 written in Demotic in K. A. Worp, *ZPE* 80 (1990) 243-44.

[32]Zauzich 1983, 77-80. The absolute numbers he gives are based on Pestman's listing in 1965 and would be much enlarged now, but their distribution has not changed. Zauzich points out that one important change from recent finds is that no longer is Upper Egypt the exclusive source for Demotic ostraka; they are now known also from the Small Oasis, Oxyrhynchos, Sakkara, Soknopaiou Nesos, and Narmouthis. Cf. Grenier 1989 for dated Demotic texts. W. J. Tait, "Demotic Literature and Egyptian Society," *Life in a Multi-Cultural Society* (SAOC 51, Chicago 1992) 303-310, provides a context for the literary texts in the temples.

[33]That small cadre was still well organized and operated schools in temples. See *P.Rain.Cent.* 5 (95/6) (cf. K.-Th. Zauzich, *Enchoria* 12 [1984] 87-90) for regulations governing temple scribes; numerous school texts, both Greek and Demotic, have been found at Narmouthis.

[34]The number of persons entitled to be called "priest" was much larger, but there is no reason to think that most were literate in Demotic. For some numbers in 113/4, see *BGU* XIII 2215.

There was no way to have an Egyptian sentence recorded except to translate it into Greek.

It would be surprising if someone had not long since thought of a solution that used the alphabetic simplicity of Greek without abandoning the national language, namely recording Egyptian phonetically in Greek. In fact, of course, such attempts go back many centuries, to the sixth century B.C., in the phenomenon of Egyptian names transcribed in Greek.[35] But only in the Roman period did they begin to show signs of a coherent attempt to create a new writing system; the first tries are all magical, astrological, or "popularly" religious in content.[36] They come from a pagan background; authors and motives are a matter for speculation, but it would be a fair guess that these texts are the surviving evidence of widespread moves to preserve traditional learning in a form that might be more widely accessible. They reveal a purist streak, for unlike Coptic they are devoid of borrowings from Greek.[37]

Coptic itself is a different matter. It was certainly invented, in the third century, with deliberateness; because its first use was for translating the Bible into the language of the Egyptian population, it is a reasonable inference that this was the motive force of its creators.[38] It cannot automatically be assumed that it is a straightforward representation of the contemporary spoken language; writing and language are not always so simply mapped to one another, and artificiality is always a possibility.[39] A striking characteristic of Coptic is its high proportion of Greek vocabulary, a feature alike of translations from Greek and original composition in Coptic.[40] In fact, it is clear that Coptic was developed, and its literature produced, predominantly in thoroughly bilingual milieus.[41] This fact deserves further reflection.

[35]Quaegebeur 1982, 128-29; there are tens of thousands of examples in the Hellenistic and Roman papyri and ostraka, the value of which for studying the development and dialects of Egyptian is stressed by Quaegebeur (133-36).

[36]See Quaegebeur 1982, 130, 133, and Satzinger 1984, 138-44, for somewhat different appraisals of the texts, which are usually called "Old Coptic"; their character, however, is very different from that of Coptic.

[37]Satzinger 1984, 137, makes this crucial point.

[38]Quaegebeur 1982, 132.

[39]Quaegebeur 1982, 126. For the same reason, Demotic should not be treated as itself a spoken language, as Harris 1989, 190, does.

[40]Cf. Lefort 1950, 66: for example, he points out, texts of Pachomius have 25 percent more Greek words than the gospel of Matthew.

[41]See Lefort 1950, 68-69, who emphasizes that the translators of the Coptic Bible had a thorough and subtle command of Greek. See also Roberts 1979, 65-66, who points out that the first known Coptic scholar had a good command of Greek science.

All the same, there are signs that Coptic reflects not some artificial choice but the contemporary realities. The most noteworthy is the existence of dialects in early Coptic texts, those of the third to fifth centuries. The characteristics of these dialects (largely phonetic) are very largely confirmed by evidence for the regional variation of spoken Egyptian provided by the transcription of Egyptian names into Greek.[42] Six main dialects are known in the early period, through the fifth century,[43] Bohairic (in the western Delta), Fayumic, Oxyrhynchite (sometimes called Middle Egyptian), Akhmimic (the popular dialect of most of the area from Panopolis to Syene), Subakhmimic (a region centered on Lykopolis), and Sahidic (originally from a zone between Memphis and Herakleopolis, but the common educated dialect of Upper Egypt). Of these, only Fayumic, Bohairic, and Sahidic were still in use in the sixth century. A particularly striking fact is that Sahidic appears to have coexisted with Akhmimic in the Theban region as early as the third century B.C.[44] Sahidic became the standard classical Coptic literary dialect, but before 1000 it was overtaken by Bohairic, probably by virtue of the use of Bohairic by the monophysite patriarchate, then based in the Wadi Natrun.

Coptic was, then, not just an artificial creation of a central group. There is no way of telling who took the lead or just when, but Christian groups in every part of Egypt took up the idea in the third century and by the fourth century there was a version of Coptic for every known dialect. It lifts the veil that partly obscures the development of the spoken language of Egypt in the Hellenistic and Roman periods, the veil of the conservatism of Demotic. In Demotic texts, Greek loanwords are rare and limited to a few predictable categories;[45] in Coptic, on the contrary, the results of a half-millennium of cohabitation are visible in a rich Greek vocabulary.[46]

The creation of this new means of expression, with its simple alphabet and rich vocabulary, was a cultural event of major propor-

---

[42]Vergote 1973, 2-4, gives a survey of the Coptic dialects; for examples of the results yielded by the study of names, see Quaegebeur 1975 and Bagnall, *Enchoria* 8.1 (1978) 143-44 (with bibliography).

[43]And attempts have been made to identify three more minor ones, but they are based on a small amount of evidence.

[44]Cf. my article cited in n. 42 above.

[45]Clarysse 1987.

[46]Crum omitted Greek words from his *Coptic Dictionary* on the grounds that "the book being a dictionary of the Coptic language, the countless Greek words, scattered through every class of text, cannot claim inclusion" (p.viii). Lefort 1950, 65 n.1, reports that Crum told him that (far from really believing in this principle) in fact he simply found it impossible after doing much of the work to change a decision made at the start of excerpting.

tions.[47] Its immediate impact, however, was limited. Pre-Constantinian Egypt did not put Coptic to use in any wide range of writings. This stratum, in fact, was made up entirely of translations of sacred texts, principally the Bible and a few postbiblical theological writings. With approximately the 330s a major watershed occurs. First, the range of religious literature (orthodox and otherwise) expands dramatically in the middle decades of the fourth century, as the Nag Hammadi "Library" shows so vividly. Second, and equally strikingly, the first secular use of the script turns up in private letters. To the long-known letters from the Melitian archive (dated by the editor to the 330s; see plate 7 for an example),[48] and the bilingual archive of texts addressed to a monk Apa Ioannes,[49] have recently been added the Coptic letters found inside the bindings of the Nag Hammadi codices,[50] and a couple of Coptic letters in the archive of Nepheros, probably from the 350s.[51] These letters all come not only from Christian contexts but from members of the clergy, and a monastic or quasi-monastic ambience can be argued for all three groups. The broadening of the use of Coptic after 330, then, must be seen still within very specific limits.

The situation remains so for quite some time: Coptic is used for theological texts and personal correspondence, always in a Christian milieu and particularly within the growing monastic establishment. It is by no means easy to be certain about the next steps, particularly because dating Coptic texts is still a very rough art and provides a rather insecure foundation.[52]

Spoken and Written Greek in the Villages

The reality of oral expression in the countryside of Egypt is not easy to recapture. It has been claimed that Greek was "rarely heard in the Egyptian countryside,"[53] but, paradoxically enough, one must rely on

[47]As Quaegebeur 1982, 135, emphasizes.

[48]*P.Lond.* VI 1920-1922.

[49]*P.Herm.* 7-10 and *P.Ryl.Copt.* 268-276; cf. the communication of P. van Minnen to the Fifth International Congress of Coptic Studies (Washington, August 1992).

[50]*P.Nag Hamm.* C4-C8, C15-C19; the mass of Greek from the bindings is of course far greater. The very limited datable material in the bindings is all from the 340s, and it is unlikely that the undatable papyri are much distant from that date.

[51]*P.Neph.* 15-16, again accompanying a predominantly Greek archive. On the date of the archive, see Bagnall 1989b, 74-75.

[52]Cf. Gascou 1989, 77, who redates a Coptic literary text from the sixth century to the first half of the fourth. For the development of Coptic literature see generally T. Orlandi, "Coptic Literature," in Pearson and Goehring 1986, 51-81. K. A. Worp, *Anal.Pap.* 2 (1990) 139-43, lists the few exactly dated Coptic texts before 641.

[53]Youtie 1975a, 181, repeated by Harris 1989, 190.

written, not oral, communications as a base of argument. It has already been remarked above that the Egyptian population was effectively unable to express its native tongue in writing. A small number of priests or scribes, groups not readily distinguished, could write Demotic in the early Roman period, but their ranks declined rapidly and were effectively extinct by the middle of the third century. Because priests in any case needed Greek to operate their temples under Roman administration, it is unlikely that there was anyone capable of writing Egyptian but ignorant of at least oral Greek.[54] There is no evidence after about A.D. 150, in fact, even for anyone literate only in Demotic, and not many such cases exist before.[55] Nor did Coptic fill that hole, it is evident; it is still relatively rare for any nonecclesiastical use in the fourth century, and it is not employed in formal legal documents until the sixth century.[56] In short, in the time of Diocletian and Constantine as for many years before, literacy required knowing Greek and, for anyone who spoke Egyptian, implied bilingualism.

The first step in seeing who in the villages could speak Greek is therefore to identify the core users who could write it as well as speak it. It is a commonplace that the majority of the rural population was unable to write and presumably unable to read as well.[57] But the evidence, which offers little hope of statistical analysis,[58] reveals on close examination a host of complexities not readily set out even in

[54]Youtie (1975a and particularly 1975b, 255) argued that "not knowing letters" referred only to illiteracy in Greek and that such a person might know Demotic. In theory this is true, but there are hardly any cases known, and in any event it cannot have been true for any significant number of people after about A.D. 50.

[55]Cf. Youtie 1975b, 258-59, for a few apparent examples from the first and second centuries. Harris 1989, 141 n.124, seems properly skeptical of Youtie's assertion.

[56]Wipszycka 1984, 281, sees Coptic as an alternative to Greek, as Demotic had been; but only after the Arab conquest were significant numbers of formal documents written in Coptic. As long as Greek and Roman rule continued, Greek was the language of official transactions and even of most formal private ones. Her statement (286) that "on y retrouve les mêmes types de textes que dans les papyrus grecs non littéraires, avec cette seule différence que prédomine la documentation des activités privées ou ecclésiastiques" is incorrect. Some document types do occur in Coptic in the sixth century, but in a restricted range. See MacCoull 1988, 36-47, for the Coptic documents in the archive of Dioskoros of Aphrodito. (The earliest precisely dated Coptic document is 569: MacCoull, *Acts of the Second Int. Congr. of Coptic Studies* [Rome 1985] 159-66.) The relationship of Greek and Coptic documentary usage would repay further study.

[57]E.g., Youtie 1975a, 180; Wipszycka 1984, 279; Harris 1989, *passim*.

[58]See Wipszycka 1984, 286-87, for a refutation of the attempt of Steinmann 1974 to demonstrate that forty to fifty percent of the Egyptian population of the eighth century was literate in Coptic. Harris 1989, 7, berates scholars for avoiding numerical estimates, but his own are throughout only guesses.

categorical terms.[59] In most cases, it is not said who wrote the body of documents drawn up in villages. Only where the writer of the text is the same as a signer does that information sometimes emerge. Some cases drawn from the village of Karanis provide precision. For example, three rent receipts from Karanis were written in their entirety by Aurelius Kasios, acting sometimes on behalf of two half-brothers, otherwise for himself and a brother.[60] He gives the impression of the family writer, called upon whenever serious writing was needed. His background is the village elite; he and his brother Isidoros were both *sitologoi*, and they jointly owned about sixty-seven arouras, putting them each about 50 percent above the average for *sitologoi*, already a comparatively well-off group within the village.[61] Unlike some liturgists, he wrote fluently, and he wrote tax receipts himself.[62] He might reasonably be described as occupying the high end of the range of village literacy, a man of comparative means who was able to write entire texts. It is hard to say how many such a village like Karanis, with perhaps 100 to 125 adult male property owners, might have, but probably only a handful. As it happens, his brother Isidoros was one of them; we have a complete document from his hand, as well as his subscription on another.[63]

Another level is occupied by those capable of subscribing documents competently, even if a bit slowly. There was no doubt a considerable range within this group, from those who barely eked out a signature to those who probably could have written simple documents in their entirety if necessary. An example is Chairemon, who was involved in the settlement of his deceased brother Kopres' estate in 297, along with a brother, a sister, and the two daughters of the late Kopres.[64] The two nieces are represented in subscription by an unidentified man, and Chairemon's siblings are subscribed for by another man. But Chairemon subscribes for himself, in a competent but not fluent hand, writing in majuscules. He was apparently thus the only member of this family capable of doing so. There is no clear evidence of the family's wealth, but Chairemon and the sisters apparently held jointly a two-aroura plot, and the movables listed in a

[59]See Youtie 1971a, 1971b, 1975a, and 1975b for various facets of the problem.

[60]*P.Cair.Isid.* 111, 113, 116.

[61]See Bagnall 1978a, 11-12.

[62]See *P.Cair.Isid.* 41.28-41, where Kasios wrote all except his colleagues' signatures. A *sitologos* might need to issue many hundreds of such receipts in the course of his year in office, depending on how many his colleagues managed to produce.

[63]*P.Cair.Isid.* 119 in its entirety; *P.Cair.Isid.* 101, subscription. He also apparently wrote all of *P.Cair.Isid.* 45, a receipt he issued with colleagues while a *sitologos*.

[64]*P.Cair.Isid.* 105; cf. *P.Cair.Isid.* 104.

petition are moderate: 100 sheep and goats, two slaves, and small amounts of money and wheat.[65] The number of Karanidian men capable of subscribing contracts, petitions, or receipts was certainly larger than the body of those able to write complete texts, but once again—though several can be identified—quantification is difficult.[66] A full analysis of village liturgists would probably show that most of them belonged to the group of those able to sign their names but relying on someone else to write the full text.

Some liturgists, however, even relatively well-off ones, might be completely illiterate; such was the Aurelius Isidoros who has left us his archive. Isidoros held some liturgical office, many of them involving tax collection, on an average of every other year over two decades.[67] Yet he was illiterate, as numerous texts say. When he was *sitologos*, the entire college of collectors was illiterate.[68] And yet Isidoros' landholdings were larger than those of the literate Kasios and Isidoros, sons of Heras. Clearly there was no necessary link between wealth or officeholding on the one hand and literacy on the other, however unlikely it may have been that the really poor could have written even a signature. Illiteracy, indeed, is the norm for villagers, and an absolute one for women in the villages.

Isidoros' grandfather had been a *speculator* in the Roman army, and it is natural to wonder if he may have been literate, unlike his grandson. The evidence on soldiers is in fact mixed: some were literate, some not. They tended to rely on literate soldier friends to help them in transactions involving documentation, and nothing suggests that literacy was linked to any particular branch of service, though clerical officers no doubt needed to know how to write.[69] Here again, as within the village landowning class, as within particular families, literacy coexisted with illiteracy.[70]

---

[65] *P.Cair.Isid.* 64 for the movables; *P.Cair.Isid.* 104 (*BL*) for the land.

[66] Some other examples: Ision son of Paesios and Pelenis, subscribers in *P.Cair.Isid.* 82, who are both known elsewhere in contexts where such literacy is assured or likely (*P.Cair.Isid.* 11.75, 41.81); Paesios son of Ision (perhaps the father of Ision above) in *P.Cair.Isid.* 86; Theodoros in *P.Cair.Isid.* 88 and 89; Paesis son of Melas in *P.Cair.Isid.* 90.

[67] *P.Cair.Isid.*, p. 16.

[68] *P.Cair.Isid.* 11.75-76.

[69] Examples of one soldier writing for another: *P.Sakaon* 62; *P.Cair.Isid.* 83; *P.Abinn.* 60 (*BL*), all sales of animals. See Harris 1989, 253-55, for a useful assessment of military literacy under the principate. He suggests (294) that soldiers' literacy declined in late antiquity, but there is no real evidence for that.

[70] Cf. Youtie 1971a, 620, the classic statement; he seems to go too far in asserting (1971b, 651) that because no stigma attached to illiteracy no one would be proud of being literate.

The picture is irreducibly complex in the sense that no other fact about a villager would suffice to guarantee his literacy, even at the level of subscribing, although being female would guarantee illiteracy. It is natural to ask if the literate were the only ones to know Greek, that is, if the complex pattern of literacy is a proxy for a similarly complicated distribution of oral knowledge of Greek. The Copenhagen papyrus in which the unknown reader is asked to translate for the women, discussed earlier (p. 234), raises this possibility, given the universal illiteracy of village women, only mildly ameliorated in the towns. If all women in the villages were illiterate, were all unable to speak Greek? Neither answer can be tested, nor can any easy way of generalizing about men be offered.

A couple of routes, however, may provide some help in approaching the problem. For one thing, it can hardly have been the case that Egyptian was a language used in military operations. The question in the army, in fact, is not whether Greek was universally used but whether Latin had any significant toehold in daily life. Latin was used even in the military only for high-level documents and correspondence; officers communicated among themselves in Greek. It is hard to imagine that they spoke to the ordinary soldiers in anything except Greek, even if some ordinary soldiers used Egyptian in conversation among themselves. But it is clear that a considerable number of soldiers was illiterate.[71] It follows that at least in the military, the number of Greek speakers was substantially larger than that of the literate. Because soldiers on the whole came from local recruitment and in many cases settled in villages upon retirement, there is no reason to believe that they represent an unusual situation or one irrelevant to the countryside.

A second institution about which something can be said is the church, and in particular monasticism. The evidence here is primarily the corpus of writing about monks, a difficult mass of material to interpret. What is most striking about both this hagiographic literature and the church fathers is how little they have to say about language or problems of communication in a polyglot society.[72] This is as true of Athanasius, who never deals with the matter, as of works like the *Historia Monachorum*, where mentions of language are rare and tend to

[71]Cf. Bowman 1991, 126, on the complexity of the military evidence and Hopkins 1991, 138, for one bit of evidence showing almost a one-third literacy rate (ability to write a receipt) in an Egyptian auxiliary cavalry unit in the second century.

[72]See generally Dummer 1968.

involve knowledge of Latin, an unusual attainment.[73] Antony was supposedly the prototypical Egyptian monk, competent only in his own language; but monasteries had bilingual monks capable of interpreting.[74] The bilingualism of the fourth-century papyrus finds connected with monastic establishments certainly shows that literate members of these communities were bilingual, but it may also point to bilingualism as a widespread—but not universal—condition of life.[75] The one Pachomian text where language plays a visible and realistic part supports this view. In the *Letter of Ammon*, the writer recounts his own first arrival in 352, as a Greek-speaking convert from Lower Egypt, at the Pachomian monastery at Pbow in Upper Egypt. The head, Theodore, though one would expect him to be able to use Greek,[76] is dealing with a largely Egyptian-speaking population of monks and consistently uses that language; but he has a bilingual monk from Alexandria translate for the newcomer, who lives in a house with another twenty Greek-speaking monks. Before long—he stayed only three years—Ammon is able to understand the "Theban dialect," that is, Sahidic Coptic.[77]

At the least, then, sweeping assertions that Greek was hardly spoken at all in the villages seem not to be supported by what can be known about the military and the monastic establishments. Neither, no doubt, was fully typical of Egyptian society, but both drew their manpower mainly from that society. The very lack of self-consciousness about language in both documentary and literary sources suggests that bilingualism was common in rural areas, despite the survival of considerable numbers of peasants who spoke only Egyptian. At its apex, in the case of a man like Dioskoros of Aphrodito, were thoroughly bilingual aristocrats (with even a touch of Latin), though

[73]Cf. Dummer 1968, 25, who remarks that the only possible explanation for this silence is that the bilingualism of the country was self-explanatory for Athanasius and that he did not regard it as in itself a special problem. See also *HM* 6.3, 10.25. Chitty 1966, 46 suggests that bilingualism was more widespread in the Delta than in Upper Egypt; if so, our largely Middle and Upper Egyptian documentation probably understates the phenomenon considerably.

[74]Cf. Dummer 1968, 34-38; Rousseau 1985, 46. See Rubenson 1990, 142-43, for a challenge to the picture of Antony as Greekless (he is so described in several sources, such as *HL* 21.15). Naqlun has yielded both Greek and Coptic texts, and one hermitage contained only Greek (T. Derda, communication to XX International Congress of Papyrology, Copenhagen, August 1992).

[75]*P.Lond.* VI, *P.Nag.Hamm.* and *P.Neph.* are the cases in point.

[76]He came from a wealthy family: *EpAmm*, pp. 213-14; cf. Goehring 1986, 244-45. On the other hand, in *EpAmm* 6 he uses an interpreter in a one-on-one conversation with Ammon, which is surprising if he knew Greek himself.

[77]See *EpAmm* 4-7, 17, 28-29.

neither Dioskoros nor Aphrodito is likely to have been typical.[78]

Greek Literacy in the Towns

There were many differences between the nome capitals and the surrounding villages, and it can hardly be doubted that they differed in the use of language and writing as well. Administrative centers, home to self-conscious Greeks, sources of most Greek literary papyri found so far, locations of schools (cf. p. 99), the cities of Egypt were in all respects more Hellenic than the hinterland. But the countryside was not far away, and it remains as difficult to be specific and precise about language and literacy in the cities as in the villages.[79]

At the top of the social pyramid, men of the bouleutic class were expected to be able to read and write,[80] and literacy was a specific requirement for some liturgical appointments.[81] Moreover, without a reasonable ability to read, at least, anyone holding such liturgies would be in real danger of being cheated or of making mistakes that could produce disaster at the hands of the imperial treasury.[82] And in fact uncounted examples of literate members of this upper class can be produced. A repayment of a loan made to a villager, for example, is signed by both the lender, a councillor of Antinoopolis, and his business agent. Both have fast, practiced hands.[83] Some rent receipts are written by a former gymnasiarch of Arsinoe, acting on behalf of his wife, the landowner in the particular case.[84] Later, their son does the same for her.[85] The case, mentioned above, of the former high priest who claimed to be illiterate shows that not all who held such municipal offices were equally competent, and some councillors probably held on at the bare edge of ability to write.[86]

[78]See MacCoull 1988, 147-59.

[79]Which is not to say that considerable progress could not be made by systematic study of the evidence; Youtie's widely cited articles (1971a, 1971b, 1975a, 1975b) are impressionistic.

[80]See *PSI* VI 716 (Oxyrhynchos, ?306), a very fragmentary text quoting an edict of a prefect of Egypt apparently forbidding illiterates to be *bouleutai*.

[81]But not all: see *P.Amh.* II 82 (*BL*; Lewis, *Cd'E* 29 [1954] 288-91), from Arsinoe, early 4c, a petition to the prefect of Egypt by a former high priest of Arsinoe, who has been nominated (without his knowledge) to be a *logographos* in attendance on the prefect's court. He protests that there are two qualifications, literacy and membership in the boule, and he has neither. Another illiterate high priest is attested in *P.Oxy.* I 71 (*BL*) (303).

[82]See Youtie 1975a, 206, on the disadvantages of illiteracy in Roman Egypt; Harris 1989, 145, also stresses the vulnerabilities it entailed.

[83]*P.Cair.Isid.* 94 (see plate VI for the hands).

[84]*P.Cair.Isid.* 114-115.

[85]*P.Cair.Isid.* 122.

[86]Cf. Youtie 1971a, 624-25: Literacy was expected of councillors, but not all were

The situation with women of this class is not so clear. There are some well-known examples of women who specify their literacy; perhaps the most prominent is the very wealthy Aurelia Charite of Hermopolis, who describes herself as literate in the self-identification at the start of two documents.[87] But in these she wrote not the body of the text but the subscription, as she did in several other surviving documents as well.[88] The hand is clear (plate 6), the letters well-formed, but it is not the practiced cursive of someone who writes every day.[89] Charite no doubt had to deal with a large volume of business—leases, receipts, accounts, and letters—and found it more practical to have her business agents write most of these; she probably had better things to do than be a scribe. She is one extreme. At the other is the sister of a deceased magistrate and councillor of Antinoopolis, who is said to be illiterate.[90] There is no way to assess numerically the relative positions held by the counterparts of these women, but Charite is a rare case, and probably most women even of her class could do little but sign their names.

Literate or not, the men and women of this class all paid other people to do most of their writing for them.[91] They did not need to resort to the ubiquitous public scribes of the towns, so frequented by ordinary folk.[92] Instead, they had business agents, stewards, and assistants. A lease application is subscribed, and several receipts in the Isidoros archive are written, by a man who styles himself a *prytanis'* assistant.[93] The governing class employed men to manage both public and private duties for them, and the same staff would generally do both types of work without distinction. Most of the staff of liturgists and local officials was literate, although there are exceptions.[94]

---

competent; cf. Youtie 1971b, 651. Harris 1989, 314, gives a measured assessment of bouleutic illiteracy.

[87]*P.Charite* 8 and 33.

[88]For a list and discussion, see *P.Charite*, pp. 2, 9-10.

[89]Hanson 1991, 174, describes the hand as "unpracticed and inelegant," true only by an inappropriate standard (cf. Bowman 1991, 127, on another such misjudgment).

[90]*P.Ant.* I 39 (cf. *CSBE* 109) (324).

[91]See Harris 1989, 249, for this general phenomenon. Cf. Baines 1983, 580, on pharaonic Egypt: "Literacy is thus necessary for high status, but writing is delegated by those who achieve that status."

[92]And a feature of Egypt into the modern period; for example, see the painting by Roberts, *Egypt*, v. 3, pl. 29, showing a woman dictating to a scribe.

[93]*P.Cair.Isid.* 99, 117, 118, 120.

[94]Compare *P.Oxy.* XXXVI 2764 (277), the oath of a clerk in the office of the *strategos* and his surety, in which the clerk is literate but the surety is not, with *P.Oxy.* XXXVI 2765 (*BL*) (303), a similar document in which both are illiterate.

It is natural to ask if the Christianization of Egypt brought any change to patterns of literacy. On the whole, it is difficult to demonstrate any great alterations and even harder to attribute them to causes.[95] Over the three centuries from Diocletian to Mauricius in the late sixth century, there is a decline in published finds of papyri, both documentary and literary.[96] But it is far from obvious what the causes of this decline are, or whether it even reflects accurately the totality of preserved documents.[97] Nor do the surviving texts allow facile generalizations. For example, the importance the church attached to sacred writings has been thought to make a growth in literacy more likely, particularly in conjunction with the translation of the scriptures into the language of the people.[98] That is possible, of course, but finding direct evidence in favor of this theory is not easy.

One aspect more susceptible to investigation is the literacy of the clergy themselves. Here the evidence supports strongly the view that the priests were largely literate: though an illiterate priest may be found as early as the fourth century,[99] there are only about six such in the entire documentation of late antique Egypt. There are also three illiterate deacons and one subdeacon, lesser orders of ministry. These can be set against some 100 texts drawn up by clerics and about 180 instances of clerics subscribing to documents.[100] In papyrus after papyrus, the witnesses are heavily dominated by clergy. Some of the handwriting of these subscriptions, to be sure, belongs unmistakably to the class of slow writers, the awkward majuscules of those who did little more than sign their names, the very bottom rungs of the "literate."[101] While most clergy were sufficiently literate to sign for

[95]The most recent survey of the evidence is Wipszycka 1984. Harris 1989, 316-22, is more pessimistic but adds little.

[96]For documents, see Bagnall and Worp 1980b; for literary texts, Treu 1986. The treatment by Harris 1989, 283 and 297, is uncritical.

[97]Wipszycka 1984, 282-83, is skeptical about most suggestions. Her own proposal, that the death of many Fayum villages is largely responsible, cannot be right, because the decline is attested in all parts of Egypt from which there are papyri; moreover, it is precisely the deaths of villages that preserved papyri in earlier centuries, from which one might conclude that sixth-century villages were very healthy. But she is no doubt correct that much of the cause lies in different processes of deposition and preservation of papyri, which are not now readily identifiable.

[98]Wipszycka 1984, 286 ff.

[99]*P.Vind.Sijp.* 4 (340).

[100]Wipszycka 1984, 288-89, esp. n.15.

[101]An illustrated example from the late sixth century can be found in R. S. Bagnall, "Two Byzantine Papyri in a Private Collection," *Studies in Roman Law in Memory of A. Arthur Schiller* (Leiden 1986) 5, with uniformly awkward writing by the witnesses and a cleric among the illiterate witnesses for whom one of these slow writers signs.

themselves, probably many fewer were capable of drafting documents. Church rank was undoubtedly a good guide to competence with letters. The lords of the threefold orders of ministry, the bishops, were certainly literate with rare exceptions,[102] the *presbyteroi* somewhat less so, and the deacons (many of whom must have spent only part of their time on church duties) still less likely to be literate.[103]

The complexity of particular situations can be seen from two examples. The first is an undertaking on oath from Arsinoe, dated 349, directed to the *praepositus* of the pagus, stating that the declarant will produce a priest of the village of Tristomos upon demand. The surety making the declaration, Aurelius Akammon, is a deacon from another Arsinoite village. Because the deacon is illiterate, a monk who is the son of a former *prytanis* signs on his behalf.[104] Both the illiteracy of the deacon and the fact that the subscriber on his behalf is the son of a member of the bouleutic class who has become a monk are noteworthy. It appears that at least in this case antecedent social and economic background plays a larger role in the distribution of the knowledge of writing than does the ecclesiastical status of the writer. Sons of privilege who became monks had been given upper-class educations; village peasants who became deacons had not. It is possible that as time went on and the church became increasingly institutionalized such differences were blurred, but that remains to be proven.

The appearance of a monk provides a bridge to the second example, a document in which the presiding priest of a monastery in the Kynopolite Nome, being called away to a church council in Syria, appoints his brother to manage the monastic establishment during his absence. The priest signs the document himself, but one monk signs on behalf of the remainder, who are illiterate; one deacon signs for himself.[105] Now monks were not mostly ordained clergy, and their level of literacy was on average certainly lower, though again many appear as signing witnesses in contracts. The evidence about their ability to read and write is complex and, where derived from literary sources, open to suspicion.[106] Some monasteries produced extensive

[102]This may have been less true in later centuries, when at least a few bishops needed interpreters to understand Greek at councils.

[103]Cf. *NewDocs* 5, 13; lectors (*anagnostai*) were still lower, not really clergy, and their title is not always to be taken literally. Cf. below, p. 256 n. 142.

[104]*P.Würzb.* 16; the monk's title and his father's title are both partly restored, but in neither case is there significant doubt.

[105]*P.Lond.* VI 1913 (*BL*) (334).

[106]See Wipszycka 1984, 291-95, arguing for more literacy than the monks are usually given credit for.

literature and copied manuscripts, and in all the Bible was read and external correspondence carried on; moreover, internal accounting was needed, and monastery walls show many informal inscriptions. Pachomius numbered the houses at Tabennesi with Greek letters.[107] But it is not clear that these activities required more than the normal minority of literate personnel found in any Egyptian village. Monks were found both in the cities and in the villages, as well as in separate monastic establishments, and it seems fair to say that their abilities to read and write depended on background more than on monastic vocation. To the extent that the villages were the primary source of recruitment (see below, p. 302), however, situations like that in the Kynopolite monastery, with only a few literates to write for the group, must have been common. It is true that Pachomius' rule (*Praec.* 49, 139) called for all entering his community to learn to read if they could not already, but the documents scarcely suggest universal compliance or enforcement.[108]

Metropolitan residents for the most part were neither members of the bouleutic class, nor clergy, nor even business agents who needed the ability to write. Women outside the upper class were no more likely to be literate than those in the villages, and those who appear in documents are almost without exception illiterate.[109] One might at first be tempted to see a literate woman in Hermione of Hermopolis, who in her husband's absence walked out on him, taking all the contents of their house including his "essential papers." These include, we are told, sales of house plots. But hopes unravel when the husband has to have someone else sign for him because he is illiterate.[110] Clearly it was possible for him to carry on a business in which documentation was essential without actually being able so much as to sign his name to a petition.

Still, it would no doubt be wrong to think that all the middle-class residents of the metropoleis were like him. An inheritance division from Hermopolis shows three sisters and a brother dividing up the family house, each receiving several rooms.[111] At the end, husbands sign for two of the women, a man of unspecified relationship for the third, and the brother for himself. In other words, at least three of the four children in this family were either literate themselves or had

---

[107]*HL* 32.4.

[108]The rule may not date from Pachomius' lifetime: Rousseau 1985, 70.

[109]Cf. *P.Abinn.* 62 (350), in which an Alexandrian brother and sister, resident in Philadelphia in the Fayum (and the sister married to a Philadelphian), draw up a property agreement; all parties are illiterate.

[110]*P.Lond.* V 1651 (363).

[111]*P.Lond.* III 978 (p. 233) (*BL*) (331).

married literate men. It must be said, however, that the brother signs in a very slow hand, as does one of the two husbands. The other husband has a well-formed cursive hand, and the signer for the third sister writes a fast cursive, perhaps professional. Of the three men identifiably part of the family, two are slow writers then, with only one likely to have been able to draft documents or do anything more than sign his name.[112] This sort of pattern was probably repeated in numerous families.[113]

Greek and Coptic, Christianity and Paganism

It is readily apparent from what has been said earlier that language, script and religion were linked. These were not, however, so simple and straightforward as one might suppose. The clearest connection was that between the use of Demotic Egyptian and the support of the old Egyptian cults. It has already been pointed out that only the temples of the Egyptian gods, in company with the funerary personnel, preserved Demotic after the middle of the second century. After the middle of the third century, in fact, there are no datable Demotic texts except the graffiti at Philai; the last datable mummy label comes from 260/1.[114] At Philai, a sanctuary on the southern edge of Egypt dominated in this period by Nubians, Demotic graffiti continue on until 452, but these texts are striking mainly in their isolation.[115] The traditional scripts, hieroglyphic and Demotic, figure occasionally in the accounts of late pagan resistance to the dominance of Christianity, and simply to know anything of them, to have books written in them, was a sign of paganism.[116]

A more difficult matter is Hellenic paganism. There were certainly pagans among the Greek upper classes, in both Alexandria and the nome capitals. The sources provide ample evidence of what has been described as academic resistance, philosophical teaching that rejected

[112]This description is based on examination of the papyrus.

[113]See Hanson 1991, 160-65, on the mediated use of writing by the illiterate. Baines 1983, 584, remarks on the pattern in earlier times.

[114]See Zauzich 1983, 77; Pestman 1967, 117-21. Both authors mention the case of a couple of Michigan papyri of the fourth century supposed to contain Demotic, both with doubt. The date of these is probably 338/9 (cf. *Enchoria* 8.1 [1978] 148 n.21; *P.Col.* VII, pp. 98-100). Thanks to photographs taken by the International Photographic Archive of Papyri, it can be said with certainty that the marks in question are not Demotic but "control marks" of the kind found on other texts in this series like *SB* VI 9436b, 9436e, etc.

[115]Zauzich 1983, 77, points out the ironic fact that the last users of Demotic may not have been Egyptians at all but Blemmyes or other Nubian peoples.

[116]See Kákosy 1984 for a description, esp. 71-72 on Philae.

Christianity.[117] A more complex question is posed by the considerable survival, in the period from the late fourth century to the time of Justinian, of classical culture in imaginative literature, particularly poetry. Poets commonly evoke the classical gods and heroes of Greece and the large body of myth and legend connected to them, just as these figures continue to appear in artistic representations, as in mosaics. Such evocation has brought on them modern judgments that they were pagans, just as their contemporary enemies sometimes accused them of being.[118] At best such a simple description is misleading. Classical culture was part of the inheritance of all educated men, pagan or Christian; acceptance or rejection of it as material for literature is not directly linked to religious belief.[119] There is, moreover, direct evidence for the Christianity of some of these figures, such as Cyrus of Panopolis.[120] Nonnos, the poet of the *Dionysiaka*, may well have written for a largely pagan audience, but there is no evidence that his own paganism, if he was a pagan, went farther than cultural—not cultic—persistence.[121] Indeed, the attribution to him of a paraphrase of the Gospel of John shows that a contrary view was possible, and there is at least some reason to think that the attribution is right.[122]

Caution is in order, then, in blithely attributing pagan beliefs, much less cultic activity, to the imaginative literary artists of the fourth and fifth century. That is not to say that there were not some such figures; and there were certainly other well-born and rich pagans active.[123] But the use of "Hellene" for pagan is itself an invention of pagan polemic against the Christians, an attempt to claim classical culture exclusively for pagan use. The predominant Greek-speaking culture of Egypt by the second half of the fourth century was Christian, and in the fifth century upper-class pagans were isolated figures.[124]

[117]Rémondon 1952, 64, and Kákosy 1984, 66, give accounts and references.

[118]E.g., Rémondon 1952, 67; cf. Alan Cameron 1982, 239.

[119]See the nuanced discussion of Chuvin 1986 and the discussion of Basil's attitude toward classical letters in Kaster 1988, 77. Averil Cameron's study of Procopius shows the complex role, even in Justinian's period, under considerable pressure, of classicizing elements in the work of a Christian literary elite (Averil Cameron 1985, esp. chapters 1-2, 7). See more generally Averil Cameron 1991, 139.

[120]Alan Cameron 1982, 239-43.

[121]See Chuvin 1986, 394.

[122]Alan Cameron 1982, 237.

[123]Cf. Kákosy 1984, 70.

[124]Chuvin 1986, 388-90, who notes acutely that the interest in classical religion on the part of Nonnos and the like does not include Egyptian religion; it is purely classicizing.

The relationship between Greek and Coptic within Egyptian Christianity is equally a complex matter.[125] As has already become clear, Coptic contains a large measure of Greek vocabulary. The absence of such Greek elements from some non-Christian "Old Coptic" texts, parallel to the exclusion of Greek vocabulary from Demotic, suggests that acceptance of Greek is in itself a religious statement and a rejection of the old Egyptian cults. Although there are good reasons to think that the development of Coptic was multipolar and that it represents fairly the spoken language of the period with all its dialects, there must remain some uncertainty about how far Greek words were actually present in such numbers in contemporary Egyptian speech. There can be little doubt that the milieus in which Coptic developed were fluently bilingual and probably of an educated social stratum.[126]

Those who created Coptic must nonetheless have expected their audience to understand these words: those who were to read the scriptures in Coptic were not those now illiterate, to be instructed in great numbers, but rather those who knew Greek letters and the Greek language, at least to some degree. It would have made no sense to create translations in which a large share of the vocabulary was incomprehensible to the audience. For that matter, one can go farther. These scripture translations were certainly intended for reading aloud in church, to a congregation whose literacy cannot be presumed.[127] If every fifth word were opaque to the listeners, the purpose of the translation would fail.[128] And the borrowings from Greek include numerous common words like prepositions and conjunctions, not merely learned vocabulary.

And yet the Egyptian congregation should not be presumed to be in all cases so simple in its composition. One of the most striking features of the surviving Coptic biblical manuscripts is the large number of bilingual texts. Those of the New Testament are largely from either

[125]For this reason the extreme views of Steindorff 1950 are not acceptable, including his claim (p. 203) that the Greek words in Coptic come in through the translation of the scriptures. Steindorff conflates many centuries of development into an undifferentiated and simplistic account.

[126]See Orlandi 1984, 183. The whole situation is badly misdescribed by Hopkins 1991, 144-47.

[127]See below, p. 256 for the difficult question of literacy in Coptic. Harris 1989, 285, points rightly to the public and oral function of much written scripture.

[128]Cf. Orlandi 1984, 196, who argues that the "Copts" of the early period participated indifferently in Greek-language culture and in Coptic; there is no need to see a sharp division at any early date. Only gradually did Egyptian Christianity acquire the characteristics that after Chalcedon separated it from international Christianity.

the gospels or lectionaries following the pericope.[129] Evidence for bilingual editions of the letters is sketchy, and that for Revelations nonexistent. With the Old Testament, the material is less abundant and more limited; only the poetic and prophetic books turn up in bilingual form, with the Psalms the dominant book.[130] The bilingual manuscripts were clearly either full texts of those books primarily used in the liturgy or else lectionaries arranged according to the pericope and made up of extracts from those books. Given the expense and time of creating books, one may reasonably assume that the physical format of our finds reflects real needs. It follows that the lectionary books used in public worship needed to have both Greek and Coptic texts; a congregation would thus have Greek speakers, Coptic speakers, and no doubt bilingual members as well. Given the monastic origin of most surviving manuscripts, in fact, one may say more specifically that this bilingual character must have obtained inside some monasteries.[131] A "saying" of the monk Pior, with his pure Egyptian name, helps to illustrate the complexity of matters. Each man, he tells his hearers, carries a pack in front full of the sins of others, one containing his own to the rear out of sight. The tale is from Aesop![132]

The situation certainly did not remain static over the centuries. Shenute was hostile to classical Greek culture, and the later monastic tradition maintained this hostility. But it did not imply hostility to the Greek language, even after relations with the exterior became increasingly strained following Chalcedon.[133] There is even some reason to believe that Shenute himself could and did compose in Greek as well as in Coptic.[134] In fact, bilingual lectionary manuscripts continue to be produced long after the Arab conquest, until at least the tenth

[129]Treu 1965 gives a survey. Bibliographic additions may be found in Nagel 1984, 231 n.2.

[130]Nagel 1984, esp. 234-36.

[131]Cf. Treu 1965, 99, on the White Monastery as the source of most of our Sahidic manuscripts; Nagel 1984, 232, points out that Sahidic is the only dialect found in Old Testament bilingual manuscripts.

[132]*ApPatr*, Pior 3.

[133]Orlandi 1984, 197, 203, notes that translation from Greek into Coptic declines after Chalcedon, but that the decline goes back really to Shenute and the development of original Coptic literature; the break with international culture reinforced the tendency. Greek culture, theological and otherwise, came to be seen as the oppressors' culture. But even after the break culture, not language, was opposed.

[134]Leo Depuydt, "In Sinuthium Graecum," *Orientalia* 59 (1990) 67-71, responding to Enzo Lucchesi, "Chénoute a-t-il écrit en grec?" *Mélanges Guillaumont. Contributions à l'étude des christianismes orientaux* (Geneva 1988) 201-10. Depuydt argues that the parallel Greek and Coptic passages he discusses were composed independently by a writer whose primary language was Coptic, probably Shenute himself.

century.[135] How far this is simply the fossilization of practice is hard to say; but at least it shows that there was no hostility toward Greek as a language long after the Greek-using government had vanished. Indeed, the monophysite Coptic patriarch Alexander II wrote his annual Paschal Letter in Greek as late as (probably) 724, using it to polemicize against attacks on the church by the Arab rulers.[136]

Language, Literacy, and Status

A distinctly mixed picture of literacy emerges. The wealthiest and most powerful class of urban society, the small group that furnished city councillors and magistrates, was expected to display universal male competence in writing. This expectation was not always met, and it was often satisfied only in the technical sense of ability to sub-scribe one's name and approval to a document drafted by someone else. This technical literacy no doubt acquired much of its accep-tability by virtue of universal practice, even on the part of those who could write fluently, of having someone else do most of their writing for them. The wives and daughters of these men were far less likely to be able to write, with a small minority really capable of writing with some fluency and most incapable even of subscribing to documents. The adult men and women of these families, however, represent no more than the tiniest fraction of society, probably less than a half of one percent of the population.[137]

A similar but not identical situation reproduced itself in the vil-lages, scaled to circumstances. Some of the wealthier landowners, perennial holders of compulsory public offices and perhaps used to generating documents in private entrepreneurial activity, became fluent at writing Greek, capable of drafting entire documents with considerable competence. Other similarly placed men did not. There is no evidence of literate women in this group. The example of Karanis suggests that such people amounted to no more than a few per hundred, but the nature of the evidence invites caution in generaliza-tion. It is possible that villages, particularly small ones, had propor-tionately fewer professional scribes available than the cities; they certainly had fewer slaves. Someone with substantial recordkeeping

[135]So Nagel 1984, 236; Treu 1965, 95, claims a range as late as the twelfth century for bilingual manuscripts.

[136]See L. S. B. MacCoull, *DOP* 44 (1990) 27-40. Cf. generally on late use of Greek in Egypt K. A. Worp, *BSAC* 26 (1984) 99-108.

[137]On the assumption that in an average nome with a population of 100,000 there would be no more than 100 to 200 families in this stratum; obviously both figures will have varied somewhat, but the orders of magnitude not.

and liturgical duties might well find it advantageous to learn to write, but it was still possible to get by without doing so.

It would be a natural suspicion, considering the more than casual link between property and literacy, that literacy ought to be associated with the more advantageous role in economic transactions. That is, lessors and lenders would both need and be more likely to possess literacy than lessees and borrowers. The evidence does not allow clear confirmation of such a hypothesis. It is indeed true that lessees and borrowers are almost invariably illiterate, except for a few cases where members of the wealthiest classes are on the disadvantaged end of a transaction.[138] But these documents only rarely provide information about the literacy of lessors and lenders. Such parties are, of course, often women and thus usually illiterate.[139] Sales provide more ambiguous evidence, because the social position of the parties is more rarely clear to the reader.

If Greek literacy seems to offer irreducible complexities, things are still less satisfactory for Coptic. First, even documents lacking any absolute dating information can be placed approximately if they are written in Greek, thanks to the relatively large volume of dated documents with which their handwriting can be compared. Second, Coptic was not used for such purposes on any large scale until after the Arab conquest; palaeographic dating is therefore complicated by the shortage of datable texts for comparison. As a result, redatings by two hundred years or more can occur.[140] At other times, very uncertain editorial estimates can be confirmed by later documents coming from an archival context.[141] With all these uncertainties, it can be said with fair confidence that the widespread use of Coptic, for both sacred literature and letters, can be identified within a decade or so of Constantine's acquisition of Egypt after the defeat of Licinius in 324. It remains to be demonstrated that there was any use of Coptic in letters before this time.[142]

[138]For example, Aurelia Charite as borrower in *P.Charite* 34 (348).

[139]*SB* IV 7445 (Oxyrhynchos, 285).

[140]A recent example in Gascou 1989, 77, where three codices are redated (*P.Bour.* 3 + *P.Achmîm* 1; BN Copte 135A; BN Copte 135B).

[141]Thus *P.Lond.* VI 1920 (*ca* 330-340) helped confirm a date to the second half of the fourth century for some Akhmimic letters in Ryl.

[142]The editor of *P.Vind.Worp* 24, written in a handwriting that he compared to Coptic uncial book hands, dated it to the late third or very early fourth century on the basis of the letter formula and one item of vocabulary. But he admits that the word in question appears in later literary texts and that the formula also may be found later. The chancery hand is not closely datable. For these reasons his dating seems to me insecure. For similar reasons, the notion of Youtie (1971a, 613) that the reader of the church of the Oxyrhynchite village of Chysis who in 304 declares himself illiterate (*P.Oxy.* XXXIII 2673) was illiterate only in Greek but could read Coptic

A salient characteristic of early Coptic letters is their nonurban context and in particular their ties to a monastic environment. The major groups—and they are not large—known so far are those from Nag Hammadi, those from the Herakleopolite in London, and those in the Nepheros archive, all monastic in character.[143] In each of these, however, the Coptic letters are a minority element in a predominantly Greek ensemble. Scattered instances give no indication of urban provenance, as in a short account on the back of a Greek letter about agricultural matters,[144] or a Coptic subscription to a Greek letter sent from one Apa Iohannes to Paulos.[145] It is immediately obvious that a generalization of this sort is largely an argument from silence, and because Coptic papyri have often been ignored in favor of prompt publication of Greek, it is hardly conclusive. All the same, at present it is prudent to suppose that the nonliterary use of Coptic was largely monastic in the fourth century and only gradually acquired a larger public.

The flowering of documentary Coptic, as already noted, comes after the end of Roman rule. It is difficult to give any coherent picture of the process because the surviving evidence for the period after 641 is even more archivally based than in earlier periods, with entire major provenances like Oxyrhynchos simply disappearing from the record. The largest body of late seventh- and early eighth-century Coptic material, that from Jeme (Thebes), has been investigated from the standpoint of literacy, with interesting results.[146] About one-sixth of the contracts were drawn up by one party to the contract, the other five-sixths by professional scribes.[147] Of the witnesses subscribing to the contracts, just under one-half sign themselves; the other half are represented by someone else.[148] It is obvious that such figures cannot be translated into statistics about Coptic urban society, let alone Egyptian society as a whole. Nothing is recorded about the status of most witnesses, except for those who identify themselves as clerics (about

---

strikes me as wholly speculative and even unlikely. Wipszycka (*ZPE* 50 [1983] 117-21) offers the hypothesis that the statement of illiteracy was false and a deliberate refusal to cooperate with the authorities' persecution of the church; but cf. doubts by G. W. Clarke, *ZPE* 57 (1984) 103-4. A lector probably cantillated the text from memory much of the time; with ancient standards of memorization and a limited body of scripture used liturgically, this is not an impossible feat.

[143]*P.Lond.* VI, *P.Nag.Hamm.*, *P.Neph.*

[144]*P.Amh.* II 143.

[145]*P.Amh.* II 145 = Naldini 49.

[146]Steinmann 1974; what follows uses his figures without accepting most of the conclusions he draws.

[147]Steinmann 1974, 103.

[148]Steinmann 1974, 104.

one-fifth of the literate witnesses, a handful of the illiterate), but it can readily be assumed that they belong to a stratum of society well above the median—that is, people of standing and property. The contracting parties certainly belong to the ranks of those with property. A more situational analysis might clarify matters, but nothing suggests any substantial growth in literacy since the fourth century, only a shift of that literacy from Greek to Coptic.[149]

The relationship between literacy and language remains a thorny problem. There are good reasons to reject mapping the one to the other globally and straightforwardly, that is, assuming that all parties to any written Greek document were competent in the oral language. Such a view, taken to extremes, necessitates accepting the virtual disappearance of Egyptian for almost two centuries. At the other extreme stands blanket skepticism, a supposition that only those individuals with a demonstrated ability to write Greek—and not only to sign their names—were actually fluent in the spoken tongue. Such a view is not only inherently perverse; it encounters serious obstacles when one tries to envisage the process by which villagers like Kasios and Isidoros of Karanis learned to write Greek fluently and competently. It requires the acceptance of a society in which many of those who wrote Greek would have had almost no one to speak it to on a daily basis. Even if well-off peasant parents sent their children to the nome capital for an extensive education in Greek—which seems highly unlikely—sustaining competence in a village where never was heard a Hellenic word would be a difficult task.[150]

Two key factors are at the base of the phenomena observed in the documents. First, economic and social stratification figures prominently. Most people lived too close to the subsistence level to be able to afford any extended education for their children; their daily activities rarely involved written texts, and when they did, someone could be found to do the necessary writing. Those who could best afford education, on the other hand, could also afford to pay or own others to do most of their writing for them in the course of managing their business affairs. It is thus hardly surprising that there was some unevenness in the literacy of the propertied class. Those in the middle learned to write or not as circumstances dictated and offered. Business agents of various sorts, clerks in public offices, professional scribes,

[149]Steinmann's conclusions (1974, 107-10) are properly dismissed by Wipszycka (1984, 287), although her own view of the impact of the Christianization of Egypt on literacy is generally favorable.

[150]See Kaster 1988, 21, on the scarcity of evidence for the education of villagers in the cities.

and those with extensive business dealings of their own found it useful or necessary to write with some degree of competence, but most craftsmen and retail merchants did not. In important legal transactions, it was worth paying a professional to do the job well and get the formulas right, even if one was thoroughly literate oneself.[151]

These economic and social factors explain why language competence is only to a limited degree correlated with writing ability, why the second factor—extensive bilingualism—had only limited effect on literacy. There is no sign, practically throughout the millennium from Alexander to the Arabs, of conflict between Greek and Egyptian languages, of sentiment that one should not use a particular language because to do so amounted to cultural betrayal.[152] A school exercise in Demotic from Narmouthis, it is true, reads "I will not write in Greek letters; I am obstinate," but the word "I am obstinate" is written precisely with a Greek word and Greek script![153] Use of languages and scripts was preeminently a practical matter.[154] A number of Greeks in the towns undoubtedly never learned any Egyptian. How many, there is no way of telling. It was probably perfectly possible in most urban communities to get by only with Greek; tradespeople and servants knew enough Greek to communicate. At the other extreme, there were no doubt many villagers who knew nothing but Egyptian. But the very absence of any sign of difficulty in daily communication suggests strongly that there were enough bilingual people in both milieus that normally inconvenience was minimal. Women might need an interlocutor more commonly than men, but village women may have gone for long periods without needing to speak to anyone who did not understand Egyptian.

This picture, of dual language communities with a substantial overlap in membership, neither separate communities nor a fully bilingual society, may help to explain what consistently seems like borderline societal literacy. This is neither a traditional Egyptian society, with highly restricted literacy, nor the ideal world of a Greek

[151]As H. S. Smith observes (oral communication, September 1990).

[152]Youtie 1975b, 262, sought to discern such an anti-Greek bent on the part of Egyptian priests in the Roman period, but even there he could not cite any convincing evidence.

[153]E. Bresciani et al., *Ostraka demotici di Narmuti* I (Pisa 1983) 10-11 no.5.

[154]Even in a highly charged environment like Judaea this seems to have been true. In a letter written in poorly spelled Greek, found at Murabba"at, Soumaios writes to Ioanathes that his letter "was written in Greek because no means were found to have it written in Hebrew." In other words, it was easier to find a scribe competent in Greek at the moment he was writing; but other letters in the same find were in Hebrew and Aramaic. Cf. D. Obbink, "Bilingual Literacy and Syrian Greek," *BASP* 28 (1991) 51-57.

democracy with a literate citizenry. Literacy was widespread, far more so than before the arrival of the Greeks, but it never approached universality. It was an attainment of which one might be proud, but that was acquired—at least outside the upper class—mainly for practical purposes. Those who needed to write, learned; the others mostly did not. Although this situation may seem paradoxical for a society so dependent on writing, it was quite manageable. Writing penetrated the everyday life even of many illiterates, but through the mediation of the literate.[155] Class structure, Hellenism, and traditional Egypt thus interacted to create a society poised on the threshold of general literacy but restrained from stepping over it.

[155]Cf. Bowman 1991, 122-23, for the notion of a literate society containing many illiterates. For a similar (but not identical: printing had intervened) situation in pre-revolutionary France, see R. Chartier, *The Cultural Uses of Print in Early Modern France* (Princeton 1987).

CHAPTER 8

This World and the Next

Temples in Trouble

The story of religion in Egypt between Diocletian and Chalcedon is dominated by the dramatic triumph of Christianity, its internal splintering, and finally the break of most of the church of Egypt away from the orthodox ecclesiastical structure presided over by the patriarch of Constantinople. The victory of the Christians[1] came at the expense of pagan religion, and naturally the tale is generally told in terms of the contest between Christianity and paganism.[2] That struggle has its reality, and it continued for many years; the rise of Christianity is treated in a later section (below, p. 278). But the old gods of Egypt and Greece, their temples and their priests, have their own history—not simply the negative and inverted image of the Christian opponents, but a history with other foes and its own dynamic. One should not assume that the decline of pagan religion and the rise of Christianity are so simply related, like children at opposite ends of a see-saw.

Even within Christianity, a religion of the book like Judaism and Islam, the centrality of doctrine has been overplayed by the theologians who have controlled the organs and councils of the church through the centuries. In paganism, what is central is action, the cult. The religion *is* the sum of the dedications, the sacrifices, the rituals: the interaction of human and divine. In Egypt that interplay had been centered for millennia on the temples—small, medium, and large, urban and village, wealthy and poor. No popular religion existed in opposition to this official, institutional one, though there were certainly popular means of expression in the home.[3] The inquiry into

---

[1]A description in itself too simple, though perhaps not so inaccurate as Averil Cameron 1991, 122, suggests.

[2]A term used here "for the sake of convenience, and with only a little sense of embarrassment" (M. Beard, *Literacy in the Roman World* [*JRA* Suppl. 3, Ann Arbor 1991] 35 n.1).

[3]See Dunand 1979, 92-96 and 133, for the congruence of what popular terracottas reveal with the religion of the temples; and cf. generally Siegfried Morenz, *Egyptian Religion* (Eng. tr. London 1973) 81-109, for the unitary character of Egyptian religious observance. For a fuller version of the argument set out in this section, see Bagnall 1992d.

the state of Egyptian paganism, then, begins with the temples and their priests. The same is partly true of the Greek cults imported centuries earlier by settlers. They were an integral part of the life of the cities; their priests were supervised by the magistrates. There is no indication, however, that the Greek elites of the cities distinguished in their own observance between native and imported cults; and the rural population similarly had a common religiosity.[4]

There are signs that all was not well in the middle of the third century. For thousands of years, kings of Egypt had recorded their contributions to the construction and decoration of temples with hieroglyphic inscriptions on the walls, composed and carved by *hieroglyphoi* on the temple staff. The Ptolemies had followed the pharaonic habit, and the Roman emperors, their successors, did the same, though one may suspect that the prefects of Egypt were acting on their behalf. Augustus, intent on a wide-ranging reorganization and revitalization of the country, and concerned to gain the good will of the priesthoods, gave to construction projects at numerous sites; his cartouches are found all over Egypt.[5] This activity continued under succeeding emperors, but at a rapidly declining rate. At Memphis there is nothing Roman except a couple of private inscriptions of Augustus' reign.[6] The last inscription at Thebes (Karnak) is of Domitian;[7] at Diospolis Parva of Hadrian.[8] There is nothing later than Antoninus in the entire Theban region or the desert oases.[9] Caracalla is the last cartouche at Philae, Ombos, and in Lower and Middle Egypt.[10] At Esna, there are a few inscriptions of Decius.[11] After that, silence.[12]

---

[4]Cf. Dunand 1979, 154 and G. Nachtergael, "Les terres cuites 'du Fayoum' dans les maisons de l'Égypte romaine," *Cd'E* 60 (1985) 223-39, on the common religious base of the chora.

[5]See in general the indices to the various volumes of Porter-Moss, and cf. L. Pantalacci and C. Traunecker, "Premières observations sur le temple coptite d'el-Qal'a," *ASAE* 70 (1984-85) 133-37, who note the extensive Augustan activity particularly in the Thebaid, site of an early revolt against Roman rule.

[6]Porter-Moss[2] III.1-2, indices.

[7]Traunecker and Golvin 1984, 24.

[8]W. M. Flinders Petrie, *Diospolis Parva. The Cemeteries of Abadiyeh and Hu, 1898-9* (EEF Memoir 20, London 1901) 54-57.

[9]Porter-Moss[2] II, index; Porter-Moss VII, index; Wagner 1987, 166. There are fourth-century datings in the Hieratic stelae from the Bucheum; cf. Grenier 1989, 85-86.

[10]Porter-Moss IV and VI, indices.

[11]S. Sauneron, *Esna I: Quatre campagnes à Esna* (Cairo 1959) 44.

[12]See Grenier 1989 for an up-to-date repertory of imperial titles in hieroglyphics, and cf. J.-L. Fournet, *REG* 104 (1991) 618, for a telling graph.

Hieroglyphic texts might not be representative; the script was in decline itself, the lore forgotten by all but a handful of specialists, and their work was itself of very low quality by the third century. But the same story is told by Greek epigraphy. A survey of Greek inscriptions dedicating sacred architecture shows nothing after 190, except for one private dedication attributable to the reign of Gallienus from a desert site.[13] In the Fayum, no pagan cultic inscription of any sort is found after the reign of Commodus, public or private.[14] It is difficult to avoid the conclusion that imperial support for the construction, renovation, and decoration of buildings in Egyptian temples declined markedly after Augustus, shrank gradually through the reign of Antoninus, fell off precipitously after that, and disappeared altogether in the middle of the third century.[15]

Stone temples normally last a long time in Egypt, and the withdrawal of capital funding would not in itself have affected day-to-day operations of the temples in the short term; at worst, some things were left unfinished.[16] As time went on, however, one might expect some signs of distress. The temple of Luxor (Thebes) was taken over in the late third century as a military fortress, with a circuit wall, streets, barracks, and other buildings added around it, the holy of holies used for imperial cult and two dozen Pharaonic statues carefully buried.[17] (For a plan, see plate 5.) Greek graffiti inside the temple show clearly that the ancient cult was effectively abandoned before the Romans reused the building, as indeed one would expect.[18] The chronology of the abandonment of the nearby Karnak temple is less clear, but it is not

[13]Bernand 1984; he omits the Trajanic dedication published in F. Daumas, *Les mammisis de Dendara* (Cairo 1959) pl. LIV (cf. p. 292) = *I.Portes* 34.

[14]Bernand 1979; he explains the fact by the decline of the Fayum, but this is surely wrong; there are large numbers of third-century papyri from the Fayum and no sign of decline until well into that century.

[15]Even with private inscriptions things are not different. See, for example, A. Bataille, *Inscr. Deir el-Bahari* (Publ.Soc.Fouad 10) xxiv-xxv, who remarks that the epigraphic record is bare after the second century or perhaps the early third. Lajtar 1991 alters that picture, but without giving any reason to think the temple was in operation. Cf. also *I.Memnon*, p. 29: the most recent date on the Colossi is to Severus (nos. 60 and 61), who restored them.

[16]Cf. Gerhard Haeny, "A Short Architectural History of Philae," *BIFAO* 85 (1985) 197-233 at 229-30 on the Augustan "Kiosk of Trajan" for an example of an unfinished building. Haeny notes (232) that the "Gate of Diocletian" at Philae is a free-standing triumphal arch, not part of the temple precinct.

[17]Golvin et al. 1986. For the statues see "The Luxor Cache," *Egyptian Archaeology* 2 (1992) 8-9.

[18]J. Bingen, "Epigraphie grecque: les proscynèmes de Louqsor," *Cd'E* 61 (1986) 330-34. Similar behavior can be seen at Palmyra, where a former sanctuary became the *principia* of the tetrarchic camp: Isaac 1990, 165.

much later.[19] At Herakleopolis, much of the temple stone was apparently removed in the third century.[20] The North Temple at Karanis was out of use by about 250, the South Temple before the end of the century.[21] Archaeology is generally a blunt weapon, and for reasons set out in the Introduction there is precise information about the abandonment of very few temples. Those visibly abandoned by the middle of the third century are all the more impressive for that reason.

A few exceptions are known. Inscriptions recording the rise of the Nile at Akoris (Tenis, Hermopolite) continue to speak of the rise of the Nile at the temple of Souchos and Ammon and Hermes and Hera there until about 295, with a priest officiating.[22] An inscription at Medamoud (5 km northeast of Karnak) from 291 records a dedication by an eirenarch to the local god.[23] And the Egyptian cults of Philae continued well into the fifth century; but that is a different story (see above, p. 146).[24]

It has long been noted that the papyri are remarkably stingy with information about temples and priests after the middle of the third century.[25] Nor is it easy to learn much about the state of the temples from what there is. For example, the Temple of Hadrian at Oxyrhynchos appears frequently in the documents in the fourth century, but because it was used as a prison and place for trials.[26] The Temple of Kore was also used for a trial: was it also no longer an active cult center?[27] Most other references to temples barely indicate what was going on in them. The list of night watchmen at Oxyrhynchos from the end of the third or early fourth century[28] includes seven guards

[19]Cf. Traunecker and Golvin 1984, 32.

[20]Petrie 1905, 28, based on deposits above the denuded foundations.

[21]Boak 1933, 16 and 21.

[22]*I.Akoris* 29-39 are from the period of Diocletian and the tetrarchs, none demonstrably later than 295: cf. Bagnall, *JAOS* 110 (1990) 754.

[23]*SB* V 8199.

[24]There are indications of pagan cults at other Nubian sites too. See, for example, Günther Roeder, *Les temples immergés de la Nubie. Debod bis Bab Kalabsche*, I (Cairo 1911) 173 on Kertassi. Greek proskynemata end in 251, but that did not mean the end of the cult; p. 145 on Taifa, where an Isis cult survived in the early fourth century, apparently with new statuary in the chapel; and vol. III (F. Zucker) 1912, 156-64, for Isis worship at Talmis in the fifth century.

[25]See already W. Otto, *Priester und Tempel* I (1905) 404-5; for a detailed appreciation of the problem see Zucker 1956.

[26]*P.Oxy.* XLV 3249.12n. collects the evidence; add *P.Oxy.* LIV 3764 and 3767.

[27]*P.Oxy.* LIV 3759 (325); cf. LIV 3757.1n., where the gymnasium, logisterion, and Capitolium are listed as the other sites for trials attested. Some similar public function is probably at stake in *CPR* VII 21 (4c), which mentions something happening in a temple.

[28]*P.Oxy.* I 43 verso (cf. above, p. 53 n. 60 for the date).

attached to each of the Sarapieion and Thoerion.[29] But guards were regularly appointed by the liturgical system for the Hadrianeion as well.[30] The Arsinoite village of Theadelphia had to provide half the cost of a workman plus the fodder for a donkey for three months in the Temple of Hermes at Memphis in 324; but what they were doing is not said.[31]

The list of buildings at Panopolis, so rich in other information, lists a number of *hiera*, sanctuaries. They include sanctuaries of Araus, Ammon, Chnoubis, Agathos Daimon, Persephone, and Hermes.[32] That they are not completely abandoned may be deduced from the mention of a vacant lot of a former *hieron* in one place.[33] All the same, hardly anything can be said about the economic health or social acceptance of these or other temples referred to. The one exception is the sanctuary of Triphis, on the left bank of the Nile facing Panopolis, which contained a *palation* by 298 and was used to house Diocletian's entourage during his visit that year: another case like the sanctuary at Luxor, evidently.[34] One undated papyrus of the third century mentions a promised contribution to a golden statue in a temple at Oxyrhynchos, showing that at least some activity in embellishing the civic temples continued.[35] In the end, there is only one direct description of the state of a temple in the period from Decius to Theodosius, a petition from Theadelphia alleging that the village has become deserted and that the petitioner and his wife are living in the temple to guard it.[36] Theadelphia, a desiccated near-corpse of a village, is no standard.

In the third century, priests of each temple were required to file an annual return listing the clergy, their children, and the temple's furnishings.[37] Not one instance after 260 has survived to show what the condition of even one temple was. There are mentions of priests in the papyri, but they are not much more helpful. Some of them concern priestly status or privileges, such as a declaration listing the minor children of some priests of a village temple in the Kynopolite Nome

---

[29]The Thoerion is still attested in 342 in *P.Oxy.* XIV 1627, in which a man agrees to guard it for eight months.

[30]See *P.Oxy.* XLV 3249 (326).

[31]*P.Sakaon* 22.

[32]*P.Berl.Bork.* (?315-330) ix.3, xiv.27, xv.27, A.ii.4-5, A.iv.12, viii.5. Borkowski (pp. 24-26) shows that *hieron* means "sanctuary," without specification of the exact architectural form. Incomplete references to sanctuaries in ii.21, vi.3-4, and xvii.3.

[33]*P.Berl.Bork.* i.8.

[34]*P.Panop.Beatty* 1.259-261; see Borkowski 1990, 29-30, who does not grasp the implications of the passage.

[35]*P.Oslo* III 158 (*BL*) (late 3rd cent.).

[36]*P.Sakaon* 93 (314-323).

[37]*P.Ryl.* II 110 (259) is the last known example. Cf. Zucker 1956, 168.

from 282,[38] a third-century report of proceedings in a dispute between priests and pastophoroi (a lower level of the priestly class[39]) over rights to property,[40] a request in 320 for the circumcision of the son of a pastophoros of Oxyrhynchos,[41] and finally a declaration on oath, dated 336 and addressed to the *logistes* of Oxyrhynchos, in which a priest of the Temple of Zeus and Hera and the gods who share the sanctuary with them states that he received his rank in succession from his father, who held the same position.[42] These show at least that official documentation and supervision of priestly status and rights continued to the 330s; the government of Constantine was apparently interested like all its predecessors in controlling privileges and status, but it did not drive the old temples "underground." Even in 371 an official of a temple of Apollo might use his title openly in a public document.[43]

Priests appear mainly as private individuals in matters concerned with property and taxes. They are designated "priest" for the sake of identification, as another man might be given a military rank or an occupation; no temple business is involved.[44] There is also sufficient documentation of the civic offices of priest, high priest, and "chief prophet," *archiprophetes*. But the instances are mostly uninformative, showing secular functions like nomination to liturgy.[45] Once again, it

[38]*P.Oxy.* X 1256.

[39]See Schönborn 1976 for the pastophoroi.

[40]*CPR* VII 13 (prov.unkn.). The editor, dating to the third or fourth century, rightly thinks the handwriting probably from the third.

[41]*PSI* V 454 (cf. *BASP* 16 [1979] 236).

[42]*P.Oxy.* X 1265. He is also *komastes* of the divine *protomai* and of their advancing Nike (an image of Victory, cf. Wilcken in *BL* 1.334).

[43]*P.Stras.* IV 243 (*BL*) (Hermopolis?, 371), a surety undertaken by a man who signs himself as holding some position in the temple of Apollo. The title and name are only partly preserved. Cf. Zucker 1956, 172, on a passage of Ammianus Marcellinus (19.12.23) showing that an oracle of Bes in the Temple of Osiris at Abydos did not close until the reign of Constantius II.

[44]Examples: *P.Stras.* VII 618 (Hermopolis, after 319; a tax list); *P.Sakaon* 84 (298, chaff receipts) and 85 (also 298, receipt for barley); *P.Sakaon* 49 (314, loan of seed), 5 (312, tax list), 19 (315-316, list of deliveries); *O.Leid.* 340 (4c, receipt for delivery by a pastophoros); *O.Bodl.* 2062 (303, wife of pastophoros pays for wheat); *P.Lond.* I 125 recto (p. 192) and *P.Lips.* 97 (cf. above, p. 127 n. 82) (Hermonthis, 336-338, payments in accounts); *P.Lips.* 101 (*BL*) (320s or 330s?, Hermopolis, priest in land account); *SB* VI 9502 (Oxyrhynchos, 296; mentions priests petitioning about a landholding); *PSI* III 215 (*BL*) (339, Oxyrynchos; parties to a loan are priests); *O.Mich.* II 939 (Karanis, 3/4c; list includes a priest); *P.Mich.* XV 721 (3/4c, priests in agricultural account).

[45]A priest as borrower in *P.Oslo* II 41 (*BL*) (Oxyrhynchos, 331); a petition about a disputed inheritance from the *archiprophetes* of Alexandria in *P.Ryl.* IV 618 (*ca* 317). The writer's appointment to the office of *kosmetes* seems to be at stake in *P.Rain. Cent.* 73 (Hermopolis, 3/4c), a letter mentioning the *archiprophetes* and *archiereus*; *P.Panop.* 29 and 30 (332) concern a priestess who improperly nominated a man to the

seems that until the 330s there was a continuing civic religious establishment; but it is hard to find much evidence of its activity or prosperity.

Another outward sign is the disappearance of the Amesysia, a festival of Isis known from the time of Augustus on; it is last attested in 257, a casualty probably of a general decline in interest within Egypt in the cult of Isis.[46]

It is difficult to avoid the conclusion that the temples of Egypt, along with their traditional scripts, personnel, influence, festivals, and wealth declined markedly in the third century; but equally, many aspects of their life were already in decline in the first century.[47] What is distinctive about the third century is that as it nears its middle the results of the long decline become manifest. There had been no more building for at least a half-century; hieroglyphics were practically extinct except at Hermonthis and Philae; Demotic was virtually gone except at Philae. It is not easy to be certain why all this happened.[48] There is no reason to think that the decline was inevitable. The temples, their cults, and their scripts (particularly Demotic) were healthy and vital in the early Ptolemaic period, and Demotic literature had enough impetus to carry forward until the second century of Roman rule, producing much of its finest work.[49]

It may be that part of the explanation lies in one symptom, the decline of construction, decoration, and inscriptions after Augustus to virtual extinction after Antoninus. It is an obvious guess that the imperial government simply did not give any more financial support to the capital needs or wants of the temples; even Augustus, after all, did not hesitate to make his contempt for Egyptian religion known.[50] He confiscated the temples' lands, giving them in return an imperial grant in the form of grain and money or, in some cases, offering the chance to lease from the treasury at preferential rates some of the land the temple once owned.[51] From the middle of the third century

---

liturgy of *ktenarchia* and is ordered to nominate someone else instead. *P.Panop.* 14 (early 4c), a land register, mentions a chief priest. On the *archiprophetes*, see A. Bülow-Jacobsen, *Actes XV Congr. Pap.* IV 124-31.

[46]See Bonneau 1985, 366, 369-70, with bibliography on the decline of Isis cults.

[47]See J. Bingen, *Egitto e storia antica* (Bologna 1989) 29, on the decline of the temples already in the Ptolemaic period and their increasing dependence on the later Ptolemies, which set the stage for the Augustan takeover.

[48]It is at least certain that it is not the result of Christianity, despite F. Daumas, in C. Aldred et al., *L'Égypte du crépuscule* (Paris 1980) 18-19; the roots go too deep.

[49]See Zauzich 1983, 78.

[50]Cassius Dio 51.16.

[51]See Johnson 1936, 639-49, and J. A. S. Evans, "A Social and Economic History of an Egyptian Temple in the Greco-Roman Period," *YCS* 17 (1961) 149-283, for the complex patchwork of revenue sources, many of them very small, on which the

onward, there is no evidence about temple income. The empire passed through a serious crisis in the third century, and it would not be surprising if emperors cut their support for Egyptian temples in order to raise funds for other purposes.[52] By the time Maximinus Daia tried to revive civic cults throughout the East in the early fourth century, it may have been too late.[53] The prominence of other economic activities in our limited documentation for priests in the third and fourth centuries may well point to their need to support themselves from sources other than the temples. There will then have been nothing dramatic about the story, simply a slow starving to death of these cults, some of them three millennia and more old.[54]

The consequences for Egyptian society of the starvation and death of the temples were more far-reaching than most moderns would suppose. If, as it seems, Egyptian society, particularly in the villages, had little internal articulation except religiously, the loss of the institutional base of religion must have been devastating to the sense of community. It is not belief that was lost; the Egyptian peasant of the fourth century believed as securely as his ancestors in the sacral character of the Nile and in the necessity of pleasing the divine to ensure fertility of fields, animals, and women.[55] But cult as an organizing principle in society was lost. It may be that this vacuum helped make the spread of Christianity in Egypt so explosive in the fourth century: it replaced that lost structure of life.[56]

Pagan Piety and Practice

With its physical base in an advanced state of decay and its organizational structure increasingly a rickety formalism, the polytheism of Roman Egypt found itself under pressure in the later third century.

---

temples subsisted in the Roman period.

[52]There is a small sign at Esna that Decius may (along with persecuting Christians) have taken some interest in an Egyptian cult: see Serge Sauneron, "Les querelles impériales vues à travers les scènes du temple d'Esné," *BIFAO* 51 (1952) 111-21, noting Decius' erasure of inscriptions of Philippus Arabs.

[53]Cf. Oliver Nicholson, "The 'Pagan Churches' of Maximin Daia and Julian the Apostate," *APA Annual Meeting Abstracts* (1990) 11, who is apparently too sanguine about the success of Maximinus' attempts to resuscitate traditional religion.

[54]Nock 1944/1972, 571, exaggerates the role of popular support in providing basic financial sustenance for the Egyptian temples.

[55]There were also, naturally, some survivals of pagan elements in the later periods; cf. L. Kákosy, "Survival of Ancient Egyptian Gods in Coptic and Islamic Egypt," *Coptic Studies* 175-78.

[56]Nock 1944/1972, 583, rightly concludes that Christianity faced little opposition when it spread in Egypt.

Nowhere is this strain more perceptible than in the scanty documentation of sacrifice, that central cult act used to test adherence to public
religion during the anti-Christian persecutions. One undated list,
headed "with good fortune; to the *beneficiarius*," enumerates articles
for sacrifice: chickens, a piglet, eggs, wine, honey, milk, oil, pine
cones, flowers. Because the sacrifice is for the month of Hathyr, it may
well be that it was part of a festival of Isis.[57] An order for payment
from the last days of pre-Constantinian Egypt, *ca* 320-324, tells a
receiver of wine to disburse some for the sacrifice.[58] It is part of the
archive of one of the wealthiest families of Hermopolis.

Sacrifice surely did not come to an end with Constantine's victory
over Licinius, but evidence for it nearly does. Because documentation
of sacrifice is for all periods scarce in comparison to the activity that
surely must have occurred, its end is only a crude indicator.[59] All the
same, the limitation of the evidence for the half-century before Constantine to a couple of documents of upper-class origin fits well with
the indications of decay in the physical support of polytheism. One
might expect, however, that even if daily cult in the temples was in
drastic decline the major festivals would have provided an occasion
for sacrifice. The evidence for festivals themselves, however, is almost
equally weak.[60] The one significant indicator is a series of four dipinti,
in bad Greek, recording apparently annual visits by the ironworkers
of Hermonthis between 324 and 357 to the abandoned temple of Hatshepsut at Deir el-Bahari, the highlight of which was the sacrifice of a
donkey. The occasion may have been an Osirian festival, but the
identity of the god to whom sacrifice was made is unknown.[61]

Virtually all the evidence for festivals is undatable, for one thing.[62]
Some evidence for festivities linked with cultural manifestations
(above, p. 101), is only vaguely to be dated late third to early fourth
century, such as the agreement to employ the services of a mime and

[57]*P.Oxy.* XXXVI 2797 (3/4c); cf. the editor's remarks on the festival.

[58]*CPR* VI 49 (cf. p. 107).

[59]K. W. Harl, "Sacrifice and Pagan Belief in Fifth- and Sixth-Century Byzantium," *Past & Present* 128 (1990) 7-27, emphasizes the centrality of sacrifice to
paganism and the indications of its continuation in some circles (he is principally
concerned with Asia Minor) until a late date.

[60]*P.Wash.Univ.* II 95, dated to 4/5c by the editors but probably a century later, is
called by them a [pagan] "festival account," but with no basis in the text.

[61]Lajtar 1991.

[62]The same is still more true for the limited epigraphic evidence for the old
gods assigned to this period, such as a statue inscription to Anoubis (*SB* XIV 12151),
assigned by the editor to the 3/4c, or a gold tablet dedicated to Zeus Helios etc. and
dated by the editor to 4/5c with much doubt (*SB* VIII 9762). These dates are of little
value.

homerist for the festival of Kronos at Lykopolis,[63] or the Oxyrhynchos festival expense list with a herald, trumpeter, comic performer, dancer, and so on.[64] A letter of Gaianus to the *praefectus* Agenor referring to the forthcoming Saturnalia and wild beast hunt is equally undatable.[65] An invitation to a festival, addressed to a woman, asks her to say whether she is coming by boat or donkey, so that she can be sent for.[66] It, too, is dated "third to fourth century."

The two last attestations of a pagan festival to which a better than approximate date can be given both come from the first quarter of the fourth century. One is an account of payments, among which is included one to a slave on the occasion of a festival of Sarapis. The evidence of price levels in this text allows it to be assigned with some probability to *ca* 312-318, certainly not later than 324.[67] Like most of the evidence for sacrifice mentioned earlier, this comes from a manifestly upper-class milieu. The same is true of the reference to constant festival processions in Pharmouthi in a letter referring to Theophanes and thus datable to the period before 324.[68]

Festivities did not cease. The festival of the Nile was still celebrated in 424, and no doubt for many years afterward, but an order in that year to supply wine for it is written by one Theodoulos, bearer of a fine Christian name.[69] This was certainly no longer the feast of the Nile as divinity, but an officially desacralized affair. Even Christians, however, could write hymns to the Nile.[70] The festivals of the church itself are barely visible in the fourth century documents, coming to prominence only in the next century. Once again, the peculiar character of the fourth-century documentation probably deserves part of the responsibility for the silences. But just as the church did not replace paganism all at once in other respects, its filling of the gaps in festivities left by the decline of observance of the cult of the gods may likewise have been gradual.

If these outward and visible signs of pagan cult are difficult to track in the evidence, it will not be expected that the inward religious

---

[63]*P.Oxy.* VII 1025 = *W.Chr.* 493; cf. above, p. 92 for the probable provenance.

[64]*SB* IV 7336.

[65]*P.Oxy.* I 122 (*BL*). The editor remarks on the Latinate quality of the handwriting.

[66]*P.Oxy.* I 112 (*W.Chr.* 488).

[67]*P.Stras.* VI 559 (cf. Bagnall 1985b, 57 on the date).

[68]*P.Herm.* 2; it is unclear whether this was written at Hermopolis or merely found there.

[69]*P.Oxy.* XLIII 3148.

[70]*P.Turner* 10 (6c). Cf. D. Bonneau, "Continuité et discontinuité notionale dans la terminologie religieuse du Nil, d'après la documentation grecque," *Mélanges Étienne Bernand* (Paris 1991) 23-35.

feelings of those who worshiped the old gods will be easily discerned. References in personal letters offer the best and usual avenue of approach, but the general reticence of papyrus letters must be borne in mind as a limiting factor. That once again the limited evidence concerns almost entirely the upper class[71] is in one sense a confirmation of the documentation of sacrifice and festivals, but those who had to have their letters written by a public scribe were no doubt much less likely to expose their feelings than those who wrote their letters themselves (or had a trusted slave write them). The inscriptions of the iron-workers show that some private observances continued, even if sporadically.

Letters also bring with them the problem of chronology; having no absolute dates, they invite an element of subjectivity in their interpretation. The formulas popular for centuries, of the "I make daily obeisance on your behalf before the god Sarapis" type, known also for other gods, disappear at some point in the late third or early fourth century.[72] But pinning down the date of the last known examples is impossible. Some have been dated by editors to the early fourth century on palaeographical grounds,[73] but the ordinary latitude of such assignments would equally well allow a late third-century date.[74] Other casual references to Hermes or Sarapis are no better dated.[75]

The most complex and best documented case is that of Theophanes, a wealthy early fourth-century Hermopolitan serving as a *scholasticus* on the staff of the *katholikos* of Egypt, whose letters and accounts are one of the richest archives of the period.[76] Most of the texts apparently come from the period in which Licinius ruled Egypt (313-324), that important period after the end of persecution of Christians but before the overt state support of Christianity brought by Constantine. The letters have given rise to elaborate theories

[71]The same is true for the circles in which the Hermetic writings were popular: see G. Fowden, *The Egyptian Hermes* (Cambridge 1986), esp. 186-94.

[72]See H. C. Youtie, *ICS* 3 (19798) 90-99 = *Scriptiunculae posteriores* I 36-45.

[73]*SB* XIV 12029, a fragment of a private letter, with a *proskynema* formula referring to the gods; *SB* XVI 12571, a *proskynema* to Sarapis; both dated by editors to the fourth century on slender palaeographical grounds. Cf. *P.Iand.* VI 121 (dated 3/4c), also with a Sarapis *proskynema*.

[74]As in the case of *SB* VI 9194, where a reference to the *epistrategos* demonstrates that the date is before 298.

[75]Two cases dated by the editor to the third century: *P.Rain. Cent.* 72 (Hermopolis), "I pray to Hermes for your safety"; *P.Mert.* I 28, "By Sarapis, I wonder that you didn't write me by Sarapion or Techosis."

[76]For a general discussion with good bibliography, see Cadell 1989. See also now *CPR* XVIIA 18.3n.; the implication clearly is that Theophanes' activities as *scholasticus* must fall in 321-324, his trip to Syria in 322 or 323.

identifying Theophanes as a pagan (specifically as a member "of a circle of pagans worshipping Hermes Trismegistus"), a supporter of
Licinius, and a representative of his fellow pagans to the emperor.[77]
This all rests on sand—letters addressed to or mentioning Theophanes, not those written by him. An examination of these undertaken without a particular view of Theophanes shows some written
by Christians,[78] others from a chief prophet and priest of Hermes who
refers to that god.[79] There is no evidence of Theophanes' own views,
although a good case can be made out that his brother-in-law was a
Christian.[80] What does emerge is a sense that Christians and pagans
coexisted in the same upper-class circles and with much the same
cultural formation, and that both could expect a friendly connection
with a man of influence like Theophanes, whatever his own beliefs.[81]

Those upper-class circles continued to include some families
attached to the old ways. The last for which good documentation survives may be the Panopolite family of Ammon, Harpocration, and
Apollon, active in the first half of the fourth century, with its literary
and administrative success at the imperial court (above, p. 109) as well
as in Egypt. One letter of this archive mentions an attempt to secure
from the chief priest of Egypt an appointment as prophet of the first-
ranked temples of Panopolis for the writer's nephew, whose father
had been chief-prophet.[82] Much remains frustratingly unclear about
this effort, most notably its reason and date. The editor suggests financial considerations as the most important, but if so, it is most unlikely
that the date can be as late as the 330s or 340s, as he supposes; by that
time, whatever revenues remained to the temples in the early part of
the century were certainly gone. A polemical reference to "the enemies
of the gods" suggests a strongly partisan, anti-Christian stance by this

[77]See Moscadi 1970, 89-100, for a summary of the bibliography. The quotation is
of B. R. Rees, but the view still followed by Cadell 1989, 320.
[78]P.Herm. 4-5 are certainly Christian, and P.Herm. 6 offers enough New Testament echoes to warrant a characterization as Christian too. Cf. Moscadi 1970, 130-46.
The attempt by Judge and Pickering 1977, 5, to explain such phraseology away has
no basis in the texts.
[79]P.Herm. 2-3; SB XII 10803 (Moscadi 1970, 117-29 nos. 2-3 and 147-49 no.12; on
the last of these see also New Docs. 1.20, which does not know Moscadi).
[80]Cf. Moscadi 1970, 92-96, for a decisive demonstration, particularly about his
no.4 (pp. 108-13) = P.Ryl. IV 624, which he shows to have no religious reference. See
G. Bastianini, Anagennesis 3 (1983) 161-65, for arguments identifying the Hermo-
doros of P.Herm. 5 as Theophanes' brother-in-law.
[81]See Dunand 1991, 237-38, for similar coexistence in the villages. On the over-
emphasis often placed on the Christian-pagan divide, cf. Averil Cameron 1991, 122.
[82]P.XV Congr. 22.

family, but it seems most likely that this is to be dated early in the century.[83]

Magic and Astrology

Whatever the date of Ammon's attempt to secure his nephew's appointment as prophet, it is likely enough that belief in the power of the old gods survived longer in some circles than did outward manifestation of that belief through public cult. Much more lasting, however, was an underlying current of thought about the unseen world, a set of beliefs and even practices that did not depend on public cult at all. To most ancient minds, in fact, these beliefs were neither specifically "pagan" nor contradictory to Christianity. Such, for example, was the awareness of a vast unseen population of demons whose activity could be felt. Ability to control and expel such spirits has a prominent place in Jesus' career, and his successors on many occasions validated their own ministries by demonstrating the same kind of power. Miraculous cures, once the province of the old gods, became the means for holy men, especially monastics, to display the power of the Christian God.[84] From Antony on, the desert monks encountered the demons in daily struggle; they certainly did not doubt their existence.[85]

A repertory of tools for direct dealing with unseen forces had long been available. Though much remains unclear, this arsenal seems by the end of the first or beginning of the second century to take on the forms that remain characteristic through the fifth century.[86] It included—along no doubt with much that was purely oral—magical gems, lead tablets with charms and curses, and a repertory of spells that survive on papyrus. One other element is the wide use of horoscopes, through which knowledge of the future could be obtained—and measures then taken to avert disaster and seize opportunities. Relatively uncommon in Greek before the middle of the first century, these attain a steady popularity in the papyri which lasts until the end of the fourth century, after which a scattering continues through the fifth century; the last known example concerns a birth in 478.[87]

[83]The editor notes this possibility, strengthened by the sense given in the text that the emperor is propagan and that Diocletian is a recent figure. The years of Maximinus, or conceivably Licinius, are surely a better bet than the later years of Constantine.

[84]Dunand 1991.

[85]See Rubenson 1990, 86-88, on Antony's demonology.

[86]See Smith 1983a, 255-56.

[87]See Neugebauer and Van Hoesen 1959 for a compilation of both documents

Although the church disapproved of horoscopes, their use by Christians was probably as prevalent in the fourth century as it is today. A collection of them from Antinoe, to be dated not long after 385, includes horoscopes for two men named Ioannes and one named Kyrillos, all of whom are virtually certain to have been Christians.[88] Nor can such use be ascribed to low estate, because the papyrus in question comes from the economic stratum that served in metropolitan liturgies. Even wealthy Christians were no doubt as little interested in theology, or concerned about theoretical contradictions between Christian faith and astrology, as their counterparts of other times and places.

Another direct means of self-protection, also rejected by the church, was the amulet. These charms, meant to defend the wearer against either specific or general ills, vary in character. Some invoke the kind of magical talk and divinities (like Adonai) who populate the magical papyri;[89] others have a vaguely Christian character or, more precisely, appropriate the name of Christ or other Christian terminology without necessarily regarding Christ as anything more than an additional divinity to invoke.[90] Still others seem purely Christian, such as the scriptural pastiches found in some papyri.[91] Editors, perhaps embarrassed by such things, tend to label them "Gnostic," but that explains nothing. There is no reason to think that ordinary Christians did not use such amulets.

The same is true of those charms aimed not at defending the wearer from harm but at producing a positively beneficial effect, victory in life's competition, whether in the stadium[92] or (most commonly) in love, a long-established and perennially popular genre.[93] When the son of a woman named Thekla uses such a charm to bind a woman to himself, the man involved is certainly from a Christian

---

and literary sources; they show the chronological distribution on 161-62. The last item known is *P.Oxy.* XVI 2060 (29 June 478 by Neugebauer and Van Hoesen's computation). *P.Oxy.* XLVI 3298 (later third century) is an interesting addition to the corpus.

[88]*PSI* I 22-24; cf. Bagnall and Worp, *CSBE* 43 n.2, on the date of this papyrus, which includes *PSI* VIII 958-960 as well as the horoscopes.

[89]E.g., *SB* XIV 11493 (Adonai) and 11214-11215; *P.Rein.* II 89; *P.Michael.* 27.

[90]Such is probably *SB* XIV 12113, using a Christian *nomen sacrum*. So also, probably, *SB* III 6584, a phylaktery for a house, despite the explicitly Christian chi-mu-gamma heading and closing invocation.

[91]Most notably, *PSI* VI 719 and *P.Princ.* II 107.

[92]*P.Oxy.* XII 1478 (= *Sel.Pap.* I 198) (3/4c); the editor calls this "gnostic."

[93]"Pagan" examples: *BIFAO* 76 (1976) 213-23; *SB* XIV 11535. Cf. *New Docs.* 1.8 for detailed commentary.

family,[94] but his magic arsenal contains the same weapons as that of his non-Christian contemporaries.[95]

Here, too, no class-based description is satisfactory. The remarkable late fourth-century Berlin codex that contains the lurid summaries of judicial sentences in crimes involving women (above, p. 197) also has two pages of magical texts, including a charm against hemorrhage, on the second of which stands an invocation of the archangels Gabriel and Michael.[96] But most of the codex is occupied with official correspondence and receipts connected with high-level liturgical posts, no doubt an accumulation of documents relevant to the owner's service. The owner was thus a wealthy landowner. Here, as elsewhere, it is difficult to see any distinctions between Christian and pagan, or rich and poor, in underlying attitudes and in resort to traditional magical lore to gain some measure of control over a threatening world. It is true that many of these measures, like horoscopes and charms, gradually disappear from the documentation, but only long after Christianity's official triumph under Constantine.[97]

It is important to keep in mind that despite church disapproval of magical practices, Christians did not disbelieve in their effectiveness. Palladius tells of a married woman turned into a horse by a magician, who had been retained by a would-be lover disappointed at her rejection of his advances. The story includes her transformation back into human form by the monk St. Makarios and his parting comment to her that this was the result of her not having received communion for five weeks.[98] The pious Palladius does not doubt the magician's powers; all he offers is the Christian's defense against vulnerability to magic, the eucharist.

The Survival of Judaism

A survey of the religious environment in which Christianity's rapid fourth-century growth took place would not be complete without some consideration of Judaism, its earliest matrix and then, as the process of distinction advanced, its rival. The large, active, and visible Jewish community of Egypt had been crushed at the beginning of the

[94]*SB* XIV 11534 (3/4c according to ed.).

[95]For the lead tablets, see now *P.Mich.* XVI 757 introd., with a thorough survey of parallels. The dating of these texts is controversial. On the Christian use of magic, see also Roberts 1979, 82.

[96]*BGU* IV 1026 (Hermopolis, perhaps 380s).

[97]Smith 1983b, 56-58, regards the decline of these forms of magic as a "comparatively immediate" consequence of the triumph of Christianity, but given the time-lag involved this is a doubtful assertion.

[98]*HL* 17.6-9.

reign of Hadrian after a bloody revolt, much if not all of its wealth confiscated. There is no way of estimating the extent of the slaughter and enslavement inflicted on the Jewish community by the Roman authorities, but it was decisive and permanent.[99] Whatever remained is largely invisible in the documentation, and the one criterion generally used to identify Jews in the period after 117, nomenclature, cannot bear the weight put upon it.

That criterion, as usually applied, has been that persons with biblical names found in papyri dating before 337, the death of Constantine, may be taken to be Jewish, while persons with biblical names after that date may be considered Christian.[100] Quite apart from the fact that such a principle prejudges the complex problem of the pace of Christianization of Egypt (below, p. 278), it is patently illogical and certainly leads to false results. Given the fact that such names rise steadily in numbers from the late third century on, application of this principle leads to a paradoxical conclusion that Jews increased steadily in number until 337, after which they disappear and—all of a sudden—Egypt is populated with large numbers of Christians. This absurdity is in itself sufficient to show that this principle does not work. But it is also important to realize that real Jewish communities of the Roman world had onomastic repertories in which biblical names played only a small role. Unless one can identify other contemporary Semitic names in the same matrix as the biblical ones, the latter have no claim to help identify Jews; and after 117 there is a great dearth of such nonbiblical Jewish names in Egypt.[101] Biblical names securely attributable to Jews are equally rare.[102] It is in fact much more likely that biblical names in post-Hadrianic documents are a sign of Christianity.

Evidence from the period after Diocletian for Judaism and Jews, once the onomastic criterion is removed, is extremely scanty, but not

[99]See Mélèze-Modrzejewski 1987 for a good general treatment of the Jews in Egypt, esp. 45-48 for the period after the revolt; in more detail on the confiscation of Jewish property, Mélèze-Modrzejewski 1989.

[100]This is the principle of Tcherikover, *CPJud.* I, xvii-xviii, invoked, for example, in the commentaries to *P.Oxy.* XXXI 2599 and XXXVI 2770.

[101]Martin 1981, 40, notes that fully half of the supposed mentions of Jews between 117 and 337 in *CPJud.* III are occurrences of the name Sambathion, which was in wide use among Jews and non-Jews alike (as Tcherikover recognized) and is thus also useless as a criterion. Once Sambathion is removed from consideration, the balance of non-Biblical Semitic names is exiguous.

[102]*P.Oxy.* XLVI 3314 exemplifies the problem of identification, with Judas, Joses, Maria, and Isaac. G. Tibiletti's argument for Jewish identity (*Scritti in onore di O. Montevecchi* [Bologna 1981] 407-11) depends on prerevolt evidence; better is the treatment by G. Horsley, *NewDocs* 1978, 100.

the less interesting for that. One key document is a manumission of 291 concerning a forty-year-old woman named Paramone and her children; those of whom mention survives are ten and four years old. Her liberty has been paid for by the synagogue of the Jews, presumably of Oxyrhynchos, through two intermediaries, one a councillor of Oneitonpolis in Palestine named Justus, the other named Dioskoros.[103] The fragmentary preservation of the document, the extremely high price paid,[104] the fact that Paramone was born a slave, and the involvement of a notable from Palestine all make the transaction both interesting and difficult to understand. At the least, it is obvious that the scarcity of documents from the Jewish community should not cause underestimation of its cohesiveness,[105] financial strength, or ties to Palestine.

The last of these aspects is reinforced by the marriage contract (*ketuba*) from Antinoopolis, dated 417, written in Aramaic and Greek but in Hebrew letters.[106] It is essentially in the tradition of the Palestinian marriage contract as reflected also in the Palestinian Talmud, but with important influences from the traditions of Greek Egypt, and its Aramaic is Palestinian in character.[107] The late antique Jewish communities of Upper Egypt, then, though significantly influenced by their proximate environment, maintained distinctive traditions through close contact with Palestine.

A humbler testimony shows that this maintenance of tradition was not effected by economic isolation from the Christian community. In 400, one Aurelius Ioses son of Ioudas, explicitly described as a Jew, leased a ground-floor room and a basement storage room in a house at Oxyrhynchos from two sisters, who are described as *monachai apotaktikai*, apotactic monastics.[108] (This probably means living in the city rather than either as part of a detached monastic community or as hermits; cf. below, p. 297.) The rent is in line with other lease payments for parts of city houses known from the period, and the whole transaction is distinguished by its routineness. All the same, the sight

---

[103]*P.Oxy.* IX 1205 (Oxyrhynchos), a manumission *inter amicos*.

[104]At fourteen talents for a woman and two (or perhaps more likely three) children, this must be the equivalent of more than 140 artabas of wheat; fourth-century slave sales seem generally not to have prices higher than the equivalent of about 25 art. for an adult slave.

[105]The bronze incense burner, almost certainly from a synagogue, dedicated by Auxanon (*SB* XII 11100), though impossible to date with any precision, deserves mention.

[106]Sirat et al. 1986.

[107]Sirat et al. 1986, 10-15.

[108]*P.Oxy.* XLIV 3203. See *New Docs.* 1.82 for detailed commentary, mainly on the monastic questions involved.

of two Christian nuns letting out two rooms of their house to a Jewish man has much to say about not only the flexibility of the monastic life but also the ordinariness of intersectarian relationships.

Nothing thus suggests that the Jewish communities of Egypt ever recovered the numbers, visibility, or Hellenic character by which they were marked before the great revolt, and from the fifth century on, pressure from the Alexandrian patriarchate and imperial edicts may have made life in Alexandria difficult for them. But the very limited evidence from the cities of the Egyptian *chora* indicates that the small numbers of Jews who lived in them managed to maintain their own community institutions, to keep up close contacts with Palestine, and yet to live routinely if not invisibly in an increasingly Christian civil society.

The Christianization of Egypt

The church of Alexandria, which dominated the church of Egypt to an unmatched degree, considered itself the foundation of the evangelist Mark. About its early history speculation outweighs evidence by a wide margin. Alexandria in the first century had an enormous Jewish community, and this is generally taken to be the basis for the earliest foundation of Christianity. The virtual extermination of the Jewish population of Egypt early in Hadrian's reign both wiped out this matrix and eliminated any possibility that Christianity could spread throughout Egypt by way of the Jewish communities in the metropoleis.[109] Egyptian Christianity survived this blow, but little more is heard for a century after the Jewish revolt. Even for the third century, documentation is thin, concentrating on the Alexandrian elite, with scattered mentions of activity elsewhere in the province.[110]

And yet much was happening, if one may judge by the state of affairs at the start of the Great Persecution in 303. The church had clearly taken advantage of the "Little Peace" following the Decian persecution to build a provincewide structure. There were bishops in the majority of the nome capitals, and the chance survival of one property declaration of 304, during the persecution, shows that there was a church in the Oxyrhynchite village of Chysis.[111] Coptic was fully developed as a language for the scriptures, and large-scale translation

[109]See generally Martin 1979 and 1981 for the early history of the Egyptian church. The extensive treatment by Griggs 1990 is uncritical and poorly informed.

[110]A comprehensive discussion may be found in G. Tibiletti, "Tra paganesimo e cristianesimo: L'Egitto nel III secolo," *Egitto e società antica* (Milan 1985) 247-69. See also Roberts 1979.

[111]*P.Oxy.* XXXIII 2673. Cf. above, p. 256 n. 142.

activity was underway. It is impossible to quantify this activity, but it is evident that the church had a network to the village level, an extensive clergy, and enough worshipers to sustain the structure.[112] The imperial government, in sum, found plenty to persecute.

Why is the church of the four decades before the persecution so invisible in the documents? Three converging factors may be adduced.[113] First, most documentary evidence for Christianity before 300 comes from private letters that use Christian expressions of various sorts, and these are almost invariably impossible to date accurately.[114] With rough dates like "third century" or "third-fourth century" little can be done. It is clear that Christianity brought significant changes in the epistolary conventions of Roman Egypt, and it is difficult to tell how far religious conversion or epistolary change is to be credited with the very rapid growth of identifiably Christian letters in the fourth century.[115] For present purposes, however, it is the chronological vagueness of these texts that offers the greatest problem.[116]

Second, there is no secure evidence before Licinius' defeat of Maximinus and subsequent acquisition of Egypt for any use of ecclesiastical terms as a means of legal self-identification. A substantial part of the fourth-century evidence for the church is in fact evidence for individual members of the clergy, who identify themselves in documents as bishops, presbyters, deacons, or lectors. In the post-313 church of Egypt, such clerical titles had official standing, just as if one were to be designated by a post in the imperial civil service or by a civic dignity like councillor. Before that time, no such official sig-

---

[112]It is interesting that the *VAnt* (2, p. 5.20) assumes that as a youth in the 260s Antony could have gone to church regularly. How much the author knew about conditions a century earlier is not determinable.

[113]Early Christianity is archaeologically invisible; cf. Wipszycka 1988, 117-18, and Bagnall, "An Early Christian Burial at Tell el-Maskhuta?" *ZPE* 74 (1988) 291-92. The claims of C. W. Griggs, "Excavating a Christian Cemetery near Seila," *Coptic Studies* 145-50 at 149 are fantasy.

[114]A useful discussion at *NewDocs* 4.16 with bibliography. It is also true that a considerable repertory of vocabulary and ideas was common to Christians and pagans, with the result that the religious identity of many writers is indeterminable. Cf. Judge and Pickering 1977, 52-53, on the Paniskos dossier.

[115]Wipszycka 1988, 119-21, gives an interesting analysis, showing that *of letters with any religious sentiment* Christian letters make up 7 percent of the total in the third century, 55 percent in those dated third to fourth century, and 86 percent of those dated fourth century. She denies these figures any validity as an indicator of Christianization, however, and that is surely right in any precise sense, given the other factors that may be operative.

[116]Occasionally a letter mentions external circumstances that allow a date, like *P.Oxy.* XXXI 2601 = Naldini 35, dated to the fourth century start on the basis of allusion to a requirement (successfully evaded) for litigants to sacrifice. Cf. Judge and Pickering 1977, 53.

nificance was attached to church titles.[117] The sole apparent exception before 313 shows the force of the rule; for the lector of the church of Chysis declares that his (former) church had no property except a bit of bronze, and his title is given precisely because he appears in connection with his ecclesiastical function. His church title would not have appeared in a tax receipt or lease.[118]

And third, parents increasingly tended to give identifiably Christian names to their children. Although a few parents did this in the third century,[119] the number is very small and cannot safely be taken as an indicator. Only in the fourth century does this habit become fashionable, and only then is there any chance of extracting useful information from onomastic practices. For developments in the third century, then, it is of no help.

If the third-century situation is totally unquantifiable,[120] the same cannot be said for the fourth.[121] A body of distinctively Christian names comes into wide use in this period, composed of biblical names, saints' names, a few names formed on the Egyptian *ntr*, "God," and several theological abstractions. Not all Christians gave all their children such names, certainly, but those bearing such names (or

[117]*P.Oxy.* XXXIII 2665 (*BL*) (305/6) is emblematic; a report from the civic archivists that one Paulos owned nothing and was not registered, it gives Paulos no title. Because he had been condemned by the famous persecutor Satrius Arrianus, governor of the Thebaid, the editor reasonably speculates that he may have been a Christian martyr; but there is no official designation to indicate his ecclesiastical status.

[118]By the editor's date, *P.Oxy.* LV 3787 would be an important exception. This list of payers of the *epikephalaion poleos* includes a deacon and a lector, given civil identification as such. The editor dates to 301/2?, on the basis of an uncertain identification of the *systates* mentioned in the heading of the document. But the amounts paid by the persons listed would fit better with the known level of the tax from 312/3 on, and such a date seems much more likely; see Bagnall, *Cd'E* 66 (1991) 293-96. Judge and Pickering 1977, 60-61, like many date *P.Oxy.* I 43 verso, with its mention of churches in an official register, to "295 or soon after," but that is without foundation; cf. above, p. 53.

[119]Cf. *NewDocs* 3.77 for a speculation that the *dekaprotos* Athanasios in the late third-century Arsinoite was a Christian, marred however by the mistaken belief that he was called Athanasios alias Philadelphos (see Bagnall, *Aegyptus* 58 [1978] 160-67).

[120]It has been argued that "unquantifiable" does not mean small, and that Christians were numerous, open, and dynamic in the years of the "Little Peace." See, e.g., T. D. Barnes, *L'église et l'empire au IVe siècle*, ed. A. Dihle (Fond. Hardt, Entretiens 34, Vandoeuvres-Geneva 1989) 306-11.

[121]The following discussion is based on Bagnall 1982a, as amended in Bagnall 1987b (a response to criticisms of Wipszycka 1986). The hasty rejoinder in Wipszycka 1988, 164-65, does not engage the issues. The balance of that article argues for the usefulness of the Christian literary sources in assessing matters qualitatively, but Wipszycka herself (122-23) shows just how full of fiction, even on background questions, these sources are. See above, p. 7.

whose parents do) form a definable cadre of Christians capable of giving a rough minimum for their share of the population at a given point (that is, the average birthdate of the living population recorded in any given body of documentation).[122] The word *minimum* deserves emphasis here. The actual number may have been significantly higher. That figure is just under 20 percent in the years right after 313, when for the first time the church received official recognition, but it seems to have at least doubled in the decade after Constantine acquired Egypt in 324. That is, it seems likely that onomastically identifiable Christians made up the majority of the population, though perhaps not by much, by Constantine's death in 337. The lack of coherent documentation makes it much harder to be specific after that time, but by the early fifth century identifiable Christians appear to make up 80 percent or more of the population.

Rough though such quantification must be at present, it corresponds to other qualitative indicators. The virtual disappearance of visible signs of pagan observance after 324 documented above, even before any significant repressive legislation, points to a society in which Christianity was predominant, even if not yet overwhelmingly so. In place of such signs come routine references to churches and ecclesiastics, taken for granted and seemingly ubiquitous, with a fully developed structure. In addition, the key persons at the center of surviving archives from the Constantinian period or later are, where religion can be determined, probably or certainly Christian.[123] It is also striking that open division in the church, first visible in organizational (but not theological) terms after the end of the persecutions, breaks forth full-blown in the 320s, precisely when Christianity has achieved official status thanks to Constantine's victory.

Christians of the first three centuries were acutely aware of themselves as a distinct group, even if individuals within the group existed in a complex cross-matrix of other ties. Perhaps the strongest signal of this self-consciousness in the documents is the development of the Christian letter of introduction, designed to give the bearer—a part of

[122]There is no way of knowing how many Christians *changed* their own names after conversion, though some certainly did; cf. Horsley 1987, 1.

[123]For Charite, see the brilliant article of J. Kramer, "Was bedeutet koimeterion in den Papyri?," *ZPE* 80 (1990) 269-72. For Abinnaeus, see Barnes 1985. Papnouthis and Dorotheos have Christian names. The Sakaon archive, largely earlier and mute on religion, shows signs of Christianity toward the end: *P.Sakaon* 48 (343). The various monastic archives discussed below are of course all Christian. Most documents, naturally, have no reason to display the religion of the persons involved (the surprise of Horsley 1987, 12, that Christians of the fourth century are not more explicit about their religion thus seems misplaced).

one Christian community—a welcome in another.[124] Before the fourth century, certainly, entry into the church was not a casual matter, but required instruction as a catechumen. This prebaptismal status, still widely observed in the fourth century, was taken seriously and is referred to in some letters of introduction, so that the recipients will know exactly how to treat the bearer.[125] There is little indication how the church, for long set up to handle small numbers of converts, managed the enormous flow of new Christians it faced in the fourth century. The ability of the clergy to give adequate instruction to the new entrants must have been greatly diminished, and the utility of monks for evangelistic instruction cannot have been great, because most of them seem to have had little theological education themselves. The sense of Christians as a distinct group may not have survived majority status by many decades, but a letter assigned by the editor to the late fourth or early fifth century (and certainly not earlier than 370) still complains with astonishment that his correspondent has mistreated someone "who is a Christian."[126]

No clear correlation of religious affiliation with other classifications of the population is defensible, though many have been tried. Some Christians, for example, were certainly wealthy; even in the third century, when Christianity would have posed some difficulties in public life, some members of the elite were adherents.[127] This is all the more true in the fourth century.[128] But no religion with more than 1 or 2 percent of the population could have been principally upper

---

[124]The most recent list and analysis, with bibliography, is at *P.Oxy.* LVI 3857 introd.

[125]*P.Oxy.* XXXVI 2785 (4c); the editor suggests that Sotas, the recipient, may be the writer of *P.Oxy.* XII 1492 (Naldini 30) and *PSI* III 208 and IX 1041 (Naldini 28 and 29, resp.; catechumens of two different levels are mentioned in the latter), and perhaps also the recipient of *PSI* IV 311 (Naldini 39). The other side of the coin may be seen in *P.Oxy.* XXXI 2603 = Naldini 47 (4c), where the writer stresses that the bearers are *not* catechumens.

[126]*P.Laur.* II 42 (Oxyrhynchite; cf. *Misc.Pap.* 317-19). The editor appears to take the phrase to refer to the addressee rather than the woman under discussion, but that seems surely wrong. The letter is on reused papyrus; for the earlier text see H. Harrauer, *ZPE* 67 (1987) 105-8. The 10th to 12th indictions in it seem likely to be 366/7-368/9 (payment levels cannot be earlier, and the method of indicating thousands is not likely to be later).

[127]For example, see *PSI* IV 299 (Naldini 8), a third-century Oxyrhynchite letter, arguably Christian in character, clearly from an upper-class family. The former gymnasiarch Ioannes (above, p. 94), attested at the start of the fourth century, is likely to have been a Christian.

[128]On Charite, cf. above n. 123; for the correspondents of Theophanes, above nn. 78-79.

class in appeal.[129] Nor can "nationality," whatever that might mean, or language be shown to have any connection to religious outlook. Classical culture, to which love of native land was no stranger, was the common inheritance of educated persons whatever their background.[130] Christianity was neither Greek nor Egyptian in any adversarial sense, and it has already become clear that the invention and use of Coptic itself is in no sense anti-hellenic.[131] Religion cut across class and language, although the particular use of Coptic to express Egyptian is distinctively Christian.[132]

One of the most obvious signs of Christianization, mentioned already, is the growing number of appearances in the documents of members of the clergy. Despite a substantial body of evidence, however, little is clear about how they were recruited and trained, nor about their numbers and structure. By the fifth century, the clergy formed a substantial cadre in the villages. A document from Karanis, dated 439, is a statement from twelve presbyters, five deacons, and "the rest, small and great, of those from the village of Karanis."[133] Karanis of the later fourth century gives the impression of a dying village, and it is scantily documented in the fifth century, but with seventeen clergy it had either managed a revival or supported too many clergy.[134] Similar terminology, but no information about numbers, appears in a fifth-century Oxyrhynchite letter from the "presbyters and deacons and the rest of the village of Akoutou."[135] These two grades of ministry thus form, with the people of the village, a community (cf. above, p. 138). Whether the deacons served independent churches or were appointed under the presbyters cannot be determined, and the documents are silent on this point. An interesting but enigmatic text of unknown provenance lists the clergy of three establishments, two monasteries and one church, each of which has

[129]The role of the village populations in conversion must not be regarded as simply passive. Cf. W. Klingshirn, "Christianity as a Community Religion in Late Antique Gaul," *APA Annual Meeting Abstracts* (1990) 12.

[130]See Chuvin 1986 for this common inheritance, and the eloquent remarks of Wipszycka 1988, 161-62, on the integration of Egyptian patriotism into panhellenism. Her attempts (145) to claim all the Egyptian poets for paganism, and yet to see them as part of the "lower strata" of the urban elite, however, are both without foundation. Cf. above, p. 252.

[131]Above, p. 253.

[132]See Wipszycka 1988, 158-64.

[133]*P.Haun.* III 58; but the interpretation of Bonneau 1979 is to be preferred to the editor's unconvincing construction of the Greek. The editor's rejection of a reading of *xi*, "60," at the end of line 7 seems correct. Cf. above, p. 138, on this text.

[134]Another fifth-century text for Karanis has now appeared as *P.Col.* VIII 242, but it has no exact date.

[135]*P.Oxy.* LVI 3863.

one deacon and two subdeacons.[136] Karanis' seventeen clergy might thus represent seventeen establishments if each deacon headed a church (or monastery), but that might exaggerate matters. Even at a minimum of twelve, one for each presbyter, and remembering that most churches of the period were (like many in the Mediterranean today) smaller than the structures westerners are likely to envisage, this text gives a healthier impression of the village than its fourth-century documents.

Such a plethora of clergy was not in all likelihood characteristic of the earlier fourth century. There are reports of clusters of ten or more villages in Mareotis under a single presbyter in the time of Athanasius.[137] Whether the concept of "parish" has any meaning in Egypt in this period is hard to say; it is perhaps closer to the mark to describe the situation as complex and fluid, with regularized structures not yet in place and the availability of clergy and churches varying from place to place. Although the general relationship of city and villages provided an early model for a regularized hierarchy of bishops supervising village churches and ordaining their presbyters and deacons, it is impossible to be certain that this model was actually employed during the era of rapid Christianization.[138]

The presbyters, who are also like the Alexandrian patriarch called *papas* (father), evince a sense of collegiality with their counterparts elsewhere, addressing them as *sulleitourgoi*, or coworkers in divine service.[139] In their own circumscriptions they were leaders, answerable only to the bishop, and the lack of evidence for any extensive involvement by presbyters in ordinary economic activity (cf. below, p. 292) suggests that they were full-time professionals supported by church revenues.

The same is not necessarily true of deacons, the lowest of the historic three orders of ministry. Their economic activity is more generally attested, and they seem more generally enmeshed in everyday life.[140] Still lower were the subdeacons, about whom virtually nothing is known, and the lectors (*anagnostai*), an order of lower clergy only

[136]*P.Amst.* I 81 (5c).

[137]Cf. Wipszycka 1983, 198.

[138]Wipszycka 1983, 197-201, discusses the issue of parishes in some detail, perhaps with too rigid and imported a definition; she emphasizes that only after mid-century does evidence for regularized structures start to be available.

[139]E.g., *P.Oxy.* VIII 1162 (Naldini 50) (4c); *SB* XVI 12304 (Panopolis?, 3/4c). The first of these includes deacons in the greeting.

[140]Cf. *P.Sakaon* 48 (Theadelphia, 343), about the family problems of a deacon, which rather suggest the latest stage of a long feud. In *P.Col.* VII 171 (Karanis, 324) a deacon and a monk in effect get involved in a brawl, rescuing Isidoros.

spottily attested in this period[141] and whose ordained status is uncertain.

The bishops, with their seats in the metropoleis, moved on a different plane altogether. There is some reason to think that they were recruited from a wealthier and better-educated stratum of society, and there is some direct evidence of their propertied character.[142] They had a staff of lower clergy. A document from the first half of the fourth century happens to preserve an agreement between Aurelius Besis son of Hakoris with a bishop (otherwise unknown) named Ammonotheon, by which Besis acknowledges that he has been ordained as deacon into the bishop's service and that he must remain in the bishop's service until and unless he is given permission to leave it; the penalties for nonperformance include excommunication.[143]

Egypt, including Libya and the Pentapolis of Cyrenaica, included about 90 to 100 bishoprics by 320, a structure that remained stable for a long time thereafter. Of these some 29 were in the Nile valley (Middle and Upper Egypt), 44 in the Delta, and the balance in Libya and the Pentapolis.[144] The Delta, closer to Alexandria and closer to patriarchate politics, was more densely dotted with bishops than the valley. In some sees, moreover, there might be multiple bishops at one time, though that was usually a temporary matter produced by formation and healing of schism.[145]

A striking feature of the Egyptian church is the lack of offices intermediate between the Bishop of Alexandria, the patriarch, and the local bishops. Though the term "archbishop" is not found until the second half of the fifth century and "patriarch" not until the sixth,[146] the Alexandrian bishop already had most of the power associated with those titles when the church first emerges into visibility, in the early fourth century. The Meletians, it is true, not only came into existence as the result of a challenge to that power but also apparently

[141]*P.Oxy.* XXXIII 2673 (304; cf. above, p. 256 n. 142); *P.Oxy.* LV 3787 (after 313? cf. above, n. 118).

[142]Cf. below p. 292. For an attempt to show on onomastic grounds that the bishops were recruited from higher-class sources, see Martin 1979, 13, and Martin 1981, 48-49. She is concerned there with clergy in general, whom she contrasts with monastics, but in fact her evidence comes from lists of bishops. The analysis is partly vitiated by her claim that Old Testament names reflect Jewish circles in the church, a most implausible notion in post-Hadrianic Egypt.

[143]*CPR* V 11 (early 4c? ed.). Cf. *NewDocs* 1.80 for commentary. Another deacon in episcopal service probably occurs in *P.Lond.* III 981; cf. Naldini 51.

[144]See the analysis by Wipszycka 1983, 183-86.

[145]Cf. van Gucht 1984, 1138-40, on the situation in Hermopolis around 350; on the complexities of the Melitian bishoprics, Martin 1974.

[146]Cf. Feissel 1989, 804-9. Patriarch in general is not used until 449, cf. W. Frend, *ZPE* 79 (1989) 248-50.

rejected altogether the identification of the head of the Egyptian church and the bishop of Alexandria, choosing different people for those roles in their own hierarchy.[147] But that challenge had no lasting effect upon the orthodox ecclesiastical structures.

The patriarch insisted on performing all consecrations to the episcopate himself, despite the lack of any theological basis for such a rule.[148] Nor was this only a matter of ceremony; the patriarch made the final decision about such appointments and probably picked the small body of electors.[149] There were no metropolitans in Egypt, only in Cyrenaica. The patriarch was personally the direct superior of every one of the roughly seventy-five bishops in Egypt, who naturally had as a result remarkably strong bonds of dependency on him. The civil administrative structures of Egypt (particularly in the third century) have been invoked to explain this remarkable autocracy, but so little is known of the third-century church that this must remain speculation.[150]

Whether or not the ecclesiastical structure owed its character to civil models, it remained largely detached from the civil government throughout the fourth century. There are scattered mentions of the church assuming functions that might be regarded as civil, such as mediation and even judgment, but these limited actions give no indication of encroaching on civil authority.[151] Far more striking, but a phenomenon apparently only of the fifth century, is the role of local clergy as village leadership, as seen in the Karanis declaration about water rights from 439 mentioned earlier (p. 283).

As the church became an increasingly powerful institution, the relationship of the higher clergy with the government became more complicated. At the pinnacles, the emperor and the most powerful bishops engaged in duels for control, with Ambrose of Milan eventually getting the upper hand in his struggle of wills with Theodosius.[152] The local churches, however, remained dependent on imperial largess for some of their major construction projects and on imperial favor for other benefits like the right of asylum. Bishops thus became in general intermediaries between people and emperor, the

---

[147]Hauben 1981, 454-55.

[148]Wipszycka 1983, 189.

[149]Wipszycka 1983, 192.

[150]Martin 1981, 46; but Cyrene was part of the structure before it had any civil administrative link to Egypt (hence perhaps the metropolitan for that area?).

[151]See Martin 1979, 18-19, properly cautious; cf. above, p. 225.

[152]Bowersock 1986 gives a compelling account of this process, though ignoring the complications visible once one descends from the Bishop of Milan to more ordinary bishops.

latest ancient manifestation of the pattern of mutual dependence between ruler and communities visible already with Hellenistic kings and cities.[153] The Egyptian bishops, however, acted in the recorded councils as a bloc under the leadership of the bishop of Alexandria, and no doubt the patriarch in turn formed their intermediary with the emperor.[154] At a more local level, church and civil officials were closely intertwined—sometimes allies, sometimes opponents—struggling for control of their communities.[155]

The evident extinction of most pagan festivals (above, p. 269) might create the expectation of their replacement by the church. Surprisingly enough, the documentary evidence for Christian festivals is mostly fifth century and later, late fourth century at the earliest.[156] But when it is found, it indicates a full calendar, with feasts of many saints—as if the festival calendar emerged full-grown. That is most unlikely, of course; parallels with other church institutions suggest that the various pieces were put in place in the second half of the fourth century, as the church became fully institutionalized as official and majority religion, and reached maturity in the first part of the fifth century. The collections of Paschal letters from the bishops of Alexandria, particularly Athanasius, show a developed sequence of Lent, Easter, and Pentecost already in the second quarter of the fourth century, and one apparent private letter referring to both a Lenten fast and Easter confirms that silence is not necessarily significant.[157]

It should be no cause for surprise that most activities of the clergy have left no traces in the documents. Except for copies of scripture, worship services probably made little or no use of writing, with clergy and people alike reliant on memory for the liturgy and hymns. Preaching is preeminently an oral activity.[158] And most daily pastoral activities, like confession and counselling, were equally oral and unrecorded. Occasionally, however, there was a reason to write something down. A complaint about a husband's behavior indicates the intervention of bishops as mediators in a marital quarrel, no doubt a

[153]See Feissel 1989, 818-26.

[154]Cf. Wipszycka 1983, 195-96, who points out also that the Delta increasingly dominates the Egyptian delegations to such outside events.

[155]A process best known from Athanasius' episcopate in Alexandria; cf. the graphic illustration given by *P.Lond.* VI 1914 (*ca* 335). For a governor apparently corresponding in respectful terms with a monk, see *P.Lond.* VI 1924 (with Bagnall 1992c).

[156]*P.Mert.* I 40 (Arsinoite?, 4/5c); *P.Laur.* II 36 (5c ed.; could be later).

[157]*SB* XII 10840; cf. *NewDocs* 1.84.

[158]Its centrality is well described by Averil Cameron 1991, 79.

commonplace occurrence.[159] More often recorded is a priest's use of writing to send a letter to someone in authority on behalf of a parishioner, a ministry of intercession with the secular power. Two letters from clergy in the Abinnaeus archive fit this mold, both trying to get special favors for soldiers (release for one, forgiveness for unauthorized absence for another).[160] Another letter to an anchorite monk asks him to write to the appropriate authority to get the writer discharged from military service, toward which end he had already paid eight solidi.[161] A fragmentary petition of the bishop of Oxyrhynchos to the nome *strategos* concerns the care of some children whose father had died.[162]

As the church became more securely implanted and better endowed, it began to create institutional means of pursuing its charitable aims; the care of the sick in hospitals was particularly important and a significant innovation, but the church also took care to feed the poor, take care of widows and orphans, and in general look after the wretched with the offerings of the more prosperous.[163] The institutional manifestations are visible in the documents of the sixth century and later, and their origins are so far impossible to trace. Literary sources indicate that at least some were in operation by the third quarter of the fourth century, but others may be a product of the fully institutionalized church of the fifth.[164]

Distinguishing the contributions of the secular clergy and of monastics to the pastoral activity of the church is relatively easy in particular cases (cf. below, p. 299, for more on monastic activity). At a global level matters are different. As already noted, the surviving literature is very heavily derived from monks and their sympathizers, and it is full of disparaging remarks about ordinary clergy, enmeshed in the world. It tends therefore to exalt the pastoral work of monks (dangerous though that could be to their monastic vocation, cf. below

---

[159]See Bagnall 1987a and above, p. 195, on this pastoral activity. Mediation in property disputes was no doubt equally prevalent; see the example involving two presbyters in *P.Oxy.* VII 1026 (BL) (5c).

[160]*P.Abinn.* 19 (*BL*; authorship by Apa Mios [cf. *P.Abinn.* 6-8] probable but not certain); *P.Abinn.* 32 = Naldini 40.

[161]*P.Herm.* 7 = Naldini 82 (2nd half 4c).

[162]*P.Oxy.* XXII 2344 (*BL*; *P.Oxy.* LIV, p. 227) (before 336).

[163]See Martin 1979, 20-25 (with a rather gloomy view of the effect of ecclesiastical accumulation of property to support charitable foundations); Wipszycka 1972, 110-19.

[164]See Feissel 1989, 825, for an epigraphical perspective. Martin 1979, 24, places the start of institutionalization of charitable activities in Alexandria in the late fourth century. That view is supported by mentions of hostels and poorhouses in Palladius, *HL* 1.1, 6.5 etc., with reference to the 380s. The Cappadocian fathers have references as early as the 360s.

p. 299) and downplay that of the secular clergy. That bias should not be taken at face value; the occasional glimpses afforded by the documents indicate that pastoral work was a staple activity of presbyters and deacons.[165]

Property and the Church

The fourth century stands between two extremes in the ownership of property by religious institutions. The (pagan) religious establishment of third-century Egypt appears to have owned little land and in general (no doubt with some exceptions) to have been short of income, with the disastrous results for the temples described above. Some individual priests no doubt prospered, but the dominant role in the documentation played by their individual economic activities strongly suggests that the temples themselves did not provide adequate support for the clergy. The economic problems of the empire in the third century do not offer a sufficient explanation for the long-term and large-scale disinvestment in the temples visible over two centuries. Even in the most difficult days of the third century, the cities of Egypt found the resources to invest in civic adornment, colonnades, baths, streets, and the like.

By the sixth century, however, substantial property holdings were in the hands of religious institutions. In the list of one class of arable land at Aphrodito, dated *ca* 525/6, corporate religious bodies own 46 percent of the total.[166] And the fifth and sixth centuries produced an enormous wave of construction of churches and monasteries, in which the physical face of Egypt was largely recast. This wave of building is difficult to date precisely, but little can be assigned to the fourth century with any confidence. Equally, the process by which religious bodies, especially monasteries, came to have extensive landholdings and other property is difficult to trace. The third-century church shows no signs of wealth. Even if the declaration by the lector of the church in the Oxyrhynchite village of Chysis that his church "had neither gold nor silver nor money nor clothes nor beasts nor slaves nor lands nor property either from grants or bequests, excepting only the bronze material which was found and delivered to the *logistes*" reflects a partial cover-up in the context of the persecutions of 303-304,

---

[165]Cf. Martin 1979, 26, on this rivalry. Wipszycka 1983, 193-94, points up the tendentiousness of the monastic sources on the subject of the qualities sought in bishops; in reality, most choices seem to have been of presbyters with pastoral and administrative skills.

[166]See Bagnall 1992b for an analysis.

it is unlikely to be false in the matter of real property, which could be checked in the registers.[167] The list, however, at least suggests what the authorities thought a church might possibly own.

There is no sign of substantial land ownership by the church before midcentury. In the Hermopolite land register, the sole entry for church land lists an amount less than thirty arouras.[168] The next document showing any ecclesiastical ownership is a fragment of a Hermopolite tax register from 367/8, in which the Pachomian monastery of Tabennesi (in the Tentyrite Nome) is shown as the owner of lands in three Hermopolite villages.[169] Amounts of taxes are missing from the text as it is now preserved, and the holdings, apparently rented out, thus cannot be estimated.[170] The monastery also owned a boat on which tax grain was transported.[171] Monastic and other ecclesiastical holdings did not enjoy tax exemption; their growth thus had no impact on imperial tax revenues, although to the extent that it came from holdings of the curial class—a matter of speculation—it could have weakened the base for civic liturgies.

Along with local churches and the monasteries, the patriarchal church of Alexandria acquired land in the nomes. For the fourth century, such holdings are known only from one complaint, submitted to the *riparii* of the Arsinoite Nome by the *pronoetes* of the revenues of the catholic church of Alexandria under the archbishop Theophilos (385-412).[172] The church itself is described as *geouchousa*, "being a landlord" in the Arsinoite, and the object of the complaint is the behavior of two subordinate *pronoetai* in the village of Boubastos, who have failed to appear in the city for a reckoning. The Alexandrian

[167]*P.Oxy.* XXXIII 2673 (304) (cf. *ZPE* 35 [1979] 128).

[168]*P.Herm.Landl.* G534; cf. Bagnall 1992b. The fragmentary *P.Stras.* VII 693, which mentions a church estate, is probably from a similar and related list (cf. *New Docs* 4.131) and may even concern the same land.

[169]Published in Wipszycka 1975 (text reprinted as *SB* XIV 11972, incorporating some of the corrections in Gascou 1976a but retaining the erroneous reading of line 19 which led Wipszycka to claim that the monastery owned an *epoikion*; cf. K. A. Worp, *Archiv*, forthcoming, for further improvements in the text). The date is assigned on the basis of the indiction and prosopographical connections but appears secure. Pachomius' successor Petronius probably brought land along with his family's movables into community ownership, cf. F. Halkin, *Sancti Pachomii Vitae Graecae* (Subs. Hag. 19, Brussels 1932) 54 §80.

[170]Wipszycka 1975, 626, suggests that the amounts were never written, but Gascou 1976a has argued that they have been lost. Inspection of the original supports his view.

[171]Cf. Gascou 1976a for this. Wipszycka (1975, 634-36) argues that the "monastery of Tabennese" refers to the entire Pachomian congregation and that the properties were worked by Pachomian monks in the Hermopolite; but there is no evidence for either proposition, and both run contrary to the direct sense of the text.

[172]*SB* VI 9527.

church was thus asking the civil authorities to arrest the church's employees and send them to the city so that they could be compelled to discharge their duty to their employers. Once again, no quantification of holdings is possible; but if two stewards were required in a single village, the acreage is unlikely to have been trivial. It is impossible, however, to guess in how many villages the Alexandrian church owned property.[173]

Most evidence for ecclesiastical ownership of land is later.[174] There are no surviving leases of land by a church or monastery earlier than the middle of the fifth century,[175] and rent receipts are later still. In general, landholdings of churches and monasteries seem to have consisted (like holdings of wealthy individuals) of a variety of small- and medium-sized plots in different locations. The process of accumulation is still largely invisible. It had begun by the middle of the fourth century, but the evidence seems to indicate that not until a century later had it become a significant and visible phenomenon.

The church accumulated other property as well.[176] Here again, however, the evidence is mostly later: a fifth-century lease of a bakery owned by the church[177] and a lease by the church of Oxyrhynchos to an ironworker, probably of a workshop.[178] The one exception is river shipping, where there is fourth-century evidence.[179] Ownership of ships has sometimes been seen as a liturgical obligation rather than an attractive investment, but there is no evidence that Nile shipping was liturgical.[180] In sea transportation, which certainly involved obliga-

---

[173]Cf. Hollerich 1982, 190, remarking on E. Schwartz's view that the church had substantial holdings already under Athanasius (who, to be sure, had a long reign). Hollerich's notions about possible use of these holdings to disrupt tax collection and shipping are fantastic. See Sirks 1991 for a comprehensive account of the legal structure of the transportation of tax grain.

[174]What follows is based on the excellent discussion of Wipszycka 1972, 34-56. Martin 1979, 10, claims *P.Gron.* 10 for the fourth century, but this is certainly later (*BL*).

[175]The earliest cited by Wipszycka is *P.Lond.* V 1832, but it has no preserved date, and the form of payment used (solidi minus carats) is not attested before the 450s.

[176]See Wipszycka 1972, 57-63.

[177]*P.Alex.* 32 (cf. *BL* 5.4, misreporting Rémondon; there is no reason to choose any particular year).

[178]*P.Oxy.* XVI 1967 (427).

[179]Apart from the boat mentioned above as belonging to the monastery of Tabennesi, see *P.Ross.Georg.* III 6 and *W.Chr.* 434, and cf. above, p. 37.

[180]Cf. Jones 1964, 830, for this suggestion, along with the confused remarks of Hollerich 1982, 203. Jones's only base for the idea, however, was that captains swore under imperial oath to deliver the tax grain loaded on their boats. That is evidence only for the seriousness with which the authorities treated the performance of duties connected with the handling of the taxes; and it tells us nothing at all about any obligations laid on the *owners* of the boats. See now Sirks 1991, 193-95.

tions—along with privileges—however, there is no indication of church involvement.[181]

Perceptions of the church's economic power in the fourth century probably depended as much on the wealth of individual clergy as on that of the churches and monasteries themselves. As in other respects, the clerical orders displayed great variation in wealth. Bishops (*episkopoi*) were, throughout the empire, often recruited from the wealthier classes, a natural outcome of a need for a good level of education, leadership experience, administrative competence, and the ability to deal with secular powers on an equal footing.[182] Several bishops appear in the Hermopolite land registers,[183] some with substantial holdings. A telling sign is the fact that bishops appear in the company of imperial officials and members of the bouleutic order as owners of Nile boats.[184] Church policy called for bishops not to become wealthier during their time in office, certainly not to become wealthier as a result of their office; such prohibitions suggest that self-aggrandizement was a regular problem.[185]

The lower clergy are unlikely to have given an impression of wealth, but their entanglements with worldly goods undoubtedly caused problems. In principle, *presbyteroi* (presbyters), the second order of ministry, were supposed to be supported by the church's resources, mainly the offerings of the faithful. It is unlikely that any such expectations were operative in the case of the third order, the *diakonoi* (deacons).[186] There is ample evidence for their involvement in civic or village liturgies,[187] giving sureties for farmers,[188] paying taxes,[189] and borrowing money.[190] Such men, probably working only

---

[181]See Sirks 1991 on this system, scarcely represented in the papyri.

[182]See generally Wipszycka 1972, 155-60. F. D. Gilliard, "Senatorial Bishops in the Fourth Century," *HTR* 77 (1984) 153-75, argues for a curial origin for most bishops of this period.

[183]See van Gucht 1984 for their identification.

[184]*P.Col.* VII 160 and 161, cf. pp. 103-4 (345-354 and 345-351) are apparently the earliest such evidence; see also *P.Harr.* I 94 (Oxyrhynchos?, late 4c).

[185]See Wipszycka 1972, 95 and 156.

[186]Cf. generally Wipszycka 1972, 154-73 on secular activities of the clergy; unfortunately, she does not routinely distinguish presbyters from deacons. Evidence for deacons as lessees is very late, not before the 490s; her example from 360, *SB* VIII 9776, is actually from 496 (*BL*).

[187]A deacon is the writer of Naldini 97 = *W.Chr.* 420 (Thebaid, 4/5c), a letter about concerns of the office of *diadotes*.

[188]*P.Oslo* III 113 (346), concerning an obscure category of land, on which see J. Gascou, *TravMém* 10 (1987) 115-16.

[189]*PSI* I 43 (Hermopolite, 5c); *SB* XVI 12828 (Hermopolite?, mid-4c).

[190]*SPP* XX 103 (381), with the deacon paying interest in tow rather than cash.

part-time for the church, supported themselves from their own property to a considerable extent. There was no ideology of renunciation of worldly goods by the clergy to interfere with such a pattern, and no doubt the presbyters too continued to draw revenues from their property.

About the church's corporate revenues and expenses there is almost no evidence before the fifth century. The later documentation indicates that particular establishments—churches, monasteries, oratories, and so on—had their own property, revenues and expenses. Episcopal seats drew revenues from not only their own property but also contributions of local churches; Alexandria in turn drew from both the dioceses and its own holdings.[191] Even in the fifth and sixth centuries much remains unknown about the degree to which bishops were able to supervise and draw revenues from establishments in their sees, particularly those located on private property and controlled by wealthy families, and the chronology of the development of private churches is obscure.[192] For the fourth century, there is virtually total silence.[193]

This persistent pattern of scarce evidence from the fourth century, followed by much more substantial (if never adequate) documentation from the middle of the fifth century on, is unlikely to be just the chance of survival, given the range of phenomena for which it can be discerned and the relative overall poverty of the fifth-century record. Rather, it is another reminder of the degree to which the fourth-century church was still in the process of institutionalization and, probably, an indication that patterns seen in the sixth-century papyri cannot necessarily be extrapolated back to the fourth century.

Monasticism

Already in the fourth century Egypt was famous as the birthplace of the two models of monastic life that captured the imagination of the Mediterranean world and its posterity. The life of the solitary ascetic, symbolized by Antony, and the common life of the cenobitic

---

[191]See Wipszycka 1972, 121-53, particularly her discussion (125-30) of *P.Bad.* IV 94, which is to be dated after 450. See also her remarks (25-32) on types of establishments and on offerings.

[192]For their sixth-century form, see L.S.B. MacCoull, "The Apa Apollos Monastery of Pharoou (Aphrodito) and its Papyrus Archive," *Revue bénédictine*, forthcoming.

[193]*P.Haun.* III 67 (Oxyrhynchos, 398) is an order to pay wheat and vegetable seed to a martyr-shrine, evidently as an offering from a well-off layperson (who also appears in *P.Mich.* XV 727, written in the same hand). It is the first such "offering" attested in the documents.

monastery, represented by the Pachomian foundations, formed the poles of this alternative world. Any approach to the subject is encumbered with a long baggage train, most of which must be left behind if there is to be any hope of understanding the role monastic life played in fourth-century Egypt.[194]

"The very fact that modern Europe and America grew out of the Christian world that replaced the Roman Empire in the Middle Ages has ensured that, even today, these notions ["of sexual renunciation, of continence, celibacy, and the virgin life"] still crowd in upon us, as pale, forbidding presences."[195] The renunciation of sexual activity is certainly a subject unlikely to find anyone without an opinion. But the heritage of monasticism interferes in more ways than that obvious one. Western ideas of monastic life are largely formed—whether favorably or not—by the western cenobitic traditions, particularly Benedictine, and it is by no means easy to shake the spell of this imagined world. The western monastic tradition owes much to Egypt, but it must not be confused with it.

For the scholar who tries to listen directly to the ancient sources, banishing the sirens of the West, the dangers are different. In the long run, the monks won. After Chalcedon, an increasingly high proportion of bishops was recruited from the monastic clergy, and the eventual move of eastern Christendom generally to draw bishops only from the celibate clergy meant that the monks controlled the hierarchy. They also displayed great ambivalence about the clergy and ordination, telling many tales about refusing the episcopate.[196] Egypt was perhaps in the vanguard of this development, which meant that the memory of posterity was largely governed by the offspring of monasticism. Even for the period from the fourth to the sixth centuries, the surviving literature (copied, to be sure, mostly by monks) is dominated by the interests and viewpoints of the monastic movement. The heterogeneity of that movement has ensured that posterity does not see with a single lens, but there is little to represent the viewpoint of the ordinary clergy, let alone the ordinary laity.

Even where good fortune does allow another glimpse, it cannot be assumed to be disinterested. The church hierarchy valued monasticism but wanted to control it, and official views of the monks tend to

[194]The subject also has an uncommonly daunting body of scholarship. Cf. Wipszycka and Bravo 1989, 9, on "the growing complexity of studies devoted to the Pachomian corpus."

[195]Brown 1988, 446.

[196]E.g., *HL* 35.10.

be colored by the need to make them fit into approved forms.[197] Monks of various strains tried to magnify the importance of their own traditions and masters.[198] Every literary source must therefore be assumed to work from a partisan perspective of some kind.[199] All of these are valuable, but none can be taken at face value.

There was an intimate link between the types of monasticism and their physical settings. Pachomian monasteries, the closest ancestors of European cloisters, were (uniquely) located in the cultivated land of the valley, sometimes taking over an abandoned village.[200] These settlements, however, play a still lesser role in what one sees today of monasteries in Egypt than they did in antiquity, because like valley villages in general they have left few visible remains; they have either disappeared entirely or are under modern villages. The other extreme, the true hermits of the "inner" or more distant desert, were by modern standards at no great remove, up to some thirty km from the cultivated land in the case of Sketis, but much nearer in others. The hermitages near Esna, for example, lie in a zone about eight km from the Nile and the town,[201] like a monastery considered too far from the cultivated land for convenient access to a bishop.[202] For ancient travelers this was a few hours' journey. Before he moved into the "inner" desert, Antony's center was a day's walk from Karanis.[203] Sketis required twenty-four hours of desert travel.[204]

---

[197]See, e.g., *VAnt* 67 (p. 66.20), with its emphasis on Antony's deference toward the clergy, and the sharp distinction between his reception of bishops and presbyters (honor) and toward deacons (love and joy). The sketch of relations between monks and the episcopate of Alexandria by G. J. M. Bartelink, "Les rapports entre le monachisme égyptien et l'épiscopat d'Alexandrie," *Alexandrina. Hellénisme, judaïsme et christianisme à Alexandrie. Mélanges offerts au P. Claude Mondésert* (Paris 1987) 365-79, is insufficiently suspicious.

[198]See Timbie 1986, 269-70, on the probable distortions and magnifications of Shenoute's activity and reputation by his followers.

[199]Barnes 1986, 368, describes the Greek life of Antony as an Alexandrian "refurbishment more attuned to the spiritual yearnings of an urban Mediterranean culture" than the Coptic. The saint needed interpretation, depending on the interpreter and the audience. Rubenson 1990, 126-44, though rejecting Barnes's views on the version and authorship of the *VAnt*, argues that its author imposes his own Christology and ecclesiology on Antony. See H. Dörries, *Wort und Stunde* I (Göttingen 1966) 145-224, esp. 163, for the greater fidelity of the *Apophthegmata Patrum* in portraying Antony. On the distortions in *HM* and *HL*, cf. Rousseau 1985, 54-55.

[200]Chitty 1966, 4, notes this as a distinctive Pachomian characteristic. Brown 1988, 245, sees this embedded environment as an important factor in the Pachomian struggle to define themselves against the world.

[201]Sauneron and Jacquet 1972, I, xx.

[202]See Krause 1985, 33.

[203]Judge 1977, 78.

[204]*HM* 23.1; the distance is measured from Nitria, just outside the Delta's edge.

The distinctively Egyptian setting that dominates the visual aspect today and appears commonly in the papyri is neither of these, however. Rather, it is on the desert fringe of the cultivated land, only an hour or two from it in most cases. The sharp divide between the black land and the red land allows the monastery to be outside settled society and yet close enough to be intimately linked to it and readily supplied by it. (See plate 9.) Even today, however, in the age of motor transport, the nearby cultivated land, though reachable in a few minutes, can seem separated from these elevated desert perches by an immense gulf.[205] In antiquity that gulf and its essential silence can only have seemed much greater.

The built environments constructed by the monks were matched to the physical settings. The cenobitic of the valley are the least well known, but they seem to have drawn inspiration partly from the regularized order of army camps, partly from the rambling assemblages of Egyptian villages.[206] Typically there was an enclosure wall, gatehouse, houses for monks, refectory, assembly hall, kitchen, infirmary, and guest house, as well as a church.[207] (See storage magazines of a monastery in plate 11.) The similarities to army camps are extensive enough that it can be difficult to be certain whether a particular archaeological site is one or the other.[208]

Of the more extreme locales, the best known is the group of hermitages at Esna, unique though they are so far. These hermitages are in effect underground atrium-style houses, with plans like normal Mediterranean houses belonging to prosperous families, but sunk in the ground.[209] (See plate 8 for an example.) Despite the pervasive attempts of the literary sources to describe a self-denying way of life for ascetics of the desert, many of them clearly lived those lives of self-

[205]Such is, e.g., Naqlun in the Fayum, now being excavated by a Polish team. On its importance for Antonian monasticism, see Rubenson 1990, 46.

[206]Cf. Robert Milburn, *Early Christian Art and Architecture* (Aldershot 1988) 148 on the casual clusters of buildings found at some sites. A useful but rather sloppy bibliography on monastic archaeology may be found in Walters 1974, 331-41.

[207]See Chitty 1966, 22, for a general description; he notes that Pachomius' military experience may have influenced his architectural choices. Goehring 1986, 255, describes excavations at the Pachomian site of Phbow, where a large (30 m in one dimension) fourth-century basilica underlay the great fifth-century structure (36 by 72 m, five aisles).

[208]See the notable example of Taposiris Magna, which J. B. Ward-Perkins, *BSAAlex* 36 (1943-44) 48-53, identified as a monastic settlement; M. Rodziewicz (1988) has more recently argued that it is an army camp with a church inside; he cites a parallel in Syria, but one can now be offered from Egypt, Abu Sha'ar on the Red Sea. See provisionally S. E. Sidebotham, "A Roman Fort on the Red Sea Coast," *Minerva* 3.2 (Mar.-Apr. 1992) 5-8.

[209]Sauneron and Jacquet 1972, I, vi.

mortification in a setting designed to remind them of wealth, not poverty.

The same is generally true of the settlements on the edge of the cultivated land, which tend architecturally as well to a middle ground. These monks had some common facilities, but they lived in small hermitages spread out over a considerable area (called collectively a *laura*), though nothing like the twenty km through which are spread the hermitages of Esna. These individual cells could be sold, allowing the monks considerable control over their lodging. The confrontation of the literary sources with the archaeological remains has made it possible to see that many of these *kellia* were elaborate, with rooms, a court, a well, and other amenities, including cool rooms for the storage of dry bread, movable doors, and even glass in some windows.[210] (An example from Naqlun is shown in plate 10.) Others were less impressive, a room or two, though still often more spacious than cells in cenobitic monasteries. In general, the physical arrangements of these *laurai* give the impression of being modeled after upper-class houses in towns, rather than after the habitations of the poor.[211] They may reflect some difference in economic circumstances between those who chose the solitary or quasi-solitary life and those who populated the Pachomian communities.

Even if these three types of monastic environment, and the ways of life associated with them, were not always as neatly separated as this description makes them seem, they had in common that they were readily distinguished from the ordinary life of town and village civil society. The same is not true of a fourth type of monasticism, a celibate and distinct life by separate communities of men and women carried on in the midst of regular society. Such an intermediate status was seen by Athanasius and no doubt most of the main monastic movement as undesirable, an unworkable compromise, and the patriarch (and later Jerome, too) denounced this way of life.[212] Despite such official disapproval, however, such urban houses for communal monastic life no doubt persisted throughout the fourth century.[213]

[210]See Husson 1979 with full documentation.

[211]Husson 1979, 207; cf. Rousseau 1985, 12-13, who thinks that these arrangements show the expectations of their inhabitants. See *ApPatr* Arsenius 36 and Romanus 1 for the outer limits of such comfort.

[212]See Judge 1977 for a thorough discussion; he argues that the term *apotaktikos* was used for this type of monasticism, but it can hardly have been limited to it to judge from the inconsistent surviving documentation.

[213]*P.Oxy.* XLIV 3203 (400), cited above for the Jewish lessee, involves two female *monachai apotaktikai*, who presumably belong to this genre of urban nuns. Cf. *NewDocs* 1.82 for commentary. A. M. Emmett, "An Early Fourth-Century Female Monastic Community in Egypt?" *Maistor. Classical, Byzantine and Renaissance Studies*

Monks could retain property. There is evidence, for example, for a monk's inheriting, for a nun's being the registered owner of urban property, and for a monk's selling a share of a house.[214] Such documentation continues in succeeding centuries, to the point that clearly monks neither had to give up their property upon entering monastic life nor cease their involvement in managing it subsequently. An anecdote about a monk who had to be told that the field he was helping harvest was his own points up the normality of continued ownership.[215] They even engaged in standard moneylending transactions, including "advance purchases."[216] It must be recognized, however, that negative evidence on this point would consist of silence, which is difficult to evaluate. In no case is anything concrete known about the style of monasticism practiced by the monks whose propertyholdings are documented, except in a few cases of urban monks and nuns. If every Pachomian monk in Egypt had renounced his property or left its management in someone else's hands, the papyri would not show any effects. No deeds of cession exist, however, in which men or women entering a community (or moving to the desert) give either to relatives or to ecclesiastical institutions their worldly possessions.[217] Such things may well have happened, but silence on this point is probably significant.[218]

Nor did being a perpetual virgin spare one from involvement in liturgical obligations incumbent on the patrimony. In an otherwise unremarkable document from the early 370s, two children of a deceased councillor of Panopolis who had held the office of *epimeletes* for military clothing for 369/370 acknowledge to a member of the governor of the Thebaid's staff that they have received from him the

---

for Robert Browning (Byz. Austral. 5, Canberra 1984) 77-83, argues that *P.Oxy.* XIV 1774 and *SB* VIII 9746 do not come from such a community.

[214]*P.Oxy.* XLVI 3311 (*ca* 373-374); *PSI* VI 698 (Oxyrhynchos, 392); *PSI* XII 1239 (cf. *BL* 3.229) (Antinoopolis, 430); *SB* XIV 12021 (Oxyrhynchos, after 377).

[215]*ApPatr* Isaac 4.

[216]*P.Köln* III 151 (Terythis, Kynopolite, 423) is a typical agreement for a loan of two solidi to a villager, with repayment in tow. *P.Lond.* III 1303 (*Tyche* 6 [1991] 197-99) (498) shows a cenobitic nun lending funds for repayment with 2,400 wine jars.

[217]See M. Krause, "Zur Möglichkeit von Besitz im apotaktischen Mönchtum Ägyptens," *Acts of the 2nd International Congress of Coptic Studies* (Rome 1985) 121-33 at 123. Krause argues plausibly that cenobitic regulations requiring renunciation were not enforced in the eighth century; he leaves the question open for earlier centuries, but cf. above, n. 213 for newer evidence; and cf. McGing 1990 and Mac-Coull 1988, 44-45.

[218]The continued ties of property and family so much in evidence make the link between monastic withdrawal and the time-honored Egyptian habit of *anachoresis* more metaphorical than not, despite the attempt of M. Naldini, *Augustinianum* 19 (1979) 75-86, to make a close connection.

receipts concerning their father's office.[219] What is unusual is that one of these children, Didyme, is described as a perpetual virgin, or nun. Her shared responsibility here suggests that she inherited her share of their father's estate and with it the encumbrances it brought.

All these matters of property, however, merely dance around the edge of a central problem for monks, their involvement in matters of the outside world. Monastic literature is clear and explicit on the subject of priorities: It is meritorious to do good in this world, to display fraternal love, hospitality, and love, to give alms, to minister to the sick, to avoid offense; but the contemplative life is better than all of these.[220] The stories of the monks are full of their attempts, sometimes successful and sometimes not, to fend off their admiring visitors. The inherent contradiction of pilgrimages to an ascetic whose virtue lay in solitary contemplation and renunciation of things of this world weighed heavily on the spiritual supermen of the literature. To the extent that they succeeded in preserving their privacy, of course, they are among the silent; such people never figure in the papyri, and only those who were visited by some admirer cut any figure in the literature.

The papyri, then, reveal those less successful or less extreme, monks down a notch or two in the spiritual hierarchy from Antony or even the towering figures of the next rung (though even Antony had a wide circle of disciples and corresponded with them[221]). It is probably no more than chance that the surviving archives of interaction between world and monastery are largely Melitian (see below, p. 308), as nothing suggests that they differed in this regard from the orthodox.[222] Pachomian literature indicates that the steady stream of visitors to monasteries was a major problem.[223] The letters of the faithful ask for prayers, above all for healing. One woman makes her suppositions explicit: "I ask and exhort you, most honored father, that you request for me [help] from Christ that I may receive healing; I believe that in this way through your prayers I am receiving healing, for by

[219]P.Lips. 60 (BL).
[220]HM 1.63-64 (John of Lykopolis).
[221]Rubenson 1990, 40.
[222]The very fragmentary letters, both Greek and Coptic, in P.Nag Hamm. are similar in kind to the Melitian archives; but of course the origin of the Nag Hammadi documents is itself much argued, and internal evidence does not settle the matter. Shelton suggests (P.Nag Hamm. p. 9) that the Coptic letters "show in general a greater tendency to express Christian sentiments and less concern with worldly affairs than the Greek texts." Greek was certainly the standard language of business, but it is hard to know if this tendency was general. P.Nag Hamm. C5 in fact seems the most businesslike of the lot.
[223]Rousseau 1985.

those who are ascetics and religious revelations are exhibited. For I am overcome with a serious disease in the form of a terrible difficulty in breathing."[224] But monks might also be asked to gather contributions for a charitable purpose, like rescuing a wineseller who has gone bankrupt and suffered the sale of his children into slavery,[225] or to stop the harassment of a tenant for his rents.[226] When monks served as presbyters for villages near their monasteries, as some Melitians are known to have done, this pastoral activity was regularized and undoubtedly much increased.[227] Pachomian pastoral work of this sort produced conflict with nonmonastic clergy.[228]

In the return direction flowed contributions to the maintenance of the monastics, largely in the form of food and drink. Letters give the impression that the monks had the wherewithal to eat at least as well as anyone else; dates, lentils, grapes, olives, raisins, and oil all figure in the letters, and no doubt other goods were sent as well.[229] Monasteries did not, however, necessarily depend only on the personal wealth of monks and the offerings of the faithful, and indeed these offerings do not seem to have sufficed. There is, for one thing, abundant mention of monks working for cash wages, particularly at harvest time.[230] And Pachomian monasteries, at least, tended to become diversified economic enterprises. Palladius mentions that the monks included tailors, metalworkers, carpenters, cameldrivers, fullers, gardeners, smiths, bakers, basketmakers, shoemakers, and copyists.[231] If this is accurate, it suggests a degree of economic self-containment, of small-scale replication of the Egyptian economy inside the community; once again, one is reminded of military parallels.

The problem of monastic ownership of land has been discussed above (p. 290). The only evidence for the fourth century is the one papyrus that shows the Pachomian foundation at Tabennesi owned lands in the Hermopolite, some 250 km away. If figures to indicate the size of the holdings had survived, much more could be inferred. But there is no reason to reject the possibility that it also had land in other nomes in the intervening space, not to mention in the nomes to the

---

[224]*P.Lond.* VI 1926 (*NewDocs* 4.123 with extensive commentary). *P.Neph.* contains several appeals to prayers for healing.

[225]*P.Lond.* VI 1915 and 1916 (*BL*).

[226]*P.Nag Hamm.* 68.

[227]See Judge 1977, 85; *P.Neph.* 12, 13, 19 (and cf. introd., pp. 6-7).

[228]Rousseau 1985, 161.

[229]Texts in *P.Lond.* VI and *P.Neph.*

[230]See, e.g., Rousseau 1985, 155.

[231]*HL* 32.9,12; cf. Rousseau 1985, 82.

south of the Tentyrite. It was evidently impossible for the monks to work land given to them if it was not virtually adjacent to the monastery, at least without giving up their presence in the monastic community. For small plots or modest or distant farms, it was not difficult to operate as other absentee landowners throughout the country did, by letting them to local tenants and receiving rents.[232] A local steward might be required, but that posed no great problems. Receiving an entire functioning estate of some size, however, posed complex problems of management that threatened the monastery's ability to distance itself from the world.[233] That severance was always incomplete, however, particularly in the case of monastic establishments in the valley or on its edges, and when in the sixth century religious establishments can be seen owning a very large quantity of land, they continue to have extensive links to "worldly" society.[234]

The economic life of monks thus gives an impression of considerable diversity of wealth and activity, both between types of establishments and within any given type. That variety no doubt reflects in part the divergent social origins of the monks themselves. Ammon came from a wealthy family, whose parents had the means to search for him all through the monasteries of Lower Egypt after he disappeared without a forwarding address.[235] So did Petronius and Theodore, among Pachomius' successors.[236] And they were not the only ones. The character of many monastic dwellings in the desert points clearly to the presence of upper-class monks.[237]

Many signs, however, indicate that the cenobitic monasteries also attracted large numbers[238] of men (and women) from lower economic

[232]Wipszycka 1975, 635, argues that the monasteries did not own land during Pachomius' lifetime, and that individual monasteries did not own land up to 368. The latter, however, is directly contradicted by the papyrus she publishes (see Gascou 1976a for corrections, and above, n. 169).

[233]See Rousseau 1985, 153.

[234]See Goehring 1986, 249-51, pointing out that the presence of seemingly unrelated economic documents like contracts in the Nag Hammadi cartonnage is paralleled by the profusion of worldly documents from the Bala'izah excavations (of a much later period). One could now point also to the contracts in the Nepheros find, which extend over a wider chronological span than the directly monastic letters.

[235]*EpAm* 30. Cf. Wipszycka and Bravo 1989, 7, on Ammon's Greek, which is competent but does not reflect high literary education.

[236]*EpAm* pp. 213-14. See Gascou 1976a, 158-59 n.2, on the inclusion in Pachomian communities of many with a strong background in Greek culture.

[237]Brown 1988, 252, notes this point among other indications that much of the leadership came from the upper classes. Cf. also Rubenson 1990, 118 (who does not distinguish sufficiently the different types of monks). He argues (esp. 141-43) that Antony came, despite the usual characterizations on the basis of *VAnt* and other sources, from an educated, bilingual milieu.

[238]There is no way of telling just how many; *HM* 5.4 and 5.6 (along with many

groups. This situation put a premium on leadership qualities, particularly the ability to make a community out of people of different backgrounds that did not simply replicate the social hierarchies of the world outside.[239] Even after more than a century of monasticism, this challenge persisted. Shenoute had serious problems in the fifth century controlling the "uneducated, undisciplined group that entered the monastery."[240] Egyptian peasants were famously given to resisting authority through sullen avoidance and passive denial of demands placed on them. Transforming their relationship to authority, even to one freely chosen, must have been an extraordinary challenge. Although the founders might, like Pachomius himself, come from relatively humble origins and draw their authority from personal charismatic qualities, the inevitable crisis of institutionalization accompanying the second and third generations of leadership is certain to have demanded education and experience more likely to be found in the upper classes than among peasants,[241] though it is a natural suspicion that these qualities tended to reinforce rather than break down historic patterns of class relations.

Class distinctions are likely also to have played an important part in the role of sexual renunciation in monastic life. The literature of monasticism, in which male avoidance of women figures largely, is largely a literature of the desert ascetics rather than of the more proximate communities of the valley and the desert fringes. Many of these ascetics came to a monastic calling only after producing a family, enabling them thus to separate sex from reproduction and societal responsibility. Even if some of the advanced ages claimed in the literature may arouse suspicion, clearly many departures for the desert were midlife decisions.[242] The thoughtful ascetics whose views survive were able to look upon sexual desire as a manifestation of remaining claims of the self against God, important as such rather than for its sexual character.[243] Their extremes of renunciation left

---

other sources) give hugely impossible numbers, which many have credulously accepted, but there is no way of estimating more accurately.

[239]See the sensitive remarks of Rousseau 1985, 73-75, 88.

[240]Timbie 1986, 265.

[241]Cf. Goehring 1986, 242-43, on the challenge of institutionalizing the Pachomian community.

[242]Cf., e.g., John of Lykopolis (*HM* 1.4), who had avoided women for forty years—and is now ninety. Even a village notable who had slept apart from his wife for thirty years starting at a relatively young age did so after producing three sons (one wonders if there were daughters also, not thought worth mentioning): *HM* 14.13.

[243]Cf. Brown 1988, 231: "But sexual thoughts had a pervasiveness and a resilience that soon led exponents of the desert tradition to place special emphasis upon them. They served as barium-traces, by which the Desert Fathers mapped out

them on the other side of a chasm from normal society, which was freed by its admiration from imitation.[244]

In the Pachomian communities, less distanced from village life, less given to the leisure of meditation, and populated in the main by those less educated to abstract thinking, it is unlikely that very many monks thought along such lines. Pachomian anecdotes, rather, indicate the pervasiveness of embodied temptations, not just the spiritual ones lurking in the desert.[245] Nearby communities of nuns or neighboring villages offered the monks female partners, while within the walls the younger recruits provided attractive opportunities for homosexual relations.[246] Sexually, too, then, the desert seems the home of the distinctive habits and preoccupations of the educated, reflective, and wealthy.

By Schisms Rent Asunder, by Heresies Distrest

Theological controversy was from the earliest days of the church among the most salient characteristics of Christianity. Disagreements among Christians about the content of their proclamation, its intended audience, and what was demanded of its adherents left a marked impress on the literature of early Christianity, both that ultimately deemed canonical and that not.[247] As Christianity emerged from persecution and then received official state support in the first quarter of the fourth century, the controversies of the day exploded into public view, occupying subsequently a prominent place in the history of the church.

Egypt occupies a privileged place in the history of heresy and schism.[248] It owes this in the first place to the personality, career, longevity, and literary fecundity of Athanasius, Bishop of Alexandria from 328 to 373, who made himself a symbol of embattled orthodoxy

---

the deepest and most private recesses of the will."

[244]Brown 1988, 208.

[245]It is, characteristically, in the *Historia Monachorum* (20.2) that one reads about nocturnal seminal emissions. Cf. Brown 1988, 230-31, who does not distinguish monastic settings sufficiently.

[246]Cf. Brown 1988, 246, particularly on the condemnation of homosexuality in this context. The Pachomian women's house was across the river, cf. *HL* 33.

[247]Cf. the general perspective on the complexity of the Egyptian situation in Brown 1988, 86 and 244.

[248]It is striking that Griggs 1990 subtitles his chapter on the fourth century "Schisms and Consolidation." The church of Egypt largely (but in a complex fashion) moved away from Chalcedonian orthodoxy after 451, a process that lies beyond the scope of the present account.

by casting his vicissitudes in terms of theological divisions, mainly the battle against Arianism. But in the last forty years of our own century Egypt has come almost to embody theological heterodoxy by virtue of the spectacular finds of texts from mythic and theological traditions rejected by the organized church and thus ultimately by orthodoxy. The most spectacular of these have been the Nag Hammadi library, commonly referred to as "gnostic,"[249] a whole assemblage of texts, and the Cologne Mani Codex, containing "On the Procreation of His Body." Both gave an original voice back to currents of thought known until then principally from the works of Christian authors attacking them. The further enrichment of the dossier for the Melitian schism (a matter of church governance rather than theology) by the archive of Nepheros and the papyri associated with it has helped to bring that division of the church into clearer focus.

These new texts have engendered vast scholarly industries, entire new subdisciplines with series, journals, congresses, institutes, and monographs.[250] There can be no question of summarizing these here. Rather, the task is to estimate their significance for the church and society. That is not a straightforward matter. First, a text, or even a whole library of texts, does not make a sect or a community. There is clear testimony in Athanasius of intelligence that the libraries of orthodox monasteries contained heterodox works.[251] Not everyone thought that reading such works posed a problem, although the patriarch certainly disagreed.[252] It is impossible to reconstruct a community on the basis of the Nag Hammadi finds, and a wide range of explanatory hypotheses is possible.[253]

[249]A designation justifiably attacked by Morton Smith, "The History of the Term Gnostikos," *The Rediscovery of Gnosticism*, ed. Bentley Layton, II: *Sethian Gnosticism* (Leiden 1981) 796-807.

[250]For the Mani codex a recent assemblage of articles, from which the bibliography can be traced, appears in *Codex Manichaicus Coloniensis: Atti del Secondo Simposio Internazionale* (Cosenza 1990). See also Stroumsa 1986. The essentials of the Nag Hammadi bibliography, much vaster still, are sketched by Rousseau 1985, 25-28. For fuller listings, see D. Scholer, *Nag Hammadi Bibliography 1948-1969* (Leiden 1971) with annual supplements in *Novum Testamentum*.

[251]In his *Festal Epistle* of 367 he ordered their removal. Cf., e.g., Rousseau 1985, 26-28, on the controversies over a possible connection of the Nag Hammadi library to Pachomian monasteries located in the immediate vicinity of the findspot of that collection. For a similar inquiry addressed to Shenoute, cf. Timbie 1986, 270.

[252]Cf. Goehring 1986, 246-47: "As difficult as it may be for us to fathom in this modern age of reason, it was not impossible for one to support Athanasius and read the Nag Hammadi texts." That was not Athanasius' view; in fact it is Goehring's view that strikes one as peculiarly modern.

[253]Cf. A. E. Samuel, "How Many Gnostics?" *BASP* 22 (1985) 297-322, arguing for a numerically marginal position. Taking the question strictly, to be sure, and in Morton Smith's sense, the answer might be zero.

Second, Christian polemicists had a tendency to carry on controversy by highly charged categorization; opponents were denounced by being called names. This tendency, which still thrives today,[254] manifested itself, for example, in the use of "Manichean" as a term of abuse, not necessarily to be taken literally.[255] In the fifth century, Shenoute routinely attacks pagans, Jews, and Arians, but how far these represent real groups of opponents it is hard to say; it has been pointed out that the specific persons described by Shenoute as "pagans" ("Hellenes") were often within, not outside, the church.[256] The perennial tendency to apply theological categories to disagreements over political power within the church only exacerbates the unreliability of ancient literature as a witness to contemporary realities.

A third pervasive source for skepticism about reconstructing the activity of heterodox groups is the role of hindsight in defining orthodoxy. This often-remarked point needs no particular stress, but it can be seen at work in something so seemingly straightforward as the wall inscription from the Monastery of Epiphanius, near Thebes, which records a letter of Athanasius.[257] The letter is headed "From Athanasius, archbishop of Alexandria, to the monks: Athanasius to the orthodox monks everywhere etc." Seemingly innocent enough, but the title "archbishop" is used in no other inscription throughout the Christian world before the second half of the fifth century, and prudent method would suggest that this inscription too was put up at least three-quarters of a century after Athanasius' death, perhaps later.[258] Editing for current needs must then be expected, or at least regarded as a possibility.

Most of the diversity of the fourth-century church finds little reflection in the documentary papyri.[259] This should not be surprising.

[254]"Gnostic," "pagan" and "manichean" are all popular terms of abuse in polemical writing today, as can be seen from a persual of the church press, from one end of the theological spectrum to the other.

[255]Cf. Stroumsa 1986, 314.

[256]Timbie 1986, 266-68; she is also skeptical about his tirades against Melitians, but they at least seem more likely to have existed in the region (cf. below, p. 307). The use of "pagan" for opponents inside the church also flourishes today.

[257]*MonEpiphanius* II 585; for bibliography, see Feissel 1989, 803 (but cf. next note).

[258]Cf. Feissel 1989, 806-9, for epigraphical usage; curiously, he does not (803) draw any conclusion about the date of this inscription. J. van Haelst, *Catalogue des papyrus littéraires juifs et chrétiens* (Paris 1976) no. 625 (with full bibliography) dates it to the 6th/7th century.

[259]An interesting case will be the finds from Kellis (Ismant el-Kharab, Dakhleh Oasis), where Manichean texts in Sub-Akhmimic Coptic have been reported in company with ordinary Greek and Coptic documents found in the excavation of a

Even for a figure so abundantly documented as Dioskoros of Aphrodito "one cannot even say with the hard-and-fast certainty of labeling by hindsight which side of the confessional fence, Chalcedonian or non-Chalcedonian, he came down on."[260] And yet for Dioskoros chance has preserved not only numerous documents but his own compositions on religious themes. If confessional allegiance is obscure for such a man, who traveled to Constantinople, was involved with provincial notables, read widely and was certainly aware of controversies, how are the theological sympathies of other Egyptians of late antiquity to be determined? Most people, then as now, were either uninterested in theological disputes or personalized them by supporting some individual figure in the church whose doctrinal position they could not possibly have summarized or even identified. One papyrus has been identified as containing instructions for delivery of a letter, probably from an Egyptian bishop, to a Syrian bishop known from other sources as an Arian supporter.[261] But there is nothing Arian about the letter, and only thanks to conciliar records can the bishop's Arian sympathies be identified.

All this should not be taken to mean that the variety of views and allegiances reflected in the literary material is not to be taken seriously. There certainly was a diverse religious climate in Egypt in the early fourth century and for some time thereafter. The memoirs of the elderly monk Ammon, who converted to Christianity around 350 and soon became a monk, record that after his baptism he had fallen in with a heretical monk, only to be "rescued" by the presbyter of an Alexandrian church, who steered him toward Theodore and the Pachomian monastery at Tabennesi.[262] Once again, however, the reference is problematic. Would Ammon distinguish in his account between doctrinal heresy, which seems indicated, and ecclesial schism, such as that of the Melitians? The polemical patterns described above would have made it easy—for both the presbyter at the time and Ammon in retrospect—to use a more theological and more highly charged term than the situation actually warranted.

The Melitians are in fact out of all the schismatics and heretics the only group to find substantial reflection in the documents. The schism of Melitios originated in the persecution of 303-305, during which Melitios, the Bishop of Lykopolis, responded to the flight of Peter, the

---

house. See C. A. Hope et al., "Dakhleh Oasis Project: Ismant el-Kharab 1991-92," *Journal of the Society for the Study of Egyptian Antiquity*, forthcoming.

[260]MacCoull 1988, 151.

[261]*PSI* IV 311 = Naldini 39 (Oxyrhynchos, before 341).

[262]*EpAm* 2.

Bishop of Alexandria, from the capital by intervening to ordain priests in the sees of other bishops in the Delta. This action may have seemed to Melitios only a responsible act to provide pastors for vacancies at a time when the local bishops were in flight or under arrest, but it was taken by Peter as a usurpation of his own authority.[263] Peter's denunciation of Melitios led in turn to a controversy over the terms for readmission to the church of those who had denied their faith during the persecutions, and then to excommunication of Melitios and a split between the partisans of Peter and Melitios.

Within a few years, Melitios had moved to construct an independent base of power by ordaining bishops (heretofore strictly the prerogative of the Bishop of Alexandria).[264] By the time the Council of Nicaea (in 325) attempted to reconcile the sides, the Melitians had thirty-six bishops in a network covering the whole of Egypt, though by no means every nome, to oppose to the Catholic body of fifty-seven bishops, similarly distributed.[265] A plan of reconciliation approved at the council called for reintegration of the Melitian bishops and clergy, and it was partially successful;[266] but the choice of Ioannes Arkaph to be a new head of the movement after Melitios' death ended any hopes of full reconciliation.[267] Athanasius' uncompromising stance drove the remaining Melitians to make common cause with his other enemies, despite a total lack of common theological ground; this, in turn, allowed him to depict them as heretics and obscure the real ground of the controversy.[268]

The movement survived all the same, and in the early sixth century "Melitian" monks were still living side by side, apparently on amicable terms with orthodox monks, sometimes changing allegiances, selling monastic cells back and forth.[269] Relations had not always been so peaceful, however; a bloody fight between the orthodox and Melitians is reported in graphic detail in a letter from

[263]There is a detailed analysis of events by Hauben 1989, but his chronology is highly speculative and leads to implausible conclusions, such as producing a controversy over readmission of lapsed church members before the persecutions had ended (cf. his own remarks, 270).

[264]See generally Martin 1974, supplemented by Hauben 1990.

[265]On the distribution, see Hauben 1990, 163-66.

[266]Cf. Hauben 1987 on the controversy over just what was required for readmission to communion with the Catholic church; his own interpretation, however, leads to logical difficulties.

[267]Martin 1974, 37; Hauben 1981, 445, describes the gradual character of the secession.

[268]Martin 1974, 45-50.

[269]McGing 1990, with extensive bibliography and discussion. On the location of the monasteries involved, see also J. Gascou, "Nabla/Labla," *Cd'E* 65 (1990) 111-15.

the mid 330s written from the Melitian viewpoint.[270] The lack of doctrinal differentiation, the similarity of ecclesiastical structure and sources of clerical recruitment[271] all make the identification of Melitians a delicate matter, depending—in the absence of direct reference—on careful analysis of numerous traits.[272] Athanasius accuses them of keeping the bodies of martyrs on view, in opposition to orthodox practice of burying them.[273] Even if true, such traits do not help identify Melitians in everyday life. Three archives, those of Paieous (mid 330s), Papnouthios (early 340s?), and Nepheros (mainly 350s), all probably concerned with various stages in the life of one monastic community on the desert edge of the Herakleopolite and Upper Kynopolite Nomes in Middle Egypt, give a vivid portrait of the Melitians in society.[274]

Much of what these documents reveal is in accord with the general picture of monasticism given above. As the editors of the Nepheros archive remark, "Not only does the world seem fully Christianized, but the Melitians openly consider themselves as entirely normal Christians."[275] The archive, however, sheds far clearer light on the monks' involvement with the world than on the monastery itself. Letters and contracts show an endless flow of goods in and out of the monastery, journeys by monks, prayers and requests for prayers of lay supporters, the borrowing of commodities, the buying and selling of real property, and the involvement of the clergy in the affairs of the neighboring villages.[276] By contrast, the exact position of Nepheros in the monastery is obscure, as is the exact significance of much of the ecclesiastical terminology in use and the whole internal power structure of the community, not to speak of its common spiritual life.[277] Though the worldly engagement of this Melitian community represents a kind of monasticism denounced by

[270]*P.Lond.* VI 1914. Cf. Hauben 1981 for discussion of the context.

[271]Cf. Hauben 1990, 166-67, rightly rejecting nationalistic interpretations of the Melitian schism.

[272]*P.Neph.* pp. 20-21 provides a good example of such analysis.

[273]*Lettres festales et paschales*, ed. L.-Th. Lefort (CSCO 151) 41-42 (A.D. 369).

[274]The first two archives are in *P.Lond.* VI, the last in *P.Neph.* (for chronology, cf. Bagnall 1989b). Cf. *P.Neph.* p. 21 on the Melitian character of the Papnouthios archive (against *P.Lond.* VI 1923 introd.). On some possible political ramifications of Papnouthios' connection with Ausonius (the governor of Augustamnica, it seems), see Bagnall 1992c.

[275]*P.Neph.* p. 5.

[276]*P.Neph.* pp. 17-18, 24-30, summarize this activity.

[277]The best evidence of internal organization, though now supplemented by information in *P.Neph.*, is *P.Lond.* VI 1913 (*BL*), from 334, in which Pageus (Paieous), styled presbyter, transfers temporary power over his monastery to his brother Gerontius during his absence at a council in Caesarea.

writers partial to Antonian or Pachomian rules (above, p. 297), it can be paralleled in orthodox circles.

Schismatics thus resemble the orthodox to the point that they are not always identifiable; they all seem to be characterized by an overwhelming ordinariness. Probably the same was true of Arians and most other groups who could be classed as heretics. That does not deny significance to their doctrinal differences with orthodoxy, any more than the struggle for control of the church in Egypt could be a matter for indifference. But it does mean that none of these groups can—in the fourth century or later—legitimately be seen as a social force distinct from the church as a whole, nor yet as a proxy for some otherwise undocumented political movement.[278]

[278]Cf. Winkelmann 1984, 14-15, citing W. Kaegi and L. MacCoull.

CHAPTER 9

A Mediterranean Society

The Agricultural Economy

The complex reality of the agricultural economy of Egypt is not readily represented by broad generalizations or simple models. A summary of the main circumstances and influences shows why a complex variety of responses necessarily ensued. The ownership of land may be the most fundamental of these elements, though certainly not independent of other variables. At least six major groups of landowners can be identified: (1) A small group of urban residents with large holdings (greater than 100 arouras), probably no more than a hundred families in most nomes; their land was usually spread over multiple locations. (2) Urban residents with holdings sufficient to provide a livelihood from their rents, but not so great as to make the owner wealthy enough to hold his own in the city council; of these there were perhaps three to four times as many as of the really wealthy. (3) Urban residents with small holdings, less than 10 arouras, which cannot have been their principal source of income. These, another 500 families or so per city, must have been partly supported by some other employment or business. (4) Rich villagers, the top 10 percent of the village population, with holdings larger than about 70 arouras. (5) A broad middle range of village owners, with enough land to support a family (10 arouras and up), amounting to three-quarters of the landowners. (6) Village smallholders, less than 10 arouras, who must either have earned part of their living by other means or leased land from others to supplement what they owned.

Overall, this system shows a considerable degree of concentration of landed wealth, although village holdings were far more equal in scale with one another than were urban ones. This concentration shows no signs of increasing at least as late as the middle of the fourth century, nor is there any indication of consolidation of what very large holdings there were. Given the peculiarly semipublic character of the great houses of the sixth century, it is difficult even then to be certain that ownership by individuals was any more concentrated than three centuries earlier.

Different groups of owners had different objectives. In the case of the rich, a secure income capable of bearing the burdens of public office and allowing a fair amount of show was the most obvious need. This is the most important political element in the situation, but it should not be forgotten that the government also needed a stable middle class in the villages, who could shoulder the numerous and sometimes bothersome tax-collection offices required. It would be unrealistic to suppose that all the urban rich were involved in public affairs to the same extent or that all responded in the same way to the stimulus of their position. Despite the well-known predilection of the rich of the Roman world for stability of income, there is good reason to suppose that some looked more ambitiously to maximize the possibilities of their holdings.[1]

Taxation also played a part. Imperial policy, more or less faithfully executed at local levels, laid most of the burden of taxation on landed wealth. It did this in a comparatively impartial manner, levying flat rates (mainly in produce but partly in money) on each unit of land in a particular category.[2] Good land and bad, successful year and poor, all paid essentially the same. Such a policy was easily administered, but it had other effects, perhaps not all foreseen. Compared to a proportionate tax system it exaggerated disparities in value between good and poor land and even led to the abandonment of marginal property.[3] This may not be a bad thing economically, as it should lead to more efficient use of capital and labor, concentrating them where the return is likely to be highest. But, especially when coupled with an administrative system that tried to avoid removal of land from the tax rolls, it could be disastrous for some individuals and offered clear potential for social problems.

The push for higher yields benefited from a long-term change in the technology of irrigation, the tendency to introduce the *saqiya*, or animal-driven waterwheel. With this device the landowner could both irrigate land lying too high to be reached by floodwaters and provide perennial irrigation in place of the annual flooding the Nile offered. Both usable area and frequency of crops could thus be increased. It is

[1]Rathbone 1991.

[2]The higher taxation of "public" land is by this date probably only a vestige of a policy that had benefited urban landowners; the low percentage of public land in fourth-century lists shows that this policy had relatively minor effects.

[3]An example may be helpful. Suppose three plots of land, one regularly yielding 10 art./ar., another 5, another 3. A system of 30 percent taxation makes their net yields 7, 3.5, and 2.1, i.e., preserving the 10:5:3 ratio in income (and something a bit more than that in capital value, to allow for differential yield on other inputs). A flat rate of 3 art./ar. makes their net yields 7, 2, and 0, changing the net income ratio to 3.5:1:0. The last plot will be worthless.

extremely difficult to discern the pace at which this technological revolution took hold. These machines required a lot of capital investment, and evidence for them unsurprisingly comes largely from documents concerning wealthy owners.

The demand of the government for taxes took particular forms, above all wheat (and its chaff), but some barley and about a third of the total in money.[4] These requirements certainly affected what was grown and how it was marketed; ready convertibility was necessary to allow an individual to make part of his surplus available to the government in the form required. This was not the only market force, however. A sizable urban population needed to be fed. Alexandria and the nome capitals together probably accounted for 30 percent of the country's total. Their food requirements certainly created an extensive market for both staples (grains, wine, oils) and other foods like fruits, vegetables, meat, and sweets. Most of this produce was sold on the spot for cash and escapes documentation altogether. Moreover, Egypt probably produced a sizable surplus of some commodities, especially wheat, for export. All of these market influences exerted pressure on the agricultural economy.

These complexities produced a rich variety of responses. Many landowners could not (or would not) work their land themselves. The very rich are the most obvious, but some smaller holders, including many women, were in this position also. Land owned by those who could not work it was easily matched by those who owned no land but needed an income, the half or somewhat more of the rural population that owned nothing. That description might lead one to expect a one-sided dependency, but things were not so simple. Large landlords had choices to make about management, taking into account the size, character, and concentration of their acreage, along with their ability and desire to invest in capital equipment. In some cases direct leasing to tenants was attractive; in others, leasing through a local farmer doubling as land agent; in others, leasing through a hired bailiff. It might seem attractive to run more concentrated estates through hired staff with paid supervisors. No simple rule says which would be more profitable or safer, or what quality would appeal more to the owner. Nor were the landless and near-landless the only lessees. The factor of entrepreneurship looms large in some surviving archives. Farmers with significant personal holdings took the land of others on lease as middlemen, hiring others or leasing it to them in turn.

---

[4]The government required this mainly in gold, but that payment was effected by collectors who took in funds in bronze currency and bought solidi, thus producing a lively internal market in currency.

Closely linked to the structures of tenancy were those of credit. For the tenant, the availability of credit from the landlord was an important attraction, even a necessity. It was not less attractive to the lender, for whom the stability of tenant relationships provided some security. A tenant-borrower would thus offer the landlord a place to put capital to work and an overall return from leasing and lending more lucrative than other means of using the land.[5] Lenders thus also had direct opportunities to restructure their loan activity to take account of changing market conditions in the cities, where most of them lived, or to engage in complex operations to hedge their risk in dealing in commodities.

Through such operations, whether direct management or leasing, the substantial part of rural land owned by city residents formed a direct part of an integrated economy of the entire nome, with choice of crops and credit terms geared to urban and even external needs. Nor were village landownings exempted from these links, for the demands of taxation, the need of credit, the leasing of land by the relatively landless, and the entrepreneurial activities of wealthy villagers all provided connections to the urban economy. The physical closeness of the cities to the countryside, even the encroachment of the rural environment into the edges of the cities, also helped cement this integration. Although virtually all village residents probably grew food for their own consumption, hardly anyone was outside the demands and opportunities of the integrated economy of the province.[6] That economy, driven by numerous stimuli and expressed in millions of transactions, could thus transmit to the village level an enormous amount of diffuse information about supply and demand of various goods and of credit. Some people naturally had more ability to adjust their responses to this information than others, and the more active part of the village population was surely not the least dynamic sector of the Egyptian economy. The *possessores* as always had more choices than others, but it would be a mistake to imagine the poor as entirely passive recipients of the decisions of others; labor was a limited good like any other, and the anger occasionally displayed by landlords and employers at having to compete for it shows the limits of their own power.

[5]See Foxhall 1990, 111-13, for the mutual advantages of the system for tenants and landlords (as well as some risks). Many of her remarks, though based on Italy, Greece, and modern comparative evidence, are directly applicable to Egypt.

[6]Cf. Foxhall 1990, 113: "However much small farmers might have preferred to be isolated from the market economy, it is likely that most tenants (and indeed all peasant farmers) were integrated into market structures, frequently to their detriment."

The Economic Life of Cities

The vertical integration of the agricultural economy had in turn a profound impact on the urban economy, or rather, had a set of effects not all in the same direction. For the elite, the "hundred families," the products of their diverse country holdings to some extent offered self-sufficiency: their own wine, oil, perhaps pottery, building materials, and much else. There is, however, little evidence that the wealthy chose the complete autarky that owning slave craftsmen in a variety of skills could have provided. And whatever choices these families made, the size of the nome capitals was such that even a hundred wealthy households could not have made up more than a fraction of their economies.

The food surplus extracted from the countryside via rents and interest extended far beyond whatever the very rich brought in. Some of it passed through (usually minimal) processing in the cities and was then exported, but probably most was consumed locally except for wheat. It was sufficient to feed a sizable population, but it did not reach that population directly as unearned income from their own rural holdings, for only 10 to 15 percent of urban households owned any noticeable amount of land outside the city.

The enormous diversity of urban occupations documented by the papyri reflects a complex array of transactions. Those with rental or interest income naturally bought goods and services from a wide range of producers and servitors, and a considerable multiplier effect must be expected. Inexpensive labor and a high concentration of wealth meant that a rich diversity of service activities is found. But these and the spending of income from wealth cannot alone explain the size of the urban economy, even taking into account its role in passing through agricultural surpluses to the outside world. For that, two other parts of the economy are essential.

First, most of the better-documented cities show clear signs of craft production of a kind and at a level suited for export, not only for local consumption. The best quantitative evidence is from Oxyrhynchos and from the second half of the third century, but qualitative signs elsewhere and later are consistent with the hypothesis that such export-directed production in textiles was found also at Arsinoe, Hermopolis, Panopolis, and no doubt in other centers not so abundantly documented. Nor would it be safe to assume that this production was limited to textiles merely because chance survivals document that industry the best. The economy of the Delta may have involved quite other products. Papyrus is the most obvious,[7] but tanning, leatherworking, and other derivatives of cattle raising are also likely to have been much more important there than in the valley. The volume of Oxyrhynchos' production of textiles seems to have been at least on a level comparable to late medieval cloth-producing cities of northern Europe. Although the number of persons employed was certainly not of the same level as the agricultural work force of a nome, within the city itself such production may have been the largest engine of the economy.

Second, the metropoleis must have had a significant role in supplying the villages with goods not produced by village workshops. The sharp decline in diversity in the village economies from the second century to the fourth is not likely to be merely a delusion produced by deceptive documentation. Matters were perhaps not so extreme as the Isidoros and Sakaon archives would suggest, but the fourth century saw all the same a continuing growth of urban and village economic interdependence. Some of the profusion of specialized work in the cities may thus have come at the expense of economic diversity within the villages. It is likely, however, that villages would have supported generalists within any given trade; the centralization of production and (equally important) of distribution in the capitals allowed the existence of specialists who could not have flourished in the villages.

The Transformation of Society

This change in the economic relationship of city and villages was not an isolated phenomenon. If the documents do not mislead, the third century witnessed the effective demolition of many structures of village life. The end of any vital existence for most village temples stripped away the literate and respected leadership class the priesthood had long provided and no doubt eliminated to a large degree the ritual occasions that lent the village a sense of itself as a community. Even spatially it is hard to imagine that abandoned and decaying temples, whether in the center of villages or integrated on the periphery, did not depress the ability to perceive the village as something more than a collection of houses. With the temples, too, went writing in the traditional Egyptian scripts and presumably the literature of those scripts, never translated into Greek. The end of the world came slowly, but it was apocalyptic all the same.

[7]See N. Lewis, *Papyrus in Classical Antiquity* (Oxford 1974) 116-17, for the Delta's apparent domination of this important industry.

Another significant element of change was the concentration of the wealthy landowners, with their Greek culture and books, in the metropoleis. As late as the second century, important families still seem in many cases to have had their principal homes in villages; the descendants of Laches in Tebtunis are perhaps the best-documented example, but they were certainly not the only ones. The elevation of the metropoleis to proper urban status, with the opportunities for official roles and all the grand display of city life in the Greek East under Roman rule, may have been the decisive factor that drew the elite to the cities in the third century, so that by the fourth there is no sign of them in the villages. One telling sign is the disappearance of Greek literary papyri from village documentary assemblages of the period.

The apparently undeveloped society of the villages, thus bereft of both Egyptian and Greek leadership, had no institutions to substitute for what had been lost. Individuals might of course grasp for positions like the komarchy, through which the coercive power of the imperial government could be used or abused for their benefit. And anyone of decent means was likely to take up roles from time to time in the structures whereby the village records were maintained, taxes were collected, and order maintained, all largely in the interests of the central government rather than of the villagers themselves. But none of this was truly local in nature; none of it created community. The villages were, by the beginning of the fourth century, essentially lacking in institutions.[8]

By that time the replacement of village institutions had begun, and it continued with decisive results during the fourth century; by the early fifth century, the characteristic structures of Byzantine Egypt had been created. The new developments were several, but they had in common that they involved integration of the villages into the world of the cities. In some ways the easiest element to trace is the church. Village clergy assumed the leadership roles vacated by Egyptian priests and elders, and by the end of the fourth century it is normal to find presbyters and deacons as the representatives of the village population. The presbyters on average had more education than most other villagers, and they certainly had a moral authority deriving from their position. But the clergy also had a direct link to outside power, being the direct subordinates of and appointees of the bishop of the metropolis. Such ties may have been a chancy matter in the earliest years, before the church itself was fully institutionalized, but by the later fourth century that process was well advanced. Pres-

[8]Such institutional weakness is found in other undeveloped societies, of course, such as eighteenth-century America; cf. Wood 1992, 44.

byters thus had a useful line of communication; at the same time, they represented that central power to the villagers. Because bishops were themselves appointed by the bishop of Alexandria, a village priest had only one intermediate step between himself and one of the great notables of the country. Such integration could be desirable or not, according to the circumstances, but it obviously represented a radical change from the far less hierarchically structured world of the Egyptian temples. The patriarch, as he sought to mold the behavior of the population after the teachings of the church, had powerful machinery at his disposal, of a kind never before seen in Egypt.[9] Even if, as is normal, most of the population disobeyed the church's wishes much of the time, the patriarch had a kind of influence hitherto unparalleled.

A second kind of vertical integration was perhaps equally important, the influence in villages of large landowners who lived most of the time in the city. Some of them, perhaps all, maintained country seats as well and spent some time there, but through most of the year they were absentees. And yet they were a presence, physically represented often by their *epoikia* and legally by their business agents. These latter lent money or commodities, leased land, negotiated problems, and interceded with the *geouchos* for more credit or whatever the villagers needed. They became, in an important sense, the economic equivalents of priests, intercessors for the petitioners before an absent deity. The entire apparatus linked the villagers to the seat of wealth and power in the city, in that relational sense of class and status that so pervades this society. Both longstanding Roman ideology and the teachings of the church pushed the notables to use their power for the benefit of their dependents, to replicate the divine work of salvation in their own relationships. It does not, to be sure, take much imagination to see the potential for abuse placed in the hands of the wealthy by this system or that conferred on their agents by the intermediary position they occupied. But it would at least be conceptualized in beneficent terms. These patterns were not entirely new, but they were greatly reinforced by the changes in the relationship of city and village and by the parallel structures of the church. They extended upward beyond the city, of course, to the provincial and imperial levels.

At the administrative level also the process of integration proceeded. The cities acquired responsibility for managing the nomes not in one act but over a long period, going back at least to the creation of their municipal status and gradually taking shape over the

9Cf. Kaster 1988, 74, on the church's tendency to match the social fabric.

course of the third century. The fourth-century creation of the pagi, governed by wealthy metropolitans, cemented the structure with an intermediate layer between the city administration and the village. The city government was both increasingly localized in personnel and yet tightly watched and managed by the provincial governors. Just as the governor held the civic notables responsible for the management of the nome, however, so also these (through the *praepositus pagi*) held the village elite responsible for the local tax collection on which the success of the nome in paying its dues rested.

In the 360s the outlines of a transformation of management of taxation and administration, leading to the privatization of public business and the bureaucratization of the private, start to be visible. The nome's wealthiest families become increasingly and more continuously responsible for village tax collections, to effect which they use private business agents. Toward the end of the century, a letter of such an agent to his superior (but still an agent, not the principal) lists the persons involved in the posting of the tax rates in a village: the landlord, the "more important men" of the village, the *nomikarioi*, and the "more important of the landowners."[10] The *geouchos* has a high-level responsibility for the village's taxes, but he operates in concert with the local leadership, both the landowners whose taxes form a large part of the total revenue and those currently serving in official roles (partly no doubt the same people), and with the ill-known *nomikarioi*, apparently rural fiscal agents with some official power but little independent importance. Public and private, urban and village, come together to fix this official matter in concert, ensuring (as they hope) the proper functioning of a vertically integrated system in which all of them are implicated and the failure of which can mean disaster for all.

One need not believe that the overall degree of economic equality in Egypt declined to see that the fourth century systematized and integrated hierarchies where before they had been far less regularized and connected. Private economic relations, official structures, and ecclesiastical hierarchy operated in concert. As the church came increasingly under the control of the wealthy, these three forms of vertical organization increasingly depended on the same people. In the fourth century, however, that process was still in an early stage.

The integration of the villages into the city economy and society certainly contributed to the dynamic and diverse character the latter possessed, and it conformed Egypt much more closely to the prevail-

---

[10]*SB* XVI 12324; cf. Bagnall 1991a.

ing mode of social and economic organization of the eastern empire. It did not, however, restore to the villages much independent structure or community. Integration thus created a type of dependence that brought with it vulnerability to any decline in the ability of the cities to provide their share of the unequal partnership.

Forms and Uses of Power

The civic elite that wielded this economic power over the village economy was not a fourth century novelty, but its ability to found urban political dominance on a rural base was developed only in the third century and reached maturity in the fourth. This elite was, because of the lack of civic institutions, slower to develop in Egypt than elsewhere in the eastern empire, but its foundations go back to the beginning of Roman rule. Still, it is striking that it comes to full flower in a century sometimes seen as marking the crisis and decline of just this group, the curial class. The translation of economic power into political power is never before so sharply visible in the metropoleis. Indeed, the growing tendency to make large landowners responsible for tax collection in the countryside linked to a remarkable degree private economy and public administration.

This linkage was a mixed blessing for those involved. There were undeniable opportunities for profit in managing the taxes, and clearly at any given time some collectorships would be safer or more profitable than others. But risks and costs were attached to all civic offices. They were the natural result of a system that personalized expenses in the form of compulsory, but conspicuous, contributions by individuals rather than collecting them in the form of taxes.[11] It did not require extraordinary intelligence for many members of this class to realize that the ideal life would be the low taxation made possible by this system coupled with their own personal exemption from the concomitant personal burdens. There were various ways of pursuing this state of bliss, so advantageous for any individual but ultimately fatal to the system. All involved exemption from curial duties, and a complex body of imperial rulings governing these attempts grew up.[12]

The search for personal exemption intersected with the growth of other forms of power: the army, the church, and the state. These hardly form a trio of council-swallowing monsters. Despite the sweeping generalizations of a Libanius, it seems clear enough that the

[11]Cf. Millar 1983, 77, pointing out that it was by personal expenditure, not by taxation, that cities of the second century elsewhere in the Empire had done so much building.

[12]Discussed by Millar 1983.

military did not grab away any substantial share of the available land, nor yet did the bureaucratic *militia*. Nor is there any good evidence to support the belief that the military establishment grew in size.[13] The bureaucracy may have gained somewhat in numbers, but even so a sober estimate shows that they remained tiny by the standards of ages with real professional administrations (above, p. 66). Bishops hardly constituted a great throng, hardly numbering a hundred in an area (Egypt and Libya) of perhaps five million population. The numbers of presbyters and deacons are harder to assess, but they neither threatened the power of the curials nor, probably, much exceeded the numbers of the priests of the Egyptian temples in earlier centuries.

Neither numbers nor absorption of wealth, then, provides an adequate explanation of the threat posed to the curial order, a threat dealt with too often by imperial edicts simply to be dismissed as the hysterical self-interest of a Libanius. Part of the answer certainly lies in the competition of other groups for the members of the curial class. Not only did becoming an imperial official (civil or military) or a bishop have significant attractions for members of this group, these other callings consciously drew from it. High imperial officers and bishops came from the same group of the propertied as did curials, and they may even have begun their careers in their local councils. The emperor and the church needed to recruit men of ability and education, and the civic elite was the natural place to look. A real competition for a limited pool of manpower could not pass unperceived, and in a council with a membership of a hundred or less the loss of even a few would seem threatening to the stability of the rest.[14]

Perhaps still more appalling to the curials, this competition was acute precisely because the civil service, the army, and the church all accumulated substantial power, power acquired in considerable part at the expense of the civic elites as such, even if all drew their membership from the same group. Even with all allowances for ancient and modern exaggerations, officers, bureaucrats, and clergy can all be seen exercising various forms of power, and at all levels of the power structure, from the village to the imperial court. It is hardly surprising that the curial elite saw this phenomenon as threatening, corrupt, and indeed evil. That is the normal reaction of aristocracies to bureaucratic gains at the expense of their own amateur rule.[15] Corruption, though

[13]Cf. Carrié 1986, 457-59, and above, p. 174.

[14]Millar 1983, 96, acutely points up this competition, although without adequately recognizing the church's place in it (cf. however 83-84).

[15]Cf. Cannadine 1990, 244, dealing, to be sure, with (as he emphasizes) an administrative class *not* drawn from the ranks of the aristocracy.

recently proposed as a candidate for chief villain in the decline of the Roman Empire,[16] was neither demonstrably greater in the late empire nor particularly different; it is always someone else acting in his own self-interest, rather than you in yours.[17] More generally, corruption is simply the evil twin of patronage, which is the inherent way of doing business in a very hierarchical, personalized, monarchical society. Where public and private are barely delimited into separate spheres and the government operates by "mobilizing the power of private persons to carry out public ends," and where public discourse lacks any conception of government but monarchy, "corruption" is the only charge available.[18]

In any case, in Egypt as no doubt in most of the empire, these bureaucrats and clerics were "one of us" for the curials, not outsiders, and the decline of the landowners' power should not be exaggerated. The documents suggest that the newer centers of power were readily, if not uncomplainingly, accommodated within the vertically integrated economic and social power structure of the nomes. Their presence may have increased the pressure on the remaining councillors, and that was no doubt unwelcome to them. But there is no reason for the outside observer to adopt their viewpoint and consider their burdens too heavy. Although it is often asserted that the middle ranks of the civic elite faded and eventually disappeared under these pressures, the evidence does not support such claims.[19]

Egypt and Mediterranean Culture

From many points of view the third century seems a decisive watershed in the history of Egypt as part of the Mediterranean world. The singularity of Egypt in earlier periods was real, if easily exaggerated.[20] It remained a distinctive place, of course, but Egypt in the fourth century had reached its maturity as a constituent of the Hellenism of

[16]MacMullen 1988. For an effective demolition of MacMullen's main thesis, see the review by Richard Talbert, *Phoenix* 45 (1991) 85-87.

[17]"In any case, the contemporary corruption that such men denounced was probably less—assuming that such comparisons can be usefully made—than that of the period from the 1780s to 1820s, when it had been the old aristocracy, not the new plutocracy, who had been most successfully on the make." (Cannadine 1990, 229).

[18]See Wood 1992, 80-82, 105, 174-75, on this matter.

[19]Nor, to be fair, can it disprove it. Neither the Apion archives nor the papers of Dioskoros of Aphrodito, the two largest masses of papyri from the sixth century, can be looked to for a portrait of this group in that epoch.

[20]Cf. Rathbone 1989 on the economic side. Such claims of uniqueness serve in many cases mainly as an apology for scholarly unwillingness to come to terms with the quantity and difficulty of the papyrological evidence.

the eastern Roman empire. Political life, agonistic institutions, and economic integration of the countryside with the cities all give the observer a sense of continuity with the world known from the inscriptions of Asia Minor and elsewhere. Even the diet of Egypt had largely completed its transformation from distinctively Egyptian forms to the repertory basic to Mediterranean life, with beer yielding to wine, oil from seeds to olive oil, other grains to wheat. The educated urban residents read the same literature that any other group of Greeks would have known.

Many of their fellow townsmen could neither read nor write Greek, and some of them may even have been unable to speak it. In the countryside around, a partly bilingual, partly Egyptian-speaking population existed with minimal diffusion of competence in writing, thanks to the ability to get by with the help of scribes and family members. The absence of documentation comparable to the papyri makes it impossible to say with any confidence how typical this situation was, but it would be surprising if places like Syria and Armenia, at least, were not broadly similar.[21] And even where no written vernacular later flourished things may still have been much the same.

Third-century Egypt was, moreover, essentially without a written vernacular. That curious state of affairs, brewing since early in Roman rule, was a breach of a tradition more than three millennia old. It is a symptom of a broader collapse of the institutional basis of separate Egyptian culture, the temples. Their neglect, decline, and abandonment over the 250 years from the middle of the first century to the end of the third, though still only a partially known story, cleared the way for the society of the fourth century and for a new form of Egyptian culture, one integrally linked to Christianity. It is impossible to assess the relative contributions to this process of imperial policy, which is unlikely to have thought matters through to such implications, and of organic internal factors.

The new Egyptian civilization, conventionally called Coptic, differs radically from its predecessor. It was, unlike the old temples, distinctively urban in origins and character. The Coptic script and the peculiar form of Egyptian it embodied were the products of an educated bilingual milieu, with 80 percent of its alphabet and 25 percent of its vocabulary taken from Greek. That bilingual milieu can originally only have been urban. It was also, unlike some of the experimentation that led up to it, closely tied to Christianity, a religion very much based in the cities through the third century and which

---

[21]For other parts of North Africa, see F. Millar, "Local cultures in the Roman Empire: Libyan, Punic and Latin in Roman North Africa," *JRS* 58 (1968) 126-34.

adopted a vertical, city-dominated power structure to govern village churches. The use of Coptic was not long, if ever, limited to the city, any more than the city was isolated from the country; but the earliest documentary uses, private letters, were apparently written to (and presumably by) monastic establishments. Because a large part of such correspondence to monks comes from the cities, it is probable enough that so too do the Coptic letters. "Coptic" art is equally a product of commissions by a wealthy city elite, rather than a manifestation of popular village taste.[22]

It may seem paradoxical to point out that precisely this wealthy city elite was the bearer of Hellenism. It is, after all, conventional to look at Coptic culture as an antithesis to the Hellenism of the powerful.[23] But that conventional view is wrong. The Egyptian elite was probably quick to seize the instrumental advantages of learning Greek already under the Ptolemies, and by the third century it had fully internalized the conquerors' culture.[24] "In language, myth, and image it [Greek culture] provided the means for a more articulate and a more universally comprehensible expression of local traditions. This became the precious mission and character of Hellenism in the Christian empire of late antiquity."[25] A look forward to a more finished product, Dioskoros of Aphrodito, confirms this understanding. Drawing on both the common culture of the Greek Mediterranean and the resources of Egyptian traditions, Dioskoros read, wrote documents, and composed original works in both Greek and Coptic. In the middle of the sixth century, he lived as a Christian in a completely Christianized society.[26] For him, Hellenism had no connection to paganism, despite his use of an entire mythological framework that derived from it;[27] the resources on which he drew were the common intellectual inheritance of all educated men.

[22]Thelma Thomas, "Greeks or Copts?: Documentary and Other Evidence for Artistic Patronage During the Late Roman and Early Byzantine Periods at Herakleopolis Magna and Oxyrhynchos, Egypt," *Life in a Multi-Cultural Society* (SAOC 51, Chicago 1992) 317-22.

[23]This viewpoint can still be seen in Irmscher 1989.

[24]Cf. the behavior of elites in British India: G. Viswanathan, *Masks of Conquest: Literary Study and British Rule in India* (New York 1989), esp. 43, 140.

[25]Bowersock 1990, 9; his overestimation of paganism in late antique Egypt does not detract from this fundamentally correct understanding of the relationship of Hellenism and indigenous culture.

[26]Dioskoros' home, Aphrodito, officially a village in the sixth century, had once been a nome metropolis and clearly still had some of the character of one.

[27]See Bowersock 1990, 55-69, for a consideration of the role of Greek literature and myth in Egypt. As he puts it (67), "The poets and artists of Egypt held on to the gods and heroes of the pagan past not to protest anything that went on in the present."

Indeed, it was—another seeming paradox—precisely Christianity that provided the integrating element in Egyptian Hellenism. Right from the start, the Christian character of Coptic and the culture it carried ensured that Hellenism as the vehicle of Egyptian culture was specifically Christian, not pagan. Only with Christianity does Egyptian culture emerge from being a survival in the near-ghetto of the temples. That does not mean, to be sure, that pagans were somehow excluded from this culture; but it does mean that Christianity was the central engine in the enterprise, and the cultivated pagans peripheral, not the reverse. For that matter, pagans who attempted to use Hellenism as the bearer of their indigenous traditions did so in isolation from the original language of those traditions; it was the Christians who actually turned Egyptian into a vehicle for a new era. In that peculiar and narrow sense, the pagans were indeed the Hellenes.

The essential configuration of this society, then, is that of late antique Hellenism. The cities remain flourishing, as for the most part they did in the eastern Mediterranean until the late sixth century.[28] Around them was a generally prosperous countryside, albeit one under constant pressure from the city for higher revenues and subject to stresses from the taxation system and changes in agriculture. This rural world was tightly knit to the cities by economic, administrative, and religious hierarchies. The papyri have not yet yielded a fourth-century counterpart to Dioskoros, someone who will allow the modern observer to see the complex strands of culture and identity gathered through the consciousness of an emblematic, well-defined individual. The fourth-century documentation, rich and urban though it is, has so far a strongly external character, and the published personal archives are village or monastic in origin. The cluster of Hermopolitan family papers comes closest, but even a composite of these reveals frustratingly little about the personal outlook and culture of the upper-class principals.

All the same, the evidence taken together points to a society consciously both Egyptian and Greek, valuing diverse elements of culture that to a modern mind might seem contradictory but that to contemporaries were simply parts of an identity binding them simultaneously to their country with its past and to the larger Mediterranean world ruled from Rome and Constantinople. This outlook,

---

[28]Cf. Charlotte Roueché, *Phoenix* 44 (1990) 298, arguing (on the basis of Aphrodisias, Sardis, and Anemourion) that it is in the third quarter of the sixth century, after Justinian's reign, that the cities of Asia seem to have lost the capability of rebounding from natural disasters. How far Egypt was on a parallel course at that period remains to be studied.

enduringly united with Christianity, is dominant in Egypt by the middle of the fourth century. For a century previously the various elements of the Egyptian late antique synthesis—political, economic, social, and cultural—were in formation, sometimes spurred and rarely deterred by the changing policies of emperors, but finally given stimulus by Constantine's victory over Licinius in 324 and the irretrievable—despite Julian—dominance of Christianity that followed. The papers of Theophanes of Hermopolis in the early fourth century (above, p. 271) show, however, that even before that time the culture of pagans and Christians had converged to a remarkable degree. The elusiveness of his own religious allegiance is eloquent testimony to the synthesis in formation.

Time

The population of the modern western world has long become ac-
customed to the convenience of having a single system for chronological reckoning, with years reckoned from the Christian era and months
and days on the modified julian calendar.[1] Fourth-century Egypt
knew nothing of the era of the incarnation, having instead a whole
collection of systems of dating old and new.[2] The documents cited in
this book sometimes derive much of their importance from their
chronological context; the brief account offered in this appendix is
intended to tell the reader how this information is determined and
how reliable it is.

Under the Roman emperors, beginning with Augustus, Egypt
continued its long-established (but in the context of the Roman
Empire, idiosyncratic) practice of dating documents by the regnal
years of the ruler. On the death of a king, his successor's first regnal
year began immediately, ending at the end of the then-current Egyptian civil year; year 2 then began on the first day (Thoth 1) of the next
year. Year 1, then, might be from a few days to almost an entire year
long. In most documents of the first and second centuries, the name of
the current emperor is given along with the date; doubt arises, then,
only if the document is badly damaged, and then only for the modern
scholar. In the third century there is a growing tendency to omit
imperial names and titles. Where reigns are of normal length (fifteen
to thirty years, say), no one but modern papyrologists would be
inconvenienced by this practice, as it was always clear to the writer
and recipient which year was meant. In the middle of the third
century, however, with numerous changes of reign, some confusion
may have arisen even for contemporaries, and it is often impossible
for us to date a text exactly.

At the beginning of Diocletian's reign, nothing changed. But when
Maximian was associated with him soon after, a novelty was introduced: Diocletian's year 2 became also Maximian's year 1, or year 2

---

[1]On the origins of the use of A.D. reckoning, see the account in Judith Herrin,
The Formation of Christendom (Princeton 1987) 3-6.
[2]A general account of the subject can be found in Bagnall and Worp 1979b; the
main reference works are Bagnall and Worp 1978 and Bagnall and Worp 1979a.

and 1. And when two Caesars were added to the imperial college in 293, the year became 9-8-1. The numerous changes of emperor in the next few decades produced constant changes of regnal years, making them far harder to keep track of and, not incidentally, leading to some truncation and errors.

At the same time that regnal dating was becoming harder to use, the imperial government was pushing the use of consular dating, a system long used in the rest of the empire. Consuls were inherently problematic as a means of dating in a far-flung empire, because their names had to be disseminated over great distances every year and remembered by thousands of scribes to whom they were unfamiliar. Nonetheless, from 293 on consuls' names are widely used to date Greek documents. Where enough of the names is preserved, identification of the year is easy enough, but broken papyri and scribal mistakes are no rarities.

Along with the consuls came the Roman calendar.[3] The Egyptians used their own calendar, based on twelve months of 30 days and a year-end period of 5 days. Augustus ended the migration of the year's start caused by the year's being approximately 365 1/4 days in length, by adding a leap-year every four years; Thoth 1 was thus frozen on 29 August (30 August in leap years). Regnal years were based on this year, consuls on the julian year with its January start.

In late 313[4] or early 314, yet another form of chronological reckoning appears, the indiction. The indiction cycle contained fifteen years and was counted from 312; a new cycle thus began in 327, 342, and so on, and the same year number would recur at intervals of fifteen years. A document dated only by indiction number, therefore, while perfectly clear in its original context, cannot be given an exact date now except by other information such as prosopography. Complicating matters further is the starting date of the indiction year, which was not standardized: coinciding with the civil year (Thoth 1) in the Oxyrhynchite, beginning two months earlier in the Arsinoite, and starting two months earlier still (Pachon 1) in the Thebaid and many other areas.[5]

Although regnal dating virtually disappeared after Constantine, there seems to have been some lingering affection for the system in Oxyrhynchos, where it was eventually blended into a type of era-year

[3]See P. J. Sijpesteijn, "Some Remarks on Roman Dates in Greek Papyri," *ZPE* 33 (1979) 229-40.

[4]*CPR* XVIIA 2.

[5]See Bagnall and Worp 1978, 17-29, for the details of this subject; add comments in *BASP* 16 (1979) 239-44.

dating based on the regnal years of Constantius II and Julian, such that, for example, 392/3 was year 69-38; this year consistently coincided with the Egyptian civil year. An era from the accession of Diocletian also appears in the last third of the fourth century, but it is not used to date papyrus documents until after the Arab conquest; in the fourth century it appears principally in horoscopes and Christian texts.

This multiplicity of systems is undeniably confusing to the user of papyri, but the only really insoluble problem is the lack of sound criteria for dating papyri in which only an indiction number appears. Palaeography is far too approximate, and only gradually does the progress of editing texts provide a context to pin down papyri with only an indiction number. For the ancients, to be sure, the indiction number was the most convenient and widely used means of identifying years, its cyclical nature being immaterial in most circumstances. It survived Byzantine rule in Egypt by many centuries, along with the Egyptian calendar.

Days themselves were identified in documents mostly just by month and day number. The seven-day week begins to occur in papyri in the early third century, but the naming of days in general remained unofficial practice, even though the government's observance of Sunday, from Constantine on, gave it greater authority.[6] Time inside the day, for the most part in the absence of accurate means of measurement, was described by hours, both in reference to past acts and in invitations to social occasions. Hour numbers are attested ranging from one to eleven; what time they refer to, naturally, varied by the season.[7] Expressions like "at a rather late hour" or "at an evening hour" also occur. Such approximation was adequate for most purposes.[8]

In this book, 367/8 denotes a regnal or indiction year beginning in julian 367 and ending in 368; 367-369 refers to a period beginning in 367 and ending in 369. Dates to centuries are given as 4c, and expressions like 4/5c refer to a date at the end of the fourth century or the beginning of the fifth.

---

[6]See *P.Oxy.* XLIV 3174.17n.; *P.Oxy.* LIV 3759.38; K. A. Worp, *Tyche* 6 (1991) 221-30.

[7]Cf. H. Harrauer, *Anal.Pap.* 2 (1990) 132-34, on the use of hours.

[8]For the social changes brought about first by the development of public clocks and then by the miniaturization—and privatization—of timekeeping, see David S. Landes, *Revolution in Time: Clocks and the Making of the Modern World* (Cambridge, Mass. 1983).

Money and Measures

From Augustus to Diocletian, Egypt was an isolated currency zone, supplied by the mint in Alexandria with a billon (small amount of silver in a base of bronze) coinage unique to the province. Whereas in the rest of the empire a standard imperial coinage was in use, in Egypt it is found only in small amounts. The monetary unit was the drachma, in official reckoning equated to the sestertius, with the tetradrachm, four-drachma piece, equated to the denarius. In papyri of the Roman period, however, the denarius is virtually absent (apart from military texts); instead, the drachma appears, and for large amounts the talent (6,000 drachmas).

All this changed with Diocletian's currency reform of 296.[1] Egypt was provided with a three-part currency: gold coins (aurei, or solidi) of about 5.45 g; silver coins (argentei), of about 3.4 g each; and three denominations of billon coins, the largest (at about 10 g) tariffed at 12.5 denarii, doubled in 300 to 25 denarii. The minting of silver soon ceased, but gold and billon coinage continued. Constantine reduced the weight of the gold solidus to about 4.5 g, where it remained throughout the period discussed in this book. The billon coinage underwent a long and complex history of weight reductions, coupled with changes in its percentage of silver, leading ultimately (under Valentinian) to a standard coin (referred to in the sources as "nummus"), which had only a trace of silver, probably an amount below what ancient technology was capable of detecting.

At any given time, gold coins, which were effectively pure, could be purchased openly for billon coinage. The amount of billon necessary to buy gold depended on two factors: the amount of silver and bronze in the coins, and the relative values of gold, silver, and bronze at the moment. Because the government announced the value of coins, the effect of reducing the size or silver content of a coin without changing its stated value was to increase the nominal value of gold stated in units of account, that is, denarii. If, let us say, a solidus was worth 1,000 den. when there was n amount of equivalent silver[2] in a

---

[1]What follows is based on Bagnall 1985b.

[2]I.e., silver plus equivalent value of bronze (the ratio fluctuated, but 1:120 is officially attested).

nummus tariffed at 25 den., it would take 40 nummi to purchase a solidus. If the amount of equivalent silver in the nummus declined to one-half n, and the value of the nummus was still officially stated to be 25 den., then any sensible owner of solidi would now charge 80 of the new coins, or 2,000 den., for a solidus. This is in fact what happened; the value of gold and of other commodities, stated in denarii,[3] took great leaps upward until the 380s. This increase followed the repeated reductions in the weight standard and silver content of the billon coinage; government action, several times increasing the official value of these miserable coins, only accelerated the process.

The results are visible in the papyri chiefly in the vast numbers appearing as the prices of goods and services as the century wears on. To moderns, traumatized by contemporary periods of inflation or their memory and used to a purely fiduciary currency printed on paper, the term "inflation" has seemed appropriate for this phenomenon. It is hard to believe that an economy would not be drastically and adversely affected by it. But the economy of fourth-century Egypt was not like the modern one. The modern economy is permeated by institutions vulnerable to inflation because they rest on fixed amounts in accounting units: bank deposits, debt instruments, and salaries. Assets and liabilities are to a considerable degree intangibles in paper form and based on long-term credit. Banking played a minor role in the Egyptian economy, loans were mostly small and for short terms (and many not in units of currency but in gold or in commodities), and most people's assets consisted of land, precious metals, livestock, slaves, and other physical goods. Even billon currency did not lose in value; the old currency was worth more than the new, so it was hoarded, melted down, or called in. Salaried employees were few apart from those of the state—soldiers and officials—and the state was at least capable of altering their pay, even if it did not always do so.

The economy, based on wheat and other agricultural commodities, continued to function. Gold became increasingly the means of making major purchases, lending money, and fixing future obligations of other sorts; it was, rather anomalously, both money and commodity itself. Uncoined precious metal was also in circulation, apparently in significant amounts. It was in the government's interest to see this metal turned over to it for coining, but it was the natural instinct of ancient individuals to hoard bullion. Various levies in bullion were tried to extract the metal, to reverse the process of hoarding. How successful they were is hard to say, but it is generally believed

[3] Or drachmas, at 4 dr. = 1 den., for the old terms drachma and talent, though representing no real coins, continued in use as accounting terms for many decades.

that gold coinage increased from Constantine onward. The papyri, however, still show numerous transactions in billon; the prices in these must always be looked at in terms of prevailing levels at the time, for the numbers mean nothing by themselves.

The following abbreviations are used for units of currency: den. (denarius), dr. (drachma), sol. (solidus), and tal. or T. (talent).

The papyri use numerous measures. Those of significance in this book, with metric equivalents and abbreviations, are the following:

Arouras (ar.), of land: 2,756 m²; a square kilometer thus contained 363 ar.

Artabas (art.), of wheat, barley, and other dry foods: Various artabas were in use, but the common one was equal to 4.5 *modii Italici*, or 38.78 liters. An artaba of wheat weighed a bit over 30 kg. Cf. Rathbone 1983. The nonstandard forty-choinix artaba sometimes referred to would thus have held about 25.2 kg (Casson 1971 consistently uses this as a standard weight).[4]

Pounds, Roman: About 327g.

Sextarius (Greek *xestes*), measure of volume: about .546 liter.

---

[4]In *M.Chr.* 342 (*BL*) (Arsinoite, 326), a boat of 200 art. burden loads 200 *centenaria* of charcoal, or 20,000 Roman pounds, about 6.5 metric tons. This figure fits well with an artaba weighing somewhat over 30 kg.

The Nomes

Egypt had from early times been organized in geographical units described in Greek as *nomoi*, called nomes in English. The list of the nomes, fixed at an early date, is transmitted unchanged in temple texts thereafter. Over several millennia, however, their numbers, names, and boundaries had altered repeatedly. What follows describes what is known of their identity and size in the fourth century. The ancient Egyptian nome numbers are given in parentheses. The Greek names of the chief cities are given next, then (in parentheses) the modern name where known. Figures for area are very approximate,[1] particularly for the poorly documented nomes, where boundaries may have moved without our having evidence of the fact. The order proceeds from south to north and sometimes back and forth across the Nile. Past Memphis, our evidence is so slender that even as imprecise an enumeration as that given here becomes impossible.[2]

Upper Egypt

Ombite (1). Metropolis: Ombos (Kom Ombo). Area: 72 km[2] (26,136 arouras).

Apollonopolite (2). Metropolis: Apollonopolis Magna (Edfu). Area: 137 km[2] (49,731 arouras). From Ombos to Apollonopolis, about 65 km.

Latopolite (3). Metropolis: Latopolis (Esna). Area: 225 km[2] (81,675 arouras) for original nome before Hermonthite created. From Apollonopolis to Latopolis, about 50 km.

Hermonthite (part of old 3). Metropolis: Hermonthis (Armant). Area: unknown. From Latopolis to Hermonthis, about 40 km.

---

[1]They are derived from Butzer 1976, 74, with modifications as individually indicated. Figures in arouras (the standard Egyptian measure of area, which equals 2,756 m[2]) are converted by multiplying the area in square kilometers by 363.

[2]The names of the metropoleis are given as used in this book, mostly (as traditionally in papyrological usage) forms that served as the stem for the nome names. But the names used in official parlance were in this period often more grandiose, like "city of the Oxyrhynchites" for Oxyrhynchos. See for "Arsinoe" most recently L. Casarico, *Aegyptus* 67 (1987) 161-70.

Diospolite/Theban (4). Metropolis: Diospolis = Thebes (Luxor). Area: 284 km² (103,092 arouras). From Hermonthis to Thebes, about 12 km.

Koptite (5). Metropolis: Koptos (Qift). Area: 331 km² (120,153 arouras). From Thebes to Koptos: 45 km.

Tentyrite (6). Metropolis: Tentyra (Dendera). Area: 300 km² (108,900 arouras). From Koptos to Tentyra: 22 km.

Diospolite Parva (7). Metropolis: Diospolis Parva (Hiw). Area: 306 km² (111,078 arouras). From Tentyra to Diospolis: 55 km.

Great Oasis. Metropolis: Kysis.

Thinite (8). Metropolis: Thinis (El Birba). Area: 613 km² (222,519 arouras). From Diospolis to Thinis: about 57 km.

Panopolite (9). Metropolis: Panopolis (Akhmim). Area: 575 km² (208,725 arouras). From Thinis to Panopolis: about 28 km.

Antaiopolite (10). Metropolis: Antaiopolis (Qaw el-Kebir). Area: 531 km² (192,753 arouras). From Panopolis to Antaiopolis: 58 km.

Hypselite (11). Metropolis: Hypsele (Shutb). Area: 125 km² (45,375 arouras). From Antaiopolis to Hypsele: about 37 km.

Apollonopolite Parva (12). Metropolis: Apollonopolis Parva (or Heptakomias). Area: 206 km² (74,778 arouras). Location unknown.

Lykopolite (13). Metropolis: Lykopolis (Asyut). Area: 250 km² (90,750 arouras). From Hypsele to Lykopolis: about 8 km.

Koussite (14). Metropolis: Koussai (el-Qusiya). Area: 272 km² (98,736 arouras). From Lykopolis to Koussai: 67 km.

Hermopolite (15 and 16). Metropolis: Hermopolis (el-Ashmunein). Area: about 1140 km² (413,820 arouras), less area of Antinoite. From Koussai to Hermopolis: 42 km.

Antinoite. Metropolis: Antinoopolis (Sheikh Ibada). Area: small tract taken from Hermopolite. From Hermopolis to Antinoopolis, about 8 km.

Kynopolite (17). Metropolis: Kynopolis (Sheikh Fadl). Area: perhaps about 110 km² (39,930 arouras).[3] From Hermopolis to Kynopolis: about 100 km.

[3]Butzer gives an area of 563 km², but it is clear from Drew-Bear 1979 and Pruneti 1981 that all of the Kynopolite's West Bank territory was divided between the Oxyrhynchite and Hermopolite in this period (roughly three-fourths to the Oxyrhynchite), leaving only a small amount of East Bank territory: how much, cannot be determined, without knowing how much the Nile may have moved its bed in the intervening time. Moreover, some of the territory of nome 18 may have come to the Kynopolite—reduced perhaps by the eastward move of the Nile. Estimates for the Oxyrhynchite and Hermopolite have been increased by about 330 and 115 km², respectively.

Oxyrhynchite (19). Metropolis: Oxyrhynchos (el-Bahnasa). Area: about 780 km² (283,140 arouras).[4] From Kynopolis to Oxyrhynchos: about 20 km.

Herakleopolite (20). Metropolis: Herakleopolis (Ihnasya el-Medina). Area: 643+ km² (233,409+ arouras). From Oxyrhynchos to Herakleopolis: about 67 km.

Arsinoite. Metropolis: Arsinoe (Medinet el-Fayum). Area: about 900 km²? (326,700 arouras). From Herakleopolis to Arsinoe: about 26 km.

Nilopolite (21). Metropolis: Nilopolis (location unknown). Area: 133 km² (48,279 arouras).

Aphroditopolite (22). Metropolis: Aphroditopolis (Atfih). Area: 200 km² (72,600 arouras). From Herakleopolis to Aphroditopolis: about 47 km.

Lower Egypt

Memphite (1). Metropolis: Memphis. Area: 281 km² (102,003 arouras). From Aphroditopolis to Memphis: about 45 km.

[4]Cf. note 3 above for the Oxyrhynchite-Hermopolite division of the West Bank part of old nome 17. The Oxyrhynchite had at one point in the fourth century 202,534 arouras of arable land taxable in grain; see Bagnall and Worp 1980a; that would represent about 72 percent of the estimated total area.

Glossary of Technical Terms

agonothetes: civic magistrate responsible for public games

agoranomos: civic magistrate responsible for supervision of markets and notarial records

anachoresis: withdrawal or flight from settled society

apaitetes: tax collector, for items other than wheat

archephodos: village chief of police

archiereus: chief religious magistrate of a city

aroura: Egyptian unit of land measurement

artaba: Egyptian (orig. Persian) unit of measurement of volume of grains

billon: mixture of bronze and silver used in coinage

boule: city council

bouleutes: member of a city council; adj. bouleutic

cenobitic: connected to a style of monastic life involving common quarters and activities as opposed to a more solitary regimen

Chalcedon: site of the fourth ecumenical council, 451

chrysargyron: a money tax on trades

curialis: Latin general equivalent of bouleutes or bouleutic

dekaprotos: third-century civic tax-collection office

dioiketes: Egypt-wide imperial financial official in third century

dux: military commander responsible for a province

eirenarch: local peace-keeping magistrates

ephebes: young men undergoing gymnasium training

ephoros: a village official

epistates: supervisor or overseer of some function or group

epistrategos: governor of a district of Egypt, under the prefect

equestrian: order in Roman society immediately below the senatorial

eutheniarches: civic official responsible for orderly food supply

exegetes: civic official with various responsibilities including record-keeping and baths

Fayum: district in central Egypt to west of Nile valley, source of large numbers of papyri; the ancient Arsinoite Nome

gnoster: a village official

gymnasiarch: office holder in a Greek city responsible for management of gymnasium and in particular supply of oil for it *katholikos*: imperial financial official responsible for all of Egypt

kephalaiotes: lit. "headman," usually a village official with tax and/or transportation duties

komarch: highest-ranking village official

komogrammateus: village secretary

kosmetes: civic official with responsibility for ephebes

liturgy: (1) compulsory public service; (2) order of religious service

logistes: imperial official in overall charge of a particular city (Latin curator civitatis)

majuscules: capital or large letters

metropolis (pl. -eis): chief town of a nome (q.v.); adj. metropolitan

naubion: unit of volume

neokoros: temple warden, honorific priestly function

nome: administrative district of Egypt; see Appendix 3

onomastic: referring to (personal) names

pagus: subdistrict of a nome

pericope: set cycle of readings for the church year

politeuomenos: member of the political elite, usually a bouleutes

praepositus pagi: governor of a pagus

praeses: governor of a part of Egypt

prefect: governor of Egypt

propoliteuomenos: principal member of the political elite, perhaps presiding magistrate

prytanis: presiding officer of the boule

quadrarius: a village tax official

riparius: magistrate with law enforcement duties for entire nome

scholasticus: imperial legal official

sextarius: unit of liquid or solid volume (for wine, oil, etc.)

sitologos: village collector of wheat and barley taxes

solidus: standard gold coin (from Constantine on, 1/72 of a Roman pound)

strategos: in Roman Egypt, governor of a nome

syndikos: imperial official with administrative and judicial duties in a particular city (Latin defensor civitatis)

systates: civic official with recordkeeping responsibilities

tesserarius: a village tax official

tetrarchic: referring to the period 293-305, when four emperors headed by Diocletian ruled by the Roman Empire

Bibliography

A general bibliography for this period, but limited to English-language works, may be found in Alden Rollins, *Rome in the Fourth Century A.D. An Annotated Bibliography with Historical Overview* (Jefferson, N.C. 1991). For abbreviations used in this book other than those listed below, see above, p. xi.

Bagnall, Roger S.
1977a	"Bullion Purchases and Landholding in the Fourth Century," *Cd'E* 52: 322-36.
1977b	"Price in 'Sales on Delivery,'" *GRBS* 18: 85-96.
1978a	"Property-holdings of Liturgists in Fourth-century Karanis," *BASP* 15: 9-16.
1978b	"P.NYU 15 and the Kephalaiotai of Karanis," *StudPap* 17: 49-54.
1980	"Theadelphian Archives: A Review Article," *BASP* 17: 97-104.
1982a	"Religious Conversion and Onomastic Change," *BASP* 19: 105-24.
1982b	"The Population of Theadelphia in the Fourth Century," *BSAC* 24: 35-57.
1985a	"Agricultural Productivity and Taxation in Later Roman Egypt," *TAPA* 115: 289-308.
1985b	*Currency and Inflation in Fourth Century Egypt* (*BASP* Suppl. 5, Atlanta).
1985c	"The Camel, the Wagon, and the Donkey in Later Roman Egypt," *BASP* 22: 1-6.
1987a	"Church, State and Divorce in Late Roman Egypt," in *Florilegium Columbianum: Essays in Honor of Paul Oskar Kristeller* (New York) 41-61.
1987b	"Conversion and Onomastics: A Reply," *ZPE* 69: 243-50.
1988	"Greeks and Egyptians: Ethnicity, Status, and Culture," in *Cleopatra's Egypt: The Age of the Ptolemies 305-30 B.C.* (Mainz) 21-27.
1989a	"Official and Private Violence in Roman Egypt," *BASP* 26: 201-16.
1989b	"Fourth-Century Prices: New Evidence and Further Thoughts," *ZPE* 76: 69-76.
1991a	"The Taxes of Toka," *Tyche* 6: 37-43.
1991b	"An Arsinoite Metropolitan Landowning Family in the Fourth Century," *Pap.Lupiniensia* 2.

1992a   "Military Officers as Landowners in Fourth Century Egypt," *Chiron* 22: 47-54.

1992b   "Landholding in Late Roman Egypt: The Distribution of Wealth," *JRS* 82: 128-49.

1992c   "Count Ausonius," *Tyche* 7: 9-13

1992d   "Combat ou vide: christianisme et paganisme dans l'Égypte romaine tardive," *Ktema* 13 (1988 [1992]) 285-96.

1993   "Slavery and Society in Late Roman Egypt," in *Law, Politics and Society in the Ancient Mediterranean World* (Sheffield) 220-40.

Bagnall, Roger S., and Bruce W. Frier
forth.   *The Demography of Roman Egypt.*

Bagnall, Roger S., and Klaas A. Worp
1978   *The Chronological Systems of Byzantine Egypt* (Stud.Amst. 8, Zutphen).

1979a   *Regnal Formulas in Byzantine Egypt* (*BASP* Suppl. 2, Missoula).

1979b   "Chronological Reckoning in Byzantine Egypt," *GRBS* 20: 279-95.

1980a   "Grain Land in the Oxyrhynchite Nome," *ZPE* 37: 263-64.

1980b   "Papyrus Documentation in Egypt from Constantine to Justinian," in *Miscellanea Papyrologica*, ed. R. Pintaudi (Florence) 13-23.

Bagnall, Whitney S.
1974   *The Archive of Laches. Prosperous Farmers of the Fayum in the Second Century* (Diss. Duke 1974).

Bailey, D. M.
1991   *Excavations at El-Ashmunein* IV. *Hermopolis Magna: Buildings of the Roman Period* (London).

Baines, John
1983   "Literacy and Ancient Egyptian Society," *Man* n.s. 18: 572-99.

Baines, John, and Jaromír Málek
Atlas   *Atlas of Ancient Egypt* (Oxford).

Barnes, Timothy D.
1985   "The Career of Abinnaeus," *Phoenix* 39: 368-74.

1986   "Angel of Light or Mystic Initiate? The Problem of the *Life of Antony*," *Journal of Theological Studies* n.s. 37: 353-68.

Battaglia, Emanuela
1989   *'Artos.' Il lessico della panificazione nei papiri greci.* (Biblioteca di Aevum Antiquum 2, Milan).

Bernand, Etienne
1979   "Epigraphie grecque et histoire des cultes au Fayoum,"
          in *Hommages à la mémoire de Serge Sauneron* II (Cairo) 57-
          76.
1984   "Epigraphie grecque et architecture égyptienne à l'é-
          poque impériale," in *Hommages à Lucien Lerat* (Centre de
          Recherche d'Histoire Ancienne 55, Paris) 73-89.
Biezunska-Malowist, Iza
1977   *L'esclavage dans l'Égypte gréco-romaine* II (Wroclaw-
          Warsaw-Krakow-Gdansk).
Boak, Arthur E. R.
1933   Ed., *Karanis: The Temples, Coin Hoards, Botanical and
          Zoölogical Reports, Seasons 1924-31* (University of
          Michigan Studies, Humanistic Series 30, Ann Arbor).
1935   *Soknopaiou Nesos: The University of Michigan Excavations
          at Dimê in 1931-32* (University of Michigan Studies,
          Humanistic Series 39, Ann Arbor).
Bonneau, Danielle
1964   *La crue du Nil* (Paris).
1979   "Un règlement de l'usage de l'eau au Vᵉ siècle de notre
          ère," in *Hommages à la mémoire de Serge Sauneron* II
          (Cairo) 3-23.
1983   "Communauté rurale en Egypte byzantine?" *Recueils de
          la Société Jean Bodin pour l'histoire comparative des institu-
          tions* 41: *Les communautés rurales*, pt. 2: *Antiquité* (Paris)
          505-23.
1985   "Les fêtes Amesysia et les jours épagomènes (d'après la
          documentation papyrologique et égyptologique)," *ASAE*
          70: 365-70.
1988   "Agrophylax," *Proceedings of the XVIII International Con-
          gress of Papyrology* 303-15.
Borkowski, Zbigniew
1990   "Local Cults and Resistance to Christianity," *JJurPap* 20:
          25-30.
Bowersock, G. W.
1986   "From Emperor to Bishop: The Self-conscious Trans-
          formation of Political Power in the Fourth Century
          A.D.," *CP* 81: 298-307.
1990   *Hellenism in Late Antiquity* (Ann Arbor).
Bowman, Alan K.
1971   *The Town Councils of Roman Egypt* (Am.Stud.Pap. 11,
          Toronto).
1974   "Some Aspects of the Reform of Diocletian in Egypt,"
          Akten XIII. Int. Pap. 43-51.

1980   "The Economy of Egypt in the Earlier Fourth Century,"
        in *Imperial Revenue, Expenditure and Monetary Policy in the
        Fourth Century A.D.*, ed. C. E. King (BAR International
        Series 76, Oxford) 23-40.

1985   "Landholding in the Hermopolite Nome in the Fourth
        Century A.D.," *JRS* 75: 137-63.

1991   "Literacy in the Roman Empire: Mass and Mode," in
        Literacy in the Roman World (*JRA* Suppl. 3, Ann Arbor)
        119-31.

1992   "Public Buildings in Roman Egypt," *JRA* 5: 495-503.

Bradley, Keith R.

1991   *Discovering the Roman Family: Studies in Roman Social
        History* (New York).

Braudel, Fernand

1981   *The Structures of Everyday Life: The Limits of the Possible*
        (Civilization and Capitalism, 15th-18th Century, I, New
        York).

Braunert, Horst

1964   *Die Binnenwanderung. Studien zur Sozialgeschichte Ägyp-
        tens in der Ptolemäer- und Kaiserzeit* (Bonner Historische
        Forschungen 26, Bonn).

Breccia, E.

1926   "Teadelfia e il Tempio di Pneferôs," in *Monuments de
        l'Egypte gréco-romaine* I (Bergamo) 87-131.

Bresciani, Edda

1968   *Rapporto preliminare delle campagne di scavo 1966 e 1967.*
        (Istituto di Papirologia della Università degli Studi di
        Milano, Missione di Scavo a Medinet Madi [Fayum-
        Egitto] = Testi e documenti per lo studio dell'Antichità
        20, Milan).

1976   *Rapporto preliminare delle campagne di scavo 1968 e 1969.*
        (Istituto di Papirologia della Università degli Studi di
        Milano, Missione di Scavo a Medinet Madi [Fayum-
        Egitto] = Testi e documenti per lo studio dell'Antichità
        53, Milan).

Brown, Peter

1988   *The Body and Society: Men, Women, and Sexual Renuncia-
        tion in Early Christianity* (New York).

Butzer, Karl W.

1976   *Early Hydraulic Civilization in Egypt. A Study in Cultural
        Ecology* (Chicago).

Cadell, Hélène

1970 "Le vocabulaire de l'agriculture d'après les papyrus grecs d'Egypte: problèmes et voies de recherche," *Proc. XII Congr. Pap.* 69-76.

1989 "Les archives de Théophanes d'Hermoupolis: Documents pour l'histoire," *Egitto e storia antica* (Bologna) 315-23.

Cameron, Alan

1976 *Circus Factions. Blues and Greens at Rome and Byzantium* (Oxford).

1982 "The Empress and the Poet: Paganism and Politics at the Court of Theodosius II," *YCS* 27: 217-89.

Cameron, Averil

1985 *Procopius and the Sixth Century* (Berkeley).

1991 *Christianity and the Rhetoric of Empire* (Berkeley).

Cannadine, David

1990 *The Decline and Fall of the British Aristocracy* (New Haven).

Carrié, Jean-Michel

1974 "Les *Castra Dionysiados* et l'évolution de l'architecture militaire romaine tardive," *MEFRA* 86: 819-50.

1976 "Patronage et propriété militaires au IVe s. Objet rhétorique et objet réel du discours *Sur les patronages* de Libanius," *BCH* 100: 159-76.

1977 "Le rôle économique de l'armée dans l'Égypte romaine," *Armées et fiscalité dans le monde antique* (Colloques nationaux du CNRS 936, Paris) 373-93.

1981 "L'Egypte au IVe siècle: Fiscalité, économie, société," *Proc. XVI Congr.* 431-46.

1982 "Le 'Colonat du Bas-Empire': un mythe historiographique?" *Opus* 1: 351-70.

1983 "Un roman des origines: les généalogies du 'Colonat du Bas-Empire,'" *Opus* 2: 205-51.

1984 "Figures du 'Colonat' dans les papyrus d'Egypte: lexique, contextes," *Atti XVII Congresso* 939-48.

1986 "L'esercito: trasformazioni funzionali ed economie locali," *Società romana e impero tardoantico. Istituzioni, Ceti, Economie*, ed. A. Giardina, 1 (n.p.) 449-88, 760-71.

forth. "Observations sur la fiscalité du IVe siècle pour servir à l'histoire monétaire," *L'"inflazione' del IV secolo d.C.* (Rome).

Casson, Lionel

1971 *Ships and Seamanship in the Ancient World* (Princeton).

Cauderlier, Patrice
   1978   "Sciences pures et sciences appliquées dans l'Égypte
             Romaine: Essai d'inventaire Antinoïte," *Recherches sur les
             'Artes' à Rome* (Publ.Univ.Dijon 58, Paris) 47-72.

Cavallo, Guglielmo
   1974   "Papiri greci letterari della tarda antichità: Note grafico-
             culturali," *Akten XIII Int. Pap.* 69-81.

Champlin, Edward
   1991   *Final Judgments: Duty and Emotion in Roman Wills 200
             B.C.-A.D. 250* (Berkeley).

Chitty, Derwas J.
   1966   *The Desert a City* (Oxford).

Chouliara-Raïos, Hélène
   1989   *L'abeille et le miel en Égypte d'après les papyrus grecs*
             (*Dodone*, parartema 30, Ioannina).

Chuvin, Pierre
   1986   "Nonnos de Panopolis entre paganisme et christi-
             anisme," *BAGB* 45: 387-96.

Clarysse, Willy
   1980   "Philadelphia and the Memphites in the Zenon Archive,"
             Studies on Ptolemaic Memphis (Studia Hellenistica 24,
             Leuven) 91-122.
   1987   "Greek Loan-words in Demotic," *Aspects of Demotic Lexi-
             cography. Acts of the Second International Conference for
             Demotic Studies, Leiden, 19-21 September 1984*, ed. S. P.
             Vleeming (Leuven) 9-33.

Clarysse, Willy, and Alfons Wouters
   1970   "A Schoolboy's Exercise in the Chester Beatty Library,"
             AncSoc 1: 201-35 and 5 plates.

Cockle, Helen
   1981   "Pottery Manufacture in Roman Egypt: A New
             Papyrus," *JRS* 71: 87-97.

Cohen, Edward E.
   1992   *Athenian Economy and Society: A Banking Perspective*
             (Princeton).

Coptic Studies
   (1990)   *Coptic Studies. Acts of the Third International Congress of
             Coptic Studies, Warsaw, 20-25 August 1984* (Warsaw).

Coulson, William D. E., and Albert Leonard, Jr.
   1981   *Cities of the Delta, I: Naukratis. Preliminary Report on the
             1977-78 and 1980 Seasons* (American Research Center in
             Egypt, Reports 4, Malibu).

Crawford, Dorothy J.
1971 *Kerkeosiris: an Egyptian Village in the Ptolemaic Period* (Cambridge).
1974 "*Skepe* in Soknopaiou Nesos," *JJurPap* 18: 169-75.
1979 "Food: Tradition and Change in Hellenistic Egypt," *World Archaeology* 11: 136-46.

Demicheli, Anna Maria
1976 *Rapporti di pace e di guerra dell'Egitto romano con le popolazioni dei deserti africani* (Univ. di Genova, Fondazione Nobile Agostino Poggi 12, Milano).

Derda, Tomasz
1991 "Necropolis Workers in Graeco-Roman Egypt in the Light of the Greek Papyri," *JJurPap* 21: 13-36.

Diethart, Johannes M., and Klaas A. Worp
1986 *Notarsunterschriften im byzantinischen Ägypten* (MPER n.s. 16, Vienna).

Dixon, D. M.
1972 "The Disposal of Certain Personal, Household and Town Waste in Ancient Egypt," in Ucko, Tringham, Dimbleby 1972, 647-50.

Dixon, Suzanne
1992 *The Roman Family* (Baltimore)

Donadoni, Sergio et al.
1974 Ed., *Antinoe (1965-1968). Missione archeologica in Egitto dell'Università di Roma.* (Università di Roma, Istituto di studi del Vicino Oriente, Serie archeologica 21, Rome).

Drew-Bear, Marie
1979 *Le nome Hermopolite. Toponymes et Sites.* (Am.Stud.Pap. 21, Missoula).
1984 "Les conseillers municipaux des métropoles au IIIe siècle après J.-C.," *Cd'E* 59: 315-32.
forth. Reedition of the archives of the city council of Hermopolis, in *CPR* (Vienna).

Dummer, Jürgen
1968 "Angaben der Kirchenväter über das Koptische," *Probleme der koptischen Literatur* (Wiss.Beitr. Halle-Wittenberg 1968/1 [K2]) 17-55.

Dunand, Françoise
1979 *Religion populaire en Égypte romaine* (EPRO 76, Leiden).
1991 "Miracles et guérisons en Égypte tardive," in *Mélanges Étienne Bernand* (Annales Litt. Univ. Besançon 444, Paris) 235-50.

Duncan-Jones, Richard P.

1981   Review of *Armées et fiscalité dans le monde antique*, in *Gnomon* 53: 80-82.

1985   "Who Paid for Public Buildings in Roman Cities?" *Roman Urban Topography in Britain and the Western Empire*, ed. Francis Grew and Brian Hobley (Council for British Archaeology, Research Report 59).

1990   *Structure and Scale in the Roman Economy* (Cambridge).

El-Fakharani, Fawzi

1983   "Recent Excavations at Marea in Egypt," in Grimm-Heinen-Winter 1983, 175-86.

Feissel, Denis

1989   "L'évêque, titres et fonctions d'après les inscriptions grecques jusqu'au VIIᵉ siècle," *Actes du XIe Congrès international d'archéologie chrétienne* I (Vatican) 801-28.

Fikhman, I. F.

1965   *Egipet na rubeje dvukh epokh* (Moscow).

1969   "Grundfragen der handwerklichen Produktion in Ägypten vom 4. bis zur Mitte des 7. Jahrhunderts u. Z.," *Jb. f. Wirtschaftsgeschichte* (1969) 4: 149-71.

1979   "Les 'patrocinia' dans les papyrus d'Oxyrhynchus," *Actes XV Congr. Int. de Pap.* IV 186-94.

Flaubert in Egypt

(1972)   *Flaubert in Egypt: A Sensibility on Tour. A Narrative drawn from Gustave Flaubert's Travel Notes & Letters*, ed. Francis Steegmuller (London).

Foraboschi, Daniele, and Alessandra Gara

1981   "Sulla differenza tra tassi di interesse in natura e in moneta," *Proc. XVI Int. Congr. Pap.* 335-43.

1982   "L'economia dei crediti in natura (Egitto)," *Athenaeum* n.s. 60: 69-83.

Foxhall, Lin

1990   "The Dependent Tenant: Land Leasing and Labour in Italy and Greece," *JRS* 80: 97-114.

Frier, Bruce W.

1982   "Roman Life Expectancy: Ulpian's Evidence," *HSCP* 86: 213-51.

1983   "Roman Life Expectancy: The Pannonian Evidence," *Phoenix* 37: 328-44.

Frisch, Peter

1986   *Zehn agonistische Papyri* (Pap.Colon. 13, Opladen).

Gagos, Traianos, and Peter van Minnen

1992   "Documenting the Rural Economy of Egypt: Three Byzantine Papyri from Alabastrine," *JRA* 5: 186-202.

Gallazzi, Claudio, and Guy Wagner
  1983   "Un lot d'ostraca grecs inédits au Musée du Caire: une archive d'un domaine privé en Thébaïde au début du Ve siècle," *BIFAO* 83: 171-89, pll. XXXII-XXXVII.

Gardiner, Alan H.
  1957   *Egyptian Grammar*, 3rd ed. (Oxford).

Garnsey, Peter, and Richard Saller
  1987   *The Roman Empire: Economy, Society and Culture* (Berkeley).

Gascou, Jean
  1976a   "*P.Fouad* 87: Les monastères Pachômiens et l'état byzantin," *BIFAO* 76: 157-84.

  1976b   "Les institutions de l'hippodrome en Égypte byzantine," *BIFAO* 76: 185-212.

  1983   "Notes de papyrologie byzantine," *Cd'E* 58: 226-34.

  1985   "Les grands domaines, la cité et l'état en Egypte byzantine (Recherches d'histoire agraire, fiscale et administrative)," *Travaux et Mémoires* 9: 1-90.

  1989   "Les codices documentaires égyptiens," *Les débuts du codex*, ed. A. Blanchard (Bibliologia 9, Turnhout) 71-101.

Gascou, Jean, and Leslie S. B. MacCoull
  1987   "Le cadastre d'Aphroditô," *Travaux et Mémoires* 10: 104-58 with 10 plates.

Geremek, Hanna
  1969   *Karanis. Communauté rurale de l'Égypte romaine au IIe au IIIe siècle de notre ère* (Archiwum Filologiczne 17, Wroclaw-Warsaw-Kraków).

  1981   "Les politeuomenoi égyptiens sont-ils identique aux bouleutai?" *Anagennesis* 1: 231-47.

  1990   "Sur la question des *boulai* dans les villes égyptiennes aux Ve-VIIe siècles," *JJurPap* 20: 47-54.

Goehring, James E.
  1986   "New Frontiers in Pachomian Studies," in Pearson and Goehring 1986, 236-57.

Goitein, S. D.
  1967-88   *A Mediterranean Society. The Jewish Communities of the Arab World as Portrayed in the Documents of the Cairo Geniza* (Berkeley). Vol. 1, 1967, *Economic Foundations*; vol. 2, 1978, *The Community*; vol. 3, 1978, *The Family*; vol. 4, 1983, *Daily Life*; vol. 5, 1988, *The Individual*.

Golvin, J.-C., et al.
  1986   *Le camp romain de Louqsor (avec une étude des graffites gréco-romains du temple d'Amon)*, by M. El-Saghir, J.-C. Golvin, M. Reddé, et al. (Mém.IFAO 83, Cairo).

Graeco-Coptica
(1984)   *Graeco-Coptica. Griechen und Kopten im byzantinischen Aegypten* (Martin-Luther-Universität Halle-Wittenberg, Wissenschaftliche Beiträge 1984/48 [I 29], Halle).

Grenier, Jean-Claude
1989   *Les titulatures des empereurs romains dans les documents en langue égyptienne* (Pap.Brux. 22, Brussels).

Griggs, C. Wilfred
1990   *Early Egyptian Christianity From its Origins to 451 C.E.* (Coptic Studies 2, Leiden).

Grimm, Günter, Heinz Heinen, and Erich Winter
1983   *Das römisch-byzantinisch Ägypten. Akten des internationalen Symposions 26.-30. September 1978 in Trier* (Aegypt. Trev. 2, Mainz am Rhein).

Hanson, Ann Ellis
1991   "Ancient Illiteracy," *Literacy in the Roman World* (*JRA* Suppl. 3, Ann Arbor) 159-98.

Hareven, Tamara K.
1991   "The History of the Family and the Complexity of Social Change," *AHR* 96: 95-124.

Harris, William V.
1988   "On the Applicability of the Concept of Class in Roman History," in *Forms of Control and Subordination in Antiquity*, ed. T. Yuge and M. Doi (Tokyo) 598-610.
1989   *Ancient Literacy* (Cambridge, Mass.).

Hauben, Hans
1981   "On the Melitians in P.London VI (P.Jews) 1914: The Problem of Papas Heraiscus," *Proc. XVI Int. Congr. of Pap.* 447-56.
1987   "La réordination du clergé mélitien imposée par le Concile de Nicée," *AncSoc* 18: 203-207.
1989   "La première année du schisme mélitien (305/306)," *AncSoc* 20: 267-80.
1990   "Le catalogue mélitien réexaminé," *Opes Atticae. Miscellanea philologica et historica Raymondo Bogaert et Hermanno Van Looy oblata* (*Sacris Erudiri* 31 [1989-90], Steenbrugge) 155-67.

Hobson, Deborah W.
1983   "Women as Property Owners in Roman Egypt," *TAPA* 113: 311-21.
1984   "Agricultural Land and Economic Life in Soknopaiou Nesos," *BASP* 21: 89-109.
1985   "House and Household in Roman Egypt," *YCS* 28: 211-29.

1993   "The Impact of Law on Village Life in Roman Egypt," in *Law, Politics and Society in the Ancient Mediterranean World* (Sheffield) 193-219.

Hollerich, Michael J.
1982   "The Alexandrian Bishops and the Grain Trade: Ecclesiastical Commerce in Late Roman Egypt," *JESHO* 25: 189-207.

Holz, Robert K., et al.
1980   With David Stieglitz, Donald P. Hansen and Edward Ochsenschlager, *Mendes* I, ed. Emma Swann Hall and Bernard V. Bothmer (Cairo).

Hopkins, Keith
1991   "Conquest by Book," *Literacy in the Roman World* (*JRA* Suppl. 3, Ann Arbor) 133-58.

Horsley, G. H. R.
1987   "Name Change as an Indication of Religious Conversion in Antiquity," *Numen* 34: 1-17.

Husselman, Elinor M.
1953   "The Granaries of Karanis," *TAPA* 84: 56-73.

1979   *Karanis Excavations of the University of Michigan in Egypt 1928-1935. Topography and Architecture* (Univ. of Michigan, Kelsey Museum of Archaeology, Studies 5, Ann Arbor).

Husson, Geneviève
1979   "L'habitat monastique en Égypte à la lumière des papyrus grecs, des textes chrétiens et de l'archéologie," in *Hommages à la mémoire de Serge Sauneron* II (Bd'E 82, Cairo) 191-207.

1983   *OIKIA: Le vocabulaire de la maison privée en Egypte d'après les papyrus grecs* (Univ. de Paris IV - Paris-Sorbonne, Papyrologie, 2, Paris).

Irmscher, Johannes
1989   "Le origini della civiltà copta," *Egitto e storia antica dall'Ellenismo all'età araba* (Bologna) 469-73.

Isaac, Benjamin
1990   *The Limits of Empire: The Roman Army in the East* (Oxford).

Jasny, Naum
1944   *The Wheats of Classical Antiquity.* (Johns Hopkins University Studies in Historical and Political Science, 62.3, Baltimore).

Johnson, A. C.
1936   *Roman Egypt to the Reign of Diocletian* (Economic Survey of Ancient Rome 2, Baltimore).

Johnson, A. C., and L. C. West
  1949   *Byzantine Egypt: Economic Studies* (Princeton University Studies in Papyrology 6, Princeton).

Jones, A. H. M.
  1964   *The Later Roman Empire, 284-602*, 2 vols. (Oxford).

Judge, E. A.
  1977   "The Earliest Use of Monachos for 'Monk' (P.Coll.Youtie 77) and the Origins of Monasticism," *JbAC* 20: 72-89.

Judge, E. A., and S. R. Pickering
  1977   "Papyrus Documentation of Church and Community in Egypt to the Mid-Fourth Century," *JbAC* 20: 47-71.

Kaimio, Jorma
  1979   "Latin in Roman Egypt," *Actes XV Congr. Int. Pap.* III 27-33.

Kákosy, László
  1984   "Das Ende des Heidentums in Aegypten," *Graeco-Coptica* 61-76.

Kaplan, Michel
  1986   "L'économie paysanne dans l'Empire Byzantin du Vème au Xème siècle," *Klio* 68: 198-232.

Karayannopulos, Johannes
  1958   *Das Finanzwesen des frühbyzantinischen Staates* (Südost-europäische Arbeiten 52, Munich).

Karpozelos, A.
  1984   "Realia in Byzantine Epistolography X-XIIc," *ByzZ* 77: 20-37.

Kaster, Robert A.
  1988   *Guardians of Language: the Grammarian and Society in Late Antiquity* (Berkeley).

Keenan, James G.
  1975   "On Law and Society in Late Roman Egypt," *ZPE* 17: 237-50.

  1980   "Aurelius Phoibammon, son of Triadelphus: A Byzantine Egyptian Land Entrepreneur, *BASP* 17: 145-54.

  1981   "On Village and Polis in Byzantine Egypt," *Proc. XVI Int. Congr. of Papyrology* 479-485.

  1984a   "Aurelius Apollos and the Aphrodite Village Elite," *Atti XVII Congr. int. di pap.* 957-63.

  1984b   "The Aphrodite Papyri and Village Life in Byzantine Egypt," *BSAC* 26: 51-63.

  1985a   "Notes on Absentee Landlordism at Aphrodito," *BASP* 22: 137-69.

  1985b   "Village Shepherds and Social Tension in Byzantine Egypt," *YCS* 28: 245-59.

1989   "Pastoralism in Roman Egypt," *BASP* 26: 175-200.

forth.   "On Egyptian Society in Late Antiquity," *ANRW* [written in 1978].

Kehoe, Dennis
1988   "Allocation of Risk and Investment on the Estates of Pliny the Younger," *Chiron* 18: 15-42.

1990   "Pastoralism and Agriculture," *JRA* 3: 386-98.

Keimer, Ludwig
1924   *Die Gartenpflanzen im alten Ägypten* I (Hamburg-Berlin).

Kemp, Barry J.
1972   "Temple and Town in Ancient Egypt," in Ucko, Tringham, Dimbleby 1972, 657-80.

Kertzer, David I., and Richard P. Saller
1991   Eds., *The Family in Italy from Antiquity to the Present* (New Haven).

Koskenniemi, Heikki
1956   *Studien zur Idee und Phraseologie des griechischen Briefes bis 400 n. Chr.* (Suomalaisen Tiedeakatemian Toimituksia/Annales Academiae Scientiarum Fennicae, ser. B, vol. 102.2, Helsinki).

Krause, Martin
1985   "Die Beziehungen zwischen den beiden Phoibammon-Klöstern auf dem thebanischen Westufer," *BSAC* 27: 31-44.

Krüger, Julian
1990   *Oxyrhynchos in der Kaiserzeit. Studien zur Topographie under Literaturrezeption* (Europäische Hochschulschriften 3 ser. 441, Frankfurt am Main).

Lajtar, Adam
1991   "*Proskynema* Inscriptions of a Corporation of Iron-workers from Hermonthis in the Temple of Hatshepsut in Deir el-Bahari: New Evidence for Pagan Cults in Egypt in the 4th Cent. A.D.," *JJurPap* 21: 53-70.

Lallemand, Jacqueline
1964   *L'administration civile de l'Égypte de l'avènement de Dioclétien à la création du diocèse (284-382)* (Mémoires de l'Académie royale de Belgique, Cl. des Lettres, 57.2, Brussels).

Lefort, L. Th.
1950   "Gréco-Copte," in *Coptic Studies in Honor of Walter Ewing Crum* (Boston) 65-71.

Lesquier, J.
1911   "Fouilles à Tehneh, 1908," *BIFAO* 8: 113-33.

Lewis, Naphtali
   1982   *The Compulsory Public Services of Roman Egypt* (Pap.Flor. 11, Florence).

Lewuillon-Blume, Marianne
   1979   "Problèmes de la terre au IVᵉ siècle après J.-C.," *Actes XV Congr. Int. de Pap.* IV 177-85.
   1985   "Enquête sur les registres fonciers (*P. Landlisten*): essai sur les titres et professions," *Cd'E* 60: 138-46.
   1988   "Enquête sur les registres fonciers (*P. Landlisten*): la répartition de la propriété et les familles de propriétaires," *Proc. XVIII Int. Congr. Pap.* II 279-86.

Lucas, A., and J. R. Harris
   1962   *Ancient Egyptian Materials and Industries*, 4th ed. (London).

Lukaszewicz, Adam
   1986   *Les édifices publics dans les villes de l'Égypte romaine* (Studia Antiqua, Warsaw).

MacCoull, Leslie S. B.
   1985   "Three Cultures under Arab Rule: The Fate of Coptic," *BSAC* 27: 61-70.
   1986   "Coptic Documentary Papyri as a Historical Source for Egyptian Christianity," Pearson and Goehring 1986, 42-50.
   1988   *Dioscorus of Aphrodito: His Work and His World* (Berkeley).
   1989   "Patronage and the Social Order in Coptic Egypt," *Egitto e storia antica dall'Ellenismo all'età araba* (Bologna) 497-502.
   1990   "Verso una nuova comprensione dell'Egitto copto," *Studi e ricerche sull'Oriente cristiano* 13: 3-17.

MacDonald, William A.
   1986   *The Architecture of the Roman Empire* II (New Haven).

MacMullen, Ramsay
   1986   "Judicial Savagery in the Roman Empire," *Chiron* 16: 147-66 (repr. MacMullen 1990, 204-17).
   1988   *Corruption and the Decline of Rome* (New Haven).
   1989   "The Preacher's Audience (AD 350-400)," *Journal of Theological Studies* n.s. 40: 503-11.
   1990   *Changes in the Roman Empire* (Princeton).

Maehler, Herwig
   1983   "Häuser und ihre Bewohner im Fayûm in der Kaiserzeit," in Grimm-Heinen-Winter 1983, 119-37.

Manfredi, Manfredo
   1985   "Cultura letteraria nell'Egitto greco e romano," *Egitto e società antica* (Milano) 271-85.

BIBLIOGRAPHY 353

Marcus, Abraham
  1989   *The Middle East on the Eve of Modernity: Aleppo in the Eighteenth Century* (New York).

Martin, Annik
  1974   "Athanase et les Mélitiens (325-335)," *Politique et théologie chez Athanase d'Alexandrie*, ed. C. Kannengiesser (Théologie historique 27, Paris) 31-61.
  1979   "L'Église et la khôra égyptienne au IVe siècle," *Revue des Études Augustiniennes* 25: 3-26.
  1981   "Aux origines de l'église copte: l'implantation et le développement du christianisme en Égypte (Ie-IVe siècles)," *REA* 83: 35-56.

McGing, Brian C.
  1990   "Melitian Monks at Labla," *Tyche* 5: 67-94.

Mélèze-Modrzejewski, Joseph
  1987   "Splendeurs grecques et misères romaines: les Juifs d'Égypte dans l'antiquité," *Juifs du Nil*, ed. J. Hassoun, 3 ed. (Paris) 17-48.
  1989   "Ioudaioi apheiremenoi: La fin de la communauté juive d'Égypte (115-117 de n.è.)," *Symposion 1985* (Köln-Wien) 337-61.

Mertens, Paul
  1958   *Les services de l'état civil et le contrôle de la population à Oxyrhynchus au IIIe siècle de notre ère* (Acad.Royale de Belgique, Cl. des Lettres, Mémoires 53.2, Brussels).

Merzagora, Maria
  1929   "La navigazione in Egitto nell'età greco-romana," *Aegyptus* 10: 105-48.

Meyer, Béatrice
  1990   "Problèmes du combustible dans les bains publics de l'Égypte grecque et romaine," *Egitto e storia antica dall'Ellenismo all'età araba* (Bologna) 565-71.

Meyer-Termeer, A. J. M.
  1978   *Die Haftung der Schiffer im griechischen und römischen Recht* (Stud.Amst. 13, Zutphen).

Millar, Fergus
  1983   "Empire and City, Augustus to Julian: Obligations, Excuses and Status," *JRS* 73: 76-96.

Moscadi, Alessandro
  1970   "Le lettere dell'archivio di Teofane," *Aegyptus* 50: 88-154.

Nagel, Peter
  1984   "Griechisch-Koptische Bilinguen des Alten Testaments," *Graeco-Coptica* 231-57.

Naville, E.
1894   *Ahnas El Medineh (Heracleopolis Magna)* (EES, Memoir 11, London).

Neugebauer, Otto, and H. B. van Hoesen
1959   *Greek Horoscopes* (MemPhilSoc 48, Philadelphia).

Nock, Arthur Darby
1944/1972 "Later Egyptian Piety," *Essays on Religion and the Ancient World*, ed. Z. Stewart (Cambridge, Mass.) II 566-74 (originally published in 1944).

Nowicka, Maria
1969   *La maison privée dans l'Égypte ptolémaïque* (Academia Scientiarum Polona, Bibliotheca Antiqua 9, Wroclaw-Warsaw-Krakow).

Oleson, John P.
1984   *Greek and Roman Mechanical Water-Lifting Devices: The History of a Technology* (*Phoenix* Suppl. 16, Toronto).

Orlandi, Tito
1984   "Le traduzioni dal greco e lo sviluppo della letteratura copta," *Graeco-Coptica* 181-203.

Palme, Bernhard
1989   *Das Amt des apaitetes in Ägypten* (MPER n.s. 20, Vienna).

Parca, Maryline G.
1991   *Ptocheia or Odysseus in Disguise at Troy (P.Köln VI 245)* (Am.Stud.Pap. 31, Atlanta).

Pearson, Birger A., and James E. Goehring
1986   Eds., *The Roots of Egyptian Christianity* (Philadelphia).

Pestman, P. W.
1961   *Marriage and Matrimonial Property in Ancient Egypt* (Pap. Lugd.Bat. 9, Leiden).

1967   *Chronologie égyptienne d'après les textes démotiques (332 av. J.-C. - 453 ap. J.-C.)* (Pap.Lugd.Bat. 15, Leiden).

Petrie, W. M. Flinders
1905   *Ehnasya 1904* (Egypt Exploration Society, Memoir 26, London).

Pleket, H. W.
1984   "Urban Elites and the Economy in the Greek Cities of the Roman Empire," *Münstersche Beiträge z. antiken Handelsgeschichte* 3: 3-36.

Pomeroy, Sarah B.
1981   "Women in Roman Egypt. A Preliminary Study Based on Papyri," in *Reflections of Women in Antiquity*, ed. H. Foley (London) 303-22.

Pruneti, Paola
1981   *I centri abitati dell'Ossirinchite* (Pap.Flor. 9, Florence).

Quaegebeur, Jan
   1982   "De la préhistoire de l'écriture copte," *OLP* 13: 125-36.

Rathbone, Dominic W.
   1983   "The Weight and Measurement of Egyptian Grains," *ZPE* 53: 265-75.

   1989   "The Ancient Economy and Graeco-Roman Egypt," *Egitto e storia antica dall'Ellenismo all'età araba* (Bologna) 159-76.

   1990   "Villages, Land and Population in Graeco-Roman Egypt," *PCPS* n.s. 36: 103-42.

   1991   *Economic Rationalism and Rural Society in Third-Century A.D. Egypt: The Heroninos Archive and the Appianus Estate* (Cambridge).

Rea, J. R.
   1984   "A Cavalryman's Career, A.D. 384 (?)-401," *ZPE* 56: 79-92, pll. 5, 15, 16.

Reil, Theodor
   1913   *Beiträge zur Kenntnis des Gewerbes im hellenistischen Ägypten* (Borna-Leipzig).

Rémondon, Roger
   1952   "L'Égypte et la suprême résistance au Christianisme (Ve-VIIe siècles)," *BIFAO* 51: 63-78.

   1955   "Problèmes militaires en Égypte et dans l'empire à la fin du IVe siècle," *RevHist* 213: 21-38.

   1965   "Militaires et civils dans une campagne égyptienne au temps de Constance II," *JSav* 1965: 132-43.

Roberts, Colin H.
   1979   *Manuscript, Society and Belief in Early Christian Egypt* (London).

Roberts, David
   1846-49   *Egypt and Nubia,* 3 vols. (London) (2 vol. edition reprint is only partial reproduction in different order).

Rodziewicz, Mieczyslaw
   1988   "Remarks on the Domestic and Monastic Architecture in Alexandria and Surroundings," Van den Brink 1988, 267-77.

Roeder, G.
   1959   *Hermopolis, 1929-1939* (Pelizaeus-Museum zu Hildesheim, Wissenschaftliche Veröffentlichung 4, Hildesheim).

Roueché, Charlotte
   1989   *Aphrodisias in Late Antiquity* (JRS Monogr. 5, London).

Rousseau, Philip
1985   *Pachomius: The Making of a Community in Fourth-Century Egypt* (Berkeley).

Rubenson, Samuel
1990   *The Letters of St. Antony* (Bibl. Historico-Ecclesiastica Lundensis 24, Lund).

Sallares, Robert
1991   *The Ecology of the Ancient Greek World* (Ithaca).

Satzinger, Helmut
1984   "Die altkoptischen Texte als Zeugnisse der Beziehungen zwischen Aegypten und Griechen," *Graeco-Coptica* 137-47.

Sauneron, Serge, and Jean Jacquet
1979   *Les ermitages chrétiens du désert d'Esna*, 4 vols. (Fouilles de l'IFAO 29, Cairo).

Schmitz, Hermann
1934   "Die Bau-Urkunde in P.Vindob. Gr. 12565 im Lichte der Ergebnisse der Deutschen Hermopolis-Expedition," *Akten III Kongr.* 406-28.

Schnebel, Michael
1925   *Die Landwirtschaft im hellenistischen Ägypten* (Münch. Beitr. 7, Munich).

Schönborn, Hans-Bernhard
1976   *Die Pastophoren im Kult der ägyptischen Götter.* (Beitr. zur klass. Philologie 80, Meisenheim am Glan).

Schwartz, Jacques
1983   "Le commerce d'Alexandrie au début du 4ème s.p.C.," *Das römisch-byzantinische Ägypten* 41-46.

Schwartz, Jacques, et al.
1969   With A. Badawy, R. Smith, H. Wild, *Qasr-Qarun/Dionysias 1950* (Institut Français d'Archéologie Orientale, Fouilles Franco-Suisses, Rapports 2, Cairo).

Shaw, Brent D.
1983   "Soldiers and Society: The Army in Numidia," *Opus* 2: 133-59.
1984   "Latin Funerary Epigraphy and Family Life in the Later Roman Empire," *Historia* 33: 457-97.

Sijpesteijn, P. J.
1964   *Penthemeros-Certificates in Graeco-Roman Egypt* (Pap. Lugd.Bat. 12, Leiden).

Sirat, Colette, et al.
1986   *La Ketouba de Cologne: Un contrat de mariage juif à Antinoopolis*, ed. Colette Sirat, Patrice Cauderlier, M. Dukan, and M. A. Friedman (Pap. Colon. 12, Opladen).

Sirks, Boudewijn (A. B. J.)
1991   *Food for Rome. The Legal Structure of the Transportation and Processing of Supplies for the Imperial Distributions in Rome and Constantinople* (Stud.Amst. 31, Amsterdam).

Smith, H. S.
1972   "Society and Settlement in Ancient Egypt," in Ucko, Tringham, Dimbleby 1972, 705-19.

Smith, Morton
1983a   "On the Lack of a History of Greco-Roman Magic," in *Althistorische Studien Hermann Bengtson* (*Historia* Einzelschr. 40, Wiesbaden) 252-57.

1983b   "How Magic was Changed by the Triumph of Christianity," *Graeco-Arabica* 2: 51-57.

Sodini, J. P.
1979   "L'artisanat urbain à l'époque paléochrétienne (IVe-VIIe S.)," *Ktêma* 4: 71-119.

Spencer, A. Jeffrey
1984   *Excavations at El-Ashmunein* I: *The Topography of the Site* (London).

Spencer, A. Jeffrey, D. M. Bailey, and A. Burnett
1983   *British Museum Expedition to Middle Egypt: Ashmunein (1982)* (British Museum Occasional Paper 46, London).

Stein, Arthur
1915   *Untersuchungen zur Geschichte und Verwaltung Aegyptens unter roemischer Herrschaft* (Stuttgart).

Steindorff, Georg
1950   "Bemerkungen über die Anfänge der koptischen Sprache und Literatur," in *Coptic Studies in Honor of Walter Ewing Crum* (Boston) 189-213.

Steinmann, Frank
1974   "Die Schreibkenntnisse der Kopten nach den Aussagen der Djeme-Urkunden," in *Studia Coptica*, ed. Peter Nagel (*Berliner Byzantinische Arbeiten* 45, Berlin) 101-10.

Stone, Lawrence, and Jeanne C. Fawtier Stone
1984   *An Open Elite? England 1540-1880* (Oxford).

Strousma, G. G.
1986   "The Manichean Challenge to Egyptian Christianity," in Pearson and Goehring 1986, 307-19.

Tell Edfou
1937   *Tell Edfou 1937*, ed. B. Bruyère et al. (*Fouilles Franco-Polonaises, Rapports* 1, Cairo 1937).

1938   *Tell Edfou 1938*, ed. K. Michalowski et al. (*Fouilles Franco-Polonaises, Rapports* 2, Cairo 1938).

1939   *Tell Edfou 1939*, ed. K. Michalowski et al. (*Fouilles Franco-Polonaises, Rapports* 3, Cairo 1950).

Thomas, J. David

1982   *The Epistrategos in Ptolemaic and Roman Egypt*, Part 2: *The Roman Epistrategos* (Pap.Colon. 6, Opladen).

1983   "Compulsory Public Service in Roman Egypt," in Grimm-Heinen Winter 1983, 35-39.

1984   "Sabinianus, *Praeses* of Aegyptus Mercuriana?" *BASP* 21: 225-34.

1985   "The Earliest Occurrence of the *exactor civitatis* in Egypt (*P. Giss.* inv. 126 recto)," *YCS* 28: 115-25.

Timbie, Janet

1986   "The State of Research on the Career of Shenoute of Atripe," in Pearson and Goehring 1986, 258-70.

Traunecker, Claude, and Jean-Claude Golvin

1984   *Karnak, Résurrection d'un site* (Fribourg).

Treu, Kurt

1986   "Antike Literatur im byzantinischen Ägypten im Lichte der Papyri," *Byzantinoslavica* 47: 1-7.

Turner, Eric G.

1952   "Roman Oxyrhynchos," *JEA* 38: 78-93.

1956   "Scribes and Scholars of Oxyrhynchos," *Akten VIII. Kongr.* 141-46.

1975   "Oxyrhynchus and Rome," *HSCP* 79: 1-24.

Ucko, Peter J., Ruth Tringham, and G. W. Dimbleby

1972   Eds., *Man, Settlement and Urbanism* (London).

Van den Brink, E. C. M.

1988   Ed., *The Archaeology of the Nile Delta, Egypt: Problems and Priorities* (Amsterdam).

Van Gucht, Wilfried

1984   "Some Egyptian Bishops and the Date of *PLandlisten*," *Atti XVII Congresso* 1135-40.

Van Haelst, Joseph

1989   "Les origines du codex," in *Les débuts du codex*, ed. A. Blanchard (Bibliologia 9, Turnhout) 12-35.

Van Minnen, Peter

1986   "The Volume of the Oxyrhynchite Textile Trade," *Münstersche Beiträge z. antiken Handelsgeschichte* 5.2: 88-95.

1987   "Urban Craftsmen in Roman Egypt," *Münstersche Beiträge z. antiken Handelsgeschichte* 6.1: 31-88.

Vergote, J.

1973   *Grammaire Copte* Ia (Louvain).

Viereck, Paul
 1928 *Philadelpheia* (Morgenland. Darstellungen aus Geschichte und Kultur des Ostens, Heft 16, Leipzig).

Wace, A. J. B., et al.
 1959 With A. H. S. Megaw and T. C. Skeat, *Hermopolis Magna, Ashmunein. The Ptolemaic Sanctuary and the Basilica* (Univ. of Alexandria, Faculty of Arts, Publ. 8, Alexandria).

Wagner, Guy
 1987 *Les oasis d'Égypte à l'époque grecque, romaine et byzantine d'après les documents grecs (Recherches de papyrologie et d'épigraphie grecques)* (Bd'É 100, Cairo).

Walters, C. C.
 1974 *Monastic Archaeology in Egypt* (Warminster).

Watson, Andrew M.
 1983 *Agricultural Innovation in the Early Islamic World* (Cambridge).

Wente, Edward F.
 1990 *Letters from Ancient Egypt* (Writings from the Ancient World 1, Atlanta).

Whittaker, C. R.
 1990 "The Consumer City Revisited: The *Vicus* and the City," *JRA* 3: 110-18.

Winkelmann, Friedhelm
 1984 "Die Stellung Aegyptens im oströmisch-byzantinischen Reich," *Graeco-Coptica* 11-35.

Wipszycka, Ewa
 1965 *L'industrie textile dans l'Egypte romaine* (Wroclaw-Warsaw-Krakow).

 1971 Review of Fikhman 1965, *JJurPap* 16-17: 271-86.

 1972 *Les resources et les activités économiques des églises en Égypte du IVe au VIIIe siècle* (Pap.Brux. 10, Brussels).

 1975 "Les terres de la congrégation pachômienne dans une liste de payements pour les apora," in *Le monde grec. Hommages à Cl. Préaux* (Brussels) 625-36.

 1983 "La chiesa nell'Egitto del IV secolo: Le strutture ecclesiastiche," *Miscellanea Historiae Ecclesiasticae* VI, Congrès de Varsovie 1978 (Warsaw-Louvain-Brussels) 182-201.

 1984 "Le degré d'alphabétisation en Égypte byzantine," *Revue des Études Augustiniennes* 30: 279-96.

 1986 "La valeur de l'onomastique pour l'histoire de la christianisation de l'Égypte. A propos d'une étude de R. S. Bagnall," *ZPE* 62: 173-81.

1988   "La christianisation de l'Égypte aux IVe-VIe siècles. Aspects sociaux et ethniques," *Aegyptus* 68: 117-65.

Wipszycka, Ewa, and Benedetto Bravo

1989   "L'Epistula Ammonis et le monachisme pachômien," *BiOr* 46: 5-18.

Wood, Gordon S.

1992   *The Radicalism of the American Revolution* (New York).

Youtie, Herbert C.

1971a   "*Agrammatos*: An Aspect of Greek Society in Egypt," *HSCP* 75: 161-76 (rpt. *Scriptiunculae* II [Amsterdam 1973] 611-27).

1971b   "*Bradeos graphon*: Between Literacy and Illiteracy," *GRBS* 12: 239-61 (rpt. *Scriptiunculae* II [Amsterdam 1973] 629-51).

1975a   "*Hypographeus*: The Social Impact of Illiteracy in Graeco-Roman Egypt," *ZPE* 17: 201-21 (rpt. *Scriptiunculae Posteriores* I [Bonn 1981] 179-99).

1975b   "'Because they do not know letters,'" *ZPE* 19: 101-08 (rpt. *Scriptiunculae Posteriores* I [Bonn 1981] 255-62).

Yoyotte, Jean

1988   "Tanis. Les particularités d'un site protégé," in van den Brink 1988, 151-57.

Zauzich, Karl-Theodor

1983   "Demotische Texte römischer Zeit," *Das römisch-byzantinische Ägypten* 77-80.

Zucker, Friedrich

1956   "Priester und Tempel in Ägypten in den Zeiten nach der decianischen Christenverfolgung," *Akten VIII. Int. Kongr. Pap.* 167-74.

General Index

Words marked with an asterisk (*) appear in Appendix 4, Glossary.

Index of Texts Discussed

Texts only cited or briefly summarized are for the most part not listed in this index, which is restricted to those texts commented on.